Folded f
Sermon

GALATIANS, EPHESIANS, PHILIPPIANS, COLOSSIANS, *and* 1st & 2nd THESSALONIANS

Paul's Letters to Churches

PCF
Practical Christianity Foundation

CREATION HOUSE

PAUL'S LETTERS TO CHURCHES–COMMENTARY ON GALATIANS, EPHESIANS, PHILIPPIANS, COLOSSIANS, AND 1ST AND 2ND THESSALONIANS
by Practical Christianity Foundation
Published by Creation House
A Charisma Media Company
600 Rinehart Road
Lake Mary, Florida 32746
www.charismamedia.com

Design Director: Bill Johnson
Cover design by Terry Clifton

Visit the author's website: www.practicalchristianityfoundation.com

Library of Congress Cataloging-in-Publication Data: 2012937903
International Standard Book Number: 978-1-61638-994-9

First edition

12 13 14 15 16 — 9 8 7 6 5 4 3 2 1
Printed in Canada

CONTENTS

Preface ix

Practical Christianity Foundation Value Statements xi

Galatians 1

- Introduction 3
- Galatians 1 7
- Galatians 2 25
- Galatians 3 41
- Galatians 4 61
- Galatians 5 83
- Galatians 6 103

Ephesians 115

- Introduction 117
- Ephesians 1 121

Ephesians 2 139
Ephesians 3 153
Ephesians 4 169
Ephesians 5 193
Ephesians 6 217

Philippians 235

Introduction 237
Philippians 1 241
Philippians 2 261
Philippians 3 283
Philippians 4 301

Colossians 315

Introduction 317
Colossians 1 321
Colossians 2 349
Colossians 3 367
Colossians 4 385

1 Thessalonians 399

Introduction 401
1 Thessalonians 1 403
1 Thessalonians 2 413
1 Thessalonians 3 427
1 Thessalonians 4 437
1 Thessalonians 5 453

2 Thessalonians 475

Introduction 477

2 Thessalonians 1 479

2 Thessalonians 2 491

2 Thessalonians 3 507

Notes 523

Galatians 523

Ephesians 524

Philippians 525

Colossians 526

1 Thessalonians 528

2 Thessalonians 529

Contact Information 530

Study Notes 531

PREFACE

From the conception of Practical Christianity Foundation (PCF), it has been the goal of the organization to convey the truth in Scripture through verse-by-verse devotional studies such as this one. As part of that goal, we agree in an attempt neither to prove nor to disprove any traditional or alternative interpretations, beliefs, or doctrines but rather to allow the Holy Spirit to reveal the truth contained within the Scriptures. Any interpretations relating to ambiguous passages that are not directly and specifically verifiable by other scriptural references are simply presented in what we believe to be the most likely intention of the message based on those things that we are specifically told. In those instances, our conclusions are noted as interpretive, and such analyses should not be understood as doctrinal positions that we are attempting to champion.

This study is divided into sections, usually between six and eight verses, and each section concludes with a "Notes/Applications" passage, which draws practical insight from the related verses that can be applied to contemporary Christian living. The intent is that the reader will complete one section per day, will gain a greater understanding of the verses within that passage, and will daily be challenged toward a deeper commitment to our Lord and Savior Jesus Christ. Also included at certain points within the text are "Dig Deeper" boxes, which are intended to assist readers who desire to invest additional time to study topics that relate to the section in which these boxes appear. Our prayer is that this study will impact the lives of all believers, regardless of age, ethnicity, or education.

Each of PCF's original projects is a collaborative effort of many writers, content editors, grammatical editors, transcribers, researchers, readers, and other contributors, and as such, we present them only as products of Practical Christianity Foundation as a whole. These works are not for the recognition or acclamation of any particular individual but are written simply as a means to uphold and fulfill the greater purpose of our Mission Statement, which is "to exalt the holy name of God Almighty by declaring the redemptive message of His Son, the Lord Jesus Christ, to the lost global community and equipping the greater Christian community through the communication of the holy Word of God in its entirety through every appropriate means available."

Practical Christianity Foundation Value Statements

1. We value the holy name of God the Father and will strive to exalt Him through godly living, committed service, and effective communication. "*As long as you live, you, your children, and your grandchildren must fear the Lord your God. All of you must obey all his laws and commands that I'm giving you, and you will live a long time*" *(Deuteronomy 6:2).*

2. We value the redemptive work of the Lord Jesus Christ, God's holy Son, for a lost world and will strive to communicate His redemptive message to the global community. "*Then Jesus said to them, 'So wherever you go in the world, tell everyone the Good News'*" *(Mark 16:15).*

3. We value the Holy Spirit through Whose regenerating work sinners are redeemed, and the redeemed are convinced of the truth of God's Holy Word. "*He will come to convict the world of sin, to show the world what has God's approval, and to convince the world that God judges it*" *(John 16:8).*

4. We value the Holy Word of God and will strive to communicate it in its entirety. "*Every Scripture passage is inspired by God. All of them are useful for teaching, pointing out errors, correcting people, and training them for a life that has God's approval. They equip God's servants so that they are completely prepared to do good things*" *(2 Timothy 3:16–17).*

5. We value spiritual growth in God's people through the equipping ministry of the church of the Lord Jesus Christ and will strive to provide resources for that ministry by the communication of God's Holy Word, encouraging them to be lovers of the truth. "*But grow in the good will and knowledge of our Lord and Savior Jesus Christ. Glory belongs to him now and for that eternal day! Amen*" *(2 Peter 3:18).*

GALATIANS

INTRODUCTION

Paul's ministry throughout the Mediterranean region and Asia Minor was characterized by two interrelated factors in his labor as an evangelist and church planter. First, God blessed his ministry among both Gentiles and Jews with a fruitful spiritual harvest *(Acts 9:15)*. Secondly, this success was accomplished in sharp contrast to his opponents who pursued him with single-minded hostility, seeking to undermine his ministry by distorting his message with false teaching. Zealous individuals commonly known as Judaizers derailed the church in Galatia with such misguided doctrine.

Much like the Jews who harassed and falsely accused Jesus, the Judaizers opposed Paul vehemently, accusing him of promoting a king other than Caesar *(Acts 17:5–7, 13)*. Although they used unfounded accusations to gain a political advantage over Paul, the Judaizers were chiefly opposed to the Gospel of Jesus Christ that Paul boldly preached. However, they could not successfully disprove the truth and many Galatians became disciples of Jesus Christ.

Since early believers came to faith in the region of Judea and Galilee, where Jesus had walked among the populace for three years, it is easy to understand that the great majority of converts were Jews.

Some converts were Gentiles who had first given their allegiance to the Jewish faith. So it was perfectly natural for them to become followers of Christ, but continue in their Jewish traditions of worship, adhering to sacrifices, dietary laws, as well as the moral structure of their culture. "At that time conversion to Judaism was accomplished through three separate steps: (1) circumcision (for males); (2) a ritual bath in water; and (3) agreement to take upon oneself the 'yoke of the law,' that is, to obey the 613 commands of the Mosaic law as interpreted and expanded in Jewish halakah (rabbinic legal decisions)."[1]

As the years passed, a growing number of Gentiles became Christ followers, creating a problem for their Jewish brethren. These people became believers, but did not follow the traditions of Judaism. What should a new convert do? Should he also follow the established rules for becoming a Jew and thereby complete his initiation into the Christian faith? Many Jewish Christians thought that the answer was, "Yes! Of course!" They simply could not think of any possible alternative to live faithfully for God unless a new Christian joined the ranks of faithful Jewish believers. For them, becoming a Christian and accepting Jesus as their promised Messiah enhanced their Judaism, but did not replace it.[2] Some Jewish Christians felt so strongly that they made this statement: "Some men came from Judea and started to teach believers that people can't be saved unless they are circumcised as Moses' Teachings require" *(Acts 15:1).*

Although Paul had been trained as a Pharisee and knew the Law of Moses as well as anybody, he took a completely different approach to this question. The letter to the Galatian church is a treatise on Paul's interpretation of Jewish law and its relationship to a believer's freedom from sin found in Jesus Christ. Essentially, Paul taught that the transformation received by believers initiated by the work of the Holy Spirit, applying the finished work of Christ to a person's life, was the only action needed to complete one's salvation. Anything other than the work of Christ alone was nothing more or nothing less than a distortion of the gospel message.

As a result of these two viewpoints, a sharp division arose in the early church, a division of such deeply felt principles that the Judaizers made every attempt to discredit Paul or have him killed. But Paul never backed down. When the Judaizers saw the power of the Gospel and the courage of Paul, they resorted to a personal attack, questioning Paul's apostleship. By attacking Paul, and therefore the credibility of the Gospel he proclaimed, these Judaizers hoped to discredit his teachings among the Gentile Christians. Alarmed by the danger of leaving young believers exposed to the deceit of this teaching, Paul sent this letter to the church in Galatia, clearly explaining the authority of his apostleship and asserting the truth of the Gospel.

On Paul's first missionary journey (A.D. 47–48) accompanied by Barnabas, the pair had traveled across the island of Cyprus and into the southern region of Galatia *(Acts 13–14)*. Shortly after their return to Antioch, Paul and Barnabas made a visit to the leadership of the church in Jerusalem, mostly comprised of Jesus' apostles. A council was convened to put an end to this debate *(Acts 15)*. This was no small matter as the Judaizers presented their side of the argument. But Paul refused to back down. In the end, Peter and James extended the right hand of fellowship and agreed that Paul was to take the Gospel to the Gentiles and Peter would do the same among Jewish people *(Galatians 2:9)*. The leaders of the Jerusalem church gave Paul and Barnabas a letter

From New American Commentary, page 19

showing the apostles' endorsement of Paul's ministry (*Acts 15:22–29*).

Armed with the endorsement of Jesus' chosen apostles, Paul and Barnabas returned to Antioch. There, in A.D. 49, Paul penned this letter to the Galatian Christians, a letter that displayed the apostle's certainty of the Gospel he had delivered to them as well as the intensity of his frustration with their defection to the errors of the Judaizers' doctrine.

Today's Christian could easily dismiss this letter as something that no longer applies, since the debate between Paul and the Judaizers no longer threatens the Christian community. But a closer look will reveal the very serious error of those who continue in some way or another to distort the Gospel by adding or taking away from the unique place that Jesus occupies in the process of a person's salvation. Like Paul, those who have been saved by the finished work of Christ alone will stand up and say loudly, "Read Paul's letter to the Galatians."

The reformer Martin Luther considered Galatians the best of all the books in the Bible. He claimed it as his own, saying, "The epistle to the Galatians is my epistle. To it I am as it were in wedlock. It is my Katherine."[3] As we enter the study of this very special letter to the Galatians, may we cling to its timeless truth in our culture with as much passion as Paul did in his day.

GALATIANS 1

Galatians 1:1–5

1:1–2 ***[1]From Paul—an apostle [chosen] not by any group or individual but by Jesus Christ and God the Father who brought him back to life [2]and all the believers who are with me. To the churches in Galatia.***

In this opening statement, Paul asserted that his apostleship was vested in him by God Who raised Jesus Christ from the dead. In every letter Paul wrote to other churches, he emphatically makes this declaration as the foundation of the authority by which he directs the churches that were established under his ministry. However, unlike his other letters, he further stated that this appointment had nothing to do with any group or individual. In doing so, he set the tone for this letter. In no other letter does Paul express himself so forcefully with so much negative criticism in which he defined the Truth of the gospel message in opposition to the false gospel of the Judaizers *(Acts 15:1)*. Throughout this letter, he often repeated this theme. Since the Gospel he proclaimed was God-given, not man-influenced, he confidently told the Galatian church that his authority could not be challenged or questioned by the Judaizers or anyone else.

Once he affirmed his divinely bestowed apostleship, Paul gives his customary greeting to the Galatian church. However, unlike many of his other letters in which he named individuals who were with him, Paul mentioned no names in this letter. He simply referred to brothers who also sent their greetings to them. Pressed by the urgency of the crisis undermining the church, Paul set aside his customary practices of naming his ministry companions.

DIG DEEPER: *WHAT IS AN APOSTLE?*

It is not hard to know what the word apostle means, because the apostles themselves made the definition very clear. [21]*He must be one of the men who accompanied Jesus with us the entire time that the Lord Jesus was among us.* [22] *This person must have been with us from the time that John was baptizing people to the day that Jesus was taken from us"* (Acts 1:21–22). Thus, we may conclude that an apostle was one who had traveled with Jesus throughout His earthly ministry. As such, an apostle was one who had heard what Jesus taught, witnessed the miracles He performed, and experienced the miscarriage of justice that resulted in Jesus' execution. An apostle would also be a witness to Jesus' resurrection and ascension. Such a man could provide reliable eyewitness testimony to Jesus' work, which provided salvation to those for whom He died.

One argument against the authenticity of Paul's apostleship appears to have been the fact that he was neither numbered among the pillars of Jerusalem *(Galatians 2:9)* nor one of the original twelve apostles of our Lord *(Luke 6:13–16)*. In Acts 2:12–26, one hundred and twenty disciples cast lots to replace Judas Iscariot. The lots were cast and Matthias replaced Judas, numbered with the Twelve. Nevertheless, Jesus Christ confronted Paul as he entered Damascus *(Acts 9:1–19)*, completely transforming his heart and redirecting his perspective about Jesus. A three-year sojourn in the Arabian Peninsula followed this encounter. During this time, Paul received intensive training in the truth of the Gospel *(Galatians 1:15–17)*. Therefore, as an apostle "*born out of due time*" *(1 Corinthians 15:8–9)*, Paul became the primary apostle appointed by God to proclaim the Gospel to those who were not Jews *(Acts 9:15–16)*.

1:3 ***Good will and peace from God the Father and our Lord Jesus Christ are yours!***

Paul addressed the Galatians with the familiar salutation that he used in all of his letters. Addressing them as God's redeemed children, Paul assured them that God's good will, His grace, had already been given to them in the peace of their Savior Jesus Christ. In this way, Paul always greeted those he wrote with this very fundamental assertion that they were reconciled to God by and through Jesus' sacrifice on the Cross. Without this grace secured through God's Son, there could never be any peace or good will from the Father.

1:4 ***In order to free us from this present evil world, Christ took the punishment for our sins, because that was what our God and Father wanted.***

Paul's salutation to the Galatians was not a casual observation about their spiritual state of affairs. Rather, it was a reassertion of the Gospel, an affirmation of the means by which their salvation was secured. Here, he reminded them that Jesus Christ gave His life by His sacrifice on the Cross to set them free from the evil of this world. How does God set people free? He sets people free by placing the burden of their sin upon Christ, Who took the punishment for man's offense.

This was no accident. Rather it was the outcome of God's sovereign plan. Jesus Christ, the Sacrificial Lamb of God by His Father's will, provided for salvation by destroying the forces of evil through His death and resurrection. Jesus suffered for the sake of sinners not only to give them eternal life, but also to keep them free from the evil influences of a corrupt world.

1:5 ***Glory belongs to our God and Father forever! Amen.***

Paul concluded his salutation by offering praise "to our God and Father." Paul praised and glorified God to remind the Galatians that their salvation was given by God's gracious will. God alone, through Jesus Christ, was the only source for their salvation. By directing the

Galatians to the praise of God in this way, he essentially laid down the foundation for the rest of his treatise for the supremacy of the Gospel.

Notes/Applications

Paul's salutation reveals three essential principles concerning God's work in the lives of the redeemed. First, God appoints the redeemed to a calling that He confers upon each one's life. Along with the general call to a life of service and care, God commissions certain individual believers to specific offices of ministry. It is His prerogative alone to commission His workers to any authority, human or otherwise. The call upon the life of the redeemed is accomplished only through divine appointment.

Second, the salvation of the redeemed is secure in the finished work of Jesus Christ. God, by His sovereign and perfect will, determined that salvation would be given to the lost through the suffering, death, and resurrection of His Son Jesus Christ. Through Christ alone the redeemed have a secure relationship with their God and Father as His ransomed children. This blood-bought position cannot and should not be undermined by the ambitious inquiries of a person's corrupt mind.

Third, the redeemed must pay close attention to the evil realities of this world, which is governed by Satan and his evil forces. Since Satan has been given the position to rule the world for a season by God Himself *(John 12:31, 14:11)*, he tries to impose his will on God's secure children. However, the redeemed have been set free from Satan's power by Christ's finished work on Calvary. Praising and glorifying the Almighty, their God and Father, believers must firmly stand upon Christ's finished work and victoriously resist the devil, recognizing that their freedom from bondage is secure in Christ and Christ alone.

Above all things God's children must fortify their hearts and minds with God's eternal truth in order to overcome the subtle deceit of the evil one.

Galatians 1:6–10

1:6 *I'm surprised that you're so quickly deserting Christ, who called you in his kindness, to follow a different kind of good news.*

Two essential elements distinguish Paul's epistle to the Galatians from any of his other letters. In other letters, he offers an elaborate commendation of the saints gathered in the church. However, Paul's remarks directly following his salutation to the Galatian church immediately addressed the problem at hand. Paul's direct assessment underscored the urgency of his warning to his "children in the faith."

Paul rebuked the Galatian Christians for deserting, not simply the message of the Gospel, but Jesus Himself. Paul's frustration with these Christians comes immediately to the forefront, a frustration often expressed throughout the rest of the letter. His rebuke was constructed in a well-choreographed argument that disputed the false logic of the Judaizers. It was flavored by affection, care, wisdom, and patience, as well as the expression of his bewilderment and furious indignation. In no uncertain terms, he told them that he was shocked at the sudden reversal of their commitment to the Gospel they first heard and believed. He was amazed at their quick desertion of their faith in Jesus Christ alone and their adoption of a different "gospel" *(Acts 15:1)*.

1:7 *But what some people are calling good news is not really good news at all. They are confusing you. They want to distort the Good News about Christ.*

Paul maintained a delicate balance in the expression of his concern. With the love of a father and the wisdom of a caring teacher, Paul tenderly nursed the doctrinally distorted understanding of the Galatians as he carefully unfolded the true nature of the Gospel. While Paul did not relieve the Galatians of responsibility for their confusion, he strategically shifted the blame for their spiritual status to the Judaizers.

He exposed their evil scheme, which was causing the Galatians to question the Gospel he had so clearly explained to them. Instead, they were being misled by a false "gospel" advanced by false teachers who had infiltrated the ranks of their church.

The false doctrine advanced by the Judaizers was a shameless distortion of the truth. Paul expected that believers should be able to discern this error by remembering the truth they had believed for their salvation. Instead, they were abandoning the Gospel of Jesus Christ to accept another "gospel." He reminded them that any teaching that exalts any religious obligation to be superior to the work of Jesus Christ distorted the truth.

1:8 *Whoever tells you good news that is different from the Good News we gave you should be condemned to hell, even if he is one of us or an angel from heaven.*

In distorting the truth, the Judaizers had charmed their way into the hearts of the Galatians. Since they did not accept Paul as a qualified apostle, the Judaizers relentlessly attempted to convince the churches to abandon his teaching.

But Paul boldly articulated his convictions about the Gospel. For him, the message was independent from the messenger. He told the Galatians that the Gospel they first heard and believed was true regardless of the messenger who proclaimed it. If on the contrary, anyone on earth or in heaven proclaimed a message that contradicted the Gospel of Jesus Christ, which he taught, that person was cursed. Even if that person was Paul himself or an angel from heaven, such false messengers should be condemned to everlasting punishment in hell. Paul was so confident about the Gospel he preached that he was willing to condemn even the angels if they opposed Jesus Christ.

1:9 ***I'm now telling you again what we've told you in the past: If anyone tells you good news that is different from the Good News you received, that person should be condemned to hell.***

Paul reiterated his condemnation of the enemies of the Gospel with a slight change in the persons he described. Now, he expressed his aversion toward the enemies of the Gospel by reiterating his disgust through an emphatic reaffirmation of his curse on them. Paul wanted the Galatians to know that the Gospel they first heard and believed from his lips provided the only accurate representation of the Gospel. Therefore, *anyone* supporting any opposing doctrine was the enemy of the Truth and should not be accepted. The enemies of the authentic gospel message had nothing worthwhile to offer to the redeemed. Those who were already saved by the work of Jesus Christ should not pay any attention to the distorted opinions of those who were already condemned.

1:10 ***Am I saying this now to win the approval of people or God? Am I trying to please people? If I were still trying to please people, I would not be Christ's servant.***

Paul paused for a moment and invited his audience to think about what he had just told them. He wondered if they appreciated the context in which he issued his swift verdict that condemned the enemies of the Gospel. He attempted to discover what they believed about the Gospel so that he could deliver them from confusion. Did they really understand his vehement defense of the validity of the Gospel he preached? Why did Paul pronounce such a terminal judgment upon those whom he viewed as the enemies of the Gospel? Was he seeking to satisfy what people wanted, or please God?

Even though his main audience was the Galatians, Paul's question was likely directed both to the Galatians and to the Judaizers. The Judaizers considered Paul's Gospel as an erroneous doctrine, wrongly attempting to relieve people from their duty to the Law. They viewed him as one who tried to please men and get their approval by reducing their requirement to obey the Law. Similarly, the Galatians were confused about Paul's purpose in teaching against the age-old Judaic tradition of accepting the Law as the non-negotiable requirement of religious practice. In both cases, unstable believers as well as the circulators of false doctrine who failed to understand the Gospel despised the message Paul preached.

Paul's answer to the shallow beliefs of the skeptics was clear and uncompromising. Neither Paul's teaching nor his commitment to the Gospel was based on human reasoning. Discretion and common sense dictate that people try to do what others want if they want to gain their approval. But Paul's reason and purpose in preaching and defending the Gospel was not motivated by human approval. Rather, his commission to proclaim the Gospel came from the Lord Himself and he decided that he would never sacrifice the integrity of the truth of the message entrusted to him. His unwavering commitment to preaching and defending the truth was, therefore, simply an expression of his loyalty to the Gospel of Jesus Christ by which he and the redeemed are saved from damnation.

Notes/Applications

In this powerful passage, Paul displays an uncompromising commitment to the truth of the Gospel. Neither the Galatians nor the Judaizers mattered much to him as he openly declared his own subjection to God's eternal truth. Rebuking the Galatians and condemning the Judaizers, Paul unashamedly declared that God's truth reigns supremely above all men no matter who they are or what they think. He condemned the enemies of the Gospel whether they came as angels, ministers, or any individual from any walk of life.

Paul's perception of the Gospel was indelibly shaped by the inherent truth embedded in its message and the absolute sovereignty of its Author. Following his Damascus Road experience, Paul immediately realized that he was no longer his own person. He understood that he had no other option but to obediently respond to the call that God had placed upon him to proclaim the Gospel to the nations. Serving the Gospel was not something left to Paul's thoughtful consideration. It was not a task he performed by his personal choice. Rather, it was a divine calling placed by divine appointment upon an individual divinely set aside for the specific task of telling others about salvation in Jesus Christ. He simply had to do it *(1 Corinthians 9:16–17).*

Paul told the Galatians and the Judaizers in no uncertain terms that the Gospel could never be subject to human scrutiny for evaluation, modification, alteration, adjustment, approval, or disapproval. God's Word judges and is never judged. It will accomplish what it was sent out to do. It will never return without accomplishing its assignments *(Isaiah 55:11).* The Gospel is the true Word of the living God spoken through the servants He appointed. Its appointed messengers are the witnesses called to spread the Good News of God's salvation. A true ambassador of the Gospel faithfully declares God's revealed redemption through Jesus Christ as imparted by the Holy Spirit. Any attempt to proclaim God's truth outside of God's message given to His appointed messengers is an act of defiance and is, therefore, worthy of condemnation. Just like the serpent in the Garden of Eden, the Judaizers were guilty of trying to undermine the truth that was preached to the Galatians. Therefore they deserved the verdict of a curse.

In a world filled to overflowing with all sorts of messages promising a better life, the words of Paul bring us to a quick halt. We listen to these messages at the peril of our eternal souls. We should forget the messenger and prove the value of the message by the words of Scripture. Then, with careful study and Spirit-guided discernment, we can join with Paul by standing boldly for the Gospel of Jesus Christ, the only way of salvation offered to a world that otherwise makes only empty promises.

Galatians 1:11–17

1:11–12 ***[11]I want you to know, brothers and sisters, that the Good News I have spread is not a human message. [12]I didn't receive it from any person. I wasn't taught it, but Jesus Christ revealed it to me.***

Paul further explained the authenticity of the Gospel by telling the Galatians the unusual circumstances by which he had received the message. Paul first assured friend and foe alike—especially the Galatians—that the Gospel he preached was not the offspring of human invention. Openly refuting the hostile claims of the Judaizers, Paul made it clear that the Gospel of Jesus Christ was completely pure and unadulterated by man's foolishness. That is, since the Gospel is God's truth revealed through His Word and committed to His appointed servants, neither its authorship nor its credibility has anything to do with human reasoning. Neither the authenticity of the message of the Gospel nor the reason for its proclamation among the nations depends on anyone's approval or endorsement. Nor is its continuing nurture affected by man's inability to understand or accept it.

Paul dismantled the accusation the Judaizers leveled against him by completely separating their faulty reasoning from the clearly revealed authenticity of the Gospel. He unashamedly affirmed that he did not receive the Gospel from any human being and he was, therefore, obligated to no one as he fulfilled his duties to the Gospel. He did not sit under any human teaching when he received instructions about the Good News he was appointed to proclaim.

Fully aware of God's hand upon his life, Paul disclosed the only true source of his enlightenment in the Gospel. He told the Galatians and the Judaizers that he received the truth directly from God through divine revelation. The Gospel he preached was divine, irrefutable, and eternal, received in a manner that could not be explained by any human reasoning. It is true! It is the only truth. It is the only eternal truth, transcending all ages and faulty human perspectives. It must never be subjected to the skeptic curiosities of the fallen human mind. Nor should its credibility be questioned on the basis of the messenger's reputation. Unlike the Judaizers who attempted to undo the Gospel in light of their own view of the messenger, Paul affirmed the truth not by his own credibility but by the credibility of the Author of the gospel message Who was the Lord Almighty, the One Whom the Judaizers claimed to worship above all else.

1:13–14 *[13]You heard about the way I once lived when I followed the Jewish religion. You heard how I violently persecuted God's church and tried to destroy it. [14]You also heard how I was far ahead of other Jews in my age group in following the Jewish religion. I had become that fanatical for the traditions of my ancestors.*

Unlike his previous religious passion, Paul's defense of the Gospel was not in any sense the fruit of an ignorant zeal. Since he himself was once like them, Paul was fully aware of the sincere motives that engaged the opponents of the Gospel in a malicious persecution of God's people. After he passionately affirmed the indisputable authenticity of the Gospel, Paul proceeded to remind the Galatians about his past and the man he had become in Jesus Christ, his Redeemer and Master.

Paul vehemently opposed the Judaizers and cursed them for their hostile attempt to undermine the true Gospel. He was perfectly aware of their motivations and objectives. Like the Judaizers who relentlessly chased him in hot pursuit, Paul too had been a zealous Pharisee who persecuted the disciples, seeking to destroy the church of Jesus Christ and annihilate the saints (*1 Corinthians 15:9*; *Philippians 3:4–6*; *Acts 22:3–4*). He was a full-blooded Jew, a Hebrew of the Hebrews, and an accomplished expert of the Law, trained at the feet of Gamaliel, one of the most respected rabbis of the time. He was unequaled by his peers in his passionate defense of the Jewish religious tradition. He was driven by a burning zeal motivated by a misguided religious superiority against anyone who had anything to do with Jesus Christ and anyone who threatened the Jewish religious establishment. In essence, Paul accompanied his instruction to the Galatians with the undeniable evidence of his own past. He had intimate, first-hand knowledge about the enemies of the Gospel.

1:15–17 ***15But God, who appointed me before I was born and who called me by his kindness, was pleased 16to show me his Son. He did this so that I would tell people who are not Jewish that his Son is the Good News. When this happened, I didn't talk it over with any other person. 17I didn't even go to Jerusalem to see those who were apostles before I was. Instead, I went to Arabia and then came back to Damascus.***

Paul effectively answered the Judaizers' accusations by offering a clear explanation of his appointment to the ministry of the Gospel. He told the Galatians how and by Whose authority his conversion and commission were executed. In spite of Paul's Judaic zeal, God moved in His own time and accomplished His eternal plan for Paul whom He had separated for His own purpose while Paul was yet in his mother's womb, indeed, even before the foundation of the world *(Ephesians 1:4)*.

God replaced Paul's misguided zeal with a life-long appointment to proclaim the Gospel of Jesus Christ. When it pleased Him to do so, God decisively interrupted Paul's zealous mission and stopped him cold in his tracks. God met Paul on the road to Damascus with the blinding Light of His glory and redirected his mission to what had been planned for him in the eternal counsel of the One Who created him *(Acts 9:3–6)*. The Lord told Paul to go into Damascus and receive instructions for his divinely preordained mission from the disciples he came to destroy. God appointed Paul to apostleship before he was born, called him to the ministry of the Gospel by His grace, and personally delivered His instructions directly from the mouth of His Son Jesus Christ. Not only did God reveal Jesus Christ to Paul, but also sent him to tell the message of His Son to the Gentiles who did not have the privilege of directly receiving the Law like the Jews.

As noted in verses eleven and twelve above, Paul did not receive the Gospel from men. He received the truth by a direct revelation from God without the agency of a human messenger. He told the Galatians that he left Damascus and went to Arabia for some time before he went to Jerusalem. He did not go to Jerusalem to confer with the apostles to affirm his salvation and call to ministry. He was led by God to go to Arabia. In essence, Paul effectively dismissed the hostile allegations of the Judaizers against him as groundless accusations. They had nothing to do with His conversion and appointment to ministry. They did not have the authority or the spiritual wisdom to hold him accountable.

Notes/Applications

For obvious reasons outlined above, Paul had absolute confidence in the message that he preached to the Galatians. His strongly worded rebuke was not merely a call to return to what they first believed. Paul also wanted the Galatians to reject the false teachings of the Judaizers for what it truly was. By sharing his personal testimony, Paul informed the Galatians that the Judaizers' accusations against him were groundless and promoted in ignorance.

Immediately following his extraordinary encounter on the outskirts of Damascus, Paul was left with no alternative but to surrender to his guides who led him into the city. There, he joined the disciples of Jesus Christ. He no longer persecuted them. Instead he became one of them. God's encounter was direct, sudden, and irresistible. Even Paul, the proudest Pharisee, the most learned theologian, the most passionate zealot, the most dedicated champion of Judaism, and a Hebrew of the Hebrews could not resist God's power and continue with his malicious persecution of the disciples of Jesus Christ. Paul later realized that his apostleship to the Gentiles was a way of life chosen for him. He recognized that a life of ministry was not a matter of choice for him. It was an irresistible calling. God's sovereign calling to spread the Gospel among the Gentiles was imposed on Paul even against his own natural will or personal desires *(1 Corinthians 9:16–17).*

The Judaizers did not know the truth that Paul had personally and directly received from God. Nor were they consulted on Paul's appointment to apostleship. Their opposition to Paul's itinerant evangelism was simply a hostile pursuit fueled by the same zeal which consumed Paul prior to his transformation. Paul, therefore, warned the Galatians that the Judaizers were not qualified to validate the truth that transformed their lives. The truth of God's Word is self-evident and affirms its own credibility by its own intrinsic merit derived from its Author. God's truth needs no defense. Its transcendence and inherent value are invincible. Paul strongly demanded the Galatians reject the false teachings put forth by the Judaizers. He urged them then, and urges us today, to fight any and all departures from the message of salvation in Jesus Christ alone by the power of the Truth instilled in the believer's heart by the Holy Spirit.

Galatians 1:18–24

1:18 *Then, three years later I went to Jerusalem to become personally acquainted with Cephas. I stayed with him for fifteen days.*

Paul continued the biographical story of his salvation and call to ministry. Three years after his Damascus Road experience and a retreat to Arabia, Paul went to Jerusalem to meet Cephas, another name for Peter *(John 1:40–42)*, where he stayed for fifteen days. Paul gave the Galatians ample information to help them understand that the Gospel he preached did not come from human sources and was not, therefore, subject to human opinion.

Paul's introduction to the disciples was not easy. In Acts 9:26–27, we read that the disciples did not immediately accept him as a fellow-believer because of his reputation as their enemy who had persecuted them relentlessly. The disciples were all afraid of him. But Barnabas took Paul under his personal care and introduced him to the disciples. Barnabas told the disciples about Paul's conversion and how God used him in spreading His Word. Even after three years of relative peace in Judea and Paul's absence from the scene, the disciples were not convinced that God could change someone like Paul. But God had a witness, Barnabas, a name meaning *the son of consolation.*

1:19 *I didn't see any other apostle. I only saw James, the Lord's brother.*

Paul's initial contact with the disciples was limited. He met Peter and stayed with him for fifteen days. During his stay, he also visited with James whom he identified as the Lord's brother. This was Jesus' maternal half-brother, since Jesus did not have an earthly father. By all accounts, it appears that Paul met only with Peter and James when he first came to Jerusalem. The rest of them were either afraid or stayed away or had no occasion to see him at Peter's home where Paul stayed. Paul tells this to the Galatians to reinforce his argument that he was not tutored in the Gospel by any human being. Therefore, the message he proclaimed should not be questioned by anyone. At best, Paul's journey to Jerusalem was a search for Christian fellowship, not instruction in the Gospel.

1:20 *(God is my witness that what I'm writing is not a lie.)*

Paul realized that the Galatians were caught between his clearly stated message of the Gospel and the misguided teaching of the Judaizers. The Judaizers certainly talked about the Law as they tried to impress the importance of their traditions on the Galatians. No matter how sincere their motivations, that message drew them away from their new God-given faith in Jesus Christ. The Galatians also heard Paul's strong reaffirmation of the Gospel and his challenge to stand firm on God's true and living Word. To the Galatians, all of this may have appeared to be a confusing exchange, making it difficult for them to know what or whom to believe.

Paul pointed the Galatians to God, the Author of the Gospel, to validate the authenticity of the Gospel he preached to them. The testimony he shared about his own conversion and call to ministry only confirmed his unique position as God's appointed messenger of this Gospel. He called upon God as his witness to publicly affirm that he spoke nothing but the truth. Even though the Judaizers had their own opinions and traditions to depend on for support, Paul assured the Galatians that he was telling them the truth as unto the Lord. That is, he spoke God's truth to them as God Himself gave it to him.

1:21 *Then I went to the regions of Syria and Cilicia.*

After his brief stay in Jerusalem with Peter, Paul went on to Syria and Cilicia, a region about 125 miles (200 km) north of Jerusalem. As an apostle to the Gentiles, Paul traveled throughout the Mediterranean basin and preached the Gospel wherever God opened doors of opportunity for him. His visit to Syria and Cilicia was the beginning of his itinerant ministry.

1:22 *The churches of Christ in Judea didn't know me personally.*

After a minimum of three years following his conversion, Paul visited Jerusalem only for fifteen days. He only met with Peter and James, the Lord's brother. Then he again traveled northward to Syria and Cilicia. Most of the believers in Judea never had the opportunity to meet him. Because of this, Paul was a stranger to the Christian churches in the center of Jewish life.

1:23 *The only thing they had heard was this: "The man who persecuted us is now spreading the faith that he once tried to destroy."*

The only thing that the disciples in Judea and Jerusalem knew about Paul was that he had been an enemy of Christ's church. But now, they heard that he was a follower of Jesus Christ and preached the Gospel he had so vehemently rejected in the past. Even though he was hardly known, his reputation had reached well beyond his immediate acquaintances. Nearly all believers in Judea knew him as the one who was once their persecutor and was now boldly preaching the Gospel.

1:24 *So they praised God for what had happened to me.*

Those who recognized the dramatic change in Paul did not need to meet him in person. They simply praised God and glorified His Name for what He did in Paul's life. Unlike the Judaizers, many of the believers in the churches of Judea had godly wisdom that enabled them to discern the transformation which had taken place. Even though they did not know him in person, Paul's notoriety in wreaking havoc among the disciples of Jesus Christ was well known to the churches in Judea. Being endowed with God's wisdom, it was not hard for them to discern the marvelous work of God's redemption in Paul. Without meeting or seeing him in person, they trusted God for His own work in Paul and praised Him for the transformation that transpired in the life of this most passionate zealot, a self-appointed persecutor of the church.

Notes/Applications

Paul shared his personal testimony with the Galatians to affirm two essential facts about his conversion and subsequent service to the Gospel. First, he wanted to assure the Galatians that God directly accomplished his transformation and instruction in God's truth without the use of any human agency including the intervention of the disciples. Second, no one had the spiritual capacity to contest the inspired teaching he had received.

No one is ever equipped to question God's direct revelation of His truth. Paul wanted the Galatians not only to believe in what he taught them, but also to reject bad teaching on the basis of the truth he had taught them. Paul encouraged the Galatians to dismiss the Judaizers' hostile accusations against him by relying on the Spirit-affirmed truth of the Gospel instilled in their hearts at the time of their salvation.

The relationship of the believer to the Lord is fundamental to the to the believer's ability to determine truth from falsehood, the difference between the unchanging Gospel and the always-changing teachings of people who do not really belong to God. Both churches and individual believers are constantly under the divine obligation to know the Word of God so that they are not deceived by those who distort the clear message of the Gospel.

So may all believers attend faithfully to the study of the Word, knowing that we walk in a world that continues to oppose Jesus and His finished work on the Cross of Calvary.

GALATIANS 2

Galatians 2:1–6

2:1 ***Then 14 years later I went to Jerusalem again with Barnabas. I also took Titus along.***

Paul continued with his explanation to show the Galatians that the Gospel he preached was revealed and given to him by God. As noted in the first chapter, he began to correct the error of their thinking by reaffirming the truth that he had already preached to them and by condemning anyone who taught anything that was different from the Gospel of Jesus Christ. He then continued to share his own experience as God's appointed apostle to the Gentiles by giving a detailed account of his testimony in the service of the Gospel. Following his three years in Arabia and his brief visit with Peter and James in Jerusalem, Paul embarked on his first missionary journey and was fully engaged in the proclamation of the Gospel throughout the Mediterranean coast for fourteen years. Then he returned to Jerusalem with his companion Barnabas. He also brought Titus along with him to Jerusalem, a Greek convert who was not raised in the Jewish tradition. Because of his specifically assigned task among the Gentiles, Paul was absent from Jerusalem for a total of seventeen years.

2:2 ***I went in response to a revelation [from God]. I showed them the way I spread the Good News among people who are not Jewish. I did this in a private meeting with those recognized as important people to see whether all my efforts have been wasted.***

Paul did not casually end up in Jerusalem without a good reason. He went to Jerusalem as a result of a specific revelation from God. Paul's God-directed visit to Jerusalem had two essential objectives. First, he wanted to glorify God with his comrades in the faith by declaring God's mighty work of redemption among the Gentiles. Second, he wanted to affirm the credibility of his work among the Gentiles to God's appointed apostles. Even though Paul's conversion, encounter with the Truth, and ultimate appointment to his work among the Gentiles did not come through human agents, Paul still held himself accountable to God through the authority of the apostles who, like him, were appointed by God to serve the cause of the Gospel.

We read in Acts 13 and 14 that Paul and Barnabas preached the Gospel in Antioch, a city in the region of Syria, and the province of Lycaonia in the respective cities of Iconium, Lystra, and Derbe in Asia Minor (what is now Turkey). God blessed their ministry with a fruitful harvest and miraculous signs everywhere, drawing the people to Himself in multitudes. However, the Jews in all of the cities violently opposed them, sometimes trying to kill them. So Paul and Barnabas returned to Jerusalem to have the Gospel officially affirmed by the apostolic leadership *(Acts 15:2)*.

2:3 ***Titus was with me, and although he is Greek, no one forced him to be circumcised.***

Paul went to Jerusalem with Barnabas, his ministry companion, and Titus, one of the early converts of his ministry among the Gentiles.

Being a Gentile convert, the Judaizers would have required Titus to be circumcised in order to secure his salvation *(Acts 15:1)*. However, instead of pressuring Titus to be circumcised, the apostles trusted Paul's testimony and accepted Titus as a believing brother without the requirement of complying with the Jewish law. God had poured out His grace on the Gentiles and presented Titus to them as the living evidence of God's saving grace. This was a vital issue to the Galatians since they themselves were Gentiles and were harassed by the Judaizers because they had not submitted to the Judaic law, which the Judaizers wrongly believed necessary to complete their salvation.

2:4 *False Christians were brought in. They slipped in as spies to learn about the freedom Christ Jesus gives us. They hoped to find a way to control us.*

Alluding to the Jews who persecuted him throughout the cities where he taught, Paul told the Galatians that his dissenters pursued him everywhere. Now these dissenters who were not Christians quietly infiltrated the assembly where Paul and the apostles were gathered. These Judaizers were not interested in hearing about God's mercy revealed among the Gentiles. They were looking for opportunities to undermine the Gospel by zealously teaching an erroneous gospel everywhere the Good News of God's redemption in Jesus Christ was preached. They relentlessly countered the message of freedom in Jesus Christ by telling the people about their responsibility to the Law as the only way to salvation. They ridiculed freedom in Jesus Christ in order to take control of the people by subjecting them to the Law.

2:5 *But we did not give in to them for a moment, so that the truth of the Good News would always be yours.*

Paul assured the Galatians that the theological perspective of the Judaizers did not deter his companions in ministry from the truth he had received from the Lord Himself. They exposed the false teachings of the Judaizers with the truth. False doctrine cannot prevail because truth always strips away the thin veneer of religious error. Because Paul refused to submit to the control the Judaizers attempted to impose on the meeting, the truth of the Good News triumphed, and that truth preserved the integrity of the message that had been delivered to the Christians in Galatia. All believers are sustained in faith because of the enduring truth of the Gospel.

2:6 *Those who were recognized as important people didn't add a single thing to my message. (What sort of people they were makes no difference to me, since God doesn't play favorites.)*

It appears that Paul recognized the need to establish the truth by additional witnesses. He told the Galatians that the apostles in Jerusalem fully agreed with his declaration of the truth. They did not have anything to add because what he proclaimed was nothing but the whole truth as given to him by God. Essentially, it was the same message proclaimed by the church leaders in Jerusalem.

In a sense, Paul indirectly again told the Galatians that the authenticity of what he preached did not depend on the opinion of any human being. He told them that the high regard the apostles enjoyed among the believers in Jerusalem did not personally matter to him. Even though he sought the affirmation of the apostles, he really did not *need* their consent. God's truth is the only truth and that truth was the same for the disciples in Jerusalem as it was for the disciples in Asia Minor. However, the consent of the apostles was still significant so that all believers could demonstrate their oneness in the Gospel. At the same time, that unity in the truth was an important part of the church's rejection of the false doctrine of the Judaizers.

Notes/Applications

Paul continued to correct the Galatians by shifting his focus to his own personal testimony. He told the Galatians that he returned to Jerusalem after fourteen years of ministry to confer with the apostles about his work among the Gentiles and to publicly declare the breadth of God's inclusive grace.

Being a Jew himself, Paul knew so well that Jewish believers struggled with the idea of salvation without the observance of Jewish rituals. He brought Titus to Jerusalem to show the apostles how God's grace had been granted to non-Jewish people in a way that demonstrated clearly that salvation through Jesus was the fulfillment of the promises given to the children of Israel. As noted in chapter 1:15–16, God had already planned to redeem children from among the Gentiles and appointed Paul to be His apostle to the people who were not Jewish even before he was born. Paul showed the apostles that God's plan to save Gentiles was not an afterthought. Rather, God's salvation was planned and accomplished eternally according to His sovereign will. Paul's personal account of his experience among the Gentiles was a powerful testimony to the apostles in Jerusalem. His report helped the apostles see beyond their Jewish religious mindset and appreciate the breadth of God's grace. Even though salvation is individual and personal, it is conferred upon all the elect by the same Holy Spirit no matter if one is a Jew or a Gentile.

Galatians 2:7–13

2:7 ***In fact, they saw that I had been entrusted with telling the Good News to people who are not circumcised as Peter had been entrusted to tell it to those who are circumcised.***

Paul told the Galatians that the apostles finally understood what God did through him and the rest of the apostles to spread the Good News of His salvation both among the Jews and the Gentiles. The apostles recognized that Paul was indeed a fellow apostle. He was assigned to preach the Gospel to the Gentiles while Peter was appointed to preach the same Gospel to the Jew, doing exactly the same thing as Paul was doing. Here, Paul showed how different apostles were appointed to minister to different people groups. The message was exactly identical. Even though Jews and Gentiles had a different heritage, God's message to both groups was the same—salvation was the gift of God through the finished work of Jesus Christ. Even though the message was delivered in the context of their respective backgrounds, the only pathway to eternal life was through the sacrifice of Jesus Christ alone.

2:8 ***The one who made Peter an apostle to Jewish people also made me an apostle to people who are not Jewish.***

The apostles in Jerusalem realized that Paul and Peter preached the same message given to them by the same Lord. They both proclaimed the finished work of Jesus Christ as the only way to the Father. They also realized that both men were appointed to their tasks by the same Lord. There is only one message given to Church of Jesus Christ, that message given by the Author of the Gospel and the same appointing Authority, even Jesus Christ Himself. So, there was no need for a different message that did not support what the Church of Christ was already proclaiming.

2:9 ***James, Cephas, and John (who were recognized as the most important people) acknowledged that God had given me***

this special gift. So they shook hands with Barnabas and me, agreeing to be our partners. It was understood that we would work among the people who are not Jewish and they would work among Jewish people.

Paul was emphatic as he showed the Galatians how he did not receive the Gospel from men no matter how well respected they were. Nevertheless, he consulted the apostles in Jerusalem for the benefit and unity of the believers–Jew and Gentile–and presented the evidence of God's redemption even among the Gentiles. Paul told the Galatians that even the chief apostles James, Cephas (Peter), and John finally realized that God had extended His redemption to the Gentiles through Paul's preaching. The apostles and the whole assembly of believers actually dispatched a letter by the hands of chosen disciples to confirm their conclusion about God's redemptive work among the Gentiles (*Acts 15:22–33*). It was necessary for the Galatians to understand this fact. The Judaizers who came to turn them against Paul's teaching were effectively telling them that the chief apostles had accepted an erroneous conclusion. By telling the Galatians that the chief apostles recognized God's power in his ministry among the Gentiles, Paul demonstrated that the Galatians were specifically involved in the same debate and should arrive at the same conclusion. Otherwise, the devious false teaching of the Judaizers would undermine their faith in the finished work of Jesus Christ.

2:10 *The only thing they asked us to do was to remember the poor, the very thing which I was eager to do.*

The apostles confirmed Paul's ministry and communicated their support by letter. This letter was carried to Gentiles outside of Jerusalem by envoys chosen from the Jerusalem assembly. They did not add to or detract from the Gospel that Paul preached to the Gentiles. There was complete unity among the leadership of the Jerusalem church. The apostles additionally asked Paul to remind the Gentile believers to remember the poor. Paul fully supported such charitable work. In short,

Paul told the Galatians that the Gospel he preached was completely in line with what God had revealed to the other apostles. That Gospel transformed people's lives so that their hearts became compassionate toward those who were less fortunate. Both Paul and the leadership in Jerusalem agreed completely in this outward demonstration of their faith.

2:11 ***When Cephas came to Antioch, I had to openly oppose him because he was completely wrong.***

Paul, Barnabas and the chosen men of the Jerusalem assembly finally returned to Antioch to present the letter sent from the apostles regarding the dispute that arose earlier between Paul and the Judaizers. The letter vindicated Paul, affirmed the Gospel, and acknowledged God's redemption among the Gentiles. The false doctrine put forth by the enemies of the Gospel was exposed for what it was. Paul's ministry among the Gentiles continued along with his companions, Barnabas, Judas, and Silas *(Acts 15:25, 32)*.

However, when Peter came to Antioch some time later, the issue again troubled the unity of the early church. Even though Peter was an apostle, Paul did not hesitate to confront him when he saw Peter behave in a way that contradicted the letter given by the Jerusalem assembly. Paul had already told the Galatians that any one who preached a different message from the Gospel that he preached was cursed regardless of who he was *(Galatians 1:8–9)*. To Paul, Jesus Christ was the only truth in Who He is—in what He said and in what He did.

2:12–13 ***[12]He ate with people who were not Jewish until some men James had sent [from Jerusalem] arrived. Then Cephas drew back and would not associate with people who were not Jewish. He was afraid of those who insisted that circumcision***

was necessary. [13]The other Jewish Christians also joined him in this hypocrisy. Even Barnabas was swept along with them.

Cephas (Peter) was in good fellowship with the Gentile Christians in Antioch during the initial period of his visit with them. He had no trouble associating with these believers—entering their homes and eating their food. However, he stopped associating with the Gentile Christians when certain Jews dispatched by James in Jerusalem arrived in Antioch. Whoever these representatives were, Peter felt constrained by their presence to withdraw from Gentile company. Peter's withdrawal so influenced other Jewish believers in Antioch that they also stopped associating with their Gentile brothers in Christ. Even Barnabas followed his example and joined with the Jerusalem representatives, abandoning their fellowship with Gentile Christians.

In spite of the conclusion reached in Jerusalem and his own personal experience, Peter was afraid of those Jews who insisted on the importance of following Jewish religious practices. This was not acceptable to Paul. Truth was truth and error was error. In Jerusalem, Peter actually defended Paul when he came to Jerusalem to present his case before the assembly and the chief apostles *(Acts 15:7–11)*. Peter argued that both Jews and Gentiles were saved by the grace of the Lord Jesus Christ. Peter's statement was so powerful that it quieted the whole assembly and gave Paul and Barnabas the opportunity to share their testimony of the Gospel's work among the Gentiles.

Peter knew the truth. He spoke it, taught it, and defended it. He heard it from Jesus' lips and was himself delivered by this truth. However, Peter was unduly influenced by his fellow Jews who imposed their Judaic precepts upon the finished work of Jesus Christ. Paul exposed Peter's hypocrisy and confronted him publicly about his unreasonable fear when he knew the truth so well. Paul showed the Galatians that, if left unaddressed, an enduring falsehood could practically keep them from understanding the truth. He encouraged them to stand firmly upon the truth of the Gospel they first heard and believed and reject any other teaching regardless of the reputation of the person presenting it to them.

Notes/Applications

Paul and Peter were both Jewish men. They were both familiar with the Judaic teachings of the coming Messiah. However, while their backgrounds and knowledge of their Jewish history and theology were absolutely necessary to present the Gospel in its entirety, the difference in the cultural backgrounds of Jewish and Gentile Christians required a focused ministry by a dedicated apostle. Therefore, God appointed Paul to preach the Gospel to the Gentiles while Peter was sent to his Jewish compatriots.

Paul and Peter were entrusted with the same message even though different points of emphasis were addressed in the process of delivering the Gospel. Peter, like Stephen, recited the entire Jewish history and the events pertaining to Jesus' crucifixion because their history and the Scriptures proved that Jesus was their promised Messiah *(Acts 2:14–36; 7)*. But Paul spoke directly about the finished work of Christ and man's fallen condition in sin when he preached the Gospel to the Gentiles *(Ephesians 2:1–10)*.

Paul made it clear to Gentile unbelievers that the Jewish heritage was not important in their understanding of Christ's redemption because they could not relate to it. Any teaching that attempted to base the redemptive benefit of Christ's work on Jewish religious practice was wrong and unfounded. Regardless of history, heritage, or pre-condition, God's redemption is given only through Jesus Christ's finished work upon Calvary and His glorious resurrection. Both in his confrontation with Peter and his exhortation of the Galatian Christians, Paul encouraged all believers to stand firmly upon God's truth and reject any distortion of this Gospel without fear or compromise.

Galatians 2:14–21

2:14 ***But I saw that they were not properly following the truth of the Good News. So I told Cephas in front of everyone, "You're Jewish, but you live like a person who is not Jewish. So how can you insist that people who are not Jewish must live like Jews?"***

Paul was uncompromisingly committed to the truth that God entrusted to him. His defense of the truth was not dependent upon other persons or circumstances. So when he saw Peter's two-faced conduct, Paul publicly exposed his hypocrisy. Why did Peter try to make the Gentiles live like Jews when he himself lived freely like a Gentile? What Peter did was far worse. He adjusted his outlook and practice according to the group that he was with at any given moment.

He comfortably ate and associated with Gentile Christians when he first came to Antioch. But when Jewish believers came from Jerusalem he abandoned his friendly companionship with Gentile believers and joined with Jewish believers in order to save face with the Jerusalem church. Paul found Peter's conduct to be duplicitous, hypocritical, and cowardly. Therefore, his question demanded that Peter stand firmly upon the truth of the Gospel both in his conversation *and* in his practice. If he believed in the truth, he must also live it out without apologizing for his faithfulness to the truth.

2:15–16 [15]***We are Jewish by birth, not sinners from other nations.*** [16]***Yet, we know that people don't receive God's approval because of their own efforts to live according to a set of standards, but only by believing in Jesus Christ. So we also believed in Jesus Christ in order to receive God's approval because of faith in Christ and not because of our own efforts.***

People won't receive God's approval because of their own efforts to live according to a set of standards.

Paul indicted Peter's behavior not just as hypocrisy, but he said that Peter should have known better. He was a Jew, the only people to whom the Law was directly given. God gave the Law to the Jews and sent His Son to earth through the Jews. The Law was given to the children of Israel as the foreshadowing representation of God's salvation that was unequivocally fulfilled in Jesus Christ within the geographic and historic framework of a Jewish setting. Paul emphatically claimed that Peter should have known this so well and should not have fallen into a mindset of duplicitous hypocrisy.

As the disciple of Jesus Christ, Peter should have known that the Son of God fulfilled the Law both through His righteous life and sacrificial death. He should have known that Christ declared freedom to those who were called unto salvation out of sin's bondage. Paul confronted Peter's hypocrisy because he was wrong in spite of the knowledge and Christian experience he had in the faith. He himself had been saved by God's grace through faith in Jesus Christ. Why did Peter behave as though the Law had not been fulfilled by Jesus Christ? Why would he by his behavior show the Gentiles with whom he had associated that he was still obligated to the Law? Why was he willing to compromise the truth in order to accommodate the wrong thinking of Jewish believers, risking the confusion of the Gentiles?

2:17 ***If we, the same people who are searching for God's approval in Christ, are still sinners, does that mean that Christ encourages us to sin? That's unthinkable!***

Paul raised a question that the Judaizers might use to rationalize their insistence for the continued observance of the Law in order to complete their salvation. Does being saved through faith alone mean that the saved are free to forget the Law and live in sin? Does Christ approve of sin by setting believers free from the standards of the Law? Paul's answer to this question was an emphatic, "NO!"

2:18 *If I rebuild something that I've torn down, I admit that I was wrong to tear it down.*

Paul publicly acknowledged that if he rebuilt what he tore down, he would be guilty of duplicity. Either he was wrong in destroying what he later determined to rebuild, or, he was in error in rebuilding what he thought should be torn down in the first place.

The point is that the Law is fully satisfied by Jesus Christ. There is nothing more to fulfill. God, by His grace called the redeemed to believe the finished work of Jesus Christ and accept His salvation. Paul reminded Peter that he could not be a child of grace and again become enslaved to the Law to get what he already had been given by Christ. One is either saved by grace or remains in bondage to the Law.

2:19 *When I tried to obey the law's standards, those laws killed me. As a result, I live in a relationship with God. I have been crucified with Christ.*

Paul employs yet another framework of explanation to clearly delineate the truth about the position of believers in Jesus Christ. Using a relational perspective, Paul outlined the two distinctly different and irreconcilable associations that the believer has with His Savior and the Law respectively. Because of sin and man's inability to satisfy the Law, the Law has already condemned everyone to death. Therefore, people are completely unable to live in such a way that they can satisfy the Law. In relationship with the Law, people are dead and not alive.

However, having paid the penalty for man's transgression, Jesus Christ revived those whom He has saved from death and set them free by the gift of His redemption. That means believers are dead to the Law but alive in Jesus Christ. Therefore, their living relationship can be shared only with their Savior in Whom they have been made alive. They can no longer share life with the Law because they are already dead to it as a result of salvation. The believer's relationship to the Law is dead not only due to transgression, but also because they have been crucified with Jesus Christ Who paid the penalty for their debt which justified their death under the Law. So, calling the redeemed back to the Law is the same as inviting them to live in death. That is the same as rejecting the salvation they have received through Christ's finished work on the Cross of Calvary.

2:20 *I no longer live, but Christ lives in me. The life I now live I live by believing in God's Son, who loved me and took the punishment for my sins.*

Being dead to the Law due to sin and having been crucified in Jesus Christ, the believer has life by Jesus Christ Who actually lives His life in the redeemed by the indwelling presence of the Holy Spirit *(John 14:17, 23)*. Paul said the life that he now lived was actually the life that Jesus was living in him. Christ's life in the believer is manifested through the steps and actions of faith taken by the child of God in every aspect of life's expressions. Jesus has full claim upon the life of the believer because He paid the full price to ransom the sinner for Himself. So the redeemed remains dead to the Law and to himself and lives only to the Lord under the full authority and direction of the Redeemer. Such a life cannot return to live for the Law against the will of the One Who paid the price to love, cherish, and purchase the redeemed by His blood.

2:21 *I don't reject God's kindness. If we receive God's approval by obeying laws, then Christ's death was pointless.*

Anyone who has been made alive by the precious blood of Jesus Christ cannot disavow the gift of eternal life given to him by God through Jesus Christ. Such an unfathomable grace cannot be fully comprehended by the human mind let alone be neglected. If believers, like the Judaizers, follow the natural patterns of human thinking and attempt to elevate the Law above the work that Christ did on behalf of sinners, they are fighting against God's salvation and, instead, embracing a life of death under the Law. If there is a need to return to the Law as the way to earn God's grace, then Jesus Christ's sacrifice is useless. In effect, people would be saying that they knew better than God Who is both the Lawgiver and the gracious Redeemer.

Notes/Applications

Paul was keenly aware of the spiritual fragility of the newly transformed believer. In 2 Corinthians 11:3, he voiced his concern that the mind of the believer might be confounded by the simplicity of the Gospel of God's grace through Jesus Christ. He knew that false teachers like the Judaizers would threaten the truth of the Gospel. They would not waste time in appealing to the thoroughly embedded sin-nature by confusing the new believer with a sense of guilt about obeying the Law. Paul clearly explained that the Law was fully satisfied by Jesus Christ and man is no longer required to fulfill it to receive God's salvation and approval.

Salvation is not given through the Law nor is it acquired by satisfying its standards because of two major reasons. First, man is incapable of meeting its demand because he is born with a sin nature. *"Behold, I was brought forth in iniquity, and in sin did my mother conceive me" (Psalm 51:5).* Second, the Law no longer requires fulfillment because it is fully satisfied by Jesus Christ.

So both to the Judaizers of old and to the legalists of all ages, Paul speaks clearly and loudly that any effort to put forth the Law as the means to secure or sustain salvation is impossible, meaningless, unnecessary, and offensive to God. Therefore, we are called to abandon ourselves to the grace of God and rest in our salvation in Christ so that He may live His life in us.

GALATIANS 3

Galatians 3:1–9

3:1 *You stupid people of Galatia! Who put you under an evil spell? Wasn't Christ Jesus' crucifixion clearly described to you?*

In the preceding two chapters, Paul used his personal history to rebut all the accusations against his apostleship to the Gentiles. He reaffirmed the authenticity and authority of the Gospel he preached. He now turned his attention to the subject matter at hand and began to outline the essentials of the Gospel. Paul told the Galatians that they were stupid when they abandoned the truth. Had they not understood the singular importance of Jesus' crucifixion in their salvation? This verse clearly reveals the level of Paul's intense frustration with the situation in Galatia.

Did Paul really think that the Galatians were stupid people? That they did not have the mental capacity to understand what he had told them? Absolutely not! Rather, he is expressing his frustration by asking how otherwise intelligent people could not see through the deceit of the Judaizers' teaching. How could people who seemed to understand clearly the importance of Christ's crucifixion even think of entertaining any other alternative for their salvation? But today's Christians often listen to differing theories or interpretations of biblically constructed messages without checking them against the infallible truth of the Scriptures—the whole counsel of God. They, like the Galatians, often succumb to the deceit of attractive philosophies that fail to uphold the central importance of Christ's crucifixion. Otherwise intelligent people often become fascinated by enticing ideas, forsake what Paul calls the foolishness of the Gospel, and in turn, they themselves become fools.

3:2 *I want to learn only one thing from you. Did you receive the Spirit by your own efforts to live according to a set of standards or by believing what you heard?*

Paul challenged the Galatians to rethink their initial experience with the Gospel and the life-changing transformation that took place in their hearts when they first heard the Good News of God's salvation. What was it like when they initially experienced their salvation? What actually took place? Did they respond by faith to the Gospel of God's salvation or did they secure God's redemption by satisfying the Law? Was their salvation secured through a contractual arrangement, or, did they receive God's gift of redemption through Christ's finished work? Which one was it? Was it faith by hearing or salvation by qualifying under the Law?

3:3 *Are you that stupid? Did you begin in a spiritual way only to end up doing things in a human way?*

The phrase *in a spiritual way* seems to imply that salvation was something that happened as a result of some inherent spiritual value within people. Other translations make it clear that, for Paul, salvation begins as a result of the work of the Holy Spirit. Example: "Are you so foolish? Having begun by the Spirit, are you now being perfected by the flesh?" *(Galatians 3:3, ESV).*

Paul demanded that the Galatians take a hard look at themselves.

What went wrong? What changed their minds? When and how did they get sidetracked from the inerrant truth of the Good News and, in fact, denied their own experience? Were they so foolish to believe that what they had received from the Holy Spirit could be improved by their human effort? How could a gift be reclaimed when it had already been given and even received? What convinced them that what they had already received from the Spirit could be reclaimed by any other means as if it had not already been given to them?

God had redeemed them by imputing His Son's righteousness to their credit. The Law had already been fulfilled by Jesus Christ on their behalf. Salvation was already given. They already belonged to God as a result of the crucifixion of Jesus Christ. What else was necessary for their salvation when the gift of eternal life had already been given by the Lord and received by them?

3:4 *Did you suffer so much for nothing? [I doubt] that it was for nothing!*

Apparently, faith in Jesus Christ was not easy for the Galatians. On the one hand, Christians were not well accepted by the pagan culture in which they lived. On the other hand, the Judaizers harassed them, insisting that they observe Judaic laws and rituals in order to complete their salvation. So Paul asked them if they suffered persecution for something they did not believe? Were they the target of the Judaizers for something they would later abandon? Paul answered his own question with an emphatic no because he knew that their salvation was unshakable if it was truly a transformation accomplished by the quickening power of the Holy Spirit. But he wondered if the Galatians realized that their attraction to the Law also implied that they had suffered uselessly for their faith in Jesus Christ.

3:5 *Does God supply you with the Spirit and work miracles among you through your own efforts or through believing what you heard?*

Paul continued to challenge the Galatians with probing questions. Did God provide them with His Spirit as a result of their works or their compliance with the Law? Did they receive faith through what *they* accomplished or as a gift from the *Spirit* through the Gospel they heard and believed? Did God make His miracles known to them to reward their performance under the Law or to affirm their faith in Jesus Christ? How could they forget their faith so quickly and easily? With this questioning method, Paul guided the Galatians back to the truth they already knew, which he prayed would revive the Gospel message in their hearts.

3:6 *Abraham serves as an example. He believed God, and that faith was regarded by God to be his approval of Abraham.*

Paul reminded the Galatians about Abraham. God considered Abraham to be righteous and was called the friend of God because he believed God and trusted His Word *(Genesis 15:1–6)*. God's favor rested on Abraham because he accepted His promise by faith, not by observing the Law. He did not acquire righteousness by what he did. Abraham, the great patriarch of the Jewish people, simply believed God and his faith was counted as righteousness. Paul's observation highlighted the obvious conclusion. Just like Abraham, the Galatians also received salvation through faith by believing the Gospel. Abraham's faith was the example that proved the reliability of the gospel message in the experience of their transformed lives.

3:7 *You must understand that people who have faith are Abraham's descendants.*

Abraham is not just an example of faith and righteousness. He is the father of those who receive God's redemption by faith. God promised Abraham that his descendants would be as numerous as the stars in the sky and the sand of the sea. God promised Abraham that He would bless him with a son in his old age. He said his wife Sarah would bear him a son. Even though he struggled with the idea of a son at his age, Abraham obeyed God and fulfilled his part of the covenant. Abraham left his country and family because God called him to a life different from the culture in which he lived. Abraham did everything as God told him by faith *(Genesis 12–25)*. Thus, Abraham's children are not those who are his biological descendants, but those who live by faith.

3:8–9 ***[8]Scripture saw ahead of time that God would give his approval to non-Jewish people who have faith. So Scripture announced the Good News to Abraham ahead of time when it said, "Through you all the people of the world will be blessed." [9]So people who believe are blessed together with Abraham, the man of faith.***

Paul interpreted God's promise to Abraham so that the Galatians could understand clearly what God had said about people who would come to Him by faith, not by the works of the Law. God told Abraham that kings and nations would arise from among his children. His descendants would be blessed. In addition, those who believe in God by faith would be blessed together with Abraham as God's children of faith. As their father Abraham was a man of faith, his descendants who believed in God and accepted His promises would also receive the privilege to be the children of God. In pronouncing His blessings upon him, God actually told Abraham that his descendants would be saved from the condemnation of the Law by faith in Jesus Christ. Even though the Law was given to the Jews as a covenantal institution, all who come to God by faith are blessed just like Abraham. Unlike the Judaizers who continued to depend on the Law to gain God's approval, all of Abraham's faith-descendants obtain their salvation only through Jesus Christ, believing the Gospel of Christ's sacrifice. God considered Abraham to be righteous, not because of obedience, but because of his faith.

Notes/Applications

Paul's challenge to the Galatians was not ambiguous. After sharing his own experience in God's redeeming and sustaining grace, he encouraged the Galatians to stop and rethink their initial spiritual experience. He wanted them to ask pertinent questions that would remind them of God's grace and remarkable provision for their salvation and ongoing spiritual nourishment. How did they receive God's redemption? How did they become God's redeemed children? Did they qualify for salvation by fulfilling the provisions of the Law, or, did they receive redemption by believing the Good News of God's salvation?

Paul knew how the Galatians became the followers of Jesus Christ. The only way to salvation is through Jesus Christ Who secured God's redemption for the lost. He Himself is the way, the truth, and the life—the only One by Whom anyone can come to the Father. Pointing to Abraham, who became the spiritual father of all who would be saved by faith, Paul told the Galatians that faith in Jesus Christ could never be replaced by obedience to the Law. The truth they first learned should not be replaced or undermined by any new teaching that would draw them away from what they initially heard, believed, and experienced.

Paul encourages all believers to grow in the knowledge of Jesus Christ in order to guard against the misleading influences of false doctrines. Believers are encouraged to remain focused upon God's Word and continue to grow in their knowledge of the truth. What they learn must remain consistent with the initial truth that quickened their heart to faith in Jesus Christ. The search is not for new information. Rather, the child of God must be nurtured by the continuing revelation of God's grace. The Holy Spirit illuminates the understanding of the believer, affirming step by step the truth that He brought into the heart of the believer when He raised the sinner to life in the light of God's redemption. The challenge encourages the believer to be diligent and consistent in the study of God's Word so that the child of God may properly understand and interpret the truth, maturing in the faith that God has already given to them.

Galatians 3:10–18

3:10 *Certainly, there is a curse on all who rely on their own efforts to live according to a set of standards because Scripture says, "Whoever doesn't obey everything that is written in Moses' Teachings is cursed."*

Paul's emphasis on faith was not a rejection of the Law. He did not tell the Galatians to despise the Law and deny its appropriate relevance to the life of the believer. However, crediting their salvation to their observance of the Law was wrong.

Any claim to salvation through the Law is wrong for two essential reasons. First, no human being is able to fulfill the Law in its entirety because people are born in sin. Second, anyone born in sin lacks the perfection required by the Law and is, therefore, cursed *(Deuteronomy 27:26)*. Paul vehemently asserted that returning to the unforgiving rigors of the Law for salvation meant that they rejected God's salvation by grace through faith. They were saved from sin's condemnation by faith and, therefore, should not even want to return to the bondage of the Law whereby they were condemned, as though the work of God's grace was not sufficient.

3:11 *No one receives God's approval by obeying the law's standards since, "The person who has God's approval will live because of faith."*

The redeemed are not only saved by grace, but also continue to grow in faith by God's grace. No Christian has ever been saved by satisfying the Law. Since all people are born in sin, they are incapable of perfectly or sinlessly observing the Law. Nor are they capable of living in perfection because of their fallen nature. Therefore, as justified saints in Jesus Christ believers live by the same faith through which they were saved *(Habakkuk 2:4)*. Given the relentless distribution of the false teachings of the Judaizers, Paul found it necessary to reestablish firmly their understanding of God's redemption and ongoing sanctification secured in Jesus Christ alone.

3:12 *Laws have nothing to do with faith, but, "Whoever obeys laws will live because of the laws he obeys."*

The Law does not require faith as its criteria for perfection. Its provisions call for a perfect score in order to receive God's approval. All of its requirements must be fulfilled without any exception *(Leviticus 18:5)*. People can earn God's approval if they perfectly live by its rules without a single incidence of disobedience. That is, those who want to live by the Law must unequivocally satisfy the Law in order to benefit from its rewards. However, if people make the choice to live by the Law, then they must be willing to be judged by the Law.

The Law does not provide for forgiveness or restoration. All violations are punishable without any opportunity for reprieve. No substitution is considered. The guilty must face the full consequences of the transgression as charged. Under the Law, guilty people do not have the benefit of faith in the perfection of Jesus Christ or God's grace. Paul reminded the Galatians that God had already redeemed them by His grace, saving them from His judgment as administered by the Law.

3:13 *Christ paid the price to free us from the curse that God's laws bring by becoming cursed instead of us. Scripture says, "Everyone who is hung on a tree is cursed."*

Even though salvation is the gift of God's grace to those whom He redeems, it does not come without cost. After fulfilling the requirements of the Law by His perfect, sinless, and righteous life, Jesus Christ gave His life to die on the Cross as One Who was cursed *(Deuteronomy 21:23)*. The penalty for sin is death. Jesus died to pay the penalty demanded by the Law for sin. Jesus Christ laid down His life on the Cross, sparing transgressors from facing death. By His sinless life and sacrificial death on the Cross, Jesus Christ sets people free from the rigors of the Law and the consequences of their transgression. Freedom in God's redemption means that God's grace is conferred upon those who do not deserve mercy because Jesus' sacrifice satisfied the requirements of the Law. There is no need to return to the Law for salvation. The Law cannot demand anything from God's redeemed people. Jesus Christ has fulfilled it on their behalf.

3:14 *[Christ paid the price] so that the blessing promised to Abraham would come to all the people of the world through Jesus Christ and we would receive the promised Spirit through faith.*

Jesus Christ's sacrifice at Calvary was the fulfillment of God's promise to Abraham. Abraham believed and God counted his faith as righteousness. God promised Abraham that the nations of the world would be blessed through him. Therefore, God settled His judgment upon sin by sacrificing His Son so that those who would believe in Jesus Christ would be His children by faith like Abraham. Those who accepted Jesus Christ by faith would receive the promised Holy Spirit through faith without having to achieve God's approval through an unattainable obedience to the Law.

The phrase *to all the people of the world* is a translation of a Greek word usually translated as *Gentile*. While Christ's sacrifice at Calvary was sufficient for the sins of the world, careful consideration of the entire body of the Scriptures makes it clear that Paul was refuting the argument of the Judaizers. Gentile people would be saved by the sacrifice of Jesus Christ just as Jewish people were.

3:15 *Brothers and sisters, let me use an example from everyday life. No one can cancel a person's will or add conditions to it once that will is put into effect.*

Paul explained his point by using an illustration referring to a familiar legal practice. Once a will is probated and enforced, no conditions can be added to its terms. Nor can there be any cancellations or additions. The will is enforced as written and cannot be changed. Once it is put into effect, the will becomes the exclusive law over the parties and interests covered by its provisions.

3:16 ***The promises were spoken to Abraham and to his descendant. Scripture doesn't say, "descendants," referring to many, but "your descendant," referring to one. That descendant is Christ.***

The will Paul had in mind was God's promise to Abraham. In that promise, God referred to Abraham's Descendant. The word is not plural. It is singular. Thus, God told Abraham that by his seed all nations of the world would be blessed. By his encounter and conversion through Jesus, Paul knew that Abraham's promised Descendant was Jesus Christ. God's promise to Abraham is fulfilled by Jesus Christ alone. That is, God's covenant to Abraham stipulated the promise of blessing through Jesus Christ. Since God already put His promise to Abraham into effect, nothing could cancel the blessing offered to the lost through Jesus Christ.

3:17 ***This is what I mean: The laws [given to Moses] 430 years after God had already put his promise [to Abraham] into effect didn't cancel the promise [to Abraham].***

Since the Promise had been given and put into effect before the Law was given to Moses, God's promise was the foundation of God's covenant with Abraham concerning the nations of the world. God's promise that all nations would be blessed through Abraham's seed could not be annulled by anything that happened prior to or following the Promise. The Law was given to Israel four hundred and thirty years *after* God put His promise to Abraham into effect. Therefore, since the Law was given after the Promise, it cannot be retroactively applied and annul God's covenant to Abraham. The Judaizers' effort to put the Galatians under the bonds of the Law was a futile attempt to annul God's promise through Abraham's Seed, Jesus Christ.

3:18 ***If we have to gain the inheritance by following those laws, then it no longer comes to us because of the promise. However, God freely gave the inheritance to Abraham through a promise.***

The idea of earning God's favor through the Law is not only unbiblical, but also spiritually impractical. Man is naturally incapable of satisfying the Law with perfect observance. Therefore, any effort to qualify oneself through the Law is futile from the start. Furthermore, desiring to receive God's favor through the Law is the same as rejecting the promise already given by grace nearly four hundred and thirty years earlier. Not only is it impossible, but also the choice of obedience to the Law was effectively a rejection to what God in His perfect wisdom and sovereign will had chosen to ordain.

Notes/Applications

Paul told the Galatians that God had prepared the way to escape condemnation by the Law. The way to gain His favor is to receive His salvation by grace through faith. Not only are God's children blessed through Abraham's Descendant, Jesus Christ, they are also blessed through their faith as Abraham was.

Man's conventional wisdom believes that hard work achieves a good reward. He is born to believe that he is in charge of his life and that he can, by his own effort, determine his destiny. Because of this innate characteristic of the sin nature, people think that nothing happens without some cost being attached. So the Judaizers were able to mislead the Galatians by appealing to their human logic. People, by their sin nature, want to work for what they get and receive the credit for their effort.

But God, Who knew our inadequacies, provided the way by which we could receive His forgiveness and come to Him. The Law is incapable of redeeming the lost because its requirements are beyond man's ability to comply perfectly. The Law condemns. But once the Law was fulfilled by His Son, God dispensed His grace to bless the lost with

His redemption. Paul was surprised that this simple truth escaped the Galatians after their initial encounter with and acceptance of the Gospel. They looked foolish to him for abandoning God's true and irrevocable promise and, instead, opted to earn what was already given by doing what was proven to be impossible. People always complicate the simplicity of God's plan of salvation.

Galatians 3:19–29

3:19 ***What, then, is the purpose of the laws given to Moses? They were added to identify what wrongdoing is. Moses' laws did this until the descendant to whom the promise was given came. It was put into effect through angels, using a mediator.***

Paul was candid in his correction of the error the Galatians were making. He knew that his strong rebuke about their attitude to the Law would raise a serious question about the purpose of the Law. If the Law had no effect on the salvation of the redeemed, then why was it given?

God reaffirmed His initial promise to save the lost *(Genesis 3:15)* by confirming His blessings to Abraham. However, the hands of Moses gave the Law to the children of Israel because of sin. God showed the children of Israel a way of life He wanted them to observe. He instituted the Law in order to instruct them how to live as His people. He gave them the Law to put behavioral restraint on them. He gave them the Law in order to explain the consequences of disobedience from the rewards of obedience. God issued the Law in order to identify clearly the presence and the manifestation of sin.

God also entrusted the Good News of His salvation to appointed messengers. The Greek word for *angels* is often translated as *messengers*. God entrusted the promise of salvation to Abraham and, throughout Israel's history, to His prophets. When the time was right, God sent His Son as the mediator to execute His redemption *(Galatians 4:4)*. God fulfilled His promise to Adam, reaffirmed His covenant with Abraham, and accomplished His plan through His Son Jesus Christ by Whom He fulfilled the Law. The Law was given to reaffirm that the only way of salvation is through Jesus Christ in keeping with the Father's will.

3:20 ***A mediator is not used when there is only one person involved, and God has acted on his own.***

A mediator cannot do his mediation with only one party. Even though God is one and the main actor in the redemption of the lost, Jesus Christ was the Mediator between God the Redeemer, and the redeemed. As the Mediator, Jesus Christ stood in the gap between His Father and the lost, making God's redemption available to the redeemed. As Simeon said, "Many will rise or fall in light of their relationship with Jesus Christ" *(Luke 2:34)*. The redemption or judgment of man is determined in light of Jesus Christ, the only One between God and man.

God is the only actor in the whole episode of redemption and judgment. He is also the only Lawgiver. If God determined to extend His redemption through the mediatory ministry of His Son, then any support of the Law as a means of salvation is a refusal to accept God's will and purpose. The Galatians had to realize that going back to the Law was not only wrong, but also, more importantly, a rebellion against God and His plan for salvation.

3:21 ***Does this mean, then, that the laws given to Moses contradict God's promises? That's unthinkable! If those laws could give us life, then certainly we would receive God's approval because we obeyed them.***

Does the Law given to Israel by the hands of Moses on Mount Sinai annul God's earlier promise to Abraham? Paul's answer to his own question was an unequivocal, "No!" God's Law is intact. Whoever desires to fulfill its provisions and benefit from it may do so. The truth is, however, man is not capable of satisfying the Law.

3:22 ***But Scripture states that the whole world is controlled by the power of sin. Therefore, a promise based on faith in Jesus Christ could be given to those who believe.***

God's Law is unassailable and stands eternally invincible. Anyone who can completely satisfy the Law without exception can earn God's favor by living according to the terms of His Law. Because of sin, however, man is incapable of satisfying its provisions without committing any transgression against the Law. The whole world is lost in sin. The power of sin prevails in man's unregenerate heart. But God chose to save people by His grace through the sacrifice of His Son. God revealed His plan of grace through the promise He made to Adam, Noah, and Abraham (*Genesis 3:15; 9:1–17; 15*). Those who accept the sacrifice of Christ are justified as though they had fulfilled the requirements of the Law. Jesus was the only One Who satisfied the Law on their behalf.

3:23 ***We were kept under control by Moses' laws until this faith came. We were under their control until this faith which was about to come would be revealed.***

All of mankind was under the condemning control of the Law because of sin. No one had a chance against the power of sin. All people have sinned and fallen short of the glory of God (*Romans 3:23*). Death has been pronounced upon the descendants of Adam. However, God took the initiative and instilled faith in the hearts of those whom He called to salvation. They could receive Christ's finished work as the fulfillment of the Law and the satisfaction of the judgment handed down by God as the just penalty for sin.

3:24 ***Before Christ came, Moses' laws served as our guardian. Christ came so that we could receive God's approval because of faith.***

The Law of Moses was the prevailing institution of godly living and worship. Its precepts served as instruction for moral uprightness and godly living among God's people. The Law served as the point of reference for God's righteousness and justice, keeping God's precepts in front of the people.

The Law was the guardian of God's righteousness, keeping sinful people under its condemning influence. But God in His grace and mercy instilled faith in the hearts of His people to believe in the sacrifice of Jesus Christ Whom He sent to fulfill the Law and to suffer the penalty for their sin. By giving faith to the lost, God redeemed His people from their deserved condemnation and accepted them into an unmerited salvation by the righteousness of His Son.

3:25 *But now that this faith has come, we are no longer under the control of a guardian.*

Once salvation is given by grace through faith, the redeemed are no longer under the condemnation of the Law. The redeemed are free from the control of the Law. They are free from condemnation. They are in the safety of God's salvation. They are secure in His redemption. The Law can no longer condemn God's redeemed children because they are made righteous in Jesus Christ. They no longer answer to the Law for their salvation and security in God's redemption. Having been justified by faith in Jesus Christ, they are at peace with God *(Romans 5:1)*.

3:26 *You are all God's children by believing in Christ Jesus.*

Paul reminded the Galatians that they were indeed God's children through Jesus Christ. They had been made God's redeemed children by faith in the substitutionary sacrifice of God's only begotten Son. Paul's encouraging words assured the Galatians that they must never return to the Law to acquire God's favor. God's mercy had already been given through His Son. There is nothing to earn! There is nothing to attain! Jesus Christ gives all of God's riches in His good will to all those He redeems without imposing the demands of the Law upon them.

3:27 *Clearly, all of you who were baptized in Christ's name have clothed yourselves with Christ.*

The redeemed are united with Jesus Christ. They are one with Him because He purchased their salvation with His precious blood. God imputed His Son's righteousness to the redeemed, clothing them in Christ's righteousness and justifying them. They are separated from their former lives and live their remaining years in the embrace of God's ongoing sanctification. They were never responsible to the Law for their salvation. The Law only condemns people. But God's redeemed people are no longer under condemnation because they are covered by Christ's righteousness. They are no longer guilty under the Law. They are covered by the precious blood of their Redeemer Jesus Christ and are, therefore, protected from the consequences of the Law.

3:28 *There are neither Jews nor Greeks, slaves nor free people, males nor females. You are all the same in Christ Jesus.*

Contrary to what the Judaizers thought, God's grace and His Law are equally applicable to all of His people regardless of their cultural or ethnic backgrounds. Likewise, all believers are saved by the same grace given through Jesus Christ. Unlike circumcision, which was specifically given to Abraham and all male descendants as a seal of their covenant with God, God's redemption was given through Jesus Christ to everyone who is saved on the basis of what He has accomplished on Calvary. There are no racial, religious, gender, or national distinctions in light of that salvation. The redeemed are given access to God's presence without any qualifying distinction other than the righteousness of Jesus Christ.

3:29 *If you belong to Christ, then you are Abraham's descendants and heirs, as God promised.*

Paul finally answered the Judaizers who were attempting to mislead the Galatians by presenting a false gospel that could never make them

Abraham's children. The Judaizers were wrong in assuming that circumcision and observance of the Law could provide any value to receiving God's approval. Circumcision was given as a seal to physically affirm God's ownership of His people but not to reconstitute one's heritage. Because of sin, no one was capable of being God's child through the Law. Therefore, the Judaizers loyalty to the Law opposed the way, the truth, and the life that God provided for salvation. All believers who accept Christ's redemption by faith are also Abraham's children because he believed in God and it was counted to him as righteousness. Therefore, all who believe in Jesus Christ are Abraham's children by faith regardless of their cultural backgrounds. What the Law could not provide was given through grace and is accepted only by faith in Jesus Christ.

Notes/Applications

As noted in the initial verses of this chapter, Paul was surprised how easily the Judaizers deceived the Galatians. Paul asked the Galatians a series of questions, helping them refocus on their initial experience with the quickening power of the Holy Spirit heard in the good news of the Gospel of Jesus Christ. He took time to reintroduce them to the salvation they received by faith through the preaching of the truth of God's redemption.

The Galatians seemed to have forgotten the salvation they received through the preaching of the Gospel. They were easily dissuaded from the truth they experienced by the deceptive presentation of the Judaizers. Because they did not grow in the knowledge of the truth, the Galatians were led to believe that their salvation remained incomplete until they satisfied their alleged obligation to the Law. They were wrongly persuaded that faith in Christ's sacrifice was insufficient for salvation and that the Law still required complete compliance in order to secure one's redemption.

The Galatians were unable to discern the difference between truth and error because they did not mature in God's wisdom. They were so deceived that they tried to earn what they had already been given. Not only did they fail to recognize the transformation that had already occurred in their hearts, the Judaizers also convinced them that God's provision for their salvation fell short of satisfying the Law. They were persuaded that their obedience to the Law was more important than the righteousness and sacrifice of Jesus Christ.

People always prefer the idea that they have something to contribute to their salvation. Deep within the core of their souls, they truly believe that they are really pretty good—that they have the intelligence to look at the Bible and make a decision to follow Jesus. But that idea is not very different from the teaching put forth by the Judaizers. In the final analysis, we add the good things that we do to the salvation that has already been given to us in Jesus Christ and conclude that we have received God's approval because of what we have done.

But the fate of the Judaizers awaits those people who do not grow in the knowledge of the truth that sets us free. Like the Galatians, we too will waver in our pilgrimage, tossed around by the raging storm of false teaching that so frequently dominates our churches today. God's living Word, Jesus Christ, must be alive in us so that we may always prove the validity of the messages presented to us. Then, searching the Scriptures, we can determine if the message is true or false *(Acts 17:11).*

GALATIANS 4

Galatians 4:1–7

4:1–2 ***[1]Let me explain further. As long as an heir is a child, he is no better off than a slave, even though he owns everything. [2]He is placed under the control of guardians and trustees until the time set by his father.***

So far, Paul dealt with the false teachings of the Judaizers by explaining the true biblical doctrine about salvation and sanctification in light of God's saving grace and the Law. Now Paul uses the essential aspects of family relationships to show the connection between the Law and grace.

The family unit consists of parents and household members including children and servants who have different positions within the family structure. Both children and servants are under the authority of the head of the household. As natural descendants, children possess ownership rights as heirs of their parents. Servants do not have this same position. Until they come of age, children and servants both live under the authority of the head of the family. In the sense of living under authority, there is little difference between children and servants while the children are still under age. Just as the servant continues to serve at his master's command unless he is set free from his obligations, the child also lives in total subjection to the parents until he attains the legal age of adulthood. The child is placed under the protective guardianship of a tutor, a guardian, or under the watchful supervision of the father until the time of the child's independence. The same authority of the head of the household is imposed on the servant, indisputably placing both a minor child and a servant under the same authority.

4:3 *It was the same way with us. When we were children, we were slaves to the principles of this world.*

Making an analogy from the above illustration, the transformation of the believer's life also passes from bondage to deliverance through a similar process. Paul said that the redeemed lived as "slaves to the principles of the world" while they were children. As lost sinners, people live in their unregenerate state, condemned to death and darkness under the bondage of the Law. There are severe consequences for believers who flirt with the Law and their former life of disobedience in spite of their deliverance from sin's damning grip. Like a child under his guardian or a servant under his master, both the unregenerate and the immature believer struggle hopelessly in a life of bondage in darkness and the Law.

4:4 *But when the right time came, God sent his Son [into the world]. A woman gave birth to him, and he came under the control of God's laws.*

In His time and according to His will and determination, God sent His Son into the world to provide the way out of sin, darkness, condemnation, and bondage. Jesus was sent to earth as human baby, born of the Virgin Mary—a young maiden living under the rules of the Mosaic Law. Jesus came into the world of sinful men as a baby and, as a Jew, was subject to Moses' Law. He was the Word Who became flesh and dwelt among men. He was born into a nation under the Law so that He might fulfill the Law with His righteousness. God sent His Son to earth to answer the condemnation of sinners by the Law.

4:5 *God sent him to pay for the freedom of those who were controlled by these laws so that we would be adopted as his children.*

Jesus Christ was sent to earth to satisfy the legitimate demands of the Law imposed on all transgressors. He came not only to fulfill the Law, but also to pay for the freedom of those under the condemning consequences of disobedience to the Law. Since He was the only One to live an absolutely righteous life, never transgressing the standards of the Law, He was the only One qualified to pay fully the cost that freed the condemned. By His atoning death, Jesus set the captives free so that those who are rescued from condemnation could be adopted as God's redeemed children.

4:6 *Because you are God's children, God has sent the Spirit of his Son into us to call out, "Abba! Father!"*

The process of being born into the family of God is not observable in the same way that a biological birth is. There is no physical infant that can be seen. In this transforming process, the Holy Spirit takes up residence in the heart of the individual He redeems. The Holy Spirit generates a spiritual sense of awareness in the heart of the believer and confirms the effective change that takes place during spiritual birth, giving the redeemed a sense of belonging to their heavenly Father. The child of God then recognizes God as his true Father both as Creator and Redeemer and in a new intimacy calls Him "Abba! Father!"

4:7 *So you are no longer slaves but God's children. Since you are God's children, God has also made you heirs.*

Paul reminded the Galatian Christians of the truth that the transformation from slavery to freedom is irreversible. Those who are set free from bondage are no longer slaves to what was holding them under the yoke of subjection. In fact, once free from bondage and condemnation, God's children become heirs of a heavenly inheritance through Jesus Christ. This was the most essential aspect of their redemption that Paul wanted the Galatians to understand. Once freed from bondage and adopted as God's children with all the privileges of a natural-born child, the redeemed are no longer accountable to the Law as the criteria for gaining God's approval. Once redeemed, believers are God's children and heirs with Jesus Christ for all eternity, free from obligation to any other authority including the Law. Once freed, the redeemed should never return to bondage.

Notes/Applications

Even though they believed the Gospel of Jesus Christ when they first heard the message of salvation, the Galatians quickly fell victim to the seduction of an appealing philosophy. They were not firmly grounded in the knowledge of the spiritual transformation that had taken place in their lives. Because they did not mature in their spiritual faith, they easily veered from the pathway of truth. Even though they knew what they heard and believed what Paul had told them, they were easily convinced about something new that sounded good and appeared reasonable, at least from the human point of view.

Paul found the spiritual laziness of the Galatians to be similar to an adult who wants to return to childhood so that he can live under the controls of guardians. The Galatians were easy prey for the Judaizers because they did not fully comprehend their identity as God's children. Even though they were set free, they were persuaded to accept slavery to the Law from which they had been freed by Jesus Christ. They did not fully grasp the magnitude of the salvation they received through Jesus Christ. They did not grow in the knowledge of the finished work of Jesus Christ by which they became God's children and heirs to heaven's treasure. They did not understand their freedom in Christ. Because they were not acquainted with the full significance of the salvation they received, they tried to build their faith by their obedience to the Law, which only condemned them. Consequently, they did not enjoy the freedom Jesus secured for them by His death and resurrection.

Paul speaks to all believers with the same passion for God's Truth. The freedom we have in Jesus Christ is eternally affirmed by the fact that we are God's children and heirs of heaven's treasure, not by our own actions, but by the grace, mercy, and faith given to us by God our Father through the death of His Son and the work of the Holy Spirit.

Galatians 4:8–16

4:8 *When you didn't know God, you were slaves to things which are really not gods at all.*

Paul reminded the Galatians that their life before their salvation was completely opposite to their new life in Christ. Prior to their redemption, they lived in slavery to the material world, which had a god-like grip on their lives. Although the world was not God, they were completely subjected to the material world as though it was God. They were not consciously aware of their condition, lost in sin. They were completely controlled by the power of their sin nature and the evil influences of a lost world that rebelled against the Creator. They did not know God because their spiritual condition was immune to any awareness of God. They knew nothing beyond the blind confines of their depravity, blinded to the reality of their situation. They lived in abject bondage, fully controlled by their human nature.

4:9 *But now you know God, or rather, God knows you. So how can you turn back again to the powerless and bankrupt principles of this world? Why do you want to become their slaves all over again?*

Why would anyone entertain the thought of returning to slavery once they had tasted freedom? Paul reminded the Galatians that God knew them, even if they did not realize fully the effects of their salvation. God knew them not only as their Creator, but also as their Redeemer Who individually saved each one of them from condemnation through the finished work of His Son Jesus Christ. God individually identified each one as the recipient of His saving grace. By His salvation, God brought His people to the knowledge of their new life in Christ. Because the redeemed are known by God, they are made to know Him as the Redeemer.

Like every saved sinner, the Galatian Christians also recognized their depravity by the conviction of the Holy Spirit. The Holy Spirit not only breathes new life into the sinner, raising the person from death in his sin nature to life in God's salvation, but also leads the sinner to repentance and a conscious acknowledgement of what they have experienced. This redemptive transformation is undeniable and irreversible. Neither the Law nor their sin-nature had the power to save them from God's judgment. Why would Christians submit again to the false promises of human effort after they had been saved by the free gift of God's grace?

4:10 *You religiously observe days, months, seasons, and years!*

The Galatians began behaving in reaction to the pressure imposed on them by the Judaizers. In spite of the profound change that occurred in their hearts, they celebrated Jewish religious holidays that the Judaizers required as a confirmation that they had accepted Jewish tradition and thereby secured their salvation. Since most of the Galatian Christians were Gentile, returning to the celebration of pagan or Jewish holidays was an offense to their salvation received through Jesus Christ. Instead of worshiping the Lord who had changed their hearts, they reverted to their former ways so quickly that they felt it necessary to earn their way to heaven by observing religious obligations even though they had already received the gift of eternal life in Jesus Christ.

4:11 *I'm afraid for you. Maybe the hard work I spent on you has been wasted.*

The Galatians' reversal irritated Paul. He was confused about the condition of their hearts. He was convinced that they had genuinely responded to the Gospel when they first heard the message and believed. He knew that no one could proclaim Jesus as Lord unless the Holy Spirit gave life to the dead human spirit. However, the regression of the Galatians was so brazen that it appeared to be more important to them than the conversion they experienced. So Paul registered his frustration by expressing his disdain for their behavior, which threw doubt on their salvation. With anguish in his heart, Paul agonized over their ignorance, which made him doubt the value of the hard work he had invested in them.

4:12 ***Brothers and sisters, I beg you to become like me. After all, I became like you were. You didn't do anything wrong to me.***

Paul concluded his stern rebuke and shifted his language to a more encouraging tone. Perhaps it was his honest effort to soften the severity of his words—to soften but not to compromise. Paul openly pleaded with the Galatians to evaluate their spiritual condition. He wanted them to recognize where they stood both in their understanding of the truth of their salvation and their knowledge of the Gospel. He assured them that his strong words were not a reaction to any criticisms directed at him. He told them that he did not feel personally offended.

Paul wanted to make sure that his strong scolding was not wrongly interpreted as an insensitive interpretation of their actions. His angry words were not a reaction to a personal offense. Paul's words were strong and uncompromising, but they were necessary to stir the Galatians out of their spiritual lethargy. Their agreement with false teaching contradicted everything they had experienced when they had received their salvation.

Paul never intended to condemn them or crush their spirits with his harsh rebuke, but he wanted them to understand what was going on. He begged them to become like him, not in the sense that he had any moral superiority. But Paul, a natural born Jew, a trained Pharisee from the tribe of Benjamin, wanted them to see that he now rejected Jewish observations and traditions because they did not have any impact on his salvation. He wanted them to follow his example and forsake their acceptance of Jewish traditions. In a sense, their paths had crossed. Paul understood that his salvation came only by the grace of God in Jesus Christ and became more like a Gentile while the Galatians had accepted their salvation in Jesus Christ and then decided to distort that salvation by observing Jewish traditions. Paul wanted the Galatians to return to the truth they first believed and grow in the genuine knowledge of the Gospel.

4:13 *You know that the first time I brought you the Good News I was ill.*

Paul reminded the Galatians what it was like when he first visited the region. He was sick! He was either sick with some disease or physically tired, perhaps as a result of the stress of his travels. Despite his illness, he presented the Gospel to the inhabitants of Galatia, people who were not Jewish and had little or no knowledge of the only living God. Like Peter's audience at Pentecost, the Galatians were cut to the heart by the redeeming message of the Gospel. The Galatians knew this all too well.

4:14 *Even though my illness was difficult for you, you didn't despise or reject me. Instead, you welcomed me as if I were God's messenger or Christ Jesus himself.*

Paul recalled the enthusiasm with which the Galatians received him in spite of his difficult condition. The Galatians did not know how to cure Paul's physical condition, but they received the Gospel he explained as if it was coming from the mouth of Jesus Christ or one of His messengers. Their whole attention was focused on the message of salvation through Jesus Christ. Paul's frailties did not blind them from the truth he proclaimed. They were able to see beyond his physical weakness and responded to the Gospel by faith.

4:15 *What happened to your positive attitude? It's a fact that if it had been possible, you would have torn out your eyes and given them to me.*

Paul was puzzled about the sudden and drastic change that came over the Galatians. Their care for him was boundless and their faith in the Gospel he preached was well established. They were so moved by their new life in Christ to which he introduced them that they responded with gratitude. Their gratitude was so intensely expressed that they would gladly have plucked out their eyes and given them to him. That is, they would give up their most treasured faculty as a token of their gratitude for the spiritual benefit they received through his ministry. What caused them to abandon the truth they so enthusiastically received? What changed their mind so quickly that they wanted to slip back into bondage? Why did their love for him disappear so suddenly?

4:16 *Can it be that I have become your enemy for telling you the truth?*

Paul candidly asked the Galatians if their opinion of him had changed. Was he now their enemy because his rebuke forced them to take a good look at themselves and evaluate their spiritual condition? Paul did not change his message. Nor did he adjust his teachings to suit the condition of his audience. He always spoke the truth with care and love. So what happened? Did the Galatians get tired of the truth? Did they feel they had learned something more important from the Judaizers?

Notes/Applications

Paul did not ask for anyone's opinion or reaction to help him diagnose the spiritual condition of the Galatians. He knew exactly what their problem was. He directly challenged their thinking by reminding them of God's saving work in their hearts. He asked them questions that exposed the blatant inconsistency expressed by their sudden change of heart. Paul tried to educate the Galatians in their understanding about the seriousness of their spiritual instability.

It is important to notice the conditions in which Paul first explained God's salvation. Paul was frail and unimpressive when he first came to the Galatians. However, his weakness was instrumental in reflecting the full power of the Gospel. The Galatians received salvation through the Good News of God's redemption despite the weakened condition of the messenger. In spite of his outward appearance, Paul's presentation of God's salvation through the sacrifice of

Jesus Christ set them free from the bondage of sin, which was clearly defined by God's Law.

The message and the messenger did not change. However, the Galatians themselves were drawn away from the truth by subsequent teachings that emerged out of unbiblical sources. Paul wanted the Galatians to understand that their spiritual distraction was not simply a matter of error. It was drastic! In sharp contrast to the seriousness of their spiritual condition, their initial response knew no bounds and they loved both the Gospel and the Lord's messenger. Sadly, however, their attitude swiftly swerved in the opposite direction so severely that they distorted the truth that had saved them. They also questioned the messenger that had suffered physically when he brought the message to them. Why?

The Galatians were ill-prepared to face the deceit of false teaching. They were no match for the Judaizers who packaged false doctrine in an impressive presentation. Consequently, the Galatians were easily led back to a mindset that enslaved them to the bondage of the principles from which they were set free once and for all.

The Galatians are not alone in succumbing to false teaching because of spiritual immaturity. Paul's message goes out to all believers who are unwittingly caught by some form of false teaching. Christians are often misled by a charismatic presentation of a message that cannot be supported by the unchanging and unchangeable truth of God's Word. However, those whom God has redeemed should avoid any deviation from the biblical truth that the Bible so clearly presents. God's Word is the *only* resource by which God's children can guard against the poisonous subtleties of false messages that seem to be exciting but are really opposed to the truth expressed in the gospel message. Every wind of doctrine must be carefully checked against the infallible reliability of God's Word. Failure to do so is catastrophic for the Christian.

Galatians 4:17–20

4:17 *These people [who distort the Good News] are devoted to you, but not in a good way. They don't want you to associate with me so that you will be devoted only to them.*

Paul wanted to show the Galatians the underlying motivation of the Judaizers. These messengers of false doctrine had a sincere devotion to their audience. The Judaizers were committed to their religious perspectives and, therefore, to those who accepted what they taught. But that apparent friendship drove a wedge between the Galatians and Paul. More important than the threat to Paul's relationship was the wedge that they drove between Christians and the truth of the Gospel. Certainly they displayed a warm, friendly attitude, but these people were fundamentally opposed to the true Gospel.

4:18 *(Devotion to a good cause is always good, even when I'm not with you.)*

Paul was careful to warn the Galatians that their devotion to the truth should not be dependent upon their attitude toward the person who presented it to them. Teachers are not relevant in determining what the truth is. While devotion to a good cause is commendable, one must be reasonably certain that one's devotion is influence by God's truth. Before committing to some goal, a Christian should evaluate the content of the subject. Nowhere is this more important than in understanding how they were saved. Paul encouraged the Galatians to apply themselves to this truth. They should do this whether or not Paul was with them. The truth of the God's Word is always supported by its own testimony. It does not need any defense or apology. God's truth is independent of human reasoning. It stands above everything and everyone. God's truth must be followed on the basis of its own self-attesting merit. But people do not automatically devote themselves to this unchanging truth.

4:19 *My children, I am suffering birth pains for you again until Christ is formed in you.*

Paul felt terrible about the spiritual condition of the Galatian Christians. His debate with the Judaizers was not merely an academic exercise in theology. Since he was their spiritual father, their spiritual well-being was his primary concern. He explained the intensity of his concern for them by comparing it to the pains a woman experiences when giving birth. Even though he knew that they were born anew in Christ, he was deeply troubled by their spiritual immaturity and instability. Even though he knew that they would not be eternally condemned, he was fully aware of the danger experienced when a child of God strays from the true teachings of the Gospel of Jesus Christ.

Paul was not interested simply in leading them to faith in Christ. He wanted them to grow in their faith until the person and character of Jesus was formed in them. He wanted to encourage them in their spiritual growth so that the life they lived was actually the expression of Jesus Christ living in them. Paul was deeply concerned for the Galatians because he knew that growth in faith gets much harder when the child of God is out of touch with the transformation taking place in his heart.

4:20 *I wish I were with you right now so that I could change the tone of my voice. I'm completely puzzled by what you've done!*

Even though Paul told them the truth in love, Paul was fully aware that his words might not be well received by the Galatians. Certainly, their precarious foothold in the Gospel puzzled him. They became unstable in their faith and were easily dissuaded from the truth. He did not necessarily think that the Galatian Christians would deliberately or maliciously argue with the content of his teachings. But he recognized the potential for their resistance to the tone of his serious but sincere rebuke. Acknowledging the Galatians might be spiritually too immature to receive his forceful rebuke calmly, Paul expressed his desire to be with them so that he could personally assess the situation as he instructed them again in the basic tenets of the Gospel they had abandoned.

Notes/Applications

Paul's corrective instruction to the Galatians had two distinct aspects. First, their belief was based on an erroneous teaching. That is, he directly exposed the doctrinal errors they had adopted as they paid attention to what the Judaizers were telling them. Second, their impression of the Judaizers blinded their ability to discern the truth. The influence the Judaizers imposed on the Galatians was so compelling that they were easily dissuaded from the Gospel. Doctrinally, Paul carefully explained the marvelous gift of salvation by God's grace and the former life of subjection to the Law from which they were set free. He further exposed how falsehood took hold of their attention because of the influence the Judaizers imposed upon them.

Paul candidly and gently unmasked the inherent flaw in the character and personality of the Galatians that caused their downfall. The Judaizers were able to persuade the Galatians because they recognized Jesus as the Messiah promised throughout Jewish history. It would not be unnatural for the Galatians to accept the Judaizers because of their heritage as Jews and their traditional association with the Law. But the natural tendencies of fallen man should not be allowed to defeat the work of the Gospel in a life that was already transformed by God's saving grace.

Paul explained that their unwarranted devotion to the Judaizers was instrumental in blinding the Galatian Christians from discerning the truth about the falsehood they were being fed. They were easily persuaded by the enticing words of the people who impressed them the most. Yes, Paul commended the Galatians for accepting the Gospel in spite of his frailties. But he rebuked them for accepting false teaching because of their devotion to people who taught false doctrine. Rather, he urged them to discern the truth without confusing the message with the messenger.

Likewise, all believers are admonished to imitate the Bereans who were always ready to receive the Word. They diligently searched the Scriptures to determine if Paul was teaching them the truth and to guard against unbiblical instruction *(Acts 17:10–11)*. Like the Galatian Christians, many believers today are influenced by exciting teachers who do not present the unchanging Truth of God's Word. These people may be pleasant and friendly, but they do so to enhance their own self-exalting ministries. In the process, believers face the dangers of living unfaithfully, proud of their knowledge of some doctrine, which is clearly in contradiction to the Scriptures. They forsake the truth of the Gospel by which they were saved.

Galatians 4:21–31

4:21 *Those who want to be controlled by Moses' laws should tell me something. Are you really listening to what Moses' Teachings say?*

Paul found it unbelievable that some of the Galatian Christians displayed a spiritually unhealthy tendency to return to the Law in spite of their security in God's grace. Did they understand what the laws or the Teachings of Moses really said? Paul did not think so. Rather, he was puzzled not only by their change of attitude toward true doctrine of God's grace through Jesus Christ, but also the ignorance with which the Galatians accepted teachings that contradicted the Gospel. What relevant truth did they learn by rejecting the Gospel and by embracing the Law?

4:22 *Scripture says that Abraham had two sons, one by a woman who was a slave and the other by a free woman.*

After disproving the false doctrine embraced by the Galatians, Paul explained the essential difference between true doctrine and the false teaching of those who opposed God's grace. Going back to the Old Testament, Paul showed the Galatians that the truth he taught them was a timeless revelation of the Gospel that was clearly seen in Abraham's life. He reminded them that Abraham had two sons by two different women, one of whom was a slave and the other a free woman. Paul was referring to Sarah, Abraham's wife, and Hagar her maid.

4:23 *Now, the son of the slave woman was conceived in a natural way, but the son of the free woman was conceived through a promise [made to Abraham].*

Abraham's first two children were sons that were conceived by Hagar and Sarah respectively. Paul told the Galatians that, even though Abraham fathered both sons, the circumstances surrounding their conception were not the same. Both sons were born through the natural process. The difference between the two births was the decisions that led to their conception. Ishmael was born as a result of decisions and arrangements made by Abraham, Sarah, and Hagar. Sarah was old, past the childbearing years. She was unable to conceive a child so she gave Abraham her servant Hagar. Hagar gave birth to Ishmael because Abraham and Sarah came to the conclusion that this was the only way that they could have a child. They did this even though God had promised Abraham a son through Sarah.

On the other hand, Sarah's son Isaac was born by the power of God's promise. Both Abraham and Sarah were old. Even though Sarah was long past childbearing age, she gave birth to Isaac under miraculous circumstances. God fulfilled His promise by giving Sarah her biological son through the natural process. So Paul reminded the Galatians that Ishmael was the son of man's decisions while Isaac was the child of God's promise. Isaac was the fulfillment of God's promise despite all the reasonable biological limitations, while Ishmael's birth was the human attempt to fulfill God's promise by human means.

4:24 ***I'm going to use these historical events as an illustration. The women illustrate two arrangements. The one woman, Hagar, is the arrangement made on Mount Sinai. Her children are born into slavery.***

Hagar and Sarah illustrate two different contexts that demonstrate the difference between the works of the Law and God's grace. As Sarah's maid, Hagar represents birth in the context of slavery because she gave birth to Ishmael while she was Sarah's slave. Because of her position as a servant, her child was also born into slavery.

Paul said that Hagar represented the arrangement that God made with the children of Israel on Mount Sinai. The children of Israel surrendered to the Law as their rule of life for serving God and to live as God's people *(Exodus 19:4–8)*. Mount Sinai represents Israel's enslavement to the Law.

4:25 ***Hagar is Mount Sinai in Arabia. She is like Jerusalem today because she and her children are slaves.***

Hagar illustrated not only Israel on Mount Sinai, but also the city of Jerusalem in Paul's time. Hagar's position of slavery did not change. She was driven out of Abraham's household because she did not have any rightful claim to freedom. She had to learn hard lessons in the Arabian wilderness. In the same way, Jerusalem remained under the Law, continuing to suffer the just consequences to the slavery imposed by Moses' Law. Having been subjected to the Law, Jerusalem continued to serve the Law, just as Hagar remained a slave even though she gave birth to her master's eldest child.

4:26 ***But the Jerusalem that is above is free, and she is our mother.***

Paul showed the Galatian Christians the difference between their position as the children of the Law and the freedom given to them in their salvation by Jesus Christ. They were not the children of the earthly Jerusalem depicted by Hagar, chained in bondage to the Law. They were the children of the heavenly Jerusalem, which is free and is represented by Isaac, the son conceived as a result of God's promise. Unlike Hagar, Sarah was Abraham's wife. In a sociological sense, Sarah was a free woman, but in a very practical sense, she was the vessel by which God fulfilled His promise to Abraham. God overruled the laws of nature He had instituted and gave her Isaac in her old age. Being the free mother of the promised child, Sarah illustrated the heavenly Jerusalem, which is the mother of all who are freed from the slavery of the Law by God's promise.

4:27 ***Scripture says: "Rejoice, women who cannot get pregnant, who cannot give birth to any children! Break into shouting, those who feel no pains of childbirth! Because the deserted***

woman will have more children than the woman who has a husband."

Paul reminded the Galatians of God's Word given to Israel in Isaiah 54:1–6. Coupled with the text of Isaiah 44:1–2, the narrative in Isaiah 54 assured Israel that God Himself is the Father of the orphan and the Husband of the widow. God promised the childless mother that she would be filled with joy. The barren woman should rejoice and break out in song because her latter years would be filled with children. God Himself would remove her shame. In the same sense, the Galatians and all who believe in Jesus Christ should rejoice and break out in songs of praise because the shame of their bondage under the Law is removed. They are set free in Christ. Having been rescued from the grip of condemnation under the Law, the redeemed have been made the children of the free woman represented by the heavenly Jerusalem.

4:28 ***Now you, brothers and sisters, are children of the promise like Isaac.***

Speaking without any ambiguity, Paul told the Galatian Christians that they were the children of promise just as Isaac was. Sarah gave birth to Isaac in a manner that contradicted the natural conditions of her aging body. She gave birth to Isaac because of God's promise to Abraham. Not only did God promise Isaac, but also brought His promise to fruition in spite of Sarah's physical condition and the unbelief in her heart. In the same sense, the Galatian Christians and all who believe in Jesus Christ are the children of God's promise to Abraham, born by God's promise by the Holy Spirit in the sacrifice of His Son. God promised that by Eve's seed salvation would come to the world *(Genesis 3:15)*. The redeemed are made God's children through the finished work of His Son Jesus Christ Whom God promised to send through Abraham's seed. God therefore decreed that through Isaac, the seed of God's promise, Abraham's children would be identified *(Genesis 21:12)*.

4:29 ***Furthermore, at that time the son who was conceived in a natural way persecuted the son conceived in a spiritual way. That's exactly what's happening now.***

Paul explained that their exposure to the poisonous teaching of the Judaizers was nothing more and nothing less than a representation of the conflict that developed between Isaac and Ishmael, the son born as a result of God's promise and the son born as a result of unbelief. The conflict between the Gospel and the Law continued to captivate the attention of the Galatian Christians. There were those enslaved to the Law and those who were the children of God's promise, set free from bondage through Jesus Christ their Savior. Just like Ishmael mocked his brother at the time of Isaac's weaning celebration (*Genesis 21:8–9*), the Judaizers tried to show Christians that they should also embrace the Law, even though the Law only condemns people to death. Ishmael's reaction to Isaac's development did not have any impact on Isaac's position as the son of a free woman. Instead, Ishmael was expelled from Abraham's household by God's direction because Ishmael was not the son of God's promise. Therefore, Ishmael did not belong in the family of those who were the children of the free woman. Paul wanted the Galatians to view the Judaizers and their false teachings in the context of their own security as children of God's promise, realizing that the Judaizers did not amount to anything more than the enemies of that promise.

4:30 ***But what does Scripture say? "Get rid of the slave woman and her son, because the son of the slave woman must never share the inheritance with the son of the free woman."***

Once again, Paul directed the attention of the Galatians to the Scriptures where God's sovereign will and action was clearly recorded regarding the conflict within Abraham's household. Here, Paul wanted the Galatians to recognize the difference between God's revealed truth concerning the redeemed and the false doctrine of the Judaizers.

Sarah was upset with Ishmael when she observed his aggressive attitude toward Isaac—her own flesh and blood son. She complained to Abraham and asked him to get rid of Hagar and Ishmael. Abraham was troubled because both Ishmael and Isaac were his flesh and blood sons. He tried to reconcile the conflict between his wife and his sons by being fair to both women at the same time. But God Himself intervened and instructed Abraham to expel Hagar and her son Ishmael from his household *(Genesis 21:8–12)*.

God told Abraham to listen to his wife. Sarah was right in arguing that Ishmael could not share the inheritance with Isaac. Sarah might not have recognized God's sovereign determination about Ishmael's and Isaac's future. She was simply jealous for her son. Nevertheless, her position was more compatible with God's plan than Abraham's was. Isaac was promised and given by God. Ishmael was procured by the human interpretation of God's promise. The two would never share God's inheritance. Likewise, the Galatians should not listen to the Judaizers because these teachers of falsehood have nothing in common with respect to the true Gospel.

4:31 *Brothers and sisters, we are not children of a slave woman but of the free woman.*

Paul brought his argument to its reasonable conclusion. He told the Galatians that they, like Paul himself and all believers in Jesus Christ were the children of the free woman. Believers are not the children of the woman in bondage. Just like Isaac, the redeemed are the children of God's promise in Jesus Christ. The parent-child connection with the bondwoman is completely severed. The children of God should never listen to Ishmael's mocking or to Hagar's complaints. Rather, believers are Sarah's children and the descendants of Isaac. They are born of the Spirit by God's grace through God's promise in Jesus Christ. They are not born into God's Kingdom by any human decision. Paul told the Galatians to reject the Judaizers totally and completely, recognizing the true Gospel as their only source of direction for their life in Jesus Christ.

Notes/Applications

So far, Paul rebuked the Galatians, consoled them, and finally explained the Gospel by illustrating the true message of God's salvation through a biblical event from the Old Testament. He showed them that they once lived in bondage as slaves to the Law. But now they were free, delivered from condemnation by God's grace through faith in Jesus Christ.

In addition to his declaration of the truth, Paul's stern scolding of the Galatians was an uncompromising call to all believers to reject any teaching that contradicted the truth of salvation in and through Jesus Christ. Instead, Christians should embrace a sincere, serious commitment to the Gospel. Paul firmly rebuked their stagnation in spiritual infancy. Even though salvation declares the ransom of the lost from eternal damnation and the believer's eternal destiny with the Lord Jesus Christ, the salvation experience is not confined to the initial event of the believer's encounter with the quickening power of the Holy Spirit.

The believer is urged to search God's Word diligently and grow in the knowledge of the truth. In his letters to Timothy, Paul counseled the younger man to be aware of those who hate the truth. The Judaizers easily confused the Galatian Christians about the true Gospel because they had accepted their salvation with childlike enthusiasm, but failed to grow up and mature in the context of God's truth. The Galatians had trouble seeing the error in the teaching of the Judaizers. They mistook their freedom in Jesus Christ for bondage under the Law. As a result, they were overwhelmed by the compelling presentation of false doctrine.

The same admonition bids us to feed on the Bread of Life and refresh our souls by the Living Water of God's Word so that we will not be confused as the Galatian Christians were. We should never be tossed around by the waves of erroneous doctrine, but instead grow in wisdom and understanding of the magnificence of our salvation provided to us by Jesus' sacrifice on Calvary.

GALATIANS 5

Galatians 5:1–6

5:1 ***Christ has freed us so that we may enjoy the benefits of freedom. Therefore, be firm [in this freedom], and don't become slaves again.***

Having concluded his stern corrections regarding the true Gospel in response to the falsehood circulated by the Judaizers, Paul then showed the Galatian Christians the practical application of God's revealed truth. Earlier in the letter, Paul told them that they should be firm in the truth that set them free from bondage. They should not listen to false doctrine and return to slavery. They should acknowledge their freedom in Jesus Christ, which freed them from slavery to the Law. Then they should grow in the faith that the Spirit had given to them until they are firmly grounded in their freedom, resisting all influences that attempt to draw them away from their liberty in Jesus Christ. The practical aspects of their lives must be influenced by a God-given attitude cultivated and nurtured by a dynamic awareness of their freedom in Christ and firmly rooted in their spirit, heart, and mind.

5:2 ***I, Paul, can guarantee that if you allow yourselves to be circumcised, Christ will be of no benefit to you.***

Candidly, Paul told the Galatians that if they chose to live according to the Law, then they could not expect to benefit from grace. If Gentile Christians felt the need to be circumcised in order to fulfill the requirement of the Law and thereby secure their salvation, then it would mean that they did not truly appreciate Christ's finished work. If they felt they could provide for their salvation by their own adherence to the Law, then it would mean that they did not benefit from the grace extended to them by Christ's death, burial, and resurrection. If they were tempted to live under the Law for their security in God's redemption, then it would mean that their love for Christ and their appreciation for His grace was sadly lacking. If Jewish Christians chose to return again to the Law, then they effectively rejected the redemption that Jesus Christ had secured for them through His own death, burial and resurrection and had been extended to them by His Father's grace.

5:3 ***Again, I insist that everyone who allows himself to be circumcised must realize that he obligates himself to do everything Moses' Teachings demand.***

The Galatians' decision to adhere to the Law and neglect God's grace had severe consequences. Observance of the Law was not selective. If they chose to live under the Law, then they accepted all parts of the Law. Allegiance to the Law could not be less than a full commitment to the total Law. Paul put the Galatians on notice that their preference for the Law would actually indebt them to the Law. If they felt obligated to be circumcised in order to satisfy the Law for their salvation, then they would be accountable to the Law in its entirety and subject to the punishments that the Law imposed on transgressors.

5:4 *Those of you who try to earn God's approval by obeying his laws have been cut off from Christ. You have fallen out of God's favor.*

Anyone who chooses to earn God's approval by obeying His laws is doomed to failure. Such people really express their indifference toward God's grace. The desire to live under the Law amounts to declaring God's grace insufficient to give and sustain salvation. Attempting to add to God's grace is the same as admitting one's continuation in bondage. It is the same as if one is lost, not having been rescued from damnation by God's grace. It is as if believing that God's grace has not been quite effective in executing His deliverance from sin. It would be the same as declaring that grace alone could not keep any one in God's favor. Looking to the Law for the security of one's salvation is the same as admitting that one has fallen out of God's favor as if grace alone could not secure a person's approval by God.

5:5 *However, in our spiritual nature, faith causes us to wait eagerly for the confidence that comes with God's approval.*

The term *spiritual nature* may be a little confusing, since it implies that human nature itself can adequately induce a confident faith in God's approval. Since Paul is talking to believers, the phrase assumes that the believer's spiritual nature is under the subjection of the Holy Spirit. However, in keeping with the Greek text and most other translations, it is probably best to state that the Holy Spirit is the One Who provides this confidence.

Paul restated his affirmation that those who are truly redeemed and have experienced the inner witness of the indwelling Holy Spirit will not suffer from any sense of unfulfilled spiritual need. Instead, their hearts would be filled with an enduring assurance of what has been done by the Lord Jesus Christ on their behalf. The redeemed patiently wait for the fulfillment of the promise of God's salvation already accomplished and given to them in Jesus Christ.

5:6 ***As far as our relationship to Christ Jesus is concerned, it doesn't matter whether we are circumcised or not. But what matters is a faith that expresses itself through love.***

Those who live by faith and wait in hope should not worry about the demands of the Law as taught by the Judaizers. Since their relationship with Jesus Christ is based on faith in His finished work, the stipulations of the Law have no significance in light of their salvation and sustenance as the redeemed of God. Therefore, circumcised or otherwise, those who are in Christ should reflect a vibrant faith driven and expressed by the love of Jesus Christ working in them.

Notes/Applications

The Judaizers pursued Paul and relentlessly tried to discredit his teachings in their attempt to scare new believers such as the Galatians into compliance with the requirements of the Law. In Acts 15:1, the Judaizers openly taught that no one can be saved without being circumcised, contradicting the Gospel of Jesus Christ which Paul preached everywhere he went. Even though the Galatians were safe and secure in their salvation in Jesus Christ, their spiritual growth was undermined by the false teachings imposed upon them by the Judaizers. That was a matter of a grave concern to Paul.

Paul was concerned that the strong, relentless circulation of a false gospel by the Judaizers coupled with the familiarity of the tradition of the Law might easily turn the Galatians from the truth. He was not worried that they might lose their salvation, needing to be saved again. But he was well aware that a life that was not firmly grounded in the true Gospel would be void of a meaningful experience as the disciple of Jesus Christ. He knew that a redeemed mind that is not equipped with godly wisdom could be tossed around by the waves of ungodly doctrine. So, instead of directly confronting the Judaizers, Paul chose to strengthen the Galatians' faith by reacquainting them with the truth about their salvation and their endurance in the faith given to them by God's grace in Jesus Christ. Paul's instruction had a single but powerful theme. He told the Galatians that they needed to be firmly grounded in the true Gospel so that they could continue in faith without being influenced by the camp of false doctrine.

The child of God is set free and is kept steady by this Truth. It is hard to understand why anyone would turn away from the grace of God's free gift of salvation in Jesus Christ. To set any hope of earning God's approval by obedience to the Law is foolishness. Life's experience proves our inability to conform to God's standards no matter how hard we try. But the human spirit, contaminated by the disease of sin, tries to earn God's favor by some set of rules. We have an unquenchable need to prove that we made some important contribution to our salvation and our subsequent growth in the faith.

However, God's Word tells us over and over again that God has freely given us His grace and mercy, saving us from the penalty of our sin, not because we obey some set of rules, but simply because He loves us. We bring nothing of our own to our salvation in Jesus Christ. Without His gift of salvation, we deserve only His justice and punishment. But for some reason unknown to the human mind, the Holy Spirit has opened our eyes to the depth of our sin and the glory of His grace. The richness of our salvation through the sacrifice of Jesus Christ is immeasurable. Our only prayer is, "*God, in Jesus Christ, be merciful to me a sinner!*"

Galatians 5:7–15

5:7 *You were doing so well. Who stopped you from being influenced by the truth?*

Again, Paul's frustration with the Galatian Christians comes to the fore. His frustration is expressed by his commendation on how well they were doing in their faith. Then he immediately throws out a question that demands an answer. They had heard the true Gospel and believed in its message. They had been set free from sin and bondage under the Law. What then diverted them from the truth? What was so enticing or compelling about the false gospel supported by the Judaizers that their allegiance to the truth was so easily compromised? What deceived them so easily that they turned away from the message that had saved them and embraced a message that would again bind them in hopeless slavery to the Law?

5:8 *The arguments of the person who is influencing you do not come from the one who is calling you.*

Paul cautioned the Galatians to take note of the author of what they were taught before passing a value judgment on the credibility of the doctrine. The true Gospel was the Good News of God's salvation based on Christ's finished work on the Cross. Then any teaching that contradicted this unchanging truth could not come from the same Author. If such teaching contradicts the truth, then it is false. It is a false religion authored by a different author other than the Author of the true Gospel. Therefore, any teaching that contradicts the truth is wrong and should not be accepted. Error never warrants the support of those whose lives have been changed by the true Gospel. Paul reminded the Galatians that they should have easily recognized the error by its glaring difference from the truth because of its origin and its content.

5:9 *A little yeast spreads through the whole batch of dough.*

False doctrine is a highly potent poison! The child of truth should not play with it under any circumstances. It is like a little yeast used to ferment an entire lump of dough. Despite its insignificant volume, a little yeast permeates an entire batch of dough and changes the taste and texture of what is being prepared for baking. In the same sense, what appears to be trite could be detrimental if left unchecked. Even though error cannot have a lasting effect on God's unchanging truth, it could easily stifle the understanding of the redeemed resulting in serious confusion about anything related to the truth. Paul wanted to help the Galatians recognize that their confusion about the truth resulted from their own tolerance of false doctrine.

5:10 *The Lord gives me confidence that you will not disagree with this. However, the one who is confusing you will suffer God's judgment regardless of who he is.*

Openly expressing his confidence in God, Paul boldly asserted that the Galatians would not disagree with what he had just told them about the Truth. The Truth is self-evident. The true Gospel is not only self-evident, but is also affirmed by the witness of the Holy Spirit in the hearts of those who have experienced His life-giving power. They should courageously resist these false teachings by the power of the Truth. However, God will deal with false teachers regardless of who they are. Speaking against God's Truth is tantamount to speaking against God Himself because Jesus Christ His Son is the Truth, the Way, and the Life. As the redeemed set free by the Truth, God's children should not pay attention to erroneous teaching let alone accept its principles. In fact, they should flee its influence leaving its fate in the hands of the Lord's judgment.

5:11 ***Brothers and sisters, if I am still preaching that circumcision is necessary, why am I still being persecuted? In that case the cross wouldn't be offensive anymore.***

Absolutely sure of his own position in God's truth, Paul asked a rhetorical question. Why would he preach *salvation by faith alone* if circumcision and the Law attained the same objective? If the message of circumcision still held true, why would he teach against it and suffer persecution? If circumcision were still necessary for salvation, he would have supported it. Then, no one would be offended by the message of the Cross of Jesus Christ. Paul wanted the Galatians to think about the reasons that he suffered persecution. Why would he risk his own life if Jesus Christ was not the Truth, the Way, and the Life? Why would he expose himself to malicious attacks by the Judaizers if Christ's finished work was not sufficient for salvation?

5:12 ***I wish those troublemakers would castrate themselves.***

Paul's aggravation with the Judaizers culminates in this intensely graphic statement. He was extremely angry with these messengers of a false gospel. The way they behaved diminished the uniqueness of the believer's new nature in Christ. Even though he held the Galatians accountable to the truth, Paul expressed his fury toward the Judaizers with language that describes a horribly painful procedure. Some Bible scholars suggest that Paul wished their instantaneous death, as in being "cut off" from life. Others suggest that Paul wished that the Judaizers would geld themselves to show their commitment to circumcision, the Law, and their Jewish traditions.

5:13 ***You were indeed called to be free, brothers and sisters. Don't turn this freedom into an excuse for your corrupt nature to express itself. Rather, serve each other through love.***

Once again, Paul reminded the Galatians that they were set free and were called to live in that liberty. They were free from the depraved influences of their corrupt nature. They were not free to do what the flesh dictates. But they were free to live in the freedom that Jesus Christ secured for them.

Freedom in God's grace should not be equated with unrestrained indulgence. Paul urged the Galatians to refrain from abusing their freedom; they should never give in to the desires of their human nature. Their freedom in Christ was freedom from sin and its consequences. It was not freedom to do whatever their sin nature dictated. Paul encouraged the Galatians to reject the desires of their corrupt nature and, instead, serve each other with the love of Christ with which God first loved them. In essence, Paul wanted them to understand that their life as the redeemed children of God was one of love and service to one another following the example of the Lord Jesus Christ.

5:14 *All of Moses' Teachings are summarized in a single statement, "Love your neighbor as you love yourself."*

Paul did not teach the Galatians to oppose the Law. The Law is holy, just, and good as Paul confirmed in his letters to the Romans and Timothy *(Romans 7:12; 1 Timothy 1:8)*. Paul never instructed anyone to neglect the Law. However, Paul did oppose the erroneous teaching about the Law that was presented by the Judaizers. The Law saved no one! The Law only showed people the depth of their sin in the sight of the holy Creator.

The Law was fulfilled by Jesus Christ, but is implemented by the manner in which the redeemed relate to one another. To do this, Paul reminded them of one of most basic principles of the Law *(Leviticus 19:18)* that was quoted by Jesus during His ministry *(Matthew 22:39)*. Paul thereby affirmed that the love of God that works in His redeemed children is actually the fulfillment of the Law in its entirety because its righteous demands were fully met by Jesus Christ. Instead of erroneously trying to secure their salvation by obeying the rules of the Law, the saints of God should try to share the fruit of Christ's satisfaction of the Law by relating to each other through God's love working in their hearts. So Paul instructed the Galatians to reject false doctrine about the Law while embracing its precepts in the practice of Christian living.

5:15 *But if you criticize and attack each other, be careful that you don't destroy each other.*

Paul also warned the Galatians about the consequences of accepting a false doctrine that contradicted their new nature in Jesus Christ. Both their freedom and the love they shared were a reflection of the new person born in their heart by the regenerating work of the Holy Spirit. Therefore, if they tried to live by the Law's rules, they would end up criticizing and attacking each other instead of loving one another. They would become victims of their own destructive behavior induced by their acceptance of false religious rules. Love always nurtures a sound Christian fellowship among believers. Paul essentially discouraged the Galatians from indulging themselves in useless arguments while encouraging them to relate to each other in a neighborly love in Jesus Christ.

Notes/Applications

Paul reminded the Galatians that their redemption was purchased and secured by Jesus Christ and by Him alone. However, Paul continued to scold the Galatians for their lack of commitment in learning more about their salvation and faith in Jesus Christ. He also instructed them about the godly attitude with which the truth of the Gospel should be applied in their lives as well as in their relationship with one another.

Paul was obviously concerned for the Galatians because of the spiritual vulnerability he observed. He wondered why the Galatians were so easily deceived and were led astray from the truth. He urged them to be diligent in their knowledge of the truth and be firmly established on the foundation of the true Gospel. He reminded them that falsehood had no place in their lives.

Paul added two important points to his admonition of the Galatians. Paul cautioned the Galatians to guard their liberty in

Christ and to conduct themselves in the love of their Redeemer. They should not abuse their liberty, nor should their liberty make them vulnerable to falsehood. Being firm and well-armed with the truth of the Gospel, they should live in the love and freedom of Jesus Christ without compromising their faith. They were free through Christ's redemption from bondage to the Law, but still called to fulfill the Law through the love of Jesus Christ.

Paul did not want the Galatians to behave like the Judaizers. He did not want them to take the truth and twist it like the Judaizers did. He did not want the Galatians to employ the true Gospel in useless arguments and selfish pursuits. Instead of arguing with the Judaizers, Paul encouraged the Galatians to take the true Gospel and apply it to their lives so that it would produce the genuine fruit of the Spirit as they lived together in the family of faith in Jesus Christ. Paul's tireless effort in correcting the Galatians was not in vain after all. He told them to recapture the truth and apply it to their lives as they shared the love of Christ. This essential message of the true Gospel echoes throughout the ages to all believers, even to us today.

Galatians 5:16–26

5:16 ***Let me explain further. Live your life as your spiritual nature directs you. Then you will never follow through on what your corrupt nature wants.***

Now Paul embarked on some very practical steps Christians should take in order to apply the truth of their salvation to their lives in a meaningful and relevant way.

Christians must live according to the dictates of the new authority in their heart. They are to conduct themselves in keeping with the principles embedded in their redeemed spiritual nature, recognizing that their revived spiritual nature is the new man brought to life by the Holy Spirit. It is the Spirit Who actually nurtures and directs the newborn in Christ. It is the Spirit Who continues to sustain and educate the maturing Christian each step of life's journey. The Holy Spirit helps the believer not only to mature in the right direction, but also to guard against slipping back into corruption. Listening to the Holy Spirit's direction to the new redeemed nature causes the believer to continue forward with faith and confidence. At the same time, the Spirit effectively guards against the constant onslaught of the sin nature, which always tries to undermine the spiritual well being of the child of God.

5:17 ***What your corrupt nature wants is contrary to what your spiritual nature wants, and what your spiritual nature wants is contrary to what your corrupt nature wants. They are opposed to each other. As a result, you don't always do what you intend to do.***

The spiritual nature of the new man in Christ is distinctly different from the old sin nature. The two are opposite. They share nothing in common except the person they seek to dominate. The new spiritual nature displaces the old sin nature from dominance as the quickening power of the Holy Spirit takes effect in the heart of the newly transformed sinner. Consequently, the war between the two natures rages even though the battle has already been won at the moment Jesus died as the acceptable sacrifice for sin.

Even though the Redeemer has sealed His eternal authority over the life He ransomed, the sin nature continues to present its own corrupt objectives, trying to assert its fading influence over the life of the redeemed individual. Consequently, the believer is often confused between the truth he knows and the corrupt influence he struggles to resist. Often, the believer ends up doing what he did not intend to do as the child of God *(Romans 7).*

5:18 *If your spiritual nature is your guide, you are not subject to Moses' laws.*

Paul promptly reminded the Galatians that the answer to their dilemma was their allegiance to the truth. If they continued to listen to the Holy Spirit as He directed their newly quickened spiritual nature, then there was no way for the corrupt nature to dominate their behavior. While believers continue to obey the precepts of the Law in Christ, the Law has no eternal impact on the lives of the redeemed because its demands have already been satisfied in Jesus Christ. There are many voices demanding the attention of God's children. But there is only one true voice that continues to echo the eternal truth of the Gospel directly to the quickened spirit of the redeemed. Paul reminded the Galatians that their attention must be fixed upon this one true voice, even the voice of the Holy Spirit.

5:19–21 [19]*Now, the effects of the corrupt nature are obvious: illicit sex, perversion, promiscuity,* [20]*idolatry, drug use, hatred, rivalry, jealousy, angry outbursts, selfish ambition, conflict, factions,* [21]*envy, drunkenness, wild partying, and things like that. I've told you in the past and I'm telling you again that*

people who do things like that will not inherit the kingdom of God.

Paul was well aware that the Galatians needed more practical guidance than just doctrinal correction. So he supported his stern instruction against corruption by identifying the specific behaviors in which the depraved qualities of the sin nature manifest themselves. Regardless of the spiritual status of any individual, the sin nature will always manifest itself through the evil works of its own fallen nature. Paul unequivocally declared that those who identify themselves with the evil works of the sin nature will not inherit the Kingdom of God.

The evil works of the sin nature are intimately related to various aspects of the human person. They emanate from the individual as a sensual, emotional, intellectual, or relational expression of the sin nature. Even though the list is not exhaustive, Paul outlined a catalog of behaviors identifying the works of the flesh that should not characterize the redeemed.

The corrupt works of evil should not become the behaviors of the redeemed spirit of God's child. The two have nothing in common. The sin nature and the quickened spirit of the redeemed are actually at enmity with each other. The sin nature fully controls the conduct, words, and deeds of the unregenerate person relentlessly exploiting evil to satisfy its lust. When the redeemed succumb to the evil works of the sin nature, they actually contradict God's Spirit Who is living and working in them. Paul told the Galatians to reject their sin nature and listen only to the Holy Spirit Who directs their quickened spirit in the righteous path of the Lord Jesus Christ. In Paul's letter to the Thessalonians, he advised: "Do not put out the Spirit's fire" *(1 Thessalonians 5:19).*

5:22–23 ***[22]But the spiritual nature produces love, joy, peace, patience, kindness, goodness, faithfulness, [23]gentleness, and self-control. There are no laws against things like that.***

Man's spiritual nature does not produce anything positive in the lives of believers, because that nature is as corrupt as man's physical nature because of sin. Rather, it is the Holy Spirit that works in the hearts of God's redeemed people, producing those characteristics which reflect the fact that Christ lives in their redeemed hearts. This is a stark contrast to the evil that results from man's sin nature. Instead of being overcome by the actions of the corrupt nature, Paul informed the Galatians that the Spirit produces these characteristics as nine integrated components of one fruit in the lives of those that He has saved. This fruit reflects the person and character of the Lord Jesus Christ living within the redeemed person.

As Jesus demonstrated the love of God to the world by His sacrificial death, so the believer reflects God's love to the world by showing how God has redeemed him. As Jesus gives His peace to those who belong to Him, so the Christian lives peaceably in a world that is generally hostile to the Gospel. As Jesus endured the cross because of the joy that lay on the other side of that suffering, so the disciple looks beyond any present circumstance, enduring suffering, because of the joy that awaits him when he meets his Savior face-to-face. As Jesus patiently taught the multitudes that followed Him and quietly instructed them in the work of His Kingdom, so the faithful follower patiently instructs unbelievers in the ways of Christ. As Jesus looked past the sin of those who asked for healing, and healed them out of the kindness of His heart, so the saved sinner engages with his neighbor out of a heart overflowing with the kindness that Jesus has given to him.

As Jesus associated with sinners, demonstrating the forgiving goodness of God, so the children of God, filled with this same goodness, share the saving message, forgiving others as Christ has forgiven them. As Jesus faithfully fulfilled the will of His Father, giving His life on behalf of sinners, so God's people submit to the will of their heavenly Father, faithfully doing those things which the Spirit directs them to do. As Jesus walked among the crowds, He always treated people gently, understanding their sin and the limitations that sin produces. So those who are called by the Spirit live in such a way that the gentleness of Christ is evident in their relationships with others. As Jesus went to the cross, His self-control is difficult to comprehend. He could have called down legions of angels to destroy His enemies. Instead, He laid down His life of His own will. So those who have been rescued by His death from the penalty of their sin submit to the control of the Holy Spirit, bowing to the authority and control of the One Who has died for them.

In contrast to the Law endorsed by the Judaizers which produces only condemnation and imposes only a death sentence on the law-breakers, Paul summarizes those characteristics that reflect the abundance of a redeemed life. There is no law that can be as effective in living the way God wants as the person whose life has been filled and continues to be filled with the fruit that the Holy Spirit produces.

5:24 *Those who belong to Christ Jesus have crucified their corrupt nature along with its passions and desires.*

Those who are renewed in God's salvation through Jesus Christ are naturally changed by the ongoing work of the Spirit, Who produces the fruit of their redemption in their lives. They are not to be easily deceived by the evil of their corrupt nature. They know they cannot trust themselves. Because of the transformation that has been effected in their hearts, believers normally develop an aversion to their sin nature. Consequently, they leave the sin nature where God put it. Jesus Christ nailed the sins of the redeemed by His body on the cross effectively killing the sin nature so that it no longer dominates the lives of those whom He saves. Therefore, beneficiaries of Christ's finished work on Calvary, the redeemed no longer surrender to their corrupt nature and enjoy its evil designs. Instead, the Spirit cultivates God's fruit in their hearts by the indwelling Holy Spirit.

5:25 *If we live by our spiritual nature, then our lives need to conform to our spiritual nature.*

If the believer is committed to a life of compliance to the spiritual transformation he experienced, then he should conduct his life in tune with the new spiritual nature cultivated in him by the Holy Spirit. Simply put, the spiritual framework of a person's new life requires corresponding behaviors that reflect the new life given as a result of the salvation experienced. The believer cannot split his spiritual allegiance to both natures–the sin nature and the new man. The redeemed nature necessarily demands a new way of life. The Galatian Christians could not live within the framework of the true Gospel while attempting to accommodate the sin nature. If they were transformed in Jesus Christ from death to life, then they must live in the newness of God's redemption. The actions of the redeemed life should correspond with the new life being nurtured by the Holy Spirit.

5:26 *We can't allow ourselves to act arrogantly and to provoke or envy each other.*

The believer should not live a life that contradicts his redemption in Jesus Christ. He should not submit to the arrogance of his sin nature. Envy should not disrupt the communion of the redeemed both with each other and with God. Arrogance and envy are not the fruit of the Spirit. They are spawned by the corrupt greed of the sin nature. So the believer is strongly urged to reject the sin nature, resist its corrupt tendencies, and renounce arrogance and envy so that the new man in Christ is kept faithful to his redeemed nature.

Notes/Applications

Paul firmly described the clear distinction between the Law and God's grace. The understanding of this distinction had a huge impact on believers' position before God as His redeemed children. In summary, the Law condemned them, but God's grace saved them. The Law required the death penalty, but Jesus' death removed that penalty and gave them abundant life in this world and the next. Man's corrupt nature produces a litany of godless behaviors, but the Holy Spirit plants, nurtures, and produces a fruit that supersedes any human law.

All believers struggle in their new life as the disciples of Jesus Christ. It is terribly difficult to abandon the human desires which have dominated life from the moment of birth. Once saved, everything is new. The light of Christ colors everything the new believer sees, hears, and understands. Many new believers blossom in the faith that Christ has instilled in them. The Word of God becomes their dearest treasure. Its precepts are planted deeply in the soil of their redeemed hearts. Others seem to blossom for a short time and then reach a plateau where further growth seems to stop. At that stage, they become vulnerable to the influences of people who, like the Judaizers, offer some tantalizing alternative to the salvation that has been given to them. This was the situation in which Paul found the Galatian Christians—redeemed, but misled because they had not matured in the faith that the Lord had given them.

So Paul reminded them of the work that the Holy Spirit continues to do in the lives of those He has saved. The Spirit convicts unbelievers of sin and judgment, and then continues to sow the seeds of His fruit in the lives of those who belong to Christ. The Law has no effect on those whose lives have been conformed to the image of Jesus Christ by the maturing fruit of saving faith. Yes, the Spirit uses God's Law to show sinners the error of their rebellion against God. But the continuing work of the Spirit so changes believers' hearts that the abundance of their life in Christ outshines the demands of the Law. The unchanging truth of God's Word becomes more precious than all the wealth the world has to offer. The influences of strange ideas become only the stepping stone to greater confidence in the abiding presence of Jesus Christ.

If the Galatians were continuously maturing in their faith and the knowledge of the true precepts of the Gospel, then they would have learned the distinction between the evil works of the flesh and the fruit of the Spirit. They would also have known that both the evil works and the fruit of the Spirit are the natural outcomes of their respective natural sources. That is, they would have understood that evil works are generated by the sin nature while the fruit of the Spirit is produced by the Holy Spirit. Ultimately, they would have known that as the redeemed children of God their unavoidable choice in all aspects of their daily lives would have been directed necessarily by the indwelling Holy Spirit. Therefore, Paul admonished both the Galatians and all believers that after knowing the truth, the redeemed must listen to the Holy Spirit so that they could live in the awareness of their redeemed life in Christ as their spiritual nature develops into a maturing disciple of Jesus Christ.

In the heart of such a believer, Christ reigns supreme, the Holy Spirit rejoices, and the Father is glorified. May the Spirit so powerfully move in believers' hearts that the fruit of their changed lives gives testimony to the glorious salvation that has been given to them in and through Jesus Christ.

GALATIANS 6

Galatians 6:1–6

6:1 ***Brothers and sisters, if a person gets trapped by wrongdoing, those of you who are spiritual should help that person turn away from doing wrong. Do it in a gentle way. At the same time watch yourself so that you also are not tempted.***

Paul concluded chapter five with a warning to the Galatians against arrogance and envy toward each other. Not only are believers to care for their own spiritual well-being, but they are also encouraged to support of one another. The alternative, enslavement to the Law and the flesh, is unthinkable among Christians. But Paul lived in the real world. He knew that God's children struggle and falter along the way. So Paul encouraged the believers to take notice of each other's predicaments and offer support as each one matures in faith.

Individual spiritual maturity is not confined to self-centered spiritual concerns. Rather, individual spiritual stability and growth are encouraged in the context of the whole body of Christ. So Paul urged the Galatians to listen to the Holy Spirit and live according to the dictates of the Spirit-directed spiritual nature. Thus each believer could effectively resist evil and become a strong link within the family of faith.

But there are dangers when the stronger Christian helps the weaker. The human spirit is extremely deceitful and the attitude of spiritual superiority can creep into the hearts of stronger believers. They credit themselves for the good that the Holy Spirit does through them toward the weaker Christian. It is also possible that the stronger believer may succumb to the same sin at some future time. Paul strongly encouraged believers to support each other on a deeply personal level, but he also offered a carefully constructed warning to those who undertook this task.

6:2 *Help carry each other's burdens. In this way you will follow Christ's teachings.*

There are tremendous rewards when Christians follow Paul's advice. He told them to bear each other's burdens, displaying the character of the Lord Jesus Christ in practical ways. Instead of demeaning one another, God's children should encourage each other with the fruit of the Spirit *(Galatians 5:22–23)*. The Holy Spirit does this so that the whole body of Christ will be strengthened, encouraged, and supported. Jesus told His disciples that the world would know that they were His disciples by the love they showed to one another *(John 13:35)*. A life, which reflects the love of Christ, certainly fulfills the law of Christ's liberty in the true Gospel.

6:3 *So if any one of you thinks you're important when you're really not, you're only fooling yourself.*

Recognizing the sinful nature in all people, Paul carefully blended his discourse with encouragements and warnings. He reminded all Christians to guard against arrogance and condescension, even as they worked at spiritual excellence so that they would not be consumed by foolish self-adulation. The Holy Spirit works in every believer's heart within the framework of the individual personality, which God created in each redeemed individual. Every incident of struggle and victory takes place within the context of the individual's unique circumstances. Even though lessons learned are needed for the edification of the whole body, whether a matter of struggle or a point of success, each experience is a "mile marker" in each individual's journey. So the Galatians were warned to watch themselves lest they misread their successes or struggles as occasions to indulge in self-praise. He cautioned them to watch their natural tendencies so that they would not be deceived by their own corrupt imagination and inclination to pride.

6:4–5 [4]*Each of you must examine your own actions. Then you can be proud of your own accomplishments without comparing yourself to others.* [5]*Assume your own responsibility.*

Even though the redeemed are called to support one another, each believer is responsible for his own spiritual journey, and must be sensitive to the internal work of the Holy Spirit indelibly impacting every aspect of the whole person. All personal experiences of the believer are processes through which the Holy Spirit accomplishes His purpose as He brings the redeemed along toward the finish line.

Each lesson learned is an aspect of God's practical truth that must be used to nurture the body of Christ in keeping with the admonitions of God's Word. Therefore, the child of God must be consciously aware of his own spiritual experience, and respond to the direction given by the Holy Spirit as He makes God's Word alive and relevant in each situation. In this sense, Paul told the Galatians to be responsible children of God under the guidance of the Holy Spirit. They should not assume a position of self-righteous importance from which they "look down their noses" at weaker believers. But they should encourage the weak with the same comforting assurance by which the Holy Spirit brought them to maturity.

Having encouraged the Galatian Christians to help each other through the difficult experiences of life, Paul then told them that each person had to take personal responsibility. If one believer helps another, both the helper and the one helped bear individual responsibility before God. Each believer is personally accountable to God. *"All of us will have to give account of ourselves to God" (Romans 14:12).*

6:6 *The person who is taught God's word should share all good things with his teacher.*

Two interpretations are derived from this verse. First, as many scholars correctly understand, Paul put a non-negotiable responsibility upon all members of the family of faith—on those who teach and those who are taught. Those who teach must declare the truth faithfully without fear, doubt, or compromise. Those who are taught must support their teachers in practical ways that meet their material needs *(1 Timothy 5:18).*

Another interpretation comes from the understanding that the Holy Spirit is the ultimate teacher. Jesus Himself assured His disciples that the Holy Spirit would give them understanding regarding all the things He told them. Therefore, all believers are instructed to share the entirety of their lives with the Holy Spirit by responding with a genuine love and obedience.[1]

Notes/Applications

Paul instructed the Galatians to be sensitive to one another. He admonished them to view each other in the context of each one's relationship with Jesus Christ. He urged all believers to consider their action toward others to be the same as that of Christ's toward them. The believer's attitude toward fellow-believers and unbelievers is the natural outpouring of the character of Jesus Christ being manifested by the Holy Spirit within them.

The redeemed are to be to one another as Christ would be, a source of comfort and strength. Believers are to be selfless, rejecting everything that produces pride. Instead, the redeemed should be consciously aware of their own spiritual journey, obeying the guidance of the Holy Spirit and responding to one another in the good things of God's grace.

Galatians 6:7–11

6:7 *Make no mistake about this: You can* *out of God. Whatever you plant is what you*

The life of the believer or any other person is an open book before God. Every word and action is fully known by Him. Paul cautioned the Galatians not to view God as a "bystander" watching from the sideline, often missing the details. God can never be deceived. Whatever the redeemed does in life, God knows it! The way a person behaves will produce a similar harvest. People reap the consequences of their actions. God is loving, caring, and gracious, but should not be taken for granted. God is never deceived by anything a person does *(Psalm 14:1).* Kenneth Wuest's translation of this verse says: "Whatever a man is in the habit of sowing, this also will he reap; because the one who sows with a view to his own evil nature, from his evil nature as a source shall reap corruption."[2]

6:8 *If you plant in [the soil of] your corrupt nature, you will harvest destruction. But if you plant in [the soil of] your spiritual nature, you will harvest everlasting life.*

In chapter five Paul contrasted the evil works of the sin nature from the fruit of the Spirit. Here Paul once again identified the source and the result of the different experiences in the life of the redeemed. In simple words, Paul told the Galatians that corruption results in a harvest from seeds planted in the soil of one's sin nature. Eternal life results from seeds planted in the spiritual nature redeemed by the work of the Holy Spirit. So, if they trusted in the Law from which they were set free, they would be disappointed, because the Law had already found them guilty. But if they continued to trust in the true Gospel, they would be strengthened even more. Despite the sin nature with which believers always struggle, Jesus Christ gives them life eternal.

Ve can't allow ourselves to get tired of living the right ay. Certainly, each of us will receive [everlasting life] at the proper time, if we don't give up.

Paul candidly reminded the Galatians that they were not to tire of living in compliance with the Gospel. The flesh might be weak but the redeemed spirit is always ready. Even though the believer will ultimately come to the final fulfillment of his redemption in Christ at a future time, there is still a life to be enjoyed on earth under the caring providence of the Lord. Paul encouraged believers not to give up but to continue as God's redeemed children, being and doing good without weariness.

6:10 ***Whenever we have the opportunity, we have to do what is good for everyone, especially for the family of believers.***

Being good to everyone, especially to fellow-believers is the normal outcome for a follower of Jesus Christ. God's goodness is expressed through the words and deeds of His children. So whenever believers encounter opportunities for exhibiting God's goodness, they must honor God by obediently sharing the goodness that God had stirred up in them. Being good to others is an active expression of obedience to God and the manifestation of His goodness toward those who benefit from our Christian conduct.

6:11 ***Look at how large the letters [in these words] are because I'm writing this myself.***

Paul wanted the Galatians to know that what he said was what he meant. He put his own personal handwritten validation to his remarks unlike his other writings, which were probably penned by a secretary. He asked them to notice the size of the letters he wrote to draw attention to the intensity of his feelings about their spiritual condition. It was his personal expression of what he would have said to them if he were with them in person.

Notes/Applications

Before recapping the essentials of the true Gospel in the closing verses of this letter, Paul addressed them about the practical aspects of the Gospel in their day-to-day experiences. Living in the world as believers and struggling with their sin nature, Christians are to persevere in faith, looking to Jesus and listening to the Holy Spirit as He guides them one step at a time. Their thoughts and conduct must be fully submissive to the dictates of the redeemed life gradually cultivated within them.

The believer, whose life is paid for by heaven's most magnificent Treasure, can no longer live in compliant partnership with the sin nature. Instead, the redeemed must continue to sow the living Word of God into the fertile ground of their changed hearts, so that they may enjoy the blessings of the fruit of the Spirit in their daily walk. All believers who have tasted God's goodness can no longer quietly avoid opportunities to let God's goodness flow through their words and actions. Paul encouraged the Galatians and all believers to walk worthy of their calling, and live their lives in a way that continues to manifest their faith and God's goodness in practical ways.

Galatians 6:12–18

6:12 *These people who want to make a big deal out of a physical thing are trying to force you to be circumcised. Their only aim is to avoid persecution because of the cross of Christ.*

In his closing, Paul presented a simplified and practical conclusion bearing on the essentials of the Gospel. He reminded them that the Judaizers who attempted to lead them away from the Gospel were selfish cowards who kept avoiding the truth. The Judaizers genuinely believed that a new Gentile convert had to adopt the precepts of Jewish tradition. Because of their intense commitment, many Jewish believers were afraid to speak for the truth of the Gospel as Paul did. Afraid of this persecution, they continued to live in the environment of an erroneous doctrine, continuing to follow their Jewish traditions, which tied them to the slavery of the Law. Paul told the Galatians to disregard the counsel of the Judaizers because they avoided the truth in order to escape persecution for the sake of Christ Who was sacrificed for their redemption. If they believed that their salvation was secured by the precious blood of the Lamb, then they had nothing to fear. The One Who did not spare His Son from death on the cross for their sake would certainly not forsake them under any circumstance. Paul showed the Galatians the true color of the Judaizers by exposing their real motive.

6:13 *It's clear that not even those who had themselves circumcised did this to follow Jewish laws. Yet, they want you to be circumcised so that they can brag about what was done to your body.*

Looking further into the motive of the Judaizers, Paul told those who were influenced by them that many had been circumcised in order to avoid persecution, not because they truly observed the Law. An underlying motivation fueled their zeal to impose their views on genuine converts. The Judaizers were caught trying to gain public notoriety at the expense of the redeemed by circumcising Gentile converts, thus showing their commitment to the Jewish Law and to the tradition of their forefathers. They wished to prove their excellence by disguising their false position. The Judaizers were serving their own interest at the expense of Gentile converts who had been delivered from bondage by the true Gospel.

6:14 ***But it's unthinkable that I could ever brag about anything except the cross of our Lord Jesus Christ. By his cross my relationship to the world and its relationship to me have been crucified.***

After exposing the self-serving motivation of the Judaizers, Paul firmly stated his own conviction regarding his relational position with Jesus Christ. Unlike the Judaizers, Paul's confidence was in Jesus Christ and His cross. The material world no longer mattered to Paul. All human relationships outside of Christ had lost their significance. He was a new man with a new purpose and destiny in life. Unlike the Judaizers, Paul no longer looked back at the Law. He kept pressing onward toward his future in Jesus Christ.

6:15 ***Certainly, it doesn't matter whether a person is circumcised or not. Rather, what matters is being a new creation.***

Paul finally declared the true message of the true Gospel in a few simple words. What matters is the new life that the Gospel brings into the heart of the redeemed. The issue was not whether circumcision is right or wrong in and of itself. Circumcision has no significance on one's salvation. Paul assured the Galatians they should not concern themselves with circumcision, since it had no impact on their new life in Christ.

6:16 ***Peace and mercy will come to rest on all those who conform to this principle. They are the Israel of God.***

Paul had just clearly summarized this letter by stating the most important principle for the believer—a person in Christ is a new creation. The essence of his statement can be viewed from two complementary perspectives. First, Paul affirmed that those who were new creatures in Christ would surely receive the peace and mercy of God given to them in Jesus Christ. Second, he affirmed that God's peace and mercy would be experienced practically in the life of those who were in Jesus Christ. He called them the Israel of God—an endearing designation for the people of God.

Those who are redeemed will not need to look for any other way of escaping judgment. They have been made free because the Holy Spirit Himself bears witness of God's redemption in their hearts. So, if the Galatians were truly saved by hearing and believing in the true Gospel, they should no longer be looking to the Law for their redemption. God's peace and mercy was already in their hearts causing them to rest in their Father's grace.

6:17 *From now on, don't make any trouble for me! After all, I carry the scars of Jesus on my body.*

Paul candidly pleaded with the Galatians to take their faith seriously. He told them not to give him any more grief. He had been suffering enough for the sake of Jesus Christ, his Master. He would rather not endure any more anguish over the relentless efforts of the Judaizers to undermine the witness of the Lord for Whom he had suffered. He yearned to rejoice with the Galatians as they continued to persevere in the truth of the Gospel, in spite of the false doctrine being propagated by the Judaizers.

6:18 *May the good will of our Lord Jesus Christ be with your spirit, brothers and sisters! Amen.*

In conclusion, Paul expressed a heartfelt amen, passionately submitting himself to the truth he proclaimed. He wished them the goodwill of the Lord Jesus Christ to bring God's grace into their spirit, so that their experience of the true Gospel would be real and meaningful. He had taught them everything they needed to know, giving them practical and timely instructions to enable them to live the life they professed. Now it was the time to pronounce the benediction, pointing them to the source of sustaining grace, even Jesus Christ, their Savior and the Sustainer of their faith.

Notes/Applications

As Paul began his letter to the Galatian Christians, he first established the authenticity of his apostleship by providing a record of his conversion, his call to service, and his response to that call. Jesus Himself had stopped Paul as he entered Damascus, intent on arresting and imprisoning Christians. In that encounter, Jesus completely redirected Paul from trusting in his observance of the Law to trusting in Jesus Christ. Although a devout Jew and a member of the Pharisees, he learned that the Law only condemned people, because no one could successfully live up to the standards God had established. Then he met Jesus, and learned that Jesus Christ had paid the penalty for his sin. For Paul, this simple truth became the foundation for his ministry among the Gentiles.

Therefore, any deviation from this simple message of salvation was wrong. Unfortunately, the Christians in Galatia had listened to people who believed that Jesus was not enough for salvation. To receive God's approval, a person also had to agree to obey the Law. That was simply unacceptable! It made Paul angry and frustrated. He called the Galatians fools—misguided fools! He berated those who urged people to adopt such a false religion, in the end wishing that they would themselves be castrated. Nothing could be done to gain God's approval except to receive the gift of salvation offered in the life, death, and resurrection of Jesus Christ. Why couldn't they understand that?

Why don't we understand this simple, saving message? Because we are so much like the Galatian Christians. We, too, have listened to the voices of today's false prophets. We have been told that we need to obey the Law, and if not the Law, at least the rules of the church to which we belong. Right away, the sin urge in us makes us believe that, because we are saved, we can show God how good we really are. But, as

Paul tells us, we cannot fool God! He sees everything! He knows that we cannot successfully follow the rules. Even though He demands our obedience, He has provided forgiveness for our disobedience. He has freely given us His Son to suffer the eternal consequences of our sin. That should be enough!

Like Paul, we should brag about nothing except the cross of Jesus Christ whereby the world and all its enticements have been crucified to us and, in turn, we have been crucified to the world. These opposing elements of the redeemed life are mutually dead to each other. This is nothing more and nothing less than what Paul wrote to the Ephesian church: "[8]For by grace you have been saved through faith. And this is not your own doing; it is the gift of God, [9]not a result of works, so that no one may boast. [10]For we are his workmanship, created in Christ Jesus for good works, which God prepared beforehand, that we should walk in them" *(Ephesians 2:8–10).*

EPHESIANS

INTRODUCTION

Ephesus was the capital of the province of Asia during Roman occupation, and enjoyed significant prosperity due to its strategic location at the mouth of the Cayster River near the modern city of Selçuk on the western coast of Turkey. During the New Testament era Ephesus was one of the largest and most important cities of the Roman Empire. It was the crossroads of the trade routes between Rome and its eastern boundaries, creating a banking and commercial empire. Because of its size and importance, people of diverse cultural backgrounds sought to share in its riches, giving the city a multicultural landscape.[1]

One of the Marble Streets in Ephesus

A huge temple dedicated to the Greek goddess Artemis, goddess of wild animals and the moon and protector of the household, dominated the city. This was the precursor to the Roman goddess Diana. At

Ephesus she was worshiped primarily as an ancient Near Eastern fertility deity, in whose honor the Greek colonists built a temple around 700 B.C. This temple, considered one of the seven wonders of the ancient world, was destroyed in 356 B.C., but was rebuilt. Worshipers carried small silver, marble, and terra-cotta images of this temple with them, to be placed inside the actual temple and possibly also in their homes as house shrines.[2] Because of the demand for these religious trinkets, silversmiths were a dominant political force in the city.

This was the environment of the city Paul visited briefly on his return to Jerusalem following his second missionary journey, A.D. 49–52 *(Acts 18:18–22)*. At that time, he promised to return if the Lord permitted him to do so. During his third missionary journey, Ephesus became the focal point of Paul's ministry, working in the city for nearly three years, A.D. 53–57 *(Acts 20:31)*. A confrontation with the silversmiths in Ephesus hastened Paul's exit from the city.

At the end of that journey, Paul was confined to a long period of imprisonment, first in Jerusalem and eventually in Rome, A.D. 59–62. Paul wrote his letter to the Ephesian Christians during his time in prison, still concerned for the spiritual welfare of those who had been saved by the Lord under his missionary endeavors. Most Bible scholars have come to the conclusion that Ephesians was written while Paul was in Rome about A.D. 61–62.

Even though Paul was in prison, the Gospel was not. Rather, the Gospel flourished during these years. Paul used the opportunities he had to mentor younger believers, witness to his guards, and write letters to encourage the churches that were established during his ministry. Paul also wrote the letters to Colossae, Philippi, and Galatia during this time. People in the emperor's household knew that Paul was in prison because of Jesus Christ *(Philippians 1:12–13)*.

Paul wrote this letter to Christians in Ephesus, a pagan, multicultural city, on the west coast of Asia Minor while imprisoned for the Gospel of Jesus Christ. It is hard to imagine that anything good could be produced from such a terrible situation. Nevertheless, Ephesians is one of the pristine jewels of Paul's New Testament letters, overflowing with the greatness of salvation in Jesus Christ and its practical application in the relationships that surround the believer in an unbelieving world.

Typical of the outline of his letters, Paul begins with the theological foundation upon which the lives of all believers are constructed. His redeemed spirit bubbles with unrestrained joy because of the blessings of redemption. He reminds believers that they have been brought near to God by the blood of Jesus Christ, made into one family by their reconciliation that breaks the conditions that normally divide the human race. Christ is the cornerstone of that family, constructing a living temple that reflects the glory of the Lord.

Building on the foundation of Christ's work of salvation, producing peace and unity in the lives of believers, Paul then urges believers to walk in that unity. He demonstrates the way in which the Body of Christ functions as the Spirit gives differing abilities to God's people so that the Church can be a faithful witness to God's saving work among the lost people of the world. Outlining the rules for the believer's new life in Christ, Paul displays the way in which relationships fulfill a positive testimony of God's work among His people—husbands and wives, parents and children, slaves and masters.

Then in a challenging conclusion, Paul describes the warfare that engages the strength and energy of His people who live in a world hostile to the One Who made them. He urges believers to look to God Who will provide them with the armor needed to defend themselves from the evil influences of the world and stand firm in the faith which God has entrusted to them.

When we read this letter, understanding the circumstances in which it was written and the culture in which the Christian was called to live, we trust that our Lord will give us better insight into our circumstances as we live in the light of Christ's redemption, shining in the dark world of our day. May the Holy Spirit employ Paul's joy, enthusiasm, and confidence as our encouragement for the battle that is set before us. May He help us to stand faithfully for our Savior as we face the world's hostility with confidence and joy, glad that we share in the work of His Kingdom.

EPHESIANS 1

Ephesians 1:1–6

1:1–2 ***[1]From Paul, an apostle of Christ Jesus by God's will. To God's holy and faithful people who are united with Christ in the city of Ephesus. [2]Good will and peace from God our Father and the Lord Jesus Christ are yours!***

Paul introduced his letter to the Ephesians with a salutation that was common in letters written in his time and culture. However, his address was not given in the language of his day. Rather, it was delivered in the framework of the Christian faith. He unashamedly pointed to God the Father and our Lord Jesus Christ His Son, effectively reflecting the Jewish and Christian perspectives of the eternal God and Jesus Christ as complementary aspects of a single expression of faith.

Paul identified himself as an apostle of Jesus Christ. He also told them that his apostleship was established by God's sovereign will. It was not a position he earned or for which he was qualified. Rather, it was God's appointment that was divinely determined even before Paul was born *(Galatians 1:15–17)*.

Paul described the Ephesians as God's people, holy, faithful, and united in Christ. The message God gave to Paul in this letter was presented to believers who were already mature in their faith. They already possessed the grace and peace from God the Father and the Lord Jesus Christ. They had already grown in the faith, and Paul considered them to be holy and faithful people fully united with Jesus Christ. They were holy because they were the temple of God in which His Holy Spirit lived. They were faithful because the faith of Jesus Christ was instilled in them by the power of the Author and Finisher of their faith. In the context of a mature and well-developed faith, God directly and personally sent this message to the believers in Ephesus.

1:3 *Praise the God and Father of our Lord Jesus Christ! Through Christ, God has blessed us with every spiritual blessing that heaven has to offer.*

Following his warm salutation, Paul broke into a joyful doxology of praise. He offered this praise to God on behalf of the redeemed, thanking Him for the blessings He gives to His children through the sacrifice of Jesus Christ His Son. God holds nothing back from those whom He chooses to save through Jesus Christ. By receiving the fullness of heaven's spiritual blessings in Jesus Christ, the redeemed came into a heavenly position of becoming joint heirs with Jesus Christ as the recipients of the entirety of God's gift *(Romans 8:17)*. Paul wanted the Ephesians to know that they are not only holy, faithful, and united in Christ, but also are divinely favored children of God fully accepted into the heavenly inheritance of God's grace, His good will, the peace of the Lord Jesus Christ, and the full measure of God's blessings.

1:4 *Before the creation of the world, he chose us through Christ to be holy and perfect in his presence.*

God bestowed the fullness of His heavenly riches on the redeemed according to His eternal purpose. God's decision to save sinners was not a reaction to man's sin or because of the death of His Son. God never reacts to any situation or event. He is never surprised by anything that happens in the world that He has created. Rather, it was a carefully ordained, planned, and accomplished eternal event executed before time began.

Before He created the world, God made a timeless decision to save a people for Himself who would be holy and perfect through the holiness and perfection of His holy and perfect Son, Jesus Christ. Then, at the exact moment God had determined, He executed this plan according to a specific process through which God's eternal will was revealed to the people of the world in time and space (*Galatians 4:4; Hebrews 1:1–3*).

1:5–6 [5]*Because of his love he had already decided to adopt us through Jesus Christ. He freely chose to do this* [6]*so that the kindness he had given us in his dear Son would be praised and given glory.*

God's sovereign determination to save a people for Himself is not just a demonstration of His authority. His authority is incontestable. Rather, His redemption is executed in the framework of His love, mercy, and grace. His love, mercy, and grace are marvelously displayed in His decision to adopt those whom He chooses to be His redeemed children in Jesus Christ. He ordained those whom He chose to see His grace revealed in Jesus Christ and praise His Name for the gift of their salvation. God's adopts those whom He chooses simply as an act of His love and His grace, executed freely out of His pleasure. It is just an awesome phenomenon, which He was pleased to do. Amazingly, this was accomplished exactly as He determined. He made those whom He loved and chose to be acceptable to Himself in, through, and for the sake of His own beloved Son, Jesus Christ.

Notes/Applications

Paul's letter to the Ephesians is a type of general circular correspondence sent to show believers the mystery of their salvation in Jesus Christ. Paul, who was God's appointed apostle to the Gentiles, saluted the Ephesians in the grace and peace of God our Father and His Son, our Lord Jesus Christ. He reminded them that they were holy, faithful, and united in Christ because of what God did in their hearts by the power of His Spirit.

Paul wanted the Ephesians to understand their salvation as the outcome of God's sovereign plan. Their salvation was the unavoidable and irresistible essence of God's timeless determination regarding those whom He chose to redeem for Himself. It is the divine expression of God's sovereign will accomplished without any consultation with anyone outside of God Himself. It is a ruling that was pronounced in eternity past before any form of existence other than Himself was ever a reality.

God decided to lavish the riches of His love, grace, and mercy upon those whom He chose to be the objects of His favor.

God's redemption is not confined to the functional rescue of the lost from deserved judgment. But it is God's gift of the full measure of His blessings in Jesus Christ to those who are chosen for such heavenly favor. The gift is not earned. Nor is it merited by an anticipated or foreseen faith or qualification. It is given out of God's pleasure and good will. It is not given as a result of any human effort. It is given only by God through the merit of the sacrifice of Jesus Christ. God's redemption is the divine expression of His love, mercy, grace, good will, and peace, effectively generating His holiness, perfection, faith, and unity in the lives of God's redeemed children. The Ephesians were exposed to the truth of their salvation so that they would know and appreciate the inexplicable extent of God's blessings given to them. All believers across the ages join the Ephesian Christians in praise of God's measureless grace.

Ephesians 1:7–14

1:7 *Through the blood of his Son, we are set free from our sins. God forgives our failures because of his overflowing kindness.*

God expressed the riches of His kindness and grace by preparing the means and paying the cost for the execution of His redemption. As the Judge, God knew exactly what was required to cancel the offense committed against Him because of sin. He knew that He was the only One Who was able to correct this situation. Therefore, He gave His only Son to be a sacrifice for sin's penalty and took the place of the sinner who legitimately and legally deserved it. God Himself secured forgiveness for sinners by shedding the precious, pure blood of His holy, perfect, and sinless Son. God's love, mercy, and grace are even more openly expressed in His unfailing forgiveness of the sins and failures that plagued the whole of mankind.

1:8–9 [8]*He poured out his kindness by giving us every kind of wisdom and insight* [9]*when he revealed the mystery of his plan to us. He had decided to do this through Christ.*

God revealed the mystery of His redemption to those whom He redeemed not only by executing His plan through and in Jesus Christ, but also by giving His children godly wisdom to recognize and acknowledge what Christ's sacrifice had accomplished on their behalf. God's redemption is an unknowable secret to the unregenerate human mind. The idea of an undeserved gift contradicts everything the human mind understands. Instead, people believe that they are worthy of the gifts they receive, that they have done something good that earned them some reward.

Humanity does not understand that they stand condemned before the throne of a just, righteous God. So God instills His Spirit in the heart of those He ransoms for Himself in order to equip His children with the resources of His wisdom. Only by the work of the Holy Spirit do the redeemed have the spiritual capacity to live in communion with their God in full recognition of the salvation that has been purchased for them *(John 16:13)*. Therefore, even though it is completely foreign to human thinking, God's children understand through God's wisdom and insight that their redemption is indeed God's gracious gift given to them according to His own exclusive purpose and pleasure. He did by Himself, for Himself, and within Himself. Paul did not have any difficulties or doubts declaring God's ordained election of the redeemed before the foundation of the world. He understood clearly that it pleased God to give His wisdom along with His living Word to His people to comprehend the mystery of their redemption.

1:10 *He planned to bring all of history to its goal in Christ. Then Christ would be the head of everything in heaven and on earth.*

Even though everyone ever born is an actor on the stage of history, each one serves God's purpose, accomplishing His plan across the ages. God purposed, planned, and executed His redemption and judgment in Jesus Christ in order to bring everything in heaven and earth to its ultimate goal in His Son Jesus Christ. By doing so, God perfected everything by His own determination, placing on His Son the full weight of man's sin and satisfying His judgment and redemption at a specific time and place in history. Christ alone is due the glory and praise of all people, both the saved and the unsaved. "[9]*This is why God has given him an exceptional honor–the name honored above all other names–*[10]*so that at the name of Jesus everyone in heaven, on earth, and in the world below will kneel* [11]*and confess that Jesus Christ is Lord to the glory of God the Father" (Philippians 2:9–11)*. Then Jesus Christ surrendered Himself with all of His glory to the Father so that God's absolute sovereignty is openly displayed. "*But when God puts everything under Christ's authority, the Son will put himself under God's authority, since God had put everything under the Son's authority. Then God will be in control of everything" (1 Corinthians 15:28)*.

1:11 ***God also decided ahead of time to choose us through Christ according to his plan, which makes everything work the way he intends.***

Jesus Christ, Whom God the Father has made the head of His entire creation, is also the One by Whom the redeemed receive the inheritance of their salvation in this world and in heaven. By ordaining Jesus Christ His Son to be the head of everything, God also determined that the redeemed would receive His salvation through the merit of Christ's sacrifice and righteousness. This is God's incontestable will executed before time to fulfill God's eternal purpose and pleasure. God chose the redeemed and the means by which they would be redeemed because He alone orchestrates everything to satisfy His will. He alone fulfills His purpose by the exclusive counsel of His own sovereign prerogatives.

1:12 ***He planned all of this so that we who had already focused our hope on Christ would praise him and give him glory.***

God determined, prepared, and extended His redemption to those whom He chose to give Him glory and to receive their praise. God purposed, planned, and accomplished His redemption before the foundation of the world so that He alone would be credited with the glory of His own determination and work. God gave the redeemed wisdom and understanding so that they would recognize His grace and offer Him praise, knowing that the gift they received in Jesus Christ was given to them by God's gracious favor and His Son's obedient and willing sacrifice. Those who trust Christ for their salvation know that nothing in them warrants their redemption. God redeems them and reveals the mystery of His redemption so that they would worship Him with sacrifices of praise and thanksgiving. "*Through him then let us continually offer up a sacrifice of praise to God, that is, the fruit of lips that acknowledge his name*" (*Hebrews 13:15*).

1:13 ***You heard and believed the message of truth, the Good News that he has saved you. In him you were sealed with the Holy Spirit whom he promised.***

Paul told the Ephesians that his doxology of praise was all about what they had received from God through the Gospel they heard. He reminded them that they were redeemed and had received God's gracious favor because they trusted in the Good News of their salvation after hearing the Gospel and believing in the redemption of Jesus Christ. The Gospel they heard was the Word of Truth. It was the Gospel of their salvation. Their salvation did not result from their rational acceptance of what they heard. Their commonsense did not generate a positive response to an offer that sounded reasonable. Rather, they were drawn to faith in Jesus Christ and were sealed in their faith by the Holy Spirit Who Jesus promised to those who would believe in Him for their salvation *(John 14:16, 26; 15:26; 16:7; Ephesians 4:30)*.

1:14 ***This Holy Spirit is the guarantee that we will receive our inheritance. We have this guarantee until we are set free to belong to him. God receives praise and glory for this.***

The Holy Spirit comes into the heart of the redeemed transforming the sinner's heart from a den of thieves into God's holy temple. The Spirit brings glory and praise to God for His gracious favor, which transforms the heart of offense into a sanctuary of worship. He brings the fullness of God into the lives of the redeemed, guaranteeing God's holy and eternal pledge to pay the total cost required to settle the debt of the sinner. The sinner is legitimately indebted to the Law because of sin. The sentence pronounced is eternal damnation to hell. But God Himself appointed His Son to offer Himself as the holy and perfect sacrifice, fully satisfying the Law for the sins of the world and thereby cancelling the debt for all offenses toward God.

The Holy Spirit seals and guarantees the pledge of God's payment for the sin of the redeemed, securing the future of His chosen people for eternity. This guarantee is absolutely essential as God guides the redeemed while they continue in the world, struggling with their dying sin nature. God also directs His people as they face the onslaught of a hostile world, bearing witness to God's redemption. So the Holy Spirit secures the guarantee of God's redemption until His people are set free from corruption to live eternally with God, their Creator, Redeemer, and eternal Father.

Notes/Applications

Paul was eager to tell the Ephesians about the mystery of God's redemption. He knew that there was much more to learn about salvation than simply telling them that it happened. He was fully aware that the mystery of God's redemption stretched the finite capacities of the human mind. Even man's wildest imagination falls miserably short in its attempts to capture a glimpse of what God has done in His redemption. Why?

Like the Ephesians, all believers across the ages are puzzled by the awesome wonders of God's redemption. Once we realize what was at stake, however, we are even more overwhelmed by the infinitely broad chasm between God's holiness and man's flawed existence. Nevertheless, Paul was absolutely certain that with the enlightening power of the Holy Spirit, God's supreme truth can be appreciated by redeemed mortals through godly wisdom and heavenly insight. Assured by God's infallible promise, Paul further explained the supreme mystery of God's redemption. So, what is God's redemption? Who did He redeem? Why?

The essence of God's redemption and judgment is simply the expression of His sovereignty. God is timeless and is absolutely complete within Himself. God is not measured by time and not marked by any point of beginning or ending. Nothing is and can be known about Him except that which He has revealed. Nothing is and can be seen of Him except that which He has unveiled.

God, Who is infinite and absolute in His eternal Being, determines within the counsel of His own sovereign pleasure to redeem a select few out of the sinful mass of humanity. He purposed, planned, and executed His redemption and His judgment in and through His Son Jesus Christ. Those whom He called to faith in His Son are those who are individually selected for salvation while the rest remain under His wrath and judgment.

God did not need anyone's advice from any authority or framework of thought outside of Himself. To be sure, God is self-sufficient. God chose those whom He redeemed for reasons that are satisfactory only to Himself. He chose the means by which He redeemed His own. In other words, God, the sovereign Lord and Creator, redeemed whomever He wanted for His own reasons by His own means. God foreordained what He wanted, foreknew what He foreordained, and actively executed what He foreordained and foreknew. He did not passively foreknow in His prescient omniscience what turned out to be the inevitable. He sovereignly and actively executed what He foreordained because He foreknew what He had already determined. God sets the course of history in motion and actively accomplishes His purpose as He ordains each event. Even though Christ's crucifixion took place in real time and space, and even though individual salvation is personally experienced at the time of confession of faith, God's decision to save or to judge accomplishes God's eternally planned purpose.

There is nothing in man worthy of his redemption, because all have sinned and fallen short of the glory of God. But God is pleased to place the burden of man's debt on His holy, perfect, and sinless Son, providing the only way by which His redemption can be conferred on those chosen for salvation. By this priceless sacrifice the legitimate demands of the Law are fully satisfied once and for all. Paul reminded the Ephesians and all believers that God's sovereign decision to redeem or to judge cannot and should not be questioned. The divine foundations for His purpose, plan, and action are rooted in Who He is. Therefore, God's children are called to join Paul in a doxology of praise to God our Redeemer Who rescued us from condemnation through His Son's finished work of love and sacrifice. Believers therefore recognize the depravity and deserved condemnation from which they have been saved and the undeserved glory into which they have been brought. In light of this glorious salvation, Paul encourages all believers to live a life of worship, acknowledging that our redemption is God's gracious gift given out of God's sovereign pleasure, unconditionally guaranteed by the seal of the Holy Spirit.

Ephesians 1:15–23

1:15–16 [15]*I, too, have heard about your faith in the Lord Jesus and your love for all of God's people. For this reason* [16]*I never stop thanking God for you. I always remember you in my prayers.*

After praising God for His redemption through His Son Jesus Christ as well as the preservation of God's elect by the Holy Spirit, Paul offered his thanksgiving to God. He especially thanked God for the testimony of faith and love observed in the Christians in Ephesus. He thanked God for their salvation as well as for their knowledge of the mystery of God's redemption. He praised God for their faith in Jesus Christ and their love for God's people. Paul continued to thank God that His foreordained redemption was revealed in the salvation of the chosen in Ephesus, just as God's salvation was revealed elsewhere among the Jews and the Gentiles. Because of such a glorious display of God's grace and mercy, Paul gave thanks to God for his spiritual children in Ephesus, always remembering them in his prayers.

1:17 *I pray that the glorious Father, the God of our Lord Jesus Christ, would give you a spirit of wisdom and revelation as you come to know Christ better.*

Paul was deeply moved by the redemptive work of the Holy Spirit in the hearts of these mature Christians. However, Paul prayed that God would continue to give them wisdom and insight to receive His revelation and understand the mystery of what He determined in redeeming them. Paul declared the truth to the Ephesians. But he looked to God for their understanding. He asked that God would transform their minds so that what He revealed would be discernable in the both spiritual and intellectual aspects of their redeemed lives. Paul prayed for godly wisdom so that they could continue to grow in their relationship to the One Who willingly and lovingly gave His life for their salvation.

1:18 *Then you will have deeper insight. You will know the confidence that he calls you to have and the glorious wealth that God's people will inherit.*

Paul told the Ephesians that when God gave them His insight, their spiritual eyes would be opened. Their minds and hearts would continue to be changed. They would discern godly things as they were revealed by God. They would understand the mysteries of God's redemption and the glorious inheritance they had been given in Jesus Christ. They would begin to capture the essence of the unity they had with Jesus Christ and, through Him, with the Body of Christ. The reality of the hope they have in Christ and their confidence in the redemption to which they had been called would become plainly obvious. Paul earnestly prayed that they would receive godly wisdom and heavenly insight so that they could more clearly understand God's redemption, the election of the redeemed, and the eternal promise of their salvation by faith in Jesus Christ. When Jesus walked among the crowds during His earthly ministry, he made this assuring comment: "[28]I give them eternal life, and they will never perish, and no one will snatch them out of my hand. [29]My Father, who has given them to me, is greater than all, and no one is able to snatch them out of the Father's hand" *(John 10:28–29).*

1:19 *You will also know the unlimited greatness of his power as it works with might and strength for us, the believers.*

These mature Christians would also realize that the power of God's greatness was unlimited. Those schooled by the Holy Spirit would be drawn to a deeper level of understanding the power of God, seeing the way that He executed His redemption exactly as He planned. Paul prayed that God would give them wisdom and insight, understanding that they were not only loved and richly blessed, but also were secure in His salvation through Jesus Christ by His power.

1:20–21 ***[20]He worked with that same power in Christ when he brought him back to life and gave him the highest position in heaven. [21]He is far above all rulers, authorities, powers, lords, and all other names that can be named, not only in this present world but also in the world to come.***

God does not dispassionately transform people's lives and promise them eternal life just because He can do so. It pleased God to redeem a chosen remnant for Himself out of the mass of sinful humanity. He revealed the immeasurable depth of His goodness by lavishing His sovereign grace on unworthy sinners. But God's favor toward the redeemed is also expressed in the nature of the power He expended to execute His plan and accomplish His foreordained purpose.

God's sovereignty is fully reflected in His power to save and execute His plan of salvation. However, His power is not manifested as a despotic autocracy. His power actually revealed His divine love and mercy toward undeserving sinners legitimately damned under the Law. God secured the redeemed in His salvation by the same power He executed His redemptive plan through His Son Jesus Christ–His virgin birth, righteous life, crucifixion, death, burial, resurrection, ascension, His second coming, and His ultimate coronation as the eternal King. In essence, Paul wanted the Ephesians to know that in redeeming them through His Son and for His sake, God used the same power to adopt them as His children, making them joint heirs with His Son Jesus Christ.

God's salvation of the redeemed is secure because His redemption is executed by the same power that brought Jesus back to life after His sacrificial death. The same power exalted His Son to be the risen conqueror, seated at His right hand. By the same power, Jesus became the head of the Church He redeemed. By the same power He raised Jesus Christ from death, God glorified His Name above all names, powers, and authorities on earth or in heaven, in this world and the next. God redeemed His elect and secured their salvation, and by the same power He will bring everyone to their knees, bowing before Jesus

Christ and confessing Him as Lord to the glory of God the Father *(Philippians 2:9–11).*

1:22–23 ***[22]God has put everything under the control of Christ. He has made Christ the head of everything for the good of the church. [23]The church is Christ's body and completes him as he fills everything in every way.***

God put His Son in charge of everything because Jesus Christ conquered all forces through His sacrifice and resurrection—all by the power of God His Father. God also made Him the head of the Church—the collective assembly of God's redeemed elect. God exalted Jesus Christ above all forces and vested in Him supreme and absolute power over every aspect of His creation, giving His people the guarantee of their position as God's elect under His authority as the head of the Church. God's redeemed elect are the prized possession of the supreme and absolute Ruler of God's entire dominion. God exalted His Son Jesus Christ to the highest and most glorious position of absolute and ultimate authority. Thus, their salvation and enduring hope in God's redemption is eternally secure. By making Christ the head of the Church, and by making the entire assembly of the redeemed His Son's living Body, God eternally sealed the inseparable union between His Son and His elect by His power.

Notes/Applications

Initiated by a warm greeting and adorned by a moving doxology, the first chapter of Paul's letter to the Ephesians echoes a simple message of supreme, eternal truth. Because the essence of the truth outlined in the text is incompatible with man's finite reason, Paul asked God to give His redeemed children wisdom and insight so that they could discern the mystery of His sovereign grace, love, and mercy by which His salvation was given to them through Jesus Christ. What the Ephesians received from God was true, eternal, and unalterable. Even though God's redemption is not humanly discernable, it can certainly be clearly and correctly understood by God-given wisdom by the Holy Spirit through the godly application of His living Word. God's children across the ages are likewise encouraged to have confidence in God's sovereign grace and His wisdom so that they can discern what they have received in Jesus Christ.

The redeemed should fear nothing because God our Redeemer is all in all. God's redemption reveals the essence of His sovereign grace. The execution of God's redemption throughout history openly displays His love and mercy. Believers in all times and places clearly see the hope and confidence to which they have been called. They rejoice in the inheritance God has given them. They revel in the wisdom, knowledge, and understanding the Holy Spirit has planted in their hearts. The immeasurable riches and spiritual blessings He graciously has given to them bring them to their knees in adoration and worship.

God planned and accomplished the salvation of His elect as it pleased Him. He appointed Jesus Christ, His holy and perfect Son, to be the agent of His plan. He chose those He wanted to be the object of His redemption. He determined the process and ordained all events that brought His plan to completion.

God's redemption is executed by the might of His sovereign power. God orchestrated the virgin birth of His Son Jesus Christ, His righteous and sinless life, ministry and proclamation of the Good News of His salvation, His miracles, His betrayal, crucifixion, burial, and death. By His power He brought Jesus back from death, demonstrating His victory over man's sin and guaranteeing eternal life to those He saves. Jesus ascended to His place at the right hand of the Father's throne where He advocates on behalf of those who belong to Him. At some future time, He will return to earth again, destroy sin and the devil, and ascend the throne, ruling forevermore as the King of kings and Lord of lords. What God did through Jesus Christ is actually the execution of His redemption.

It must then necessarily follow that the salvation of the redeemed is secured by the same power that executed God's plan of redemption through Jesus Christ. The salvation of the redeemed is, therefore, as sure as the resurrection of Jesus Christ since it is guaranteed by the same power of the same sovereign God.

To argue otherwise is to deny God and to turn away from His purpose, plan, and power. Since God's foreordained redemption and plan is secured by the supreme power, which transcends all powers and forces, then God's people can rest in the One Who has given them so much evidence of His unsurpassed glory and power.

Praise be to God forever. Our hope in Jesus Christ has already been accomplished by God's sovereign plan and executed by matchless power.

EPHESIANS 2

Ephesians 2:1–10

2:1 *You were once dead because of your failures and sins.*

After explaining God's eternal plan to redeem sinners, Paul reminded the Ephesians of their spiritual status prior to their salvation. They were dead in their sins before they were transformed into a new life in Christ by the redemptive favor of God's sovereign grace. Born in sin into a state of condemnation like all of Adam's children, the Ephesians lived in death both temporally and eternally. They existed in bondage to sin completely incapable of knowing God's saving grace and loving care. They lived under God's judgment, condemned to eternal damnation. In a simple statement of godly truth, Paul reminded the Ephesians that prior to their salvation, they were dead in their sins and lived in death as unregenerate sinners well on their way to hell.

2:2 *You followed the ways of this present world and its spiritual ruler. This ruler continues to work in people who refuse to obey God.*

As unregenerate sinners, the Ephesian Christians lived in the corrupt environment of the ungodly world and the devil, the ruler of this present world. Because they lived outside any fellowship with the God, they were fully controlled by sin, the human spirit, the ungodly perspectives of the world, and the evil forces of the devil. Being spiritually dead to godly direction and void of godly wisdom, unregenerate sinners live in disobedience in full subjection to the controls of the devil. Paul told the Ephesians that, before their redemption, they lived dead in sin serving the master of disobedience.

2:3 *All of us once lived among these people, and followed the desires of our corrupt nature. We did what our corrupt desires and thoughts wanted us to do. So, because of our nature, we deserved God's anger just like everyone else.*

The Ephesians were not alone in their desperate condition while they were in sin's bondage. Because Adam sinned and fathered his descendants in his status as dead in sin, all of humanity was born in a state of condemnation judged for inherent disobedience and consequently open rebellion. Paul affirmed to the Ephesians that all, including himself, were born in sin and walked in disobedience prior to God's redemption.

While still in sin, even those who are now redeemed once lived according to the dictates of their corrupt nature. The affairs of daily life were carried on under the constraining force of the ungodly desires of the unregenerate heart. Every one wanted to satisfy the lustful appetite of their sin nature. While under the bondage of their evil nature, everyone lives in disobedience, willfully following the dictates of their evil thoughts. Whether the sinner knows it or not, the unsaved has a relationship with God only as the object of His wrath. Such was the status of the redeemed before they were rescued by God's saving grace.

2:4 *But God is rich in mercy because of his great love for us.*

God, Who is just in His judgment, is also gracious in His redemption. Even though the redeemed justly deserved His wrath, He saved each one from condemnation by His grace simply because it pleased Him to do so. God showed the unsearchable extent of His mercy by lavishing His love on undeserving people who were already condemned to hell. God's sovereign grace is openly displayed not only in what believers receive–His gift of eternal life, but also in what they did not receive–the punishment for their sin. God, in His great mercy, rescues the lost from their deserved condemnation.

2:5 *We were dead because of our failures, but he made us alive together with Christ. (It is God's kindness that saved you.)*

All have fallen short of the glory of God *(Romans 3:23)*. All were dead in sin deserving the full punishment prescribed by the Law. But God, Who is pleased to lavish His favor upon the dead, made those whom He redeemed alive in Christ Jesus simply by His grace. God redeemed some of the dead and made them alive by removing the cause of their death and putting the whole weight of the Law on Jesus Christ. The dead were made alive by the grace of God, Who condemned His own sinless Son to suffer the death of the sinner.

2:6 *God has brought us back to life together with Christ Jesus and has given us a position in heaven with him.*

God made those whom He redeemed alive through the resurrection of His Son Jesus Christ Who died in their place. God removes the death sentence from the redeemed and gives His people a new life in Jesus Christ. God accomplished everything in and through His Son. He sets the sinner free by substituting His Son as the only acceptable sacrifice that satisfies the demands of the Law imposed on those who were legitimately condemned under its provisions. God also imputed the righteousness of His Son to those who are set free from condemnation and qualifies them as the rightful recipients of the new life that Christ earned for them by conquering death through His resurrection. God sets His people free and raises them to new life in Christ, pronouncing them just because God is now at peace with them. Paul showed the Ephesians that their salvation meant that they were free from their sin, made new, reconciled to fellowship, and pronounced just before God in and through Jesus Christ.

2:7 *He did this through Christ Jesus out of his generosity to us in order to show his extremely rich kindness in the world to come.*

God is not under any obligation to do anything. Nor must He answer to any one. He does not have to satisfy any reason or system of thought. But God laid the burden of sin upon His Son and blessed the redeemed with His righteousness showing His love and care toward sinful man. He saved whom He chose as He pleased. He dispensed His mercy and redeemed the lost at His own cost in His own way, reflecting the immeasurable richness of His grace both now and for eternity.

2:8–9 [8]*God saved you through faith as an act of kindness. You had nothing to do with it. Being saved is a gift from God.* [9]*It's not the result of anything you've done, so no one can brag about it.*

Salvation is completely the gift of God. The recipient has nothing to do with God's redemption in any sense at all. The redeemed are saved by God's grace through the agency of the faith instilled within the heart of the sinner by the work of the Holy Spirit. Glory and praise is fully ascribed to God the Father, Jesus Christ His Son, and the Holy Spirit for the salvation executed according God's eternal plan and foreordained purpose *(John 6:44).*

Once redeemed, the sinner will recognize the value of their salvation after the fact, no one can take credit for personal wisdom when God gives them the gift of new life in Jesus Christ. Paul had carefully explained the condition in which the people live before their salvation.

The sinner is completely incapable of any positive response toward God (*Romans 3:10–11; Psalm 14:1–3*). Their spiritual capacities were nonexistent toward the things of God. Since no one is capable of positively responding to God's redemption, the salvation cannot be the result of human wisdom. No one can claim credit for making the right choice. It is God's gift and, therefore, it will eternally stand as the evidence of His sovereign grace.

2:10 *God has made us what we are. He has created us in Christ Jesus to live lives filled with good works that he has prepared for us to do.*

Like all human beings, the redeemed are also created by God. Every individual human being is endowed with similar traits and qualities, which distinguish them from other creatures. Furthermore, each one is uniquely and individually given special talents, gifts, and capabilities that would set one apart from others.

Even though born into a state of condemnation, all human beings are created to live and function as men and women. And as such, everyone lives in rebellion while functioning properly in keeping with God's creation. However, the redeemed are regenerated into new life in Jesus Christ by God's redemption. Therefore, those who were created as human beings and lived in rebellion because of sin, are now made new in Jesus Christ and are empowered by the indwelling Holy Spirit to live in compliance to the purpose for which they were created and redeemed. That is, the redeemed are first created to behave and conduct themselves as human beings. Then, they are made new creatures in Christ to do what they were ordained to do as the children and servants of God, their Creator and their Redeemer. They are created and redeemed to be intelligent, obedient individuals, living to fulfill the good work God ordained them to do.

Notes/Applications

Paul's explanation of the mysteries of God's redemption has two aspects. In the first chapter, he focused on God's sovereign grace. He explained God's absolute authority and sovereign pleasure in His determination to offer redemption at His own cost to undeserving sinners of His choice. Earnestly asking God to impart His wisdom and understanding, Paul courageously explained God's eternal truth without hesitation even though the human mind cannot comprehend it.

Paul revealed the second aspect of his teaching in the preceding ten verses of this chapter. The salvation of the redeemed is also the rescue of the lost out of a deserved status of lawful condemnation to eternal damnation. Every single redeemed individual was born condemned to death because of man's inherent sin nature. Prior to one's redemption everyone lived according to the dictates of sin and disobedience.

The condition of the condemned could not prevent God from graciously extending His redemption toward those whom He chose. God was pleased to save some from His own just judgment. He prepared the way, fulfilled the non-negotiable requirements of His own Law, and revived the spirit of those whom He chose to save by imparting the Holy Spirit to incite conviction, generate faith, and to facilitate responsive obedience in the hearts of persons who lived previously unacquainted with obedience to Holy God. By clearly outlining both aspects of God's redemption, Paul helped the Ephesians and all believers know, understand, and appreciate the riches and the depth of God's love toward the redeemed. We know that God not only saved us, but also loved us. He did not merely rescue us. But He lavished His favor on us. We are not just given a second chance. But we are saved from deserved wrath at the hands of an omniscient, Holy and Almighty God. Knowing that we had nothing to do with our salvation and understanding that God took our redemption upon Himself will ultimately encourage us to forsake all including ourselves and fully commit our lives to the One Who purposed to make us His own children.

Ephesians 2:11–22

2:11 ***Remember that once you were not Jewish physically. Those who called themselves "the circumcised" because of what they had done to their bodies called you "the uncircumcised."***

The opening sentence of this verse seems to say that the Ephesian Christians were not Jews before they became believers. However, when they became Christians, they physically became Jews. This implication may lead some to conclude that Paul had changed his mind. In his first letter to the Corinthians, Paul boldly stated: "Circumcision is nothing, and the lack of it is nothing. But keeping what God commands is everything" *(1 Corinthians 7:19)*. It is better to understand that Paul was talking about the Ephesians' genetic heritage. This was how the Jews looked at them. They were not Jews, but Gentiles, and now that they were believers, they were still Gentiles.

Paul reminded the Ephesians of the cultural barriers that separated Jews from Gentiles. The Jews were proud of their history and the heritage that had been handed down to them for nearly two thousand years. They were the people of God. God had called their fathers, Abraham, Isaac, and Jacob. God had given them His covenant, sealed by circumcision. He had rescued them from slavery in Egypt and given them the Law. They lived under the blessing of the living God. They were God's chosen people.

Everybody else was a pagan and the Jews derogatorily called them "the uncircumcised." No one else had God's blessing. No other nation or people could say that they were God's chosen people. Everyone else was excluded from the privileged position the Jews enjoyed. They were lost!

2:12 ***Also, at that time you were without Christ. You were excluded from citizenship in Israel, and the pledges [God made***

in his] promise were foreign to you. You had no hope and were in the world without God.

Prior to their salvation, the Ephesians did not belong to God. Spiritually, they did not know about the salvation that God offered to them. Physically, they were not a part of the Jewish covenant of circumcision. They were strangers to God's promises. They were excluded from the God's family. They were in reality outcasts. They were lost. They were the living dead.

2:13 ***But now through Christ Jesus you, who were once far away, have been brought near by the blood of Christ.***

But now that they were redeemed, they were drawn away from the world and close to God. They had been made God's redeemed children by Christ's sacrifice on the cross. They were no longer excluded from God's blessing. Every provision of the Law, which excluded them from the blessings of God's redemption, was fulfilled by the blood of Christ shed for the forgiveness of sin. Christ's death broke every barrier that separated people from their Creator, and brought those who were once excluded into the family of God.

2:14 ***So he is our peace. In his body he has made Jewish and non-Jewish people one by breaking down the wall of hostility that kept them apart.***

The sacrifice of Jesus Christ was not only a judicial satisfaction of the divine requirements of God's inalterable Law. It is also the means by which God's peace is instituted where hostility once reigned. Since He was the Prince of Peace, Jesus Christ brought peace between God and sinners as well as between those who were separated by the laws of circumcision. By shedding His blood and by paying for man's transgression, whether Jew or Gentile, Jesus Christ removed the wall of separation which stood between God and man as well as Jews and Gentiles. Christ's sacrifice reconciled former enemies into one Body of which He is the head. Jesus Christ not only established His peace between former enemies, but also made them one by His peace. Therefore, He is our peace—the peace of God's redeemed children.

2:15 *He brought an end to the commandments and demands found in Moses' Teachings so that he could take Jewish and non-Jewish people and create one new humanity in himself. So he made peace.*

Jesus Christ brought peace where hostilities reigned by abolishing sin, which was the reason for the barriers that separated Jews and Gentiles. Sin separated everyone from God because of disobedience to the Law. Sin also was the reason that Jews and Gentiles fundamentally distrusted each other, causing contention between the two.

When God offered His covenant to Abraham and instituted circumcision as the mark of His covenant among Abraham's biological descendants, Gentiles were not included. The Jews believed that Gentiles did not possess God's blessing and were therefore under His judgment. But by His sacrifice, Jesus Christ removed the cause for both forms of hostilities by fulfilling the Law on all accounts with His righteous life and sacrificial death. Because of Jesus Christ, the Law no longer condemns those who have been set free by Christ. Christ stands triumphant at the center of all of creation-time and eternity-giving His peace among all of God's saved children. In Him, a new people, a redeemed people, live side-by-side peacefully, since they have been made one family.

2:16 *He also brought them back to God in one body by his cross, on which he killed the hostility.*

Christ's eternal victory over the forces of evil was accomplished historically on the cross at Calvary. As the sinless and righteous sacrificial Lamb of God, Jesus Christ shed His blood at Golgotha, settling the debt owed by sinners to the holy and just God. It was there on the cross that God's redemption and His judgment were fully revealed and enforced.

The Law was fully satisfied at Calvary. It has no claim over those who are redeemed by and through the finished work of Jesus Christ on the cross. The redeemed are no longer God's enemies because they are at peace with God through Jesus Christ. Because the cause for judgment is removed and paid in full, enmity with God is not just annulled but is actually eradicated—put to death on the cross never to rise again. Therefore, having destroyed the wall of separation, Jesus Christ brought the redeemed to God as one Body in Himself.

2:17 *He came with the Good News of peace for you who were far away and for those who were near.*

The Good News of Christ's victory is sent out as the Gospel of God's redemption for everyone. God's living Word of His peace is preached both to those who were close to God through the covenant of circumcision, the Jews, and to those who were not included, the Gentiles. Regardless of any distinction, the saved are redeemed only by the finished work of Jesus Christ and are brought to God as one unified Body in Christ. Paul assured all believers that we are brought into God's salvation by and through Jesus Christ in spite of our past position with God.

2:18 *So Jewish and non-Jewish people can go to the Father in one Spirit.*

Because of Christ's uniting work of salvation, Jews and Gentiles have come together in Christ and are, therefore, one in Him. They are one Body in Christ. All who belong to God in Jesus Christ have the same access to God by and through the same Spirit Who works in everyone without. They are no longer divided by the Law or by the requirements of circumcision. There is one Redeemer, and all who are brought to God are one. No more distinction or hostilities! For God's people, hostility itself is replaced by God's peace, because all enmity is put to death by Jesus Christ Who nailed the condemnation of the Law to His cross *(Colossians 2:14)*. The Law can no longer be invoked as a qualifying barrier because it cannot require anything out of those who have been redeemed. Because the Law is fully satisfied, all who are redeemed in Christ are united in Him as one Body beyond the scope of the Law and its commandments.

2:19 ***That is why you are no longer foreigners and outsiders but citizens together with God's people and members of God's family.***

Paul assured the Ephesians that they were no longer alienated from God. There was nothing that could separate them either from God or from one another within the family of faith. Unlike the Jews who were marked by circumcision as God's covenantal people, all who are redeemed are sealed by the blood of Jesus Christ as God's people regardless of their unregenerate past. Sin's power, death's grip, hell's sting, and the devil's evil scheme are all destroyed by Christ's power revealed on the Cross and confirmed by His resurrection. Because God's redemption and peace reign, all who belong to God in Jesus Christ are united both with God and with one another in the unity of Christ's victory.

2:20 ***You are built on the foundation of the apostles and prophets. Christ Jesus himself is the cornerstone.***

What Paul taught the Ephesians was not a new doctrine. It was the eternal truth. It was the same message proclaimed by the apostles and the prophets of old. It was the same truth that both Jews and Gentiles had heard throughout the ages. It was the foundation of God's revealed love and grace openly declared by Jesus Christ Himself. He was the Rock of their salvation, which was the cornerstone upon which their faith was constructed. The Psalmist agrees: "The stone that the builders rejected has become the cornerstone" *(Psalm 118:22)*. This is the theme of the entire scriptural narrative.

2:21–22 [21]***In him all the parts of the building fit together and grow into a holy temple in the Lord.*** [22]***Through him you, also,***

are being built in the Spirit together with others into a place where God lives.

God's living temple is built, nurtured, and held together in Christ and in Him alone. Being the chief cornerstone, Jesus Christ holds the whole building of His Body together. He causes each member of His Body to flawlessly fit together as the perfect building block of God's living temple. Including the Ephesians, all who are saved have been made the constituent building blocks of Christ's Body. As Jesus Christ—the head of the Body—holds the building together and nurtures it, the Body grows into a holy temple in which God dwells and is worshiped. Bringing forth the temple of their individual heart revived, cleansed, and consecrated by the Holy Spirit, God's redeemed children constitute the Church universal as the one Body of Christ built and held together by Him as its head.

Notes/Applications

Paul certainly recognizes the limitations of man's understanding to fully capture God's unsearchable truth. With this in mind, he prays that God Himself would give His own wisdom and open the understanding of His children to know the truth and to grow in the knowledge of what He has revealed. This is an enduring and encouraging aspect of the Christian experience in all believers. We should not be discouraged by our inabilities to grasp God's divine mystery. He reveals His truth and imparts the wisdom necessary for the correct and practical understanding of what has been revealed.

Paul teaches us in the first two chapters of Ephesians that our redemption is foreordained, planned, and accomplished by God our Father through our Lord and Savior Jesus Christ. He unequivocally affirms that the salvation of the lost is God's gracious gift of eternal life to undeserving sinners who are justly condemned to damnation because of disobedience. The promise of God's redemption is not just the future eternal hope we have in Christ, but the present abiding peace that surrounds our lives. Paul speaks of an actual surpassing peace, which comes into the life of the redeemed when the Holy Spirit takes up residence in the heart of the person He regenerates.

This peace is Christ's peace. It surpasses all understanding. It destroys all the forces of evil. The peace of Christ brings down all walls of separation and ends all hostilities. The turmoil raging in the heart of the individual believer is silenced by the calming power of the Prince of peace. Differences and animosities among the redeemed become unimportant. Enmity between God and the redeemed is forever reconciled.

The redeemed become one in Jesus Christ by God's power. Those who were divided in the past by human divisions actually come together as one Body comprising the universal building of God's temple with Jesus Christ at its head. Those who despised each other are now united in Christ's love and worship the Lord as one Body. God's redemption brings real, practical, and relevant peace into the lives of those who are saved by God's grace. The redeemed are not just appeased by the hope of a future assurance, but they are truly blessed by the security of their redemption in Christ.

EPHESIANS 3

Ephesians 3:1–6

3:1 *This is the reason I, Paul, am the prisoner of Christ Jesus for those of you who are not Jewish.*

Paul told the Ephesians of his own experience that drove him to bring the Gospel to them. For Paul, his redemption was not based on some vague theory. He wanted the Ephesians to know about his personal experience of salvation and his subsequent appointment to preach the Gospel of Jesus Christ to the Gentiles.

Paul wanted the Ephesians to realize that his ministry to them was costly as well as irresistible. Costly, because the Jewish authorities persecuted him; but irresistible, because he could not resist God's call on his life. Therefore, Paul's letter came to the Ephesians while he was a prisoner in a Roman jail. He was a prisoner in that jail as surely as he was the prisoner of God's will and His eternal truth, hated by the Jewish religious men but redeemed and appointed by God to tell the Gentile people about God's salvation in Jesus Christ.

Paul suffered imprisonment at the hands of Jewish religious authorities and their Roman masters for bringing the Gentiles into the fold of God's favored. He was rejected by Jewish religious authorities wherever he preached. He was persecuted and imprisoned for preaching Jesus Christ. He was accused of rejecting his Jewish heritage, endorsing a message, which contradicted the known traditions of rabbinical practice *(Acts 22–24)*.

Paul was not even born when God determined that he would be His messenger of Good News to the Gentiles. Paul openly gives testimony to his unavoidable commitment to Jesus Christ because of the irresistible calling God had placed upon him even before his earthly birth *(1 Corinthians 9:16)*.

3:2 *Certainly, you have heard how God gave me the responsibility of bringing his kindness to you.*

Somehow the Ephesians were already informed about Paul's appointment as God's messenger to the Gentiles. Therefore, this should not come as a surprise to them. Paul carefully told the Ephesians about his commission to preach the Gospel of God's saving grace to them.

He was not sorry that he was imprisoned by earthly authorities. He was not disgruntled because God had appointed him to preach the Gospel. His circumstances and conditions had no effect on his task. He did not solicit pity from anyone. He taught the Gospel because that was what he was appointed to do. This was the responsibility God placed on his shoulders. God gave him no alternative. He was a prisoner for Christ's sake. Now he wrote this letter to the Ephesians, assuring them that, contrary to the Jewish religious mindset, God's grace and kindness in Jesus Christ was also available to the Gentiles as well. The Good News of the salvation of the Gentiles was just as sure as his appointment to preach the Gospel.

3:3 *You have heard that he let me know this mystery through a revelation. I've already written to you about this briefly.*

Paul reminded the Ephesians that he had already informed them about this through an earlier communication. He had received a revelation from God about the Gospel that must be preached. This could have been one of the letters Paul sent to the churches for general circulation among the believers. It is also possible that he sent an earlier letter directly to the Ephesians. Nevertheless, the emphasis of Paul's reminder is to underscore that the message he preached to them was the Gospel of the Lord Jesus Christ directly revealed to him by God. His message was not contrived, and therefore should not be challenged by anyone. The Ephesians should not struggle to accept Paul at his word. They had already been informed that he declared the truth that was directly revealed to him by God.

3:4 *When you read this, you'll see that I understand the mystery about Christ.*

Paul expressed an openly optimistic hope affirming that the Ephesians would understand the truth of what he taught them when they read the letter he sent to them. Taking his cue from his Lord, Paul confidently asserted that what Jesus promised to His disciples would be practically true of the Ephesians as well *(John 16:7–13)*. He knew that, as the Author of God's Holy Word, the indwelling Holy Spirit would reveal the truth in His Word when read by those who are redeemed and endowed with understanding and godly discernment. By discerning the truth, the Ephesians would not only understand the meaning of what they heard and believed, but would also affirm that Paul had indeed received a uniquely revealed revelation into the mysteries of the Gospel and had taught them the truth with godly wisdom and understanding. Consequently, they could courageously reject any attempt to undermine Paul's credibility and the integrity of his teachings.

3:5 *In the past, this mystery was not known by people as it is now. The Spirit has now revealed it to his holy apostles and prophets.*

The mystery the Ephesians ultimately understood was a newly revealed aspect of God's eternal truth. Paul told the Ephesians that God endowed the apostles of the New Testament with new insights which enabled them to discern the mystery of the gospel more clearly than the prophets of old and the redeemed of past generations. That is, while the prophets of old foretold the future fulfillment of God's eternal redemption, the apostles became the witnesses of the execution of the Lord's salvation. While the prophets of old received the words of God's promises and observed the types and shadows of His redemption, Paul and the apostles were commissioned to spread the Good News of the deliverance of the chosen as witnesses. Having seen God's redemption in the sufferings and victory of the Lord Jesus Christ and having been guided to the truth by the Holy Spirit, Paul assured the Ephesians that the Gospel was preached to them by an appointed apostle and a commissioned witness.

3:6 *This mystery is the Good News that people who are not Jewish have the same inheritance as Jewish people do. They belong to the same body and share the same promise that God made in Christ Jesus.*

God has always spoken through His Holy Word about His redemption and His judgment. He commissioned prophets and apostles to declare His message across the ages. Each one of God's called spoke verbally to his contemporaries and to all men across the ages through sacred writings preserved throughout history.

The prophets foretold about the fulfillment of God's eternal plan while the apostles confirmed the execution of what was predicted. That was exactly what Paul wanted the Ephesians to understand. The Prophets spoke of the coming Messiah Who will fulfill the Law and be offered up as the sacrifice to take away sin's guilt upon the lost. However, since most prophecies were directly associated more with the children of Israel than with other people, the inclusion of Gentiles in God's redemption was not viewed as a plausible proposition.

Just what was this newly revealed timeless truth? The mystery of God's grace was revealed and fully displayed in Jesus Christ. God's peace and His goodwill were expressed toward men in Jesus Christ, causing all who believe in Him to receive eternal life through His death and resurrection. Even though this enduring truth has always been eternal, it was not apparent to the prophets of old because they did not yet witness the physical fulfillment of the coming of the Messiah about Whom they prophesied. They faithfully declared God's truth looking forward to its fulfillment. But Paul and the apostles saw God's mercy and His saving grace revealed in Jesus Christ toward sinful men regardless of heritage or any other distinction except faith in the Son of God. Paul earnestly sought to encourage the Ephesians by assuring them that, regardless of their Gentile heritage and contrary to the opinion of the Judaizers, they were saved from condemnation through faith in Jesus Christ.

Notes/Applications

Paul explained two important aspects of his ministry among Ephesians. First, he told them that he was a prisoner of the Gospel of Jesus Christ. He was a purchased possession of Jesus Christ commissioned to preach the Gospel of God's salvation. Notwithstanding earthly persecutions, Paul was God's bondservant born, redeemed, and commissioned to spread God's Good News of salvation by grace through faith on the basis of Christ's sacrifice and righteousness.

Second, the mystery of God's salvation was openly revealed on Calvary as our Lord Jesus Christ shed His blood to fulfill the demands of God's Law upon Adam's sinful descendants. Salvation from condemnation is given by God to persons of His sovereign choice on the basis of His grace and mercy. Jewish prophets of old delivered messages from God to the children of Israel. All prophecies about the coming Messiah pointed to God's eternal promise revealed in Jesus Christ for all of God's people throughout the ages transcending any human qualifications.

Paul explained that his excitement about the Gospel was not the insane trait of an eccentric zealot. He was happily God's bondservant commissioned to bring the Good News of God's salvation to the Gentiles. He was the prisoner of the Gospel called to a life of service to Jesus Christ Who paid the ultimate price for his redemption. As for the Gospel, it was never the exclusive domain of the Jews. God has chosen to redeem people from the nations of the world throughout the ages regardless of any earthly designation. This mystery was revealed to Paul by God in a special revelation when he entered Damascus many years earlier. Throughout his subsequent ministry, he faithfully recorded God's message by writing letters so that believers across the ages could also be encouraged by God's revealed grace.

Just like Peter, his fellow servant of the Gospel of Jesus Christ, Paul told the Ephesians that the salvation of God's people had been foretold by the prophets who did not live long enough to personally witness the historic fulfillment of their prophecies. Peter, Paul, the apostles, and the believers of Ephesus lived during the historic period during which the mystery of God's faithfulness was openly revealed through the historic Cross upon which the promised Messiah was sacrificed *(1 Peter 1:10–12).*

As he did for the Ephesians, Paul continues to speak to believers of all ages through his many letters, encouraging us to press onward, confident that our salvation is secure in Jesus Christ.

Ephesians 3:7–13

3:7 *I became a servant of this Good News through God's kindness freely given to me when his power worked {in me}.*

Recalling his own salvation, Paul related to the Ephesians that his own experience was not much different from theirs in substance except in the way it occurred. Paul confessed that he was captured by God and was made a prisoner of the Gospel when Jesus confronted him on his way to Damascus to arrest Christ's disciples. The blinding light of God's glory struck Paul and purged his destructive drive, bringing him to his knees in complete surrender to the Lord Who spoke to him. Paul not only received salvation at that time, but also became captive to the Gospel. God promptly assigned Paul to the commission for which he was created and redeemed *(Acts 9:1–20; Galatians 1:13–16)*. Paul ascertained that the Gospel he preached to the Ephesians was given by revelation and was confirmed by his own experience.

3:8 *I am the least of all God's people. Yet, God showed me his kindness by allowing me to spread the Good News of the immeasurable wealth of Christ to people who are not Jewish.*

Paul openly admitted that he was the least of the people that belong to God. He did not deserve anything good from God. Not only was Paul the chief among sinners *(1 Timothy 1:15)*, but he persecuted the Church, pursuing and arresting the followers of Jesus Christ. In spite of Paul's unworthiness, God showed His mercy and grace by redeeming him and employing him in His service. God appointed Paul to preach the Gospel to the Gentiles even though there were other apostles who had been coached by Jesus Christ personally. As God chose Paul despite his grievous sin, so He saved Gentiles even as He had saved Jewish people despite the sin that permeated their souls.

3:9 *He allowed me to explain the way this mystery works. God, who created all things, kept it hidden in the past.*

Paul appreciated the privilege he was given by God to be the messenger of the Gospel to the Gentiles. Despite his past, God commissioned him to declare the unsearchable mysteries of His salvation. God's salvation for the Gentiles was not fully revealed to the prophets or even Christ's disciples. But God handpicked Paul to understand and explain God's planned salvation to the Gentiles. Paul was fully persuaded that the revelation and his commission proved that God's blessing had rested upon him, confirming that the Gospel he preached to the Ephesians was the truth, which was entrusted to him.

3:10 *He did this so that now, through the church, he could let the rulers and authorities in heaven know his infinite wisdom.*

God's choice to redeem and commission Paul for His service was not a random exercise of sovereign power. God executed His eternal plan concerning His servant, undoubtedly affirming His sovereignty, eternal will, and incontestable power to rulers and authorities in heaven and earth. In this way, God showed His glory for all to see including the Sanhedrin, the disciples, and all other authorities. Through the Church universal, the Body of Christ, comprised of the redeemed out of every nation, tribe, and language, God's grace and redeeming mercy is seen. The chief priest and the rulers in Jerusalem who sent Paul to silence the disciples of Christ, the disciples of Jesus Christ who questioned Paul's credibility to preach the Gospel to the Gentiles, and all authorities now knew that God was sovereign, gracious, and just simply by observing God's work in Paul's life and in his ministry.

3:11 *This was God's plan for all of history which he carried out through Christ Jesus our Lord.*

God's plan of redemption has been planned and accomplished by God within the framework of His eternal timelessness. God's salvation is the expression of His eternal plan carried out through the life, death, and resurrection of the Lord Jesus Christ. God consulted no one about His plan. He simply conceived the plan within His own exclusive counsel and pleasure. The unveiling of this plan occurred over many centuries in concert with God's will through the mouths of His prophets and apostles. Then, at the time determined by God *(Galatians 4:4)*, the extent of His redemption was fully revealed in Jesus Christ at a specific moment and location. Then the salvation of His elect out of all nations, tribes, and languages through all the ages became fully knowable and understandable by those He saves. This revelation was not an afterthought. Rather, Paul affirmed that, contrary to the claim of the Judaizers or the leadership of the Jewish disciples in Jerusalem, Christians were selected for salvation before the foundation of the world *(Ephesians 1:4–5, 13–14)*.

3:12 *We can go to God with bold confidence through faith in Christ.*

The Ephesians had nothing or no one to fear. They could courageously stand before God's throne of grace because of Jesus Christ. They were justified by Jesus Christ. God was at peace with them. Because of their faith in Jesus Christ, they could confidently go to God as His children and as His servants.

3:13 *So then, I ask you not to become discouraged by the troubles I suffer for you. In fact, my troubles bring you glory.*

Starting from the time of his conversion, Paul had suffered rejection and persecution for the sake of Jesus Christ. At first, even the disciples who should have been familiar with God's transforming power doubted his conversion to faith in Jesus Christ. They did not trust him. The Jews and their religious authorities hated him and tried to kill him. He was ultimately imprisoned and brought before the Sanhedrin and then the Roman authorities. But Paul considered these hardships as marks of his service to God. He did not want the Ephesian Christians to be upset by his suffering. Quite the contrary!

They should be confident in Jesus Christ and should feel honored that someone was appointed to bear suffering so that they could hear the Gospel of God's salvation.

Notes/Applications

Paul encouraged the Ephesians by explaining a new outlook about the true value of his suffering on their behalf. Paul relieved the Ephesians of any concern about his imprisonment. He had endured the relentless persecution of the Jews for years because he included the Gentiles as objects of God's redemption. To the Jews, even many Christian Jews, the conversion of the uncircumcised pagan was unthinkable. But Paul's suffering was for their glory and the Ephesian Christians should rejoice in their redemption instead of worrying about his present circumstances as an inmate in a Roman prison.

Paul considered his present situation the outcome of his faithfulness to the task to which God had appointed him. He realized that he had completely misunderstood the Scriptures before Jesus met him on his way into Damascus. He regretted his actions that opposed the Church of Jesus Christ, which in truth demonstrated his rebellion against Christ Himself. Because of these actions, Paul felt that he was the biggest sinner in the world. He certainly was not worthy of God's salvation, let alone the task of carrying the Gospel to the people of the Roman Empire.

But then, no one is really worthy of the salvation that God bestows on those He saves. Nevertheless, Paul wants believers to understand their suffering, like his suffering, pales in significance to the light of the mystery of God's redemption. The redemption of all people, both Jews and Gentiles has been part of God's eternal design, which He planned and accomplished through Jesus Christ. God kept this eternal truth to Himself until it was openly revealed in Jesus Christ at Calvary. God conferred His grace upon Paul whom He created, redeemed, appointed, and commissioned to be the bearer of the Good News of God's salvation to the Gentiles.

As Paul's suffering was the fruit of fallen man's reaction to the mystery of God's infinite grace, so believers should not to be distracted from the marvelous grace of God's redemption by man's opposition and rebellion to God's salvation *(Philippians 1:28–29).*

Ephesians 3:14–21

3:14–15 *[14]This is the reason I kneel in the presence of the Father [15]from whom all the family in heaven and on earth receives its name.*

Paul's comforting words to the Ephesians regarding his suffering were true and heartfelt. For him, his suffering was a marvelous experience that fulfilled God's commission and brought glory to His name. Paul taught the Ephesians with patience and care so that they could understand the wonders of God's glory for their redemption, declared to them by the Lord's suffering servant. To this end, Paul bowed down before the Lord to intercede for the Ephesians in the name of Jesus Christ. In this Name alone God's children including the Ephesians and the hosts of heaven are identified.

3:16 *I'm asking God to give you a gift from the wealth of his glory. I pray that he would give you inner strength and power through his Spirit.*

What did Paul ask God on behalf of the Ephesian Christians? He asked God to grant them a gift out of the rich resources of His glory and grace. He asked God to enrich their faith, not by the merit of their human effort, but by the power of the Holy Spirit. Paul depended on God to strengthen their faith. He knew that human attempts to bolster faith always met with failure. But God, in His grace and glory, never failed to enrich the lives of those He saved. So Paul prayed that God would enable them to walk by faith as God's redeemed children, strengthened by the riches of His glory. Paul pleaded with God to fortify the Ephesians by His power so that they would not be led away from the truth of their salvation in Jesus Christ.

3:17 *Then Christ will live in you through faith. I also pray that love may be the ground into which you sink your roots and on which you have your foundation.*

Paul's earnest prayer for the Ephesians was that they would continue to grow in faith. In this way, they would be more intimately bonded with Jesus Christ as the object and the substance of their faith. But Paul wanted them to understand something more than Jesus Christ simply as the object of faith. He wanted them to realize that Christ lived in them as the substance of their faith in God, reflecting His person and character in their daily life.

Paul prayed that the Ephesians would ultimately understand that the person and character of Jesus Christ lived out His life through them *(Galatians 2:20)*. As the power of Christ's presence generates godly actions and thoughts, the Ephesians would express God's love among the family of faith and toward unbelievers as well. Built on this foundation and deeply rooted in God's love, the life of Christ in them would bear God's true fruit of the Spirit in their actions and relationships. In this way, the Ephesians would have a mature faith reflecting the reality of a life well grounded in God's love.

3:18 *This way, with all of God's people you will be able to understand how wide, long, high, and deep his love is.*

Paul prayed in faith and with confidence that the Ephesians, through a genuine and deeply personal experience in Christ, would discover a fresh realization of God's divine love, which reconciled them to the Father, the Son, and the Holy Spirit. Surely, unbelievers understand and experience the emotion of love among families and friends. But this love is not common among the human population. Rather, it is the unparalleled expression of God's gift to His redeemed people. It is this gift that all of God's people understand. It is in the context of this fathomless love that all believers share the deep and abiding fellowship of the Holy Spirit.

God's love is wide, covering all peoples of the world. It is long, enduring through time and reaching into eternity. It is high, reaching to the heavens. It is deep, so deep that Jesus left heaven and suffered the depth of man's sin on the cross. Paul wanted the Ephesians to comprehend the love that caused Jesus Christ to obey His Father even to death on the cross. The love of God for His people paid the penalty for their sin so that they could receive the salvation He bought for them with His precious blood. Ultimately, this was the width, length, height, and depth of God's love. This was the root of their new life in Christ, which the Holy Spirit rooted deeply in the core of their being.

3:19 *You will know Christ's love, which goes far beyond any knowledge. I am praying this so that you may be completely filled with God.*

Paul promised that, through the Holy Spirit *(3:16)*, the Ephesians would know and understand God's unique and unparalleled love. Through that love, they would possess knowledge that could only be understood as the indwelling Holy Spirit showed it to them. It far surpasses any earthly expertise or the dynamics of human knowledge. This is the essence of Christ's love, a love that fills the believer's life with the all the fullness of God Himself. This was the essence of Paul's prayer for the Ephesians.

3:20–21 *[20]Glory belongs to God, whose power is at work in us. By this power he can do infinitely more than we can ask or imagine. [21]Glory belongs to God in the church and in Christ Jesus for all time and eternity! Amen.*

Paul concluded his prayer with a resounding doxology of praise to God affirming His power, glory, and eternality. Paul was fully confident that his prayer was already answered. He knew that God accomplishes His will in His own sovereign way providing for everything beyond the finite concerns of human desire. In thanking God, Paul expressed a strong faith that confirmed everything he asked in his prayer was ultimately fulfilled in Jesus Christ by God's power working in His Church.

Thus, the Church, the community of those redeemed by the work of Jesus Christ and instructed in the Holy Spirit, exalts the Name of God and His Son, Jesus Christ, in this world and for all eternity.

Notes/Applications

Paul was always concerned about the welfare of those who were redeemed through his ministry. This burning zeal for God's people was an important aspect of his love for the Lord and his commitment to his appointment in His service. He loved his spiritual children so much that he constantly prayed for them. On his knees, Paul interceded with his heavenly Father on behalf of His spiritual children.

Prior to telling the Ephesians the substance of his prayer, Paul reminded the Ephesians that they were a redeemed member of the larger family of saints identified in heaven and on earth by the work of Jesus Christ. Paul affirmed that all of God's children are one in Jesus Christ regardless of heritage or any other distinguishing factor. Having been made God's redeemed children by the atoning sacrifice of the Lamb of God, Paul's assures all believers of their identity in Jesus Christ. Those who belong to Christ are called by His name and depend on Him for their salvation and sanctification in this present life and for all eternity.

All believers are strengthened in their faith by God's power. As God's power works within them, they exhibit the reality of their faith in Jesus Christ openly as a living witness of the life of Jesus Christ in His children. Paul asked God to grant His power out of the riches of His glory to His children. The Holy Spirit is the source of spiritual vitality in all matters of faith and life. Paul's prayer was not only an exercise that petitioned God for something important for the redeemed. It was also an affirmation of God's accomplished will for everything His people need for faith and life, which had already been granted in Jesus Christ. Recognizing the continued work of God's grace in them, Paul encourages all believers because Christ has overcome the world and granted His victory so that we might continue as

His ambassadors, living in His love and in His grace while declaring His message of salvation for unbelievers.

As Christ's Church recognizes the immensity of God's love given to them in Jesus Christ and fulfills their appointed task by telling others of God's salvation, God is glorified and the Name of Jesus is exalted. The whole creation then joins Paul in his doxology:

> [20]*Now to him who is able to do far more abundantly than all that we ask or think, according to the power at work within us,* [21]*to him be glory in the church and in Christ Jesus throughout all generations, forever and ever.* Amen. *(Ephesians 3:20–21,* ESV*)*

EPHESIANS 4

Ephesians 4:1–6

4:1 *I, a prisoner in the Lord, encourage you to live the kind of life which proves that God has called you.*

The first three chapters of Paul's letter to the Ephesians focused on doctrinal issues that establish the immeasurable love of God that brought salvation to sinners. Then he explained how the substance of faith in Jesus Christ and the assuring presence of the Holy Spirit facilitate the believer's conduct as a member of the redeemed family. Beginning with chapter four, Paul embarks on a practical challenge to all believers to live a godly life in which the person and character of Jesus Christ is proven true at every level of the believer's experience. The transforming power of God's redemption is reflected in the life of the redeemed in the context of the believers' relationship with God, within the Body of Christ, within one's family, and with the rest of the world.

Paul's first challenge encourages the redeemed to live a life that affirms the reality of God's redemption in their lives. Their life and conduct should outwardly reflect their inward experience of salvation and faith in Jesus Christ. Here, Paul is not talking about a life that provides evidence of one's faith. Rather, the believer should be open to the full power of the transformation that accompanies God's redemption. Believers should listen to the guiding voice of the Holy Spirit as He continuously reaffirms the truth of His Gospel through His living Word. Since Paul himself was constrained by the bonds of love and obedience to His master, so he encouraged the Ephesians to walk in tune with their position in Christ as God's redeemed children.

4:2 *Be humble and gentle in every way. Be patient with each other and lovingly accept each other.*

Walking in one's identity in Christ is not a puzzle riddled with mystery. Living as a Christian is not really hard to understand. Assured by the absolute certainty of the fruit of the Spirit, Paul encouraged the Ephesians to reflect outwardly visible virtues, which confirm the ongoing work of God's transforming power in their hearts. Those who continue to walk in Christ should be humble, gentle, loving, and patient with one another. The life of God's redeemed children should reflect the dynamic inner transformation effected by the Holy Spirit through outwardly visible attitudes and conduct that bring glory to God and edifies the Body of Christ.

By behaving in this way, God's children truly reflect the person and character of the Lord Jesus Christ in a practical way. By being humble, God's children always place the godly pursuits and dreams of others with higher priority than their own. In this way, everything they do gives glory to God by crediting their actions to His goodness. By being gentle, the redeemed treat one another with respect and care, knowing that they are fragile and are easily broken. By being loving and patient, God's children demonstrate God's goodness and mercy that they have experienced at the hand of God.

The identity of the redeemed with Jesus Christ affirms the inner witness of one's redemption. The practical outcome of this inner witness brings the blessings of God's redemption to fellow believers. With this in mind, Paul told the Ephesians to let their faith in Christ produce humility, gentleness, love, and patient with one another by the power of the Holy Spirit. Since these actions are generated by the Holy Spirit, they will certainly demonstrate the ongoing work of God's redemptive transformation in the lives of His redeemed children.

4:3 *Through the peace that ties you together, do your best to maintain the unity that the Spirit gives.*

Humbleness, gentleness, love, and patience are outwardly visible virtues, which reflect the ongoing transformation of God's people by the power of the indwelling Holy Spirit. These virtues not only reflect the inner victory of God's work in the believer's life, but also draw the assembly of the redeemed together into a spiritually dynamic oneness, united in God's peace, which works together to nurture the Body of Christ. Paul showed the Ephesians how the practical reality of God's redemption brings them to a mature, selfless, respectful, caring, and patient community of faith. In this way, the Holy Spirit keeps the unity of the Body of Christ through the peace He instills in the hearts of the redeemed.

4:4 *There is one body and one Spirit. In the same way you were called to share one hope.*

There is one Body—the Body of Christ—into which believers are called. There is one Spirit even the Holy Spirit by Whom they are drawn into God's salvation and are sealed in God's redemption. Therefore, all believers are called into God's redemption by the same hope in Jesus Christ by which each one is saved. The reality of God's redemption is, therefore, openly reflected by the unity of the redeemed in the Body of Christ held together by the Holy Spirit. By serving one another with God-given actions cultivated by the continuing work of the Holy Spirit believers share the joy and fellowship that is found only within God's family of faith.

4:5–6 *[5]There is one Lord, one faith, one baptism, [6]one God and Father of all, who is over everything, through everything, and in everything.*

The nature of the unity into which the redeemed are joined stems from God's own absolute and perfect oneness, the unity of the Father, the Son, and the Holy Spirit. God reconciled the lost with Himself through His redemption, drawing those He saved into the concord of a blessed harmonious whole under the headship of Jesus Christ. Although this gift originates in the counsel of God in heaven, the Lord instills this gift in His people, bringing to earth the fellowship of one faith and one baptism.

God draws the redeemed through His Son Jesus Christ by the Holy Spirit, reconciling the sinner with Himself. He brings individual believers into the one Body of Christ and bonds them together as one by the Holy Spirit. Pointing the redeemed to their one sure hope in Jesus Christ, God purchases His saved children as the prized possession of one Lord who live together in one baptism and one faith so that God's absolute sovereignty encompasses and permeates everything He has created.

Notes/Applications

Following his doctrinal discourse in the first three chapters of the book, Paul then instructed the Ephesians in the practical aspects of their redeemed life in Jesus Christ. He began by demonstrating the indispensable outcome that affects the redeemed child of God. With firmness, Paul urged the Ephesians to prove their conversion by exhibiting the practical fruit of their faith in Jesus Christ. In this way, he challenged them to walk worthy of their identity in Christ their Savior.

Paul's strong challenge was not a call for an action initiated by the human will. Fully aware of the flawed quality of the human spirit, Paul urged believers to keep the human will under control and obediently surrender to the governing power of the Holy Spirit. Contrary to the self-serving motivation of man's natural will, the Holy Spirit will produce His fruit in the life of God's redeemed child thereby bringing the person and character of Jesus Christ to the foreground of the believer's daily walk gradually replacing the natural inclinations of the dying sin nature.

The godly virtues identified by Paul secure at least two essential objectives of practical Christian living. First, each virtue will eventually replace the opposing traits of the sin nature from the life of the believer. Second, the believer will be simultaneously integrated into the one Body of Christ as a viable redeemed member, sharing in the united work of the Holy Spirit.

The believer will turn away from human pride by submitting to God-given humbleness. A meek Christian enriches the lives of fellow believers with a gentle and respectful disposition. Godly patience cleanses the redeemed from a vengeful attitude. The spirit of a merciful forbearance will make the child of God a dependable source of comfort not easily offended by the restless, unregenerate actions of others.

As God's redeemed children, we are encouraged to be transformed by the godly virtues instilled in our hearts by the Holy Spirit as He cultivates godly love, humbleness, meekness, patience, and forgiveness into our Christian experience. In this way, the unity of the Body of Christ is enjoyed genuinely by each member of the Body. Called to live in a peaceful disposition, we are invited to flourish in the unity of the Body of Christ, continuing in a harmonious whole of one faith, looking toward one hope in our Lord Who has revealed to us the only perfect and absolute God. This is a comforting assurance given to us so that we can live in a redeemed community that shares their human frailties, rejoices in their saving and sustaining Lord, and looks forward to that day when faith will be made perfect in the presence of their Lord.

Ephesians 4:7–16

4:7 *God's favor has been given to each of us. It was measured out to us by Christ who gave it.*

Godly virtues are the traits of a transformed life. Generated by the Holy Spirit, they serve as indicators of God's steady work of sanctification in the life of the redeemed as well as the nurturing ministry of the Holy Spirit in the edification of the Church. Humbleness, gentleness, love, patience, forgiveness, forbearance gradually displace the traits of the sin nature progressively transforming the life of the child of God into a dynamic experience characterized by the fruit of the Holy Spirit, effectively causing the redeemed to walk worthy of their redemption in Christ.

Because godly virtues function in opposition to man's fallen nature, the proof of one's faith and the cultivation of godly virtues are not caused by the action of the human will. But Paul assured the Ephesians and all believers across the ages that God poured out His favor upon the redeemed. This, too, is God's gift through Jesus Christ Who gave a measure of His grace to each believer, supplying sufficient faith to receive and experience the transforming work of His redemption. God gives His gift to each believer according to His pleasure, accomplishing His will by the particular gift He gives to each one. Because the Author, Administrator, and Operator of all the gifts is God Himself, all of His people share in Christ's bounty, and are united in the exercise of God's gifts toward the fulfillment of His purpose in the Church.

4:8–10 *8That's why the Scriptures say: "When he went to the highest place, he took captive those who had captured us and gave gifts to people." 9Now what does it mean that he went up except that he also had gone down to the lowest parts of the*

earth? [10]The one who had gone down also went up above all the heavens so that he fills everything.

Paul showed the significance of God's gift of grace by alluding to Jesus Christ's victory over every aspect of His creation. Taking on the form and nature of a human being, Jesus Christ obeyed His Father even to death on the cross in order to fully satisfy the judgment of God's Law and become the Way by and through which God's redemption was fully executed. Quoting the Scriptures, Paul assures believers that Jesus Christ destroyed the combined forces of sin, death, hell, and the devil by His suffering, death, burial, resurrection, and ascension, conferring God's sovereign grace upon the redeemed *(Psalm 68:18)*. Jesus became the eternal victor over the captors of the lost by filling the depth, height, breadth, and length of His Creation—from heaven to hell—with His presence. Finally, Christ will submit Himself and His conquest to His Father so that Jesus will be in absolute control of His entire creation *(1 Corinthians 15:28)*.

When Jesus Christ conquered the masters of bondage, He secured the gift of eternal life for His redeemed people, and sent the Holy Spirit to be the resident Lord of God's redeemed. With the Holy Spirit, God gave His children gifts of every kind suitable to His purpose. He determines the gifts He gives and selects the recipients of those gifts. Paul wanted believers to realize that God gave sufficient grace through His Son Jesus Christ and by the ongoing work of the Holy Spirit so that they were equipped to live in a manner worthy of His redemption. God sent His Son to secure freedom for the lost, to conquer sin, death, and hell, and to give His people a life worthy of being lived as the redeemed of God.

Paul is telling believers that what Christ has done—in His cross, in His condescension to His humanity, in His ascension to the right hand of the Father, in His victory over the enemies of His redeemed people, in His gift of the Holy Spirit by which His people fulfill their identity in Christ—essentially encapsulates them completely within the purpose of God the Father. There are no alternatives! There is only

Christ! He alone fills the believer's life even as He fills all dimensions of His creation.

4:11 *He also gave apostles, prophets, missionaries, as well as pastors and teachers as gifts [to his church].*

God gave His Spirit to everyone whom He called out of bondage into His blessed redemption. Then He assembled the redeemed into a single universal union of His Church to perpetuate itself as the Body of Christ held together by His Son as the head. Whereas God blessed each individual believer with natural talents and spiritual gifts, He also gave some individuals varying capabilities to collectively serve the Body of Christ.

God appoints individual believers in local assemblies to serve various purposes within the church. God continues to nurture His Church by furnishing local assemblies of His children and the Church universal with: apostles, prophets, missionaries, pastors, and teachers. Some, like Paul, are appointed as itinerant ministers serving the community of believers and spreading the Good News of God's salvation on a worldwide scale. Apostles are those who were called directly by Jesus Christ–His disciples and the apostle Paul. These men were personally instructed and commissioned to make Christ known to the world. Prophets are those who have spiritual discernment and wisdom, directly instructed to proclaim what has been revealed as future events or biblically sound interpretation of God's declared truth. Missionaries are those who are appointed to take the Gospel to the unbelieving world both near and far. Pastors are those who are entrusted with the care of God's people purchased with the precious blood of His Son Jesus Christ. Teachers are those who are endowed with keen understanding and exceptional skill to instruct God's people with godly knowledge.

4:12 *Their purpose is to prepare God's people, to serve, and to build up the body of Christ.*

God nurtures His Church through the services of the several officers He appoints to positions of ministry and authority within the assembly of believers. The gifts and capabilities conferred upon each servant are given for the benefit of the Church. These ministers are called and equipped to build up the Church by nurturing and maturing the members in the knowledge and practice of their faith in Jesus Christ so that they might walk worthy of God's calling. They are appointed to serve God in the Church by providing guidance, sound biblical teaching, proper instruction, and godly encouragement. The combined outcome of God's servants in the Church results in the edification of the whole Body of Christ, the vibrant ministry of the Church, and the continued sanctification of the believers toward their ultimate perfection in Christ. The purpose of God's appointed leaders is to engage the whole body of believers in the work of Christ's Kingdom—sustaining and equipping each member for God's appointed purpose and telling unbelievers of Christ's salvation.

4:13 *This is to continue until all of us are united in our faith and in our knowledge about God's Son, until we become mature, until we measure up to Christ, who is the standard.*

God's appointment of ministerial officers and their designated services will continue as an integral aspect of the life of the Body of Christ. Because the welfare of the Church unequivocally depends on God's providence and His unfailing care, the ministers and Christian workers He appoints should continue to cultivate the Church, nurturing a more dynamic and vibrant assembly of believers. As a spiritual living organism, the Body of Christ continues to develop as it is nurtured by the services of God's appointed servants toward a fully developed maturity in Christ. Even though the perfection of Christ could not be contained in the mortal frame of fallen man, the services of God's appointed stewards and workers should direct the redeemed on a stable course steadily advancing toward the perfection that is already secured by Jesus Christ. As the redeemed press on to the finish line, they become more and more united in the faith and the knowledge of Jesus Christ, experiencing the unique oneness of the Body of Christ. As the redeemed collectively and individually grow in the faith and the knowledge of Jesus Christ, they mature and become more and more like the Son of God to Whose image they are being daily conformed by the Holy Spirit.

4:14 *Then we will no longer be little children, tossed and carried about by all kinds of teachings that change like the wind. We will no longer be influenced by people who use cunning and clever strategies to lead us astray.*

A maturing believer is one who has his eye set on the finish line. He is faithful, passionate, and focused. As he continues to grow and gradually becomes more like Christ, his association with the sin nature and his fallen inclinations will slowly begin to diminish. When the redeemed are strengthened by the transforming knowledge of God's truth, their vulnerability to the cunning craftiness of clever strategies steadily lessens, no longer influenced by deceptive teachings. They will not become the victim of the destabilizing influences of unsound doctrine.

4:15 *Instead, as we lovingly speak the truth, we will grow up completely in our relationship to Christ, who is the head.*

Instead of falling victim to ungodly influences, the maturing believer will continue to advance in the development of his relationship with Jesus Christ. As a member of the Body of Christ, a spiritually well-nourished child of God becomes more conformed to the image Jesus Christ as his living head. He will continue to grow in the godly knowledge of the truth. He will proclaim God's revealed precepts against all falsehood courageously and with love. Both the personal relationship of the redeemed with Christ and his ministry to others will be vigorously advanced when the believer is nurtured by the knowledge of God's truth and reinforced by a thriving faith.

4:16 ***He makes the whole body fit together and unites it through the support of every joint. As each and every part does its job, he makes the body grow so that it builds itself up in love.***

Christ, Who is the head of His own Body, the Church, keeps His Body together by individually nurturing each member both by the indwelling Spirit, the instruction of His living Word, and the support of their relationships with other believers. He unites the Body into a single unit comprised of mature members who nurture the Body through their mutual faith, knowledge, wisdom, and courage. Christ nourishes His Church through the gifts He gives to His people by instructing its members through the services of God's servants and engaging the support of all God's people by the power of the Holy Spirit.

Notes/Applications

Paul portrayed Jesus Christ's surpassing preeminence by describing how high He ascended and how low he descended in His conquest of those who kept His people captive *(Psalm 68:18)*. He descended to earth when He took on a human form to accomplish God's plan to save a people for Himself. He descended further when He was laid to rest in the grave experiencing the death and burial of mortal man. But He triumphantly came to life again in His resurrection. He later returned to His Father as He emerged from the grips of death, eternally overcoming sin, death, hell, and the devil. Jesus accomplished His Father's will and paid the price of sin with His life by purchasing the redeemed, paying the ransom for the captives, saving them from their just condemnation.

Jesus Christ, our triumphant Lord and eternal Victor, became the only way for our salvation by providing the ransom for our redemption by God's sovereign grace. But God did not save us and leave us alone, struggling to survive by our own ingenuity. God sent His Holy Spirit to permanently indwell and seal the redeemed after the Lord Jesus Christ ascended to His Father, after He accomplished God's redemptive purpose and plan *(John 16:7–15)*.

The call to walk worthy of one's redemption by one's own ingenuity is a humanly unattainable ideal. But God in His wisdom made it possible for His children to grow into a life that is pleasing to Him. He gave His Holy Spirit to His redeemed children to cultivate the person and character of Jesus Christ in their hearts and lives. But He also appointed and commissioned certain people within the Church to facilitate the work of the Holy Spirit on the human level as they serve God by caring for His people under the direction and control of the Holy Spirit. God assembled His redeemed children into the Body of Christ and nurtured His people by the power of the Holy Spirit through the services of its appointed members.

Why God's people struggle with God's purpose for His Church is difficult to understand. God's purpose cannot be clearer than it is in this passage. Nevertheless, all of God's people are urged to walk worthy of their position in Jesus Christ and Paul makes it clear that Christ has provided the necessary resources to make it possible.

Ephesians 4:17–24

4:17 *So I tell you and encourage you in the Lord's name not to live any longer like other people in the world. Their minds are set on worthless things.*

Continuing to speak with compelling frankness, Paul urged the Ephesians to be different from the unsaved people of the world. Paul had explained how they had been redeemed by the precious blood of the Lamb of God. They had been indwelt and sealed by the Holy Spirit. They had been transformed from within and without by the Holy Spirit, and He had equipped His Church with the services of God's appointed servants. Therefore, God's redeemed children should be aware of the change taking place in their lives and should be the pliable beneficiaries of God's sanctifying work in them. They should focus on the worthwhile things of God's redeeming work actively taking place in their lives, and no longer cling to the worthless things this world offers. In Christ, they are both the recipients of His grace and the means of God's nurturing care in the Body of Christ.

4:18 *They can't understand because they are in the dark. They are excluded from the life that God approves of because of their ignorance and stubbornness.*

The new man in Christ and the unregenerate have nothing in common. The lost remain in darkness languishing in sin's bondage. Because they are in darkness, they are unable to see the light of God's redemption and live without any spiritual understanding. They are shackled with the fetters of ignorance regarding God's redeeming love and His sovereign grace. They are entrenched in their lost ways and persist in an intractable obstinacy.

4:19 ***Since they no longer have any sense of shame, they have become promiscuous. They practice every kind of sexual perversion with a constant desire for more.***

Hopelessly enamored with their own obstinate disposition, the unregenerate remain bewitched by sin's tantalizing allurements. Taunted and provoked by the unregenerate cravings of their flesh, they are shamelessly drawn to the depth of their depravity, driven by lust that can never be satisfied. They not only live in perversion, but indulge their whole being in the pursuit of their lustful appetite. Living in the grip of unrestrained lust, the unregenerate are ultimately reduced to a sensual organism hoping for an unattainable thrill from its own depraved nature.

4:20–21 ***20But that is not what you learned from Christ's teachings. 21You have certainly heard his message and have been taught his ways. The truth is in Jesus.***

Paul reminded the Ephesians and believers of all ages to take notice of the difference between the unregenerate and themselves. What the redeemed have in Jesus Christ is absolutely incomparable to the nature and the position of the lost. The sure promises of the Gospel of Jesus Christ openly proclaimed the Good News of God's deliverance of the redeemed from the depravity and the condemnation to which the unsaved are condemned. The redeemed know that the truth of their salvation and the condemnation of the lost is in Jesus Christ *(John 3:16–18)*. Knowing that the Lord had chosen them from among the people of the world and brought them into His Kingdom, the redeemed are consciously aware of their call to walk worthy of their salvation. They actively separate themselves from the ways of the world as the truth of the Gospel is rooted deeply in their redeemed hearts.

4:22–23 ***22You were taught to change the way you were living. The person you used to be will ruin you through desires***

that deceive you. [23]However, you were taught to have a new attitude.

Paul identified the changes that a God-given transformation produces in the lives of the redeemed. Paul's explanation of the changes is underwritten by two fundamental principles he has explained earlier in this letter: (1) believers living their lives in a manner worthy of their identity with Christ; and (2) living thereafter under the inescapable experience of the fruit of God's transformation. The Ephesians had been taught to turn away from their old ways. When they first heard the Gospel of Jesus Christ and believed in Him for their salvation, they were called out of sin's bondage and ushered into the liberty of a new life in Jesus Christ. They were delivered from the shackles of their unregenerate existence and set free to enjoy the fullness of Christ's freedom in God's redemption.

The old nature is deceitful and attempts to keep the lost trapped in their depraved appetite, subject to its own lust. Having been instructed to recognize both the characteristic of the old nature and his freedom from the grip of its depraved passion, the child of God is directed to heed what he has been taught by the Gospel and walk worthy of the Name by which he is saved by consciously rejecting the sinful ways of the old nature. The Holy Spirit consistently directs, guides, and instructs God's people through His living Word, transforming their minds and attitudes by the refreshing truth of the Gospel *(Romans 12:1–2).*

The redeemed must never forget that the old nature will not voluntarily withdraw from the new man. They must, therefore, walk away from the influences of their dying nature by being consistently renewed in the refreshing truth of the Gospel. Paul instructed the Ephesians to be aware of their old nature and its deceitful ways, faithfully striving to change their ways and renew their attitudes by observing the precepts of the Gospel in a practical way. They should feed upon the truth of God's Word so that the new man can receive the maturity to stand firmly against the unwholesome influences of their sin nature.

4:24 *You were also taught to become a new person created to be like God, truly righteous and holy.*

The purpose of Christ's suffering and victory is not simply to reform a person. The changes fashioned in the believer's life are not designed to achieve some desirable level of spiritual maturity. Rather, Christ became God's sacrifice that sets the redeemed free and restores them to righteousness and holiness. Thus satisfying His absolute justice, God executed a divine exchange, placing the sin of the world on His Son and giving the righteousness of His Son to those whom He chose to redeem. Because of this exchange, believers can stand before the Lord clothed in the holiness and righteousness of Jesus Christ. They are now holy and blameless *(Colossians 1:22)*. Understanding this, Paul instructed believers to grow in the righteousness of their Savior Jesus Christ and be holy even as God their Redeemer is holy *(1 Peter 1:15–16)*. The righteousness and the holiness which God has bestowed on the redeemed is gradually fostered in the believer as the Holy Spirit faithfully cultivates the person and character of Jesus Christ throughout their lifetime *(Galatians 2:20–21)*. In addition to being rescued from God's just judgment, the deliverance of the redeemed also means a summons by the Father to live in righteousness and holiness in Jesus Christ by the direction and power of the Holy Spirit. In Christ, a person is not reformed, but transformed from sinner to saint by what God has done on behalf of sinners.

Notes/Applications

The call to walk worthy of one's redemption is a pervasive stipulation that permeates every aspect of one's experience in God's redemption. Paul recognized this and addressed the issue of the believer's transformation in all of its aspects. He unashamedly declared that God's redemption must be reflected in the change of one's attitude, personality, and character. He asserted that the transforming impact of God's redemption draws the redeemed into a harmonious whole of the Body of Christ the head of which is our Lord Jesus Christ Himself.

The redeemed will certainly experience the promises of God's redemption because He has provided His unfailing resources by the direct, personal action of the Holy Spirit and His work through those who are appointed to serve under His direction. He further exhorted believers to recognize the distinction between the lost and the redeemed, and consciously separate themselves from the unregenerate ways of the world. Paul's encouragement is to: reject darkness and walk in the light of God's redemption; defeat ignorance with the knowledge of godly wisdom instructed by God's Word; destroy shameless indulgence by godly integrity and holy decency; cure intractable obstinacy by godly meekness; and tear down selfish condescension with a hospitable sense of unity and godly harmony. In other words, we are called to live a dynamic life in Christ, visibly reflecting the Christ-like distinction of the redeemed from our unregenerate past and actively affirming our onward journey toward our future with Christ. We are called to abandon our sin nature and rejoice that we are clothed in the righteousness of Jesus Christ.

Ephesians 4:25–32

4:25 *So then, get rid of lies. Speak the truth to each other, because we are all members of the same body.*

A person who is fundamentally transformed by God's redemption is saved from sin to live in truth. The believer, indwelt by the Holy Spirit, shares something far more important than factual information. They also share the common experience of the Spirit's work in their lives. The people of God are also filled with the Person of Jesus Christ Who is the "way, the truth, and the life" *(John 14:6)*.

A person living in the truth of Jesus Christ also converses with others, both believers and unbelievers, in the context of that unchanging truth. As a member of the Body of Christ, anything a believer says or does affects the whole community of believers. A lie told by God's child distorts the reputation and witness of the Body of Christ, undermines trust within the Body of Christ, and ultimately grieves the Holy Spirit, compromising the testimony of Jesus Christ. So Paul asked the Ephesians to stop telling lies and, instead, speak to each other in the light of God's truth.

4:26–27 *26Be angry without sinning. Don't go to bed angry. 27Don't give the devil any opportunity [to work].*

As members of the human race, all of God's children are born with a sinful nature. As a result, they live with an overwhelming inclination to respond negatively to the circumstances around them. Even though it is normal to react this way, Paul instructs God's children to temper their reactions by the biblical precepts instilled in them by the teaching, guidance, and instruction of the Holy Spirit. The sinful qualities of anger should at least be mitigated if not completely erased by the power of God's transforming redemption.

At times there are appropriate circumstances that legitimately require righteous indignation toward some ungodly behavior or situation. Nevertheless, such occasions should not become an opportunity for the devil to cultivate his evil schemes among believers who are joined in one Body by the Holy Spirit. Satan has already lost his power in the Church by the redeeming victory of Jesus Christ. Not a single incident of anger should be left unresolved any longer than necessary to resolve the issue that gave rise to the difficulty. To make sure that anger has a time limit, Paul told the Ephesians that situations that give rise to anger should be resolved before the sun sets. That does not necessarily mean that all contentious issues be resolved within a single day. His counsel is directed more toward the individual rather than a negotiated settlement between adversarial groups of people. The child of God should resolve his anger before his forgiving Father and with his adversary as soon as possible by the power and ministry of the Holy Spirit. Anger should not be allowed to fester and become a tool of the devil by changing righteous indignation into a sinful rage. Instead, godly indignation fully controlled and directed by the Holy Spirit should be used as an effective means for godly correction under the authority of God's Word *(2 Timothy 3:16–17)*.

4:28 *Thieves must quit stealing and, instead, they must work hard. They should do something good with their hands so that they'll have something to share with those in need.*

Like lying and anger, thievery is also the fruit of an unregenerate life. Therefore, Paul forbids the believer from engaging in such conduct. As speaking the truth is to lying and righteous indignation to sinful rage, so working with one's hands in order to earn one's keep is a more commendable behavior than stealing. A believer who works is able to do far more than simply earn his livelihood. He would have the financial means of sharing God's blessings with those who are less fortunate. Instead of resorting to thievery, the former criminal who is now redeemed should become a productive citizen, an honest worker, and a living testimony of God's transforming redemption. Instead of stealing the property of others, the thief who is redeemed becomes a redeemed giver. Within the Body of Christ, he becomes the source of God's blessings to those in need. The robber who wallowed in his greed now serves God by sharing His goodness with others. Believers should recognize thievery as the unwholesome practice of the unregenerate past, consciously renounce it, and replace it with a productive life that is honoring to God.

4:29 *Don't say anything that would hurt [another person]. Instead, speak only what is good so that you can give help wherever it is needed. That way, what you say will help those who hear you.*

Just like a thief is transformed into a profitable member of Christ's Body, the tongue should also be changed from a harmful weapon to a source of encouragement to others *(James 3:10–18)*. Words hurt others, sometimes deeply, so Paul instructed the Ephesians to be careful about what they say. Believers should speak good and encouraging words that are helpful to their hearers. The redeemed, motivated and controlled by the Holy Spirit living within them, should communicate with others in a way that exemplifies their redeemed spirit rather than echoing the evil that rises from the sin nature. The believer should speak gracious words of godly thoughts to any one who is listening and communicate the godly love, care, and correction, which they have experienced in their walk with the Lord.

4:30 *Don't give God's Holy Spirit any reason to be upset with you. He has put his seal on you for the day you will be set free [from the world of sin].*

The transformation of the redeemed may often be observed through the changes which take place in the personality, attitudes, and overall conduct of the believer. However, the reason for the change is more important than the change itself or the results that can be expected from such progress. It is more important to understand that God Himself is the source, the reason, and the executor of the changes effected in the hearts of His people. Having paid the price of redemption with the blood of His Son to ransom the redeemed, God placed the Holy

Spirit in the heart of the redeemed to eternally secure His possession. The Holy Spirit works out the redemptive transformation that occurs in the lives of His elect. In this way, God claimed those whom He redeems as His own possession and appoints His Holy Spirit to be the resident authority Who governs, directs, and nurtures the new creation in Christ.

The Holy Spirit faithfully draws the redeemed toward God through the precepts and instructions of God's Word. The Holy Spirit instills biblical principles in the heart of God's child to cultivate the character of Christ, which is seen by others. Thus, believers live in compliant obedience to the Holy Spirit instead of disappointing Him by resorting to the familiar ways of their sinful past. Believers should never challenge the patience and love of the Holy Spirit by resorting to the behaviors of their sin nature.

Since God stamps His seal of ownership on the heart of the redeemed, any form of allegiance to the old nature has no eternal consequences. However, such disloyalty grieves the Holy Spirit and temporarily discourages the new man because his conduct reflects a momentary triumph by the old nature over the new man. The Holy Spirit grieves over any breach in fellowship between the redeemed and his Redeemer. Nothing less than God's sovereign will, eternal purpose, perfect plan, loving grace, and merciful redemption pleases the Holy Spirit. Christ's disciples should be aware of God's Lordship over His possession and the merciful love that flows out of His sovereign grace. They should never grieve the Holy Spirit by falling back to their old dying nature.

4:31 *Get rid of your bitterness, hot tempers, anger, loud quarreling, cursing, and hatred.*

Paul first instructed believers to deal with their ungodly attitudes, which still defined their character and demeanor *(vv. 17–29)*. He urged them to examine their behavior and replace their old ways with the attitudes and characteristics of the new man in Christ. Paul then addressed the way they treated each other.

Paul directed the Ephesians to govern the bitterness that often arises between people, even those who have been saved and belong to the Body of Christ. This bitterness erupts into behaviors that tear relationships apart. Hearts that are out of control, that are not under the authority of the Holy Spirit and God's Word, result in hot tempers, volatile anger, quarreling, cursing, and hatred. Those who are renewed in Jesus Christ should never harbor such animosity toward believers or unbelievers. Such ungodly conduct displays a heart that brings the person's redemption into question.

4:32 *Be kind to each other, sympathetic, forgiving each other as God has forgiven you through Christ.*

Human capabilities, permeated by sin, can never deal with the traits of the old nature. Since the depraved character of the old nature is the distinguishing quality of human nature, urging fallen man to deal with the flaws of his own sin nature is an exercise in futility. Paul therefore encouraged the Ephesians to remember the forgiveness they received from God so that the Holy Spirit working within their hearts could displace the traits of the old nature by the godly attributes of the new man.

Believers should be kind to each another instead of treating each other with hatred. Paul instructed Christ's followers to be tenderhearted and sympathetic toward each other instead of being angry with each other. Remembering their own sinful past, believers should look at each other through the eyes of their salvation. God's forgiveness through the finished work of Jesus Christ should be the only motivation to love each other with patient sympathy.

Notes/Applications

Paul's instruction to walk worthy of one's faith in Christ is accompanied with specific instructions, which promise a genuinely profitable experience of God's redemption. First, believers should listen to the teachings and guidance of God's appointed leaders in the Body of Christ as they, by the power of the Holy Spirit, nurture the redeemed into their unity in the Spirit. Second, believers should recognize the spiritual distinction between the redeemed and the unregenerate. Then, God's children should comply with the Holy Spirit as He executes God's redemptive transformation on the personality, attitude, and conduct in the lives of His people.

We learned that we were delivered out of bondage by God's grace through Jesus Christ from a life of depravity and disobedience *(2:1–5)*. Prior to our salvation we are enslaved to sin and obeyed the devil. But now our life no longer belongs to the devil or to us. It has been purchased by God with the precious blood of His Son Jesus Christ. Therefore, believers are instructed to reject the ways of sin and live in the righteousness of Christ. As the Holy Spirit continues to refresh our spirit with biblical precepts, we should comply with His instructions and stop appeasing our sin nature.

All people, even those who have been saved, recognize the depravity of their souls when they lie and resort to angry outbursts. We are only too familiar with our old nature and its deceits. Believers must always be on guard, realizing that the sin nature never relents from its attempt to betray the new creature redeemed by Christ. Therefore, listening to the still voice of the Holy Spirit, believers should faithfully follow the transforming instructions of God's living Word, observing and assimilating each precept into their lives moment by moment.

EPHESIANS 5

Ephesians 5:1–7

5:1 *Imitate God, since you are the children he loves.*

At the end of chapter four, Paul instructed believers to forgive one another just as God pardons those He saves, setting them free to reject their self-centered sin nature and be renewed in the freedom of Christ's redemption. In that statement, Paul reflected the words of Jesus: "[14]For if you forgive others their trespasses, your heavenly Father will also forgive you, [15]but if you do not forgive others their trespasses, neither will your Father forgive your trespasses" *(Matthew 6:14–15)*. It is in the framework of forgiveness that believers can best get rid of bitterness, hot tempers, anger, loud quarreling, cursing, and hatred *(Ephesians 4:31)*. Forgiveness is the antidote to such conduct.

As chapter five opens, Paul urges believers to imitate their Father in heaven Who has shown His love to people even though they were still sinners *(Romans 5:8)*. It is perfectly natural for believers to reflect the traits and character of their Father in heaven that the Holy Spirit cultivates under His direction and power. Here, he echoes Jesus' instruction: "[44]But I tell you this: Love your enemies, and pray for those who persecute you. [45]In this way you show that you are children of your Father in heaven. He makes his sun rise on people whether they are good or evil. He lets rain fall on them whether they are just or unjust. [46]If you love those who love you, do you deserve a reward? Even the tax collectors do that! [47]Are you doing anything remarkable if you welcome only your friends? Everyone does that! [48]That is why you must be perfect as your Father in heaven is perfect" *(Matthew 5:44–48)*.

But how can any human being, even though redeemed, imitate the eternal, transcendent God? How can anyone be perfect as the heavenly Father is perfect? That seems like an unreasonable request, an unattainable goal. It is painfully obvious that no one can begin to imitate God. But Paul is not telling believers to be sinlessly perfect. Rather, he is telling believers to imitate that aspect of their Father that they understand best–His love. This is the premise upon which he builds the practical application of godly living, which he explains in the following discourse.

5:2 *Live in love as Christ also loved us. He gave his life for us as an offering and sacrifice, a soothing aroma to God.*

God's love for His redeemed people was revealed at Calvary when Jesus Christ was offered up as the only sacrifice acceptable to satisfy God's just Law *(Romans 5:8; John 15:9–17)*. Jesus pleased His Father by giving Himself on the cross. Jesus also laid down His life for those whom His Father gave to Him. These believe in Him for their salvation by the regenerating power of the Holy Spirit. Therefore, as the children of the Father, the redeemed should reflect God's love to one another. The reflection of the Christ's person and character should be practically seen in the life, attitude, and conduct of God's children. The offering and sacrifice of Jesus Christ rises to the Father as a *"soothing aroma."* Clothed in the aroma of Christ's sacrifice, God's redeemed people live in the love that Christ has showered upon them and that is pleasing to God.

5:3 *Don't let sexual sin, perversion of any kind, or greed even be mentioned among you. This is not appropriate behavior for God's holy people.*

Paul's insistence to live in the framework of Christ's love also brings out his strong censure against those behaviors that fail to reflect the change brought about by the new life that the Spirit instills in the redeemed. The premise of Paul's aversion to ungodliness is simple. Once the sinner is redeemed and drawn into God's family of faith, the believer is instructed and empowered to recognize and reject the allurements of the old sin nature. The behaviors of the sin nature are no longer the conduct of the new man in Jesus Christ. Perversion and greed must be rejected not only because they are inherently sinful behaviors, but also because they are not appropriate for the new man born in the heart of God's redeemed child. The life of the believer should be so encompassed by the soothing aroma of Christ's sacrifice that these behaviors are not even mentioned in the Body of Christ.

5:4 *It's not right that dirty stories, foolish talk, or obscene jokes should be mentioned among you either. Instead, give thanks [to God].*

All conversations among God's children should be clean and honoring to God. God's children should not indulge in the conversations of the sin nature. The believer should be very uncomfortable in the perversion, obscenities, and silliness, which appeal to the pleasures of the flesh. These sinful distractions are simply wrong for God's redeemed children. This kind of behavior causes the indwelling Holy Spirit to grieve. It undermines the witness of Jesus Christ. It dishonors the Name of God, Who sacrificed His Son on the Cross to save the redeemed. The lives of God's chosen children should be characterized with praise and thanksgiving continuously offered to God from a grateful and obedient heart.

5:5 *You know very well that no person who is involved in sexual sin, perversion, or greed (which means worshiping wealth) can have any inheritance in the kingdom of Christ and of God.*

Paul did not expect the Ephesians to be puzzled by his instructions. As God's redeemed children, the believer should know that those who continue in sensual indulgences, perversion, and greed cannot simultaneously claim to be changed by God's redemption. If they were truly redeemed, they would not continue to indulge in sin, perversion, and greed. Such behavior denies the sovereign will of the Creator and the Redeemer Who paid the price for their salvation. It is logically and practically impossible to serve sin and expect to serve God with the same perverted heart at the same time *(James 3:9–12)*. Those who continue to appease their sin nature remain dead in their sin, and those who have been delivered from bondage reject sin in spite of the underlying yet dying sin nature.

5:6–7 *Don't let anyone deceive you with meaningless words. It is because of sins like these that God's anger comes to those who refuse to obey him. [7]Don't be partners with them.*

Paul instructed the Ephesians to refrain from any relationship with those who speak in a way that denies the truth they already knew. Such indifference to the truth not only breeds complacency, but also leads to an attitude of rebellion portrayed in a life of defiance. When the life of God's redeemed child is deeply influenced by such conditions, God will unleash His chastisement upon His wayward children. God is displeased about this kind of rebellion in His children, and He is angry enough to stretch out His hand and discipline them.

Paul reminded the Ephesians that any falsehood spoken against the truth is ultimately meaningless. The believer should not give in to the unregenerate influences of the enemies of the Gospel. Instead, the redeemed are encouraged to be faithful to God's revealed truth, recognizing that the empty words of the unregenerate heart are meaningless. Such words could easily entice the redeemed to return to sin's allurements if it were not for God's Word, which is faithfully and carefully applied to their hearts and lives by the Holy Spirit.

Notes/Applications

Paul's instruction to "imitate God" is often viewed as an insurmountable burden on the life of God's redeemed children. Such a perception is often the result of a guilt-ridden idea that the believer must grow into a Christ-like perfection, that the redeemed are supposed to be little Christs, or Christ-like, or even like Christ. If we are not instructed to be Christ-like, then why are we instructed to "imitate God"?

Even though God's redemption reconciles the sinner to God through Christ's finished work, the believer is never transformed into a Christ-like person while still on earth. Everyone is born in sin, condemned to die under God's judgment. But God in His mercy redeemed a people for Himself, justifying the lost by having His judgment completely satisfied by the perfect sacrifice of Jesus Christ. God does not make little Christs out of every convert. Instead, He ransomed the lost from their bondage to redeem a people for Himself by providing the means of their salvation through the life, death, and resurrection of His Son Jesus Christ. What then does "imitating God" mean?

At the moment of salvation, the Holy Spirit executes God's sovereign right of possession over the child He redeems. The experience of such a profound transformation is in itself the framework and substance of the spiritual process through which the redeemed begins to imitate God. Instead of remaining deeply involved with their sin nature, the Spirit will slowly begin to direct the will and emotions of His children toward their new life in Christ. This unstoppable transformation causes the redeemed to recognize and reject sin and its corrupt ways. The desire to please God will slowly become the new objective of the redeemed life. Paying attention to the instructions of God's Word becomes a way of life for God's redeemed child. Then, as godliness is steadily cultivated in the new man, the admonition to "imitate God" is meaningfully experienced as the redeemed live together in Christ's love, and their lives are continuously nurtured by the Holy Spirit. The call to "imitate God" is then a distinct instruction to live a godly life of love and obedience, reflecting the person and character of Jesus Christ, consciously rejecting the corrupt ways of the sin nature by the power of the Holy Spirit. Then, the child of God will attempt to observe these instructions without ever forgetting that, apart from the Holy Spirit, his life remains suspended between God's ways and the reality of his sin nature.

Ephesians 5:8–14

5:8 *Once you lived in the dark, but now the Lord has filled you with light. Live as children who have light.*

Once redeemed and enlightened by the Holy Spirit, the child of God realizes that the transformation taking place in His life persistently pulls him away from the old ways of his sinful nature and steadily draws him into his new life in God's redemption. Paul's encouragement to "imitate God" is no longer a puzzling spiritual platitude. Since believers once lived in bondage and were familiar with the shackles of darkness, they know the difference between the old realities of darkness and the new ways of life in Christ. The redeemed recognize the depravity of the dark past out of which they have been ransomed.

This fundamental knowledge becomes the means by which the Holy Spirit drives believers to reject the old ways and urges them forward to their new life they have in Christ. The new life in Jesus Christ is consummated when the believer is welcomed to his eternal home following the end of his earthly journey. However, the deliverance of the lost is also manifested in this present world through a life lived in the light of God's redemption. In that light, sin and darkness are consciously rejected and life in Christ is diligently pursued in love and obedience. Paul's admonition to live as the children of light and to separate themselves from the children of darkness is really his encouragement to recognize, accept, and observe the transformation that God has already accomplished in the life of believers through His irreversible regeneration.

5:9 *Light produces everything that is good, that has God's approval, and that is true.*

The redeemed are the children of light. Their life is influenced by the light of God's truth. They have nothing to fear because they are free in Christ and are called to live in the light of God's redemption. The new man in the believer yearns for more of God's light because God's light is good and true, always pointing to all the riches given to him in the light of God's redeeming grace. The Holy Spirit produces an irresistible attraction that moves believers toward God's light. That light reveals the goodness of God's grace given to the redeemed through Jesus Christ, showing them those things that are good, right and true.

5:10–11 ***[10]Determine which things please the Lord. [11]Have nothing to do with the useless works that darkness produces. Instead, expose them for what they are.***

The redeemed should do those things that demonstrate that they belong to the Lord, to God's family of faith. In the light of that redemption, God's people are to reject darkness and confess their allegiance to the light of their new life in Christ. Living in the light of God's redemption is more than a passive recognition of sin and the darkness that sin produces. Rather, the children of light are instructed to learn, understand, and prove the truth about their new life in Christ. Once filled with God's wisdom, equipped with godly knowledge, and enlightened with godly understanding, the redeemed are spiritually prepared to discern and observe what is pleasing to God and exposing and rejecting the ways of darkness and sinfulness.

5:12–14 ***[12]It is shameful to talk about what some people do in secret. [13]Light exposes the true character of everything [14]because light makes everything easy to see. That's why it says: "Wake up, sleeper! Rise from the dead, and Christ will shine on you."***

Paul expresses the shamefulness of secret sins that turn people away from the Lord. These deeds are so distasteful that it is shameful to speak about them publicly. However, every believer should understand that the depraved appetite of a sinful life cannot escape the scrutiny of God's light.

The children of light should not only reject darkness, but should avoid any potential for complacency or compromise with sin by consciously and knowledgeably turning away from its allurements and subtle influences. Because the light of God's living and dynamic Word unveils the true nature of sin and darkness, God's redeemed children should never be deceived by the deeds of the sin nature.

God's redeemed children are called to live in the light of God's Word so that they are awake and alert both to their spiritual growth and to their rejection of their former lives. Life in Christ is the only normal behavior for God's redeemed people. The most casual attention to sin often results in ungodly conduct and unwholesome practices. Those who have passed from darkness to light–from death to life–are to live in God's light and sever all relationships with the past world of darkness.

Notes/Applications

Paul reminds us that all of God's redeemed children are children of light. Jesus Christ our Savior is the Light of the world *(John 8:12)*. Saved by the true Light, we are, in turn, appointed by God to be a light to the nations, reflecting the light of God's truth *(Matthew 5:14)*. Believers are called to live in the light of God's truth so that they might openly reflect the testimony of our Savior. They are God's testimony to the power of the Gospel in Jesus Christ, living within the boundaries established by the precepts of God's declared truth.

However, a life overshadowed by the influences of sin and darkness is filled with shame and distress. The children of sin avoid the light so that their evil works will not be exposed *(John 3:19–20)*. But those who are redeemed and nurtured by the truth of God's Word are not afraid to come to the light thereby affirming God's work in them *(John 3:21)*.

God's living Word, Jesus Christ, Who is the fulfillment of God's written Word, shines the light of God's redeeming grace upon the lives of the redeemed. Through Paul, the Savior urges His people to be awake, enabling them to discern the truth and reject darkness. Any casual inclination toward sin and darkness makes the redeemed susceptible to indifference, apathy, and dangerous insensibility toward

God's transforming redemption working in their lives. Believers who fail to commune with the Lord through His Word are as good as dead unless they are awakened by the light of God's truth. Believers are called out of their slumber and are encouraged to come to the light of the Gospel instead of living a life of spiritual apathy. They are encouraged to rise out of the ruins of their unsaved life and come to the light of the Jesus Christ so that they can see and comprehend the reality of their transformation from death to life and from darkness to light.

Ephesians 5:15–20

5:15 *So then, be very careful how you live. Don't live like foolish people but like wise people.*

The world in which the children of light live is infested with depravity spawned by sin and darkness. Paul has instructed the children of light to do more than recognize and understand the wickedness surrounding them.

God's chosen people should live carefully, diligently guarding their outlook toward the world and understanding the threat of darkness that can influence their redeemed spirit. They should not underestimate the poison that resides in the darkness of the world. They should not be mesmerized by deception of sin's nuances. Rather, Christ's disciples should listen to the warnings in the Scriptures. The children of light should live like wise people, that is, in the wisdom imparted to them by the Holy Spirit. Any other way is pure foolishness.

5:16–17 *[16]Make the most of your opportunities because these are evil days. [17]So don't be foolish, but understand what the Lord wants.*

One of the distinguishing qualities of God's redeemed children is that they have the promise and the provision of God's wisdom to discern and to deal with the circumstances in which they live. With that in mind, Paul encouraged the Ephesians take advantage of every opportunity to do what God wants them to do. The gift of faith that saves also enlists believers in the work of Christ's Kingdom *(Ephesians 2:10)*. God has saved them for a purpose, for His purposes. God's wisdom is readily available to the children of light so that they can understand and do what is pleasing for their Lord and Master. The people who God has saved through the sacrifice of His Son should discern the times in which they live and watch themselves so that they do not waste their lives in the foolishness of the world. They are equipped to recognize their responsibility to live for God and spend their lives for His purpose as He directs each step of the way. God's redeemed children are enabled by the Holy Spirit to know and to make the most of the opportunities that God puts before them for His own purposes.

5:18–19 ***[18]Don't get drunk on wine, which leads to wild living. Instead, be filled with the Spirit [19]by reciting psalms, hymns, and spiritual songs for your own good. Sing and make music to the Lord with your hearts.***

Wine was a part of every meal throughout the Roman Empire. It was not viewed as something that was inherently evil. But everyone knew that excessive amounts of wine resulted in wild parties that characterized so much of high society in Rome. Roman emperors and their colleagues often threw extravagant parties. The whole purpose of the party was to revel in drunkenness and sexual promiscuity.

Paul spoke clearly against drunkenness, knowing that the outcome of such behavior was an offense to the Lord, Who had purchased them with His own blood. Instead, they should, for their own good, be filled with the Holy Spirit. When the Holy Spirit fills believers' hearts, they surrender control of their lives to their Lord. He saturates their hearts with praises to God and melodies of thanksgiving to their Redeemer.

From the moment of the salvation experience, the Holy Spirit works in the heart of the redeemed, destroying the old ways of the natural man and instilling the godly ways of new life in Jesus Christ. The antidote to the lure of sin and darkness is the Holy Spirit. The children of light are to let the Holy Spirit produce praises and continuous worship to God through songs, hymns, and spiritual melodies that glorify God the Almighty. By actively rejecting the tendencies to behave in the wild ways of the natural man, the child of God submits to the irresistible authority of the Holy Spirit. The redeemed gradually experience freedom from the influences of the past and enjoy the blessings of their sanctification in Jesus Christ.

5:20 *Always thank God the Father for everything in the name of our Lord Jesus Christ.*

Paul provided clear guidance for believers, naming specific behaviors that are to be avoided. Perhaps a thankful heart is the environment that enfolds the Christian's spirit, keeping them in tune with those things that God wants and avoiding those behaviors that reflect the sinful past. That spirit of thankfulness is not some general feeling of well-being—that all is right with the world. That perspective demonstrates one's bondage to the old ways. Rather, the focus of the believer's thankful heart is Jesus Christ Himself. Without Jesus, there is no salvation. Without Jesus, people stand condemned before the just and righteous Creator. Without Jesus there is absolutely no reason to be happy or joyful or obedient. All thanksgiving is focused only in Jesus Christ.

Notes/Applications

The redeemed are restored to life from the death of their sinful past. This transaction is revealed to the believer in light of God's eternal truth as conveyed by the living Word of Jesus Christ through the agency of the Holy Spirit. Once awakened, the redeemed are no longer the children of darkness. Instead, they become the children of light forever. This transaction was accomplished for all eternity at the Cross.

Consequently, Paul's teaching simply asks God's people to behave according to their new life in Christ. Not only has it already been purchased by Christ at the Cross, it continues to be ingrained in their new lives by the ongoing work of the Holy Spirit. The experience of the Christian life demonstrates only too clearly that no one is perfect, no one lives without sin. God's people struggle in the divine tension that exists between the old nature and the new creature. But they will one day be everything the Lord made them to be when He saved them. At that moment, they will be like their Savior, because they will see Him as He is *(1 John 3:2)*.

The practical manifestation of the fruit of God's redemption can be observed in the conduct and demeanor of the believer's daily walk.

The choices, decisions, and conduct of believers will eventually display the evidence of the Spirit's work taking place in their lives. The influences of the sin nature will continue to die as the new man in Christ is nurtured in the truth of God's Word. Believers are not only snatched out of the jaws of death, but they are transformed from darkness to light and from death to life. The Lord gives them the privilege to enjoy the redeeming blessings of God's grace in all its fullness. They are the recipients of the righteousness of Jesus Christ, and their lives are enriched through the light of His truth. This is the rich inheritance that God's people receive from the Lord throughout their earthly lives.

Ephesians 5:21–27

5:21 *Place yourselves under each other's authority out of respect for Christ.*

The preceding verses encouraged the children of light to be filled with the Holy Spirit rather than being controlled by a craving for wine. Believers are to walk with Christ, taking advantage of every opportunity the Spirit brings them rather than passing through life foolishly. This same godly wisdom is also the fundamental cause for reshaping the framework and substance of our thinking and reasoning. Believers think and act on the basis of what Christ's truth instructs whether or not the rationale contradicts our natural ways.

Christian relationships are then characterized by the godly attitude of love and service as seen in Jesus' relationship with His Father. Jesus loved His Father so much that He obeyed Him even though it led Him to a cruel death on the cross. Like Jesus, believer's place themselves under each other's authority for the sake of Christ. God's children relate to one another in an attitude of humbleness and respect as a living, dynamic witness of the person and character of Jesus Christ within them. Believers view each other with a submissive outlook, recognizing the power and authority of God at work in all of His children.

5:22 *Wives, place yourselves under your husbands' authority as you have placed yourselves under the Lord's authority.*

Unlike the cultural practices of many social groups, in Christ the relationship between a married couple is characterized by mutual respect and love. Wives are instructed to place themselves under the authority of their husbands. This does not mean that the husband is superior to the wife. Nonetheless, wives should submit to their husbands as the natural outcome of their submission to the Lord Jesus Christ. The wife's submission to the Lord produces a continued attitude of respect for her husband. The direct, personal relationship of the wife with Jesus Christ directly impacts her relationship with her husband.

5:23 *The husband is the head of his wife as Christ is the head of the church. It is his body, and he is its Savior.*

As the sovereign Creator Who planned all things according to His pleasure, God designed a definite structure of authority for His creation. Just as Jesus Christ is the head of the Church, so the husband is the head of his wife. In the same way, wives are instructed to submit to their husbands in obedience to God's created order. Jesus Christ offered Himself as the sacrifice for the salvation of the redeemed, which became the Church—the Body of Christ. Jesus Christ is, therefore, both the Savior and the head of the Church. Likewise, God instituted the marriage structure in which the husband is the head of the wife. God first created the man, and then created woman from man's rib. In simple, plain language, Paul defined the husband's position of authority within the family structure. He calls upon the husband to recognize it, instructs the wife to respect it, and instructs both to live within the boundaries of His created order.

5:24 *As the church is under Christ's authority, so wives are under their husbands' authority in everything.*

God's created order affirms the headship of Christ over the Church and that of the husband over his wife. The same created order also institutes the position of the Church under the headship of Christ and that of the wife under the husband. The wife must recognize God's created order and submit herself to the authority of her husband just as the Church submits to the authority of Jesus Christ its Savior. God's created order clearly identifies the authority under which the Church and the family are structured.

5:25 *Husbands, love your wives as Christ loved the church and gave his life for it.*

Whereas respect to her husband is required of the wife, the husband is instructed to love his wife just as Jesus Christ loved the Church—His Body. Christ's love for the Church is expressed through His selfless sacrifice of death on the cross for the salvation of the redeemed. The husband's responsibility in the relationship is to love his wife selflessly and sacrificially. The husband should follow the example of Jesus Christ and love his wife, even to the point of dying for her.

5:26–27 *26He did this to make the church holy by cleansing it, washing it using water along with spoken words. 27Then he could present it to himself as a glorious church, without any kind of stain or wrinkle—holy and without faults.*

Jesus' love for the redeemed is expressed through the uncommon display of His divine care, unreserved obedience, unquestioned submission, perfect righteousness, definite purpose, ultimate selflessness, and certain victory. Jesus offered Himself on Calvary to remove the wages of sin and the sting of death from the redeemed who are called into His salvation by the grace of God's mercy. In doing this, Jesus cleansed the redeemed from all unrighteousness, making them fit to be His Body. Jesus Christ loved the redeemed so much that He bore the wrath of God's judgment and set them free from the just judgment they truly deserved. Jesus was not stained by sin, but took the place of the cursed and suffered the fury of the Law. The Father loved Him so much that He made Him the head of those whom He ransomed so that they could be with Him forever. The Church is a glorious reflection of the unmatched glory of its Redeemer.

Notes/Applications

The opening verses of this chapter instruct the believer to live as practical followers of Jesus Christ, to emulate Him and His love, and to reject sin and its manifestations. As practical followers of God, the redeemed are called to live as the children of light, effectively reflecting the person and the character of Jesus Christ in their demeanor as well as their relationships with each another. One way of reflecting the person and the character of Jesus Christ is to recognize the authority of God and live with each other in active, submissive obedience to God's ways as displayed in His created order.

When God created the heavens and the earth, He implemented a structure by which all people are to live. This divine order was given by God for the benefit of mankind, establishing boundaries by which everyone is constrained. Even though God is the ultimate authority, believers should recognize that this authority is often expressed through the correction of fellow disciples. The structure of this relationship is most clearly seen in the marriage relationship. The relationship between husband and wife should always be viewed as a union based on mutual love and respect under the authority of the Lord.

The wife should respect her husband recognizing that God has determined that her husband should be her head. By respecting her husband, the wife recognizes God's will and honors His created order by her obedience, primarily in agreement with His design. Because of her submission to God, she holds her husband in higher regard than herself. She views him with a selfless attitude of respect as her expression of obedience to the Lord. Because her obedience to her husband is also her expression of love for her Redeemer, the wife who respects her husband also loves him with a selfless love.

Paul instructs husbands to love their wives as Christ loved the Church. The husband should hold his wife in higher regard than himself, viewing her with a selfless and sacrificial love, strong and deep enough to make him willing and ready to die for her as Christ did for His Church. In loving his wife with such a sacrificial love, the husband recognizes God's will and purpose in her and honors Him by loving her with real, practical love.

When godly respect and love is exchanged within the marriage relationship, a truly indivisible union takes place. The relationship is held together by God and continues to develop by the precepts of His

Word. Respect will naturally lead to love and love to respect as the husband and wife express their care for each other cultivated in their hearts by the Holy Spirit. For a redeemed couple, placing one another under each other's authority is the natural outcome of placing oneself under the authority of God Who brought them together according to His perfect will and sovereign grace. In a manner of speaking, a marriage characterized by respect and love reflects a life of godly, conscious, and active obedience expected of all of God's redeemed children.

Ephesians 5:28–33

5:28 *So husbands must love their wives as they love their own bodies. A man who loves his wife loves himself.*

Husbands are to emulate Jesus Christ in His relationship to the Church. The Church is the Body of Christ. Jesus Christ not only died for His Church, but also nurtures and cares for it as His own Body. In the same sense, husbands are encouraged to care for their wives as their own bodies. By loving his wife and caring for her, the husband actually expresses his love for himself.

5:29 *No one ever hated his own body. Instead, he feeds and takes care of it, as Christ takes care of the church.*

The husband should care for his wife as his own body for two essential reasons. First, all human beings are naturally designed to care for their bodies, because of self-preservation. It is natural for human beings to love themselves. Therefore, Paul instructed husbands to love their wives in the same way he loves himself. Second, the husband is directed to look at Christ and learn from Him. By knowing how much he is loved by God through Jesus Christ, and by learning how to apply Christ's love to his own life through God's Word, the husband is equipped to extend God's love to his wife.

5:30 *We are parts of his body.*

The instruction to love one's wife as one loves himself may seem impossible and unnatural. But that should not pose any problem for the child of God ransomed by the precious blood of the Lamb. Following the example of the Savior, those who have been redeemed give of themselves as Christ gave His life for others. The redeemed are members of the Body of Christ. Saved from sin's bondage, God's redeemed children have become members of Christ's living, dynamic Body held together as one by their Redeemer. As members of the Body of Christ, each redeemed child is spiritually equipped to do what the Lord instructs by the power which flows from their head, Jesus Christ.

5:31 *That's why a man will leave his father and mother and be united with his wife, and the two will be one.*

The individual's union with Christ and the consequent communion of the saints as one Body of Christ make the redeemed members of a single entity held together by Jesus Christ. This means that, for the redeemed, all relationships are formed, shaped, and characterized by the union the believer has with his Savior. This takes the meaning of marriage to a higher lever. The marital union between a man and a woman is the reflection of the couple's union with their Savior. When those who have been individually made one with Christ come together in marriage, they are united and bonded into a single whole by the uniting power of Jesus Christ Who is the head of the Church both in their assemblies and their relationships.

Marriage is, therefore, a wholesome union instituted by God. For this reason, the man leaves his parents and joins his wife as one integrated whole in marriage. The man does not abandon his parents. Rather, he moves out of the familial union in which he was raised and is inaugurated into the new union in which he will live the rest of his days. He was once the child of the parental union into which he was born. Now the man becomes an integral part of his union with his wife, creating a new family.

5:32 *This is a great mystery. (I'm talking about Christ's relationship to the church.)*

It appears that Paul is aware of the possibility to misunderstand his illustration. So he further clarified the unparalleled significance of the union between Christ and His Church even though he has used the marital union as an example. Even though a man and a woman become one when joined in marriage, their matrimony does not fully explain the relationship between Christ and His Church.

The union between Christ and His Church is mysterious. Language is incapable of fully reducing it to an understandable human expression. No intellectual articulation can fully capture the divine intricacies, which explains the depth and beauty of God's redemption. The union between Christ and His Church is deliberately planned and accomplished by God in keeping with His own incontestable will and pleasure. It is a divinely devised and pre-ordained process by which God ransomed a people for Himself, reconciled to Him by and through the all-sufficient sacrifice of His righteous Son. This assembly of redeemed believers comprises a singular entity under the headship of Christ the Redeemer into the consecrated Body of the elect. Christ the head loved the redeemed with an immeasurable love and consecrated them for His own purposes. They submit to Him with respect and obedience as part of His Body. It is this aspect of the relationship between Christ and His Church, which clearly delineates the relationship between a husband and a wife.

5:33 *But every husband must love his wife as he loves himself, and wives should respect their husbands.*

The instruction to the married couple is clear and concise. The husband should learn from Christ and love his wife with the love which God extended toward him. Likewise, the wife should submit herself to her husband and obey him with respect. The husband's selfless love will lead him to respect his wife as his own body. The respect of the wife will lead her to love her husband as her provider, protector, and nurturer.

Notes/Applications

Paul's instruction to all believers is to live as the children of light who follow Jesus Christ in practical ways. The true doctrine learned by the children of light must also be expressed in the practical aspects of life itself. In this respect, a major area of serious concern to Paul is the Christian quality of relationships within the community of believers.

The relationship within the marital unit is a crucial one. Both the husband and the wife are instructed to emulate Jesus Christ in their behavior toward each other. They should express Christ in them as they treat each other in and through the life that Christ is living in them. The husband should love his wife even as Jesus Christ loved the Church. The wife should respect and obey her husband even as Jesus Christ submitted Himself to His Father. These qualities of Christ do not make the husband or the wife unequal. Rather, their Christian conduct will reflect the Christ Who lives in them, living submissively and obediently. So is the call to all believers as they live within the framework of Christ's Body, loving and supporting each other through all circumstances, encouraging to look toward their hope and salvation in Jesus Christ.

EPHESIANS 6

Ephesians 6:1–9

6:1 *Children, obey your parents because you are Christians. This is the right thing to do.*

Paul continues his practical instruction about the way Christians relate to each other with submissiveness. After discussing the unique relationship between husbands and wives, he turns his attention to children within the family structure. The Greek word *téknon*, translated *children*, refers to young children still under the care and authority of their parents.[1] Young children should be characterized by obedience to their parents.

Paul cites at least two major reasons for requiring children to obey their parents. First, children must obey their parents because it is the right thing to do, and second, it is the Christian thing to do. Obedience is the right thing to do because it is God's direct command *(Exodus 20:12)*. It is the Christian thing to do because Jesus obeyed His Father as He served the purpose for which He was sent to earth *(John 4:34; Philippians 2:8)*. Jesus' example on earth sets the standard for everything both right and Christian. Children should be raised in the framework of obedience, answering to authority within the family structure. Children should be raised with the same attitude as Jesus was—obedient to both His earthly parents and His Father in heaven *(Luke 2:51–52; Philippians 2:8).*

6:2–3 *[2]"Honor your father and mother [3]that everything may go well for you, and you may have a long life on earth." This is an important commandment with a promise.*

Obedience is a commandment issued by God centuries earlier. "[12]*Honor your father and your mother, so that you may live for a long time in the land the Lord your God is giving you*" *(Exodus 20:12).* The instruction to honor one's parents is the only commandment that includes a promise. God rewards those who honor their parents with a lengthy, joyful life on earth. The term *honor* includes the idea of holding one's parents in high regard. Children who honor their parents will naturally want to obey them. Paul is simply using the same instruction that he expressed when he began his instruction about the way Christians are to treat each other: "[20]Always thank God the Father for everything in the name of our Lord Jesus Christ. [21]Place yourselves under each other's authority out of respect for Christ" *(Ephesians 5:20–21).* Raising children with godly authority, teaching them to obey, provides a solid foundation of respect for all authorities.

6:4 *Fathers, don't make your children bitter about life. Instead, bring them up in Christian discipline and instruction.*

Paul has told children to honor and obey their parents. He now tells fathers to provide Christian discipline and instruction for their children. Christian parents are God's stewards over their children. As Creator, God is the sovereign sustainer of all mankind. Here, however, Paul is instructing Christian parents, those who have been redeemed. They belong to God, not simply because He created them, but because He redeemed them and purchased them through His sacrificial death and resurrection. Paul therefore instructs fathers to bring up children in the nurture and admonition of God's Word, instilling in them godly wisdom and knowledge. Fathers are specifically instructed to rear their children with godly principles, consciously aware that they are entrusted with the care of precious jewels. Fathers are the ministers of God's nurturing love and care. They should make every effort to avoid making them angry and ultimately rebellious. They are to rear their children by the living power of the Holy Spirit working in them through His Holy Word.

6:5 *Slaves, obey your earthly masters with proper respect. Be as sincere as you are when you obey Christ.*

Like parents and children, masters and slaves should also recognize God's sovereign authority over them. They should consciously be aware of God's authority over their respective positions within the context of their relationships. Every individual human being is assigned a station in life through which God accomplishes the purpose which He intends. In this sense, slaves or modern day employees must recognize their station in life as God's will for them. People in the employment of another individual must render their service in a manner that reflects their acknowledgement of God's will and authority in what they do. The response of slaves to their masters and employees to their employers should be respectful, sincere, and proper, demonstrating a realistic acknowledgment of God's will, reverence for His sovereignty, and obedience to His precepts.

6:6 *Don't obey them only while you're being watched, as if you merely wanted to please people. But obey like slaves who belong to Christ, who have a deep desire to do what God wants them to do.*

The obedient attitude portrayed by slaves or employees toward their bosses must be genuinely motivated from the heart. Tasks should not be performed simply as an outward display of obedience. Rather, their service should be a heartfelt response toward God. Both their attitudes and performances should openly prove their passionate desire to please God. It should be a biblical manner of living practically expressed in the daily conduct of life in which every duty represents a loving obedience toward God.

6:7 *Serve eagerly as if you were serving your heavenly master and not merely serving human masters.*

Slaves or employees should serve those over them with eagerness. Their love for God should influence their desire to serve, recognizing that God had placed them in this position for His own reasons. If they recognize this, then their passion to serve should be motivated by a joyful eagerness to please God by doing what He equipped them to do. They should be eager to serve men in light of their desire to serve God.

6:8 *You know that your heavenly master will reward all of us for whatever good we do, whether we're slaves or free people.*

The instruction to serve others should be observed with a deeper understanding of God's unfailing providence. God blesses those who obey and honor His commandments. He rewards those who observe His precepts and conduct every aspect of their lives and services in the light of His instruction. Every good service is rewarded by the abundant harvest of God's goodness given to them through God's providence. God owes no one anything. But those who obey Him shall enjoy the abundance of His goodness. "[18]*Come now, let us reason together, says the Lord: though your sins are like scarlet, they shall be as white as snow; though they are red like crimson, they shall become like wool.* [19]*If you are willing and obedient, you shall eat the good of the land;* [20]*but if you refuse and rebel, you shall be eaten by the sword; for the mouth of the Lord has spoken*" (*Isaiah 1:18–20*).

6:9 ***Masters, treat your slaves with respect. Don't threaten a slave. You know that there is one master in heaven who has authority over both of you, and he doesn't play favorites.***

Paul instructs masters (employers) to understand their mandate from God who put them in charge of their servants (employees). They must recognize that their position of authority was assigned to them as a stewardship over God's possessions. In discharging their duties as masters or employers, persons of authority must be conscious of two fundamental truths.

First, masters should realize that they are God's stewards over those who serve them. Second, as God's stewards, they should also understand that God's authority also guides their lives. Even though they are placed in a position of authority, they serve God in their capacity as His appointed officers. Therefore, masters discharge their duties realizing that God rules over them as well as the servants over whom they are appointed. They should treat the servants in their charge with respect, realizing that God holds them accountable for their actions.

Notes/Applications

Paul's instruction to believers is clear. After reminding them of the basic fundamentals of the Gospel, he focused on the practical outcome of a life transformed by the power of God's Word. The blessings of God's redemption are far broader than rescuing a sinner from deserved judgment. The disciple of Jesus Christ receives new life in Christ along with the precepts, which offer direction for His people. The redeemed in Christ are transformed into a new person in Christ. When this happens, they immediately begin a new life in Christ that is dramatically different from the old ways. New precepts and principles bring different ways of thinking and behaving.

This new life in Christ the whole framework for understanding what life is all about. Since the believer is made God's prized possession because of and through salvation, the entire thought process and the resulting behavior takes on a new perspective guided by the Holy Spirit. God Himself becomes the point of reference, the reason for action, and the purpose for living. For the redeemed, God Himself and His precepts will be the only guide for all future decisions and actions. With this in mind, Paul instructs husbands and wives, parents and children, masters and slaves, employers and employees, to live as God's redeemed people, abiding by the biblical precepts by which the Holy Spirit instructs their hearts. Regardless of who they are and where people are placed in their social positions, those who have been made new in Christ should respect and care for one another because of God, living for Him by His unfailing power. It is Christ who lives in His redeemed people, giving them the abundance of His life even now while they still live on this earth *(Galatians 2:20–21)*.

Ephesians 6:10–17

6:10 *Finally, receive your power from the Lord and from his mighty strength.*

Paul was well aware that his instructions were very difficult for people to follow, even people who had been redeemed. Because he knew that those instructions were foreign to the human spirit, he promptly pointed believers to look to God for His strength to apply God's instructions to their Christian walk. Believers quickly learn that they must rely on God's strength in order to live the Christian life in the midst of an unbelieving world. Paul told Christians how to relate to each other in their relationships with other believers, and then told them to receive God's strength and wisdom to apply His teachings in the every day experience of their lives. Christian living can only be attained by God's strength through the effective application of His power.

6:11 *Put on all the armor that God supplies. In this way you can take a stand against the devil's strategies.*

God not only provides His strength that helps believers to live according to His instructions, He also provides those resources that His people need to withstand the devil's strategies. Paul uses the metaphor of battle armor to describe those resources God supplies to those He has saved. The word picture Paul draws in the following verses helps believers understand everything the Lord gives them during their lifelong battle against the wiles of the enemy. The Lord provides everything needed to ward off the attacks of the enemy and causes the life of Christ to become the spiritual reality of the believer's daily experience. This armor is Christ Himself, Who never leaves His people unprepared for battle.

6:12 *This is not a wrestling match against a human opponent. We are wrestling with rulers, authorities, the powers who*

govern this world of darkness, and spiritual forces that control evil in the heavenly world.

Before Paul begins to explain the resources God supplies His people, he describes the enemy with which God's people struggle. He has encouraged believers to experience their new life in Christ with a practical awareness of what God has given them in Christ. He has shown them how to live together in the community of faith, submitting to one another in the same love that Christ has shown them. Now Paul wants Christians to know that the battle is not between them and the material world. Rather, the battle is warfare raging in the spiritual realm as the devil and his evil forces work in the world to resist the victory of Christ over darkness. The world of Satan and his followers operate in darkness with its own rulers, authorities, powers, and spiritual forces. These forces live to serve the evil purposes of the devil, desperately trying to destroy everything that is good. They try to undermine the redeemed in an effort to oppose God and His redemption. Because the believer stands as a testimony of God's redemption in the face of the devil, Satan and his evil forces try to deceive the redeemed in a futile effort to destroy the indisputable evidence of God's grace and His sovereignty.

6:13 ***For this reason, take up all the armor that God supplies. Then you will be able to take a stand during these evil days. Once you have overcome all obstacles, you will be able to stand your ground.***

Because the spiritual warfare is real, and the devil and his evil forces relentlessly target the redeemed, Paul strongly urges believers to realize that God gives them this armor. He does this because the believer needs God's resources to effectively withstand the evil onslaught of the devil and his evil forces. Evil cannot overcome the redeemed because Christ has already sealed the victory. However, since evil must be effectively answered, God strengthens the redeemed by His armor, which He supplies. Only by being fully outfitted in God's spiritual armor can the believer stand firmly against the enemy. That is the only way that God's people can effectively stand their ground, remaining faithful to their salvation in Christ while living in a world that is hostile to the Gospel.

6:14 *So then, take your stand! Fasten truth around your waist like a belt. Put on God's approval as your breastplate.*

In the midst of this battleground, Paul encourages believers to take a stand against the enemy, assuring the redeemed that the strength of God's power supplied through the spiritual armor He provides is the only way to engage in this battle.

The first two pieces of the spiritual armor he identifies are: the belt of God's armor, which is truth, and the breastplate, which is Christ's righteousness through which believers receive God's approval. The girdle or belt, in physical warfare, was fastened or buckled around the short tunic worn by the soldier.[2] Metaphorically, the belt of God's truth strengthens the waist and the back of the believer while the breastplate of Christ's righteousness shields the heart of the redeemed from the arrows of the devil. The believer is instructed to strengthen himself by wearing God's truth as a belt and by protecting himself with Christ's righteousness.

God approves sinners that He redeemed on the basis of the righteousness of His Son Jesus Christ. God brings them into His Kingdom after justifying the lost by the righteousness of Jesus Christ. Jesus said that He is "the way, the truth, and the life" *(John 14:6)*. Paul's statement ultimately means that the believer must be dressed in the truth and the righteousness of Jesus Christ. God supplies His strength to the redeemed through the Gospel of Jesus Christ Who is the truth and the righteousness of God.

6:15 ***Put on your shoes so that you are ready to spread the Good News that gives peace.***

A believer who is strengthened by the truth of the Gospel and protected by the righteousness of Jesus Christ should not be discouraged by evil because that evil has already been put to rout by the sacrifice of Jesus Christ. God's people are given shoes that prepare them to venture into the fray with the Gospel of peace. Even though the spiritual world is fully engaged in a battle of cosmic proportions and the material world is permeated by wars and rumors of war, the redeemed of the Lord go into this hostile environment with words of peace. The Prince of Peace offers the divided, warring world a peace that can only be found in the Good News of redemption and reconciliation *(John 14:27)*.

6:16 ***In addition to all these, take the Christian faith as your shield. With it you can put out all the flaming arrows of the evil one.***

Christ's righteousness closely guards the heart of the redeemed, and faith is a gift from God, spiritual armor that shields believers from the flaming arrows hurled at the redeemed by Satan. Christ's righteousness keeps the heart holy and at peace with God by protecting it from its sinful nature and from all external evil forces. Armed with faith instilled by God, the believer stands firm on the promises and provisions of God, warding off all hostile actions by the evil one. Faith shields the believer from the evil influences of the devil and the enticing allurements of the world by causing the believer to draw closer to God.

6:17 ***Also take salvation as your helmet and the word of God as the sword that the Spirit supplies.***

Paul identifies the final two pieces of the spiritual armor supplied by God—the helmet of salvation and the sword of the Spirit, which is the Word of God. God's salvation is depicted by a helmet, protecting the head, the command center of the human body. God's salvation secures the entire riches of God's gift through Jesus Christ. God's salvation holds the unassailable answer to every question and doubt regarding the grace the believer has received from God.

The final piece of armor is the only weapon of offense in the entire arsenal catalogued by Paul. Paul encourages the believer to be armed with the Word of God. God's Word is the only reliable point of reference available to the believer for wisdom, knowledge, and understanding. Only by looking to God's Word can the believer give the reason for his faith, because God reveals Himself, His plan, His decrees, His judgment, and His redemption through His Word. God's Word is the only weapon of absolute truth by which the strongholds of the enemy can be effectively destroyed. Whereas the other pieces of God's spiritual armor provide protection for the believer, God's Word is given to destroy evil forces and to affirm God's revelation about His redemption and His judgment.

Notes/Applications

The whole tone of Paul's letter to the Ephesians is bathed in the glory of the preeminent Christ and His glorious Body, the Church. Paul then explains how this impacts believers in all of their relationships—all Christians with each other, husbands and wives, parents and children, masters and slaves. All of these relationships are based on the fact that Jesus Christ has made His people one Body, asking them to submit to each other just as He had already submitted to His Father. In this way, the doxology and praise of the early chapters gives way to a practical application that shows the world that Christ's salvation overcomes Satan, the world, and sin.

However, Paul wants to make sure that God's people understand that the Christian life is not a playground, but a battleground. Christ redeems and plants His Church in enemy territory. Christ's Church is positioned at the intersection where God's grace answers God's judgment. The Church stands firmly entrenched in their salvation, facing sin, death, and the devil as evidence of God's grace through which His redemption is offered to a lost world. This is a consistent, ongoing battle that engages believers until their final breath. Peter reminds the Church that Christ's enemy, our enemy, roars like a lion seeking whom he may devour.

Even though the battle is won, the enemies of the Gospel continue to wage war against the family of faith. This war is waged in the spiritual realm against the intellect, will, and emotions of the believer in an attempt to undermine the foundation upon which the Church has been constructed. But that foundation, Jesus Christ, is unmovable, unchanging, and forever sits at the right hand of the Father. The Church is bathed in the gift of His salvation, clothed in His righteousness, and equipped for the battle by the armor of God. Just as Christ's righteousness is given to the redeemed *(2 Corinthians 5:21)*, so the Christian soldier is clothed in the armor God supplies. As the pieces of armor are described, it is clear that Paul is telling God's people to "put on Christ" *(Galatians 3:27)*.

Each piece of armor equips the Christian to take his stand in whatever circumstance and location God has placed him. Each piece is a gift from God, given to the believer at the time of his salvation. Christ not only saves us, but He equips us for the struggles of this life, not only to stand against the deceit of the devil, but to enjoy the blessings of our salvation. Look at the armor and rejoice in its provision:

• The belt of Truth	• Jesus Christ	• John 14:6
• The breastplate of righteousness	• Jesus Christ	• 1 Corinthians 1:30
• Shoes for the gospel of peace	• Jesus Christ	• Ephesians 2:14
• Faith	• Jesus Christ	• Hebrews 12:2
• Helmet of salvation	• Jesus Christ	• Acts 4:12
• Sword of the Spirit	• Jesus Christ	• Revelation 1:16; Hebrews 4:12

This is the promise of God's Word. "*Clearly, all of you who were baptized in Christ's name have clothed yourselves with Christ*" (Galatians 3:27). So, Believer, stand! Be strong! Be of good courage! Rejoice in Jesus Christ your Savior—clothed in His righteousness and the armor He provides.

Stand up, stand up for Jesus,
stand in his strength alone;
the arm of flesh will fail you,
ye dare not trust your own.
Put on the gospel armor,
each piece put on with prayer;
where duty calls or danger,
be never wanting there.

Stand up, stand up for Jesus,
the strife will not be long;
this day the noise of battle,
the next the victor's song.
To those who vanquish evil
a crown of life shall be;
they with the King of Glory
shall reign eternally.[3]

Ephesians 6:18–24

6:18 *Pray in the Spirit in every situation. Use every kind of prayer and request there is. For the same reason be alert. Use every kind of effort and make every kind of request for all of God's people.*

Finally, Paul encourages believers to continue in prayer. After describing the battle and the Christian's armor, Paul reminds believers to submit every situation to the Lord in prayer. Throughout the believer's life prayer remains the one consistent line of communication with Jesus Christ in the Spirit, That ongoing conversation sustains, guides, and encourages believers in every battle, through every struggle, and in every endeavor. This is prayer for self, for others in the faith, and for the Church.

Believers are to pray in the Spirit. Prayer is an aspect of worship during which the believer is guided by the Holy Spirit to acknowledge God as the Provider and Giver of everything needed for this life. Equipped with spiritual armor means more dependence on the strength and power of God for receiving personal strength to face each trial. This can only be accomplished as the redeemed continue in a living, dynamic communion with God through prayer, the study of the Word, and the fellowship of other believers.

6:19 *Also pray that God will give me the right words to say. Then I will speak boldly when I reveal the mystery of the Good News.*

Paul asked for the Ephesians to pray for him. He is not in a good situation. He is under arrest and physically constrained by his circumstances. Nevertheless, he asked the Ephesians to ask God to give him the right words to speak and the courage to declare the truth. Paul was well aware that the proclamation of God's redemption as well as His judgment could not be carried out in human strength. He knew that the enemies of the Gospel were fueled by the wicked influences of the evil forces functioning in this world.

6:20 *Because I have already been doing this as Christ's representative, I am in prison. So pray that I speak about this Good News as boldly as I have to.*

Paul's insistence on his need for genuinely Spirit-guided prayer came out of experience. God had revealed the truth to him, appointing him to be His ambassador of the Gospel to the Gentiles. However, he learned quickly that living as God's ambassador was costly. He had preached the Gospel with courage and spoke the truth boldly wherever he went. Nevertheless, he paid the price for such boldness with imprisonment. He suffered at the hands of the enemies of the Gospel. But Paul understood that his suffering was also an aspect of his service to the Lord. So, despite his circumstances, Paul asked his fellow believers to intercede for him, asking the Lord for strength to continue to speak the truth boldly regardless of his suffering.

6:21–22 [21]*I'm sending Tychicus to you. He is our dear brother and a faithful deacon in the Lord's work. He will tell you everything that is happening to me so that you will know how I'm getting along.* [22]*That's why I'm sending him to you so that you may know how we're doing and that he may encourage you.*

Paul told the Ephesian Christians that he was going to send Tychicus to them so that they could be fully informed about Paul's personal condition and the Lord's work. This information would help them know Paul's specific needs and intercede with the Lord on his behalf. Paul introduced Tychicus as a dearly beloved brother. Tychicus was, therefore, a trusted co-laborer in the Gospel. Tychicus would share the testimony of God's power in the ministry of the Gospel and encourage them with the truth that Paul had just expressed in this letter. Paul was anxious to bring the Ephesians along in their knowledge of the full essence of a life lived in and for the Gospel.

6:23–24 ***[23]May God the Father and the Lord Jesus Christ give our brothers and sisters peace and love along with faith. [24]His favor is with everyone who has an undying love for our Lord Jesus Christ.***

Paul concluded his letter to the Ephesians by praying that God would give them peace, love, and faith. Paul knew that only God's peace can give believers the confidence and courage to continue as God's redeemed children in this hostile world. Equipped with God's peace, the believer could be confident and resilient in declaring the Gospel of God's peace to those whom He reconciled through Jesus Christ. Filled with God's love, the redeemed could ward off the hostility hurled at them by the enemies of the Gospel. With God-given faith, God's children could take God at His Word and become fearless in their dealings with a lost world and the forces of evil.

Paul knew that love and faith come only as God's strength generates courage and perseverance in facing the evil forces at work in this world. In praying that they receive peace, love, and faith, Paul effectively asked God that the Holy Spirit would work in the hearts of the Ephesians and generate His fruit in them so that their lives would truly manifest the power of God. Paul assured the Ephesians that those who sincerely love God have the assurance of God's grace to carry them through the trials of their earthly pilgrimage. So Paul encouraged the Ephesians to put their worries to rest knowing that God's peace, love, faith, and His grace are theirs in Jesus Christ.

Notes/Applications

Paul assured believers that the security of Christ's victory in their lives has been fully realized by God's power. However, the reality of God's power can be truly experienced only when the life of the believer begins to reflect the fruit of the transforming work of the Holy Spirit. When God's power is fully functional in the heart of one who is redeemed, aspects of the fruit of the Spirit such as peace, love, and faith will characterize the attitude and the conduct of the individual transformed by God's redemption.

Such persons become prayerful and watchful. They persevere and continue in communion with the Holy Spirit. They are courageous and will not hold back from speaking the truth boldly and clearly. They commune with God in a life of persistent prayer watching everything and everyone. They never lose sight of who they are, nor are they overwhelmed by the realities of evil around them. They support and encourage each other within the family of faith, because they know that the promise of God's grace and power to those who have been redeemed never fails.

PHILIPPIANS

INTRODUCTION

Philippi was an ancient city located in eastern Macedonia, what is now eastern Greece. It was located ten miles (16 km) north of the port city of Neapolis, now known as Kavalla, on the Aegean Sea. Before 400 B.C., the region was well known for its gold mines. In 359 B.C., Philip of Macedonia, the father of Alexander the Great, annexed the region and renamed it for himself. Armies and expeditions were expensive, and Philip needed the gold to finance his ventures. Two centuries later, Rome conquered Macedonia and in 146 B.C. it became one of the six provinces governed by Rome.[1]

Over the centuries, the gold mines were depleted and the city began a slow decline. Under Rome, the city again became the center of the province and, as a colony, the residents enjoyed the benefits of citizenship *(Acts 16:12)*. Many veterans of the Roman army retired to this region, making it a virtual replica of the capital city of Rome itself. Latin was the spoken language. "The city enjoyed not only economic privileges, such as exemption from tribute and the right to acquire, hold, and transfer property, but also political advantages, such as freedom from interference by the provincial governor, and the right and responsibility to regulate their own civic affairs."[2]

Paul arrived in this city on his second missionary journey, A.D.

50–53. Paul had retraced the steps of his first journey through Asia Minor, visiting the churches in Derby, Lystra, and Iconium. He then came to the port city of Troas on the northwestern coast. There he had a vision of a man in Macedonia, asking him to come to his country and tell them about Jesus *(Acts 16:9–10)*. Without any hesitation, Paul set sail with his companions, Silas and Timothy, stopping at the island of Samothrace, and then sailing the next day to Neapolis.

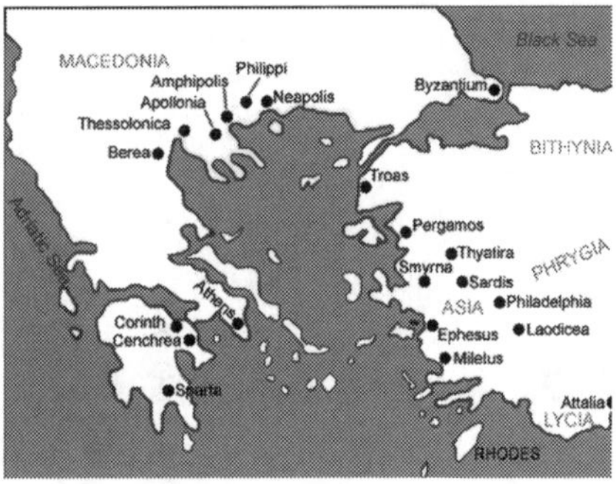

After several days in the city, Paul walked out of the city on the Sabbath and met a woman by the name of Lydia on the banks of the Gangites River. Luke states: "She was listening because the Lord made her willing to pay attention to what Paul said" *(Acts 16:14)*. She believed the Gospel and was baptized immediately, becoming the first Christian in Europe.

Shortly afterward, Paul commanded a demon to leave a young slave girl who told fortunes and made a lot of money for her owners. The owners blamed Paul for their loss of money, had him beaten, and thrown into prison. An earthquake opened the doors to the prison, but Paul and Silas refused to leave. As a result of Paul's testimony, the jailer became a Christian. When the magistrates discovered that Paul was a Roman citizen, they apologized for his treatment and set him free. Paul returned to Lydia's home, encouraged the saints, and left the city.

Following his third missionary journey, Paul was confined to a long period of imprisonment, first in Jerusalem and eventually in Rome, A.D. 59–62. During that time, Paul wrote several letters to churches that had been established during his missionary journeys—Colossians, Ephesians, Philippians, and Philemon. Most Bible scholars have come to the conclusion that these letters were written while Paul was in Rome about A.D. 61–62.[3]

Now, ten years after his first visit to the city, Paul pens this letter to the church that had flourished in Philippi. He remembered them fondly and rejoiced in the relationship he had with them. At the outset, he wrote about his situation in Rome and the proclamation of the Gospel in the capital city. He wept over the divisions that had arisen in the Roman church. Nevertheless, he remained optimistic because the Gospel was preached despite these divisions. He was happy that his imprisonment had led to the salvation of some in Caesar's household.

Paul then asked the Philippian Christians to follow Christ's example, living out their salvation in unity, humility, and selfless service to others. He promised that such a life would give them great happiness. To help them toward this end, he promised to send Epaphroditus back to them as soon as possible. He wanted them to understand the evil of the world in which they lived. He wanted them to imitate his life—a man who was well educated, a Jew from the tribe of Benjamin, a Pharisee, who considered these human achievements as rubbish compared to knowing Christ and His resurrection.

Finally, with words of love and longing, Paul urged the Philippian Christians to stay firmly rooted in the faith. They could do this by being watchful and prayerful, living in the peace of God that cannot be calculated by the human mind. Christ was their source of strength and comfort in all circumstances, just has He had been for Paul.

Though he was in prison, Paul wrote this letter with a tone of confident joy and thanksgiving, expressing how Christ was more valuable than anything the world had to offer. If one did not know Paul's circumstances, one might think that he was living the life of a wealthy man. And, indeed, he was! He was rich beyond human measure. Christ's grace had bestowed an inheritance that was more valuable than all the treasures of this life.

Christians would do well to emulate Paul, living in the contentment of their salvation in Jesus Christ, confident of His goodness, His strength, His supply. His Name be praised for all eternity by the saints who have been lifted from the depth of their sin to see the unsurpassed glory of their risen Lord, those who find in Jesus Christ the supreme satisfaction of their redeemed lives.

> Let me learn of Paul
> whose presence was mean,
> his weakness great,
> his utterance contemptible,
> yet thou didst account him faithful and blessed.
> Lord, let me lean on thee as he did,
> and find my ministry thine.[4]

PHILIPPIANS 1

Philippians 1:1–11

1:1–2 ***[1]From Paul and Timothy, servants of Christ Jesus. To God's people in the city of Philippi and their bishops and deacons—to everyone who is united with Christ Jesus. [2]Good will and peace from God our Father and the Lord Jesus Christ are yours!***

Paul opened his letter to the Philippians with a salutation that often characterized his writings. Together with his spiritual son Timothy[1] *(1 Timothy 1:2; 2 Timothy 2:1)*, they saluted the elders and deacons of the church along with the saints who were united in Jesus Christ. They invoked God's favor on the church, asking for God's grace and peace to be abundant in their lives.

Paul and Timothy were the servants of Jesus Christ. Paul acknowledged the unity they enjoyed with the saints in Philippi along with their bishops and deacons. They were God's people who had been joined together as one in the faith Jesus Christ gives. Even though he was an apostle appointed by God, Paul preferred to identify himself with his spiritual children. His message was important to the officers of the church and to the members of the body of Christ. Therefore, instead of talking down to the Philippians, Paul fondly greeted them with God's grace, favor, peace, and goodwill.

Paul left no doubt in the minds of the Philippians that his letter was Christ's inspired Word conveyed to God's people in the authority of God the Father, His Son Jesus Christ, and in the power of the Holy Spirit. Paul wrote with a dedication defined by his relationship to his Master Jesus Christ, his loyalty to the office to which he was appointed, his unreserved surrender to the Lord, and his passionate care for God's people. As God's children united in one faith in Jesus Christ, he expected the Philippians to receive his epistle with the same dedication, a genuine surrender to the instruction of God's Holy Word, and an unqualified reverence for the Author of the Gospel.

1:3–4 [3]*I thank my God for all the memories I have of you.* [4]*Every time I pray for all of you, I do it with joy.*

Paul was fond of the saints in Philippi. His memory of the believers there produced warm sentiments toward them. Paul personally rejoiced in the grace that God gave him when the Spirit called him to Philippi. He actually thanked God for the personal experience he had while serving God in Philippi and for the joy that filled his heart as he thought about their spiritual welfare.

Paul was filled with joy every time he prayed for these dear friends. Praying for his spiritual children was not a cumbersome duty for Paul. His heart was continuously refreshed by the joy of the Lord as he observed God's redeeming love work in the lives of those to whom he was sent to preach the Gospel. He always prayed for the Philippian saints with rejoicing and God-given enthusiasm.

1:5 *I can do this because of the partnership we've had with you in the Good News from the first day [you believed] until now.*

Paul realized that rejoicing over someone else's good fortune was foreign to the deep-seated human impulse. Therefore, he explained the reason for his joyful attitude when he prayed for them–their partnership in Jesus Christ through the fellowship they shared in the Gospel.

Paul appreciated the excellency of Jesus Christ Who changed his life from a persecutor to an apostle of the Good News of God's redemption. The same transforming work of the Gospel occurred in everyone in whom the Holy Spirit accomplished God's salvation. Knowing that the same Spirit brought the joy of God's salvation to all of them, Paul showed them how the union they had in and through Christ also produced the love and care they had for each other. They rejoiced with each other in the fellowship of the Gospel. Paul rejoiced with these dear brothers and sisters, because the Holy Spirit generated an unfeigned joy in all believers as they worshiped the Lord together.

1:6 *I'm convinced that God, who began this good work in you, will carry it through to completion on the day of Christ Jesus.*

Paul rejoiced with the Philippians not only because they were rescued from condemnation but also because he knew what God had prepared for them. Paul wanted the saints to know that God was their eternal Father. He would be faithful to the end. What He had begun in them He would bring to a glorious conclusion. Paul wanted them to share his confidence in God. He rejoiced over their common destiny in Christ. The Lord Who delivered them from eternal death is also able to sustain them until that day when they see Jesus face-to-face. Paul's joy was fostered by his knowledge and confidence that God is faithful to bring His redemption to its glorious conclusion.

1:7 *You have a special place in my heart. So it's right for me to think this way about all of you. All of you are my partners. Together we share God's favor, whether I'm in prison or defending and confirming the truth of the Good News.*

Paul was especially fond of the Philippian Christians. They should not be surprised by the way he viewed them. He loved them in the Lord. He shared their joy about the marvelous work of God's grace in them.

So he assured them that it was natural for him to be excited about their spiritual well-being.

Paul considered the Philippians to be bonded with him in a true fellowship both in his suffering and in the service of the Gospel. Because of the union they had in Christ, they shared in the calling of the defense and confirmation of the Gospel. Even though they were not called to apostleship as Paul was, their life as the redeemed children of God provided a viable evidence for the Gospel that was committed to Paul. So Paul rejoiced with the Philippians not only as his spiritual children, but also as fellow laborers for the Gospel. God's all-sufficient grace given to him to persevere in all circumstances for the sake of the Gospel was also given to them.

1:8 *God is my witness that, with all the compassion of Christ Jesus, I long [to see] every one of you.*

Paul truly loved the Philippian Christians. He loved each member individually and as an assembly of the body of Christ. He considered them as his partners both in his suffering and in the service of the Gospel. He had a special place for them in his heart. He missed them. He often longed to see them. Remembering his experience in Philippi while a prisoner in Rome, Paul yearned for the day of his freedom so that he could go and visit them personally. He loved them in the compassion and care of Jesus Christ. He was passionate and caring for their spiritual well being in and through the power of Christ's love. His care for them was more than ordinary human emotional fondness. This was truly a God-given love demonstrating the power and love of Jesus Christ working through him toward the Philippian believers in a practical way.

1:9–10 *[9]I pray that your love will keep on growing because of your knowledge and insight. [10]That way you will be able to*

determine what is best and be pure and blameless until the day of Christ.

Paul's prayer for the Philippians surpassed the expression of his fond love for them. He wanted their love to reach beyond a commonplace conduct of Christian care and compassion toward one another. Paul fervently prayed that the love of the Philippians would also turn into a sincere desire toward gaining godly knowledge and wisdom. He wanted them to be lovers of people and lovers of the truth.

Paul encouraged the Philippians to be more than believing and loving Christians. He prayed that they would gain a viable spiritual maturity. As he did in Ephesians 1:17–18, Paul prayed that the Philippians too would receive wisdom and knowledge, and that the eyes of their understanding would be enlightened by the Holy Spirit toward the things of God and the mystery of His redemption. He wanted the Philippians to be discerning and insightful believers so that they might be able to live for Christ in the power of God's purifying and sanctifying truth. Even though loving and dedicated, Paul recognized that the Philippians and all believers need to realize that their new life in Christ must be nurtured into a life of godly excellence and holiness.

1:11 ***Jesus Christ will fill your lives with everything that God's approval produces. Your lives will then bring glory and praise to God.***

Paul assured the Philippians that their lives will be transformed by the power of their Redeemer in a practical way. Godly excellence, holiness, truth, love, and faith will certainly be cultivated into their new life as the Holy Spirit Himself nurtures their growth with God's eternal truth. The fruit of Christ's righteousness will gradually begin to fill their lives. They will be drawn to the things that please and glorify God. They will ultimately live for the glory and praise of God. As Christ encouraged His disciples, they will deny themselves for Jesus Christ's sake and love Him with all of who they are and what they have.

Notes/Applications

Paul knew that God's wisdom, knowledge, and understanding work effectively in setting the hearts and affections of the redeemed on their heavenly riches in Jesus Christ. So he encouraged the Philippians to be forward looking in their pilgrimage, unequivocally certain that He Who began the good works in them will bring everything to a sure completion. Paul's focus was not just the beginning and the end of the life of the redeemed. The process of their new life in Christ is just as significant as their moment of redemption and ultimate consummation into the glory that God has prepared for them.

The church at Philippi appeared to be structurally quite organized, vibrant, and had the distinguishing marks of an assembly of loving, obedient, and faithful believers. However, even though he dearly loved them and unequivocally commended them for their love and faith, Paul was uncompromising in his assertions that their Christianity is of no heavenly value without the redeeming grace of God the Almighty, the eternal sacrifice of God the Son our Lord Jesus Christ, and the irresistible power of the Convictor and Enabler, God the Holy Spirit. God Himself is the Initiator, Sustainer, and the Finisher of the salvation He extends to the redeemed among the lost according to His sovereign choice and pleasure.

Paul encouraged the Philippians by affirming them in the faithfulness of the God Who inaugurated them into His redemption. He also assured them that their lives would be enriched by the righteousness of Jesus Christ. Their hearts and minds would be transformed by God's wisdom and knowledge, maturing to discerning and insightful disciples of Jesus Christ. In essence, the fruit of the righteousness of Jesus Christ would gradually become the unavoidable reflection of a life over which the Holy Spirit is in charge. The same truth keeps the redeemed looking forward to the undeniable hope of our redemption in Jesus Christ.

God Who initiates His redemption in the saints is completely faithful to finish what He has started. The righteousness of Jesus Christ enriches the lives of all His people. He transforms their hearts and minds with the truth of God's wisdom and knowledge, bringing His people to a maturing faith where they are equipped to discern what is best and pure and blameless until Christ comes again. The fruit of the righteousness of Jesus Christ will gradually become the reflection of a life over which the Holy Spirit is in charge. The same truth keeps the redeemed looking forward to the undeniable hope of their redemption in Jesus Christ.

Philippians 1:12–19

1:12 *I want you to know, brothers and sisters, that what happened to me has helped to spread the Good News.*

Many Bible scholars suggest that Paul sent his letter to the Philippians while he was in prison in Rome. We recall from the book of Acts that Paul was taken to Rome as a prisoner because he appealed the false accusation leveled against him by the Jewish religious authorities in Caesar's court at Rome (Acts 25:9–12; 28:16–17). Even though Paul's words were encouraging, it appears that the Philippians were disheartened by Paul's imprisonment.

Paul was fully aware of their unwillingness to accept God's will and His sovereign authority over everything. Every time his imprisonment is discussed, the Gospel of Jesus Christ remains front and center on the minds of Paul's friends and foes, God's appointed and anointed servant. He wanted them to know beyond the shadow of any doubt or any sense of despair that his situation actually helped the unfettered proclamation of the Gospel of Jesus Christ. They should actually rejoice in how God used Paul to unfold the mystery of His gracious redemption. Paul told them that his imprisonment was not outside of God's will for his life. Instead, it was a God-authored catalyst for the advancement of the Gospel.

1:13 *As a result, it has become clear to all the soldiers who guard the emperor and to everyone else that I am in prison because of Christ.*

The cause for Paul's imprisonment was certainly not a secret. Everyone who heard of Paul realized he was in prison because he preached Jesus Christ. Even the soldiers who protected Caesar knew that Paul suffered for the sake of the Gospel of Jesus Christ. The authorities of the Roman Empire recognized that the Jews leveled false accusations against Paul because they could not tolerate the message of salvation through Jesus Christ. Paul badly wanted the Philippians to understand that his imprisonment and appearance in the courts of the Roman authorities afforded rare opportunities to present the Good News of redemption along with his own personal experience in Christ at places that were ordinarily inaccessible. God takes His servants to places of His choice by means He determines including imprisonment. In Paul's present circumstances, the Good News was presented to the highest authorities in the Roman Empire *(Acts 9:15)*.

1:14 ***So through my being in prison, the Lord has given most of our brothers and sisters confidence to speak God's word more boldly and fearlessly than ever.***

Furthermore, his imprisonment became a source of encouragement to his fellow-believers. They proclaimed the Gospel of Jesus Christ fearlessly. They were no longer intimidated by the possibility of imprisonment or ridicule at the hands of those who opposed the Gospel. Paul told them that his suffering at the hands of the Jews and the Romans had actually helped the Gospel of Jesus Christ to spread into Caesar's household, not only by his situation, but also by the faithful witness of many believers.

1:15–17 ***[15]Some people tell the message about Christ because of their jealousy and envy. Others tell the message about him because of their good will. [16]Those who tell the message about Christ out of love know that God has put me here to defend the Good News. [17]But the others are insincere. They tell the message about Christ out of selfish ambition in order to stir up trouble for me while I'm in prison.***

Paul was absolutely realistic in his assessment of the varied behaviors of those who presented the Gospel. These people did not present God's message from the same outlook. Not everyone presented the Good News with pure motives. Those who were truly redeemed understood by the Spirit of truth the reason for Paul's circumstances. They presented God's Good News of salvation with knowledge and conviction.

Others presented the Gospel only with the intention of undermining Paul's position of apostolic authority. Paul was nevertheless content that his imprisonment brought the Gospel to the forefront of every conversation about him.

Genuine disciples of Jesus Christ love God's truth and often interpret personal situations as indicators of God's will. With love and obedience, they acknowledge God's sovereign authority in everything that happens in their lives. The disciples in Rome at this time spoke of Paul's imprisonment as a worthwhile suffering for the sake of the Gospel of Jesus Christ and continued to proclaim the truth without fear. They recognized that Paul was suffering for the sake of the Gospel because he was appointed by God from his mother's womb to spread the Gospel (*Galatians 1:15–16*). Paul proclaimed and defended its cause even at the cost of his own personal freedom.

Certainly, the enemies of the Gospel had pursued Paul from one end of the empire to the other. They tried to discredit Paul on the basis of the message that he presented and because he welcomed Gentiles into the family of God through Jesus Christ. These people intended to aggravate Paul's alleged criminality. They raised the name of Jesus Christ and His Gospel only as objectionable subjects, which were preached by Paul. Paul's accusers relentlessly tried to aggravate Paul's situation by attempting to raise the level of opposition to Paul's message. They hated both the message and the messenger.

However, we may be shocked by the sad irony implied in Paul's statement recorded in these verses. Paul confessed that he was pleased with the preaching of the Gospel in spite of their motivations. He could not have been happy by such teachings if the presentation was not truthful. Consequently, his affirmation meant that there were some who preached the truth with motivations incited by jealousy. There were some brethren within the body of Christ who preached the Gospel in an attempt to discredit Paul. However, the presentation of the truth of the Gospel was in the hands of God Who directed every aspect of the spread of the Gospel.

1:18–19 ***[18]But what does it matter? Nothing matters except that, in one way or another, people are told the message about Christ, whether with honest or dishonest motives, and I'm happy about that. Yes, I will continue to be happy [19]for another reason. I know that I will be set free through your prayers and through the help that comes from the Spirit of Jesus Christ.***

Paul did not seem to be discouraged by either his imprisonment or the varied motivations for preaching the Gospel. Instead, he openly and boldly declared his joy in spite of his suffering. To him, the only thing that mattered was the unhindered proclamation of the Gospel of Jesus Christ.

Paul was hardly affected by the motivation of those who preached the Gospel. He was not fazed by those whose efforts tried to silence him. On the contrary, he was encouraged by the boldness of the true disciples of Jesus Christ who fearlessly proclaimed the Gospel. He was happy that there was nothing that could restrict the declaration of the Truth. Paul rejoiced that the Good News of God's redemption was proclaimed, transcending personal animosity and ambition.

Paul was confident that he would be freed from prison in God's time. He knew that the prayers offered by fellow-believers on his behalf would be answered. The Holy Spirit would bring about his release. Paul accepted his time in prison as God's will for his life. The Lord used this experience to bring him to Rome to testify about Jesus Christ to Caesar and his household *(Acts 23:11)*. However, the prospect of his release from prison and the return to his apostolic calling was another reason for great joy. For Paul, his greatest happiness came from sharing, preaching, and teaching the Good News of salvation through Jesus Christ.

Notes/Applications

Even though it is perfectly natural to view imprisonment with distaste, Paul tried to correct this perspective. Humanly speaking, arrest and imprisonment is a discouraging and humiliating situation. But for

Paul, his suffering was viewed not as a disappointment but a conviction of God's direction in his life. He told the Philippians that, despite his imprisonment, his continued defense of the Gospel became a source of encouragement to those who loved the truth and spread the Good News of God's redemption. Even his enemies were forced to speak of the Gospel of Jesus Christ because of Paul's indictment as the messenger of a doctrine that contradicted Jewish law as viewed by traditional Judaism *(Acts 18:13)*.

Paul's heart was fully consumed by his love and unreserved commitment to God Who called him to a life of service. Because his heart and attention were firmly fixed on Jesus Christ, Paul was able to behold the magnificent glory of the Lord he was called to serve. Paul discounted the significance of his own suffering for the sake of Jesus Christ. He did not deny the reality of his painful experience. He did not like his present circumstances, but Paul considered his suffering as a gift from God's providence for the sake of the Gospel. He was irresistibly compelled by his consuming love for his Redeemer and considered his circumstances to be the hallmark of God's blessing.

Paul was well aware that new life in Christ was not conferred on him exclusively. Rather, the gift of God's grace and providential direction is also given to all God's redeemed people. This blessing includes the special privilege to suffer for the sake of the Gospel and the Name by which sinners are saved.

Philippians 1:20–26

1:20 *I eagerly expect and hope that I will have nothing to be ashamed of. I will speak very boldly and honor Christ in my body, now as always, whether I live or die.*

Even though the enemies of the Gospel succeeded to imprison Paul by false accusations, he was absolutely sure that he had nothing to be ashamed of. So, he reconfirmed his commitment to continue to honor Jesus Christ in his body. He was not afraid of their threats of physical suffering. He continued to stand firmly in his commitment to Jesus Christ even though he suffered physical hardship for the sake of the Gospel.

Paul informed both friend and foe that his physical confinement actually brought glory to Jesus Christ by lifting the Gospel to a prominent point of public attention. The enemies of the Gospel had hoped to stop the spread of a message that conflicted with their religious sensibilities, but the harder they tried, the more they succeeded in answering Paul's prayer for the message of salvation in Jesus Christ to be proclaimed to all nations. Paul was, therefore, bold, courageous, unashamed, and joyful in all the circumstances by which God used him to fulfill His purpose. He was committed to magnifying the name of the Lord Jesus Christ either by living for Him or by dying for the cause of Christ.

1:21 *Christ means everything to me in this life, and when I die I'll have even more.*

Nothing else mattered to Paul other than Jesus Christ Who called him into the service of the Gospel even before he was born. Once rescued by Jesus Christ's redeeming power, Paul's outlook changed dramatically. He never looked at himself in the same way. Life was no longer about himself and what he wanted, but about Jesus Christ and what the Lord asked him to do. Life itself meant belonging to Christ and doing whatever He asked. During his lifetime, Paul honored his

Lord by dying to himself and living for Christ in total surrender and obedience. When his life on earth ended, he knew he would go to be with Christ his Master and Savior. This was an unprecedented gain. Whether he lived or died, he would always be with Christ. Therefore, Paul lived and served Christ with complete confidence that neither life nor death could ever in any way affect his security in Christ. He lived with the unwavering realization that the Lord who saved, anointed, and appointed him would never forsake him.

1:22–24 ***22If I continue to live in this life, my work will produce more results. I don't know which I would prefer. 23I find it hard to choose between the two. I would like to leave this life and be with Christ. That's by far the better choice. 24But for your sake it's better that I remain in this life.***

Having expressed the essence of his redeemed life in Jesus Christ, Paul seemed untouched by his earthly conditions and circumstances. However, he showed a strong emotional dilemma, caught between his own longing for heaven and God's definite call on his life on earth. He felt hard pressed to choose between the two. He admitted that he was torn between his personal preference and God's will for his life.

Paul knew that this world was not his home. He was well aware that his absence from this world meant a definite, instantaneous presence with the Lord in heaven (*2 Corinthians 5:8*). But he also recognized that God kept him on earth for his continued service to which He had appointed him. He was unapologetic about his earnest desire to leave this world and be with the Lord in his eternal rest. He longed to be free from his suffering and enter into eternal peace with Christ. But he was fully submitted in his loyalty and unreserved obedience to God. He actually acknowledged the necessity of his continued life on earth for as long as God would have him stay for the benefit of the saints whom he served in the Lord's Name.

1:25 *Since I'm convinced of this, I know that I will continue to live and be with all of you. This will help you to grow and be joyful in your faith.*

Strongly declaring his confidence in God's plan and purpose for his life, Paul acknowledged the essential reason for the continuation of his life of service on earth. Even though he wanted to be with the Lord in heaven, he was convinced that the Lord would sustain his life for their sake. Since God appointed him to preach the Gospel to the Gentiles, he would continue to live and serve until God's plan for him and his ministry to the Gentiles was fully accomplished. It was right and necessary for his life to continue until that time when the Lord called him home. He was content to live on in spite of his suffering, simply because his ministry to them would nurture their faith in Christ in a growing and joyful confidence in the Lord.

1:26 *So by coming to you again, I want to give you even more reason to have pride in Christ Jesus with me.*

Besides their joy in Christ and their faith in His Gospel, Paul emphasized that his return to the Philippians would give them more reason to rejoice in what Jesus Christ had done through him. Paul was confident that his life would reflect Christ when they saw him again. They would see that his personal suffering and trial did not in any way extinguish the light of the Gospel from his life. He hoped that his return would encourage their hearts, which questioned Paul's imprisonment. By seeing Christ in him, Paul expected that the Philippians would acknowledge that Paul's misfortune was indeed God's designed plan for affirming the Gospel to men of every walk of life, including Caesar's household.

Notes/Applications

Paul's words of encouragement to the Philippians were far reaching. He commended them for their faith and love toward one another. He also urged them to be filled with godly wisdom, practical knowledge, and sound understanding of the truth. Paul was deeply moved by the maturity of the Philippian believers and wanted them to excel in their understanding of the marvelous ways of the Lord.

The Philippians loved him so much. They were upset because they realized that he was unjustly accused and imprisoned. They felt powerless to do anything to help their beloved teacher. They probably wondered why God would allow such a dedicated servant to be subjected to the malicious schemes of God's enemies. Even though their faith in God was strong, the Philippians were puzzled by Paul's suffering, even more so by his joyful attitude.

By describing his own transformed attitude in light of his suffering, Paul portrayed a victorious life, which reached far beyond his own self-interest. Paul understood that his suffering in the service of the Gospel became a powerful means of proclaiming the Good News of God's salvation in a practical, discernable way. Paul showed that he belonged to God, and he was owned by God. He was God's treasured possession, bought and paid for by the precious blood of Jesus Christ. To be the redeemed child of God also meant to be His selfless servant, joyfully living in the fullness of His providence with a transformed perspective of God's wisdom, knowledge, and understanding. With that understanding, Paul preferred to die and be with His Savior in heaven. But he also understood and gladly accepted imprisonment knowing that God used the resources of the enemy to take him to different places to preach the Gospel and testify about Jesus Christ before his accusers and their authorities. His suffering was a good and necessary hardship, which facilitated the accomplishment of God's will and purpose in and through him. That was not only good, but also the evidence of Paul's self-denial and the Lord's will.

Philippians 1:27–30

1:27 ***Live as citizens who reflect the Good News about Christ. Then, whether I come to see you or whether I stay away, I'll hear all about you. I'll hear that you are firmly united in spirit, united in fighting for the faith that the Good News brings.***

Paul was very cautious in his encouragement to the Philippians. Even though he wanted to return and visit them, he did not want to disappoint them if the Lord prevented him from coming. So Paul encouraged them to direct their attention to Jesus Christ their Savior. He did not want them to prove themselves to him. He wanted them to continue to grow in their understanding of the truth. Then they would conduct themselves as transformed children of God, reflecting the Gospel of Jesus Christ in their lives. He implored them to be rich in God's wisdom and knowledge.

Paul promised the Philippians that, if they continued to grow in faith, the witness of their transformation would be visible to everyone around them. He would hear about it whether or not he visited them. Paul loved the Philippians very much. However, he wanted them to develop a direct and personal relationship with Jesus Christ. He wanted them to mature in their faith in Jesus Christ and be united in Him. Their transformation by the truth of the Gospel would then produce a practical outcome that impacted their fellowship and their community, striving for the faith of the Gospel. Paul wanted them to depend on each other, on the Word, and on the work of the Holy Spirit rather than rely on his continuing influence. Paul's future was uncertain. The Lord's faithfulness was rock solid.

1:28 ***So don't let your opponents intimidate you in any way. This is God's way of showing them that they will be destroyed and that you will be saved.***

Paul hoped that the Philippians would be encouraged by his experience in prison. It was an opportunity to tell the Gospel to Caesar's household. Perhaps in an effort to wean them from their dependence on him, he told them not to be intimidated by their enemies. Those who opposed the Good News might attempt to frighten them by bullying them into submission. They might teach false doctrine, attempting to lead them away from their faith and hope in Jesus Christ. But the saints should not be scared of these people because the ultimate power rests with God Who will never abandon them. Only God has the power to give or take life away.

The saints needed to understand that the hostilities directed at them by the world are unavoidable. The world rejects God's children because they no longer belong to it. Therefore, the world is the enemy of the gospel, fighting the message of Jesus Christ and those who followed Him. The very behavior of these enemies, seen in their pursuit of believers, provided ample evidence that God's people were saved and their enemies were condemned.

1:29 ***God has given you the privilege not only to believe in Christ but also to suffer for him.***

Paul was certainly aware of the difficulty to accept the above doctrine at its face value. He had endured terrible suffering throughout his Christian life. Suffering cannot be ignored. It is very real and has significant consequences. Paul did not want the Philippians to deny the realities of the suffering they faced as God's redeemed children living in the midst of the unsaved world. He wanted their understanding to be guided by God's perspective as reflected in the Gospel of Jesus Christ. That perspective, Paul's perspective, showed that such suffering was a privilege.

God's redemption and His judgment are pre-ordained

determinations established by God according to His sovereign pleasure. When God revealed His sovereign grace and justice in Jesus Christ, he also unveiled His gift of faith and new life. He revealed His power by drawing to Himself those whom He saved by the work of the Holy Spirit. The Philippians should not be discouraged by the prospect of facing the hostilities of the world or surviving in their own strength. Christ had already overcome the world. The faith to believe unto salvation and the ability to endure suffering was given to them by their Father Who planned, purposed, and accomplished their redemption and new life in Christ.

1:30 *You are involved in the same struggle that you saw me having. Now you hear that I'm still involved in it.*

Pointing to his own experience again, Paul encouraged the Philippians to be at peace. He assured them that their suffering would not be so different from his own. Not all Christians would necessarily go to jail for believing in Jesus Christ. But whatever form of suffering they might endure, God's power would be revealed through their experiences in the same way as in his own life. He encouraged them to expect God to give them the power to endure. They could see God's mighty power in his own life as he continued to be a living witness for the Gospel in spite of what was happening to him.

Notes/Applications

Paul's instruction to the Philippians was realistic and practical. Their life as God's redeemed children living in this world is characterized by events and processes authored and executed by God. Believers must realize the following principles put forth in God's Word. First, nothing happens outside of God's will, purpose, and his active sovereign administration. Second, God works through every event and process that affects every person's life.

The world's rebellion against God will be reflected in the way that the unregenerate relate to the people in whom the Holy Spirit has taken up residence. The depraved human spirit of the unregenerate life will always react in opposition to God wherever it encounters the presence of the Holy God. This is why they react with such animosity toward those who have been redeemed. Therefore, believers should not be surprised when they are confronted by the hostile behavior of the enemies of the Gospel. In fact, the redeemed should understand this antagonism as normal and look for God's hand as He accomplishes His will in and through each situation. Then and only then can we truly join Paul as he rejoiced when he suffered for the sake of Christ.

PHILIPPIANS 2

Philippians 2:1–11

2:1–2 ***[1]So then, as Christians, do you have any encouragement? Do you have any comfort from love? Do you have any spiritual relationships? Do you have any sympathy and compassion? [2]Then fill me with joy by having the same attitude and the same love, living in harmony, and keeping one purpose in mind.***

Expanding on the thought he introduced in the previous passage, Paul expressed his desire to visit the Philippians and minister to them face-to-face. He wanted their faith in Jesus Christ to be displayed in their words, deeds, and relationships both individually and collectively. He encouraged them to stand firmly together as people united in mind and spirit—in faith, in suffering, and in the service of the Lord.

The opening words of this chapter reveal Paul's passion for the unity of the Philippian church in their Christian testimony. He probably had some concerns about their commitment to the Gospel. So he asked, "*Do you have any encouragement? Do you have any comfort from love? Do you have any spiritual relationships? Do you have any sympathy and compassion?"* In other words, Paul asked the Philippians if their lives reflected any sign of their faith in Jesus Christ. His question was couched in the context of their reaction to the persecution and struggle they faced as they lived in a hostile world as the followers of Jesus Christ.

This translation uses the phrase *spiritual relationships*. Other translations say: "if any fellowship with the Spirit" *(Philippians 2:1,* NIV*).* It is clear that the thrust of Paul's encouragement is fundamentally built on the witness of the Holy Spirit in the lives of believers. It is the Holy Spirit Who instructs believers in the truth of Jesus Christ *(John 16:13).* It is the Holy Spirit Who produces the fruit of the Spirit in which believers share their lives within their redeemed community *(Galatians 5:22–23).*

Paul was not accusing the Philippians of disharmony in the church as he did in his letter to the Corinthians. However, he insisted that the power of the Gospel of Jesus Christ and His redemption should be displayed in a life of vibrant service. Paul drew their attention to these indicators of Christian witness within their church and their community. If, as the redeemed of God, they affirmed Christ' finished work, then they should be encouraged in spite of the world. If they were filled by the love of Christ, then they should support each other in this same love. If the Holy Spirit lived in them, then they should experience a consecrated relationship in the unity of Jesus Christ. If they were transformed by God's gracious loving-kindness and mercy, then they should treat each other with sympathy and compassion out of a changed heart strengthened by Christian confidence.

With care but firmness, Paul reminded the Philippians that if the above Christian characteristics were evident in their lives, then the fruit of the Gospel and the work of the Holy Spirit would also be seen in their lives. Paul appealed to their transformed conscience, asking them to make him happy and prove him right by the evidence of their life of faith and service. He wanted them to fulfill his joy as their spiritual father, demonstrating their redeemed lives by their unity in the Holy Spirit and the love of Christ. The essence of Paul's appeal asked believers to surrender their own individuality to the unity cultivated by the Holy Spirit Who indwelt them and sealed them as one body until the day of their redemption.

2:3–4 ***[3]Don't act out of selfish ambition or be conceited. Instead, humbly think of others as being better than yourselves. [4]Don't be concerned only about your own interests, but also be concerned about the interests of others.***

The change cultivated in the sinner's heart by God's redemption does not exclude believers' earthly lives until the time they leave this world. Christians are indwelt by the Holy Spirit Who is greater and stronger than the collective strength of all the forces of evil. They are strongly urged to emulate the person and character of Jesus Christ Who, by the Spirit, lives His life in the hearts and minds of God's elect. To show the world that they belong to the Lord, Paul urges the saints to live with humility, selflessness, and service to others.

Redeemed by the same Lord, chosen by the same Father, and sealed by the same Spirit, God's saints are instructed and empowered to serve God in a way that elevates the importance of others and reduces the importance of self. Instead of self-seeking motives, those who have tasted the love of God should consider the needs and interests of others as the substance of their service. Instead of poisoning their relationships with an arrogant attitude, they should think of others as better than themselves and treat them with respect and compassion. Instead of acting with a belligerent, contentious attitude, those who are washed in the blood of the Lamb of God should be humble and generous in their relationships. The essence of Paul's instruction urges believers to be united in the expression of their faith in Jesus Christ, showing their love and obedience to Him through an observable character and way of life.

2:5 *Have the same attitude that Christ Jesus had.*

Paul was well aware that his encouragement could not be followed merely by human effort. He promptly pointed to Jesus Christ Who is the example for all believers. Jesus Christ is the model for the Christian's life. Those who place their faith in Him can learn His ways by studying His life as recorded in the Scriptures. Even though all power and authority belongs to Him, Jesus Christ was unreservedly obedient to His Father. He came to serve and not to be served. He was compassionate and encouraging in His ministry. He was never conceited or self-seeking. He said that His work was to do His Father's will. Such an attitude of life and service was what Paul wanted the Philippians to understand. He wanted them to conduct themselves the way Jesus Christ did.

It is obvious that there is only one Savior. His name is Jesus. Jesus is the One Who died for the sins of the world. There is no other name under heaven by which people can be saved *(Acts 4:12)*. Nevertheless, Paul has asked believers to follow Christ's example. It is certain that no one can be like Christ in this way. But one thing they can and should do—they should serve one another as Christ has served them. One of the most memorable narratives in the gospels is the description of Jesus, removing His clothes, wrapping a towel around Himself, kneeling at the feet of His disciples, and washing their feet *(John 13:1–14)*. *"If I then, your Lord and Teacher, have washed your feet, you also ought to wash one another's feet"* *(John 13:14)*. Paul is saying that Jesus followers should do no less.

2:6 *Although he was in the form of God and equal with God, he did not take advantage of this equality.*

Even though Jesus Christ is God the Son, He did not use His deity to avoid His mission as the Lamb of God. He did not take advantage of His sameness with God to question His appointment to be clothed in flesh and live among sinful men *(John 1:14)*. He did not turn away from serving His Father in unreserved love and absolute obedience in a lesser position as a human being.

2:7 ***Instead, he emptied himself by taking on the form of a servant, by becoming like other humans, by having a human appearance.***

Jesus Christ left the splendor of heaven and came to earth to serve His Father's will as a human being. He emptied Himself of His rightful position as God and became flesh, dwelling among men, fulfilling righteousness, and satisfying the requirements of the Law. Jesus Christ the Master became servant. Jesus Christ, the eternal, transcendent God, took on the form and appearance of men. Jesus Christ, the Creator, was born of a human mother whom He created. He Who is the Master submitted Himself to a position of servitude in order to fulfill the will of His Father.

2:8 ***He humbled himself by becoming obedient to the point of death, death on a cross.***

Jesus' humbleness was not simply an aspect of His demeanor. Rather, His humbleness was the expression of the Lord's willingness to leave heaven and come to earth for the sake of lost sinners. His obedience was not reflected by the tasks He performed—His miracles or His teachings. Rather, Jesus' obedience was absolute and unrestrained. It is measured by the extent to which He was obedient to His Father, even to His death on the Cross.

Jesus' death at Golgotha was not the ordinary end of a human life. Rather, it was the sacrifice for sin by the One Who did not sin. It was an undeserved death, but one which was accepted willingly and obediently. In His obedience to His Father's will, Jesus submitted Himself to the full force of God's wrath, accepting the punishment that men deserved. It was the most extreme form of humbleness and obedience in which the guiltless was treated as guilty in order that the guilty might be made free from guilt.

2:9–11 ***9This is why God has given him an exceptional honor— the name honored above all other names— 10so that***

at the name of Jesus everyone in heaven, on earth, and in the world below will kneel [11]and confess that Jesus Christ is Lord to the glory of God the Father.

God the Father openly declared that Jesus Christ is His Son in Whom He is pleased. John the Baptizer as well as Peter, John, and James were privileged to witness this divine declaration (*Matthew 3:17; Matthew 17:5*). The Father is pleased with the Son because the Son lived on earth as the only human being who lived a perfectly righteous life without sin. The Father was pleased because Jesus Christ obeyed His Father's will to the bitter end.

The Father exalted His Son above everything in heaven and on earth. He gave Him the Name, which is exalted above all names. Even though Jesus Christ is God, the Father gave the man, Jesus Christ, the name that is revered throughout His creation. Redeemed or condemned, everyone will recognize and confess the power and glory that is inherent in the Name Jesus Christ. Everyone will acknowledge His majesty and bow down before His authority, glory, and power. While the redeemed will rejoice in His presence and worship the Lord of lords, the condemned will bow down at this holy Name in awesome fear and trembling.

Notes/Applications

In his exposition of the idea of Christian unity he originally introduced in 1:27, Paul explained the practical manifestations of a life transformed by the sanctifying work of the Holy Spirit. Paul's explanation demonstrated a Christian conduct dramatically different from the ways of a world filled with competing individuals who advance their interests at the expense of others. The essence of Paul's teaching reveals the transforming work of the Holy Spirit Who cultivates Christ-like traits in the conduct of God's redeemed people.

Paul encourages the saints to live in the world, but not like unsaved people. They are to be a community of like-minded believers following Christ's example of service to others. Paul is not suggesting that

Christians should isolate themselves. Instead, he encourages believers to live in the world as members of the body of Christ, governed and directed by the Spirit. While Christians are citizens of this world and members of their individual communities, they should reflect those characteristics that express their identities as the followers of Jesus Christ by the way they relate to each other.

Unlike the fierce, self-serving competitiveness of unbelievers, the followers of Christ should exhibit the person and character of Jesus Christ. Like the Lord Himself, the redeemed should be humble, loving, kind, encouraging, sacrificial, caring, comforting, nurturing, and selfless. They should be likeminded in thought, word, and deed as Jesus Christ lives His life through them by the work of the Holy Spirit.

Following the example set by Jesus Christ, Paul urges the redeemed to submit to the work of the Holy Spirit. Jesus told His disciples that the Holy Spirit testifies about Him and will show them the truth about their sin and Christ's righteousness. By submitting ourselves to the leading and authority of the Holy Spirit, we will become less self-centered and more committed to the service of others.

Paul has been consistent about the unity of believers through a meaningful, practical Christian fellowship under the direction and teaching of the Holy Spirit. His letters to the Christians in Rome, Corinth, Ephesus, and Colossae echo the same instruction, encouraging the redeemed to share their redeemed lives with each other. Together they are the witness of the Gospel of Jesus Christ. Paul is not interested in advocating a social structure constructed in some sort of "Christian society" that excludes the rest of the world. Instead, he firmly tells the redeemed to reflect the evidence of God's reconciliation through words and actions, which exhibit the virtues and character of their Redeemer. Exhibiting the truth of the Gospel in attitude and conduct, they demonstrate that the real essence of Christianity is the unity of the redeemed community, living in Christ-like service to one another.

Philippians 2:12–18

2:12 ***My dear friends, you have always obeyed, not only when I was with you but even more now that I'm absent. In the same way continue to work out your salvation with fear and trembling.***

Paul's teaching about unity in the faith was based on a firm belief that the Gospel of Jesus Christ was of supreme importance to them. He expressed his confidence in their commitment to obedience both in his presence and his absence. Their redemption in Jesus Christ was not a temporary impulse based on unrestrained emotion. Paul knew very well that the outcome of his instruction was not the result of his efforts on behalf of the Gospel or a commendable attitude on the part of the saints in Philippi.

Even though he was aware of the difficulties associated with living for Christ in a world hostile to the Gospel, Paul nevertheless encouraged the saints to stay the course and work out their salvation in fear and trembling. He encouraged them to continue living in obedience as they had in the past. In this way their lives became the expression of their new life in Christ. They should continue to build on the faith that had been given to them, walking in humility among the saints and wisely among unsaved people. These relationships were the hallmark of the redeemed by which they worked out their salvation, always conscious of God Who saved them through the Lord Jesus Christ Who shed His blood for their redemption.

***DIG DEEPER**: FEAR AND TREMBLING*

Fear is a fundamental aspect of true worship. The fear of the Lord is the beginning of wisdom (*Psalm 111:10; Proverbs 1:7*). Many Christians would question this idea. Does not Christ's sacrifice reconcile the redeemed to their Creator? Does not Jesus call His disciples friends? This is absolutely true! But Paul is teaching Christ's Church that they should not look at their salvation only from the perspective of the benefits they receive. Rather, they should also see the holiness of the Lord God Who did not spare His Son, Jesus. He abandoned His Son on the cross to pay the penalty for man's sin. The depth and height of the Lord's grace is beyond human comprehension. But His judgment on those who refuse His grace is also severe and frightening. Even though saved by God's grace, those who are called by His Name should also see the glory of the Lord, and seeing His majesty and power, bow their faces to the ground in fear and trembling. God's people should never embrace the benefits of His salvation in such a way that they cannot see the One Who has saved them. It is the Lord Jesus Christ Who is to be worshiped, not the benefits of salvation.

[13]*After having heard it all, this is the conclusion: Fear God, and keep his commands, because this applies to everyone.* [14]*God will certainly judge everything that is done. This includes every secret thing, whether it is good or bad"* (Ecclesiastes 12:13–14).

2:13 *It is God who produces in you the desires and actions that please him.*

Paul reminded the saints that God was the One Who produced the actions that bring glory to His Name. Believers should not feel that the demands on their lives as Christians were burdensome. Paul knew that the Christian attributes listed above did not come out of the sinful motives of an unregenerate heart. He also knew that the same sinful traits continued to harass the heart of the redeemed person who was only too familiar with his human nature.

In light of their sinful tendencies, Paul promptly assured the Philippians that God stirred the heart of His redeemed children to obedience. The same God Who saves sinners by His grace also provides the desires and actions that please Him. The same Jesus Christ Who shed His blood for the remission of their sin also lives out His person and character through those whom He has redeemed. The same Holy Spirit Who brings sinners from death to life also nurtures them as they grow in faith in Christ. The Lord Himself produces the saint who is wise and knowledgeable in matters of faith, obedience, unity, like-mindedness, humbleness, compassion, respect, and the fear of God. Only the Lord can convince a redeemed sinner of the infinite worth and significance of His salvation.

2:14 ***Do everything without complaining or arguing.***

Paul had already complimented the Philippians for their faithfulness and obedience. But he also knew that the ongoing work of the Holy Spirit would continue to increase their faith as they worked out their salvation in fear and trembling. So, he urged them to obey God and observe His Word without complaint or argument. The saints should be prepared to face life's challenges without disputing or murmuring. They should not allow their human attitudes to influence God's work negatively. They should not be suspicious when their experiences appeared to be unusual. They should not question when confronted by their weakness in responding to life's circumstances. Instead, they should do everything for the sake of their Lord, recognizing that God Himself produces the will to do what He has determined.

2:15–16 ***15Then you will be blameless and innocent. You will be God's children without any faults among people who are crooked and corrupt. You will shine like stars among them in the world 16as you hold firmly to the word of life. Then I can***

brag on the day of Christ that my effort was not wasted and that my work produced results.

In counseling the Philippians to take God at His Word without complaint and argument, Paul was teaching them to trust God and press onward by faith as they faced the challenging circumstances of their pilgrimage. This trust will put their spirits at ease and cultivate confidence in their hearts, teaching them to believe, trust, and obey.

Nothing can turn them away from trusting God and obeying His Word. No foe can defeat their faith in the Lord, because God Himself has molded their hearts to do His will. For this reason, they will be blameless and innocent. The righteousness of Jesus Christ is always working in them. For this reason, the redeemed will stand without blame before God in plain view of a world of crooked and perverse people. Their witness of God's faithfulness can never be hidden, because the light of the Gospel will shine through their godly character and quiet strength.

By becoming one in their faith in Jesus Christ and by conducting themselves with quiet confidence in everything they do, believers will present a powerful witness for the Gospel of Jesus Christ. They will exhibit the person and character of their Savior in the practical circumstances of their lives to believers and non-believers alike. Their witness will shine like the stars for everyone to observe. The truth of the Gospel of Jesus Christ will be displayed in real ways. Then, Paul had a real reason to rejoice in God's work through His ministry. His labor would not be in vain. His imprisonment for the sake of the Gospel would be worth his suffering for the cause of God's eternal truth. His joy would be fulfilled as he was blessed to see the fruit of his labor in the lives of those whom he served as the messenger of the Gospel.

2:17 ***My life is being poured out as a part of the sacrifice and service [I offer to God] for your faith. Yet, I am filled with joy, and I share that joy with all of you.***

Paul frankly assessed the hardship he was suffering for the sake of the Gospel. He realized that his life could possibly end in the near future. Yet he was not really concerned about his personal safety. Rather, he accepted God's will in this situation. If he died, he considered everything that happened as a sacrifice and service to his Lord on behalf of the faith that he saw in the Philippian Christians. Because of his appointment by Jesus Christ to this ministry, the Lord had instilled His redemption in the hearts of these dear friends.

Actually, Paul's life was no longer his own. Jesus Christ Himself had confronted Paul on the road to Damascus and appointed him to this ministry. He now belonged to the Lord. Thereafter, the Lord used him to present the message of Christ's salvation throughout the Roman world. After he presented the Gospel, Paul continued to teach, encourage, and strengthen those who came to Christ. In spite of the hardship he faced, Paul's heart was filled with joy because of the impact of his service to God upon those who heard his preaching and received the Lord's salvation. His service to them was actually his offering to God. In spite of the persecution he faced, he was overjoyed that his sacrifice was nurturing their faith. He rejoiced in what God did for the Philippians through his ministry and happily shared his joy with them.

2:18 ***For this same reason you also should be filled with joy and share that joy with me.***

Paul invited the Philippians to join him in the joy of the Lord, happy that God redeemed them through the preaching of the Gospel. There was ample reason to rejoice and share that joy because of the redeeming truth of the Gospel. Indwelt by the Holy Spirit, their sense of joy and assurance was easily shared although many miles separated them.

Paul and the Philippians rejoiced in the unity of their faith as members of the Body of Christ.

Notes/Applications

Viewed from the human perspective, Paul's teaching could easily be mistaken as unprofitable advice. People, even God's redeemed people, do not readily give up their personal desires. Nevertheless, Paul asks Christians to be like their Lord by suppressing their selfish desires and, instead, serve others. However, Paul knew that a selfish life influenced by incurable skepticism, belligerence, and resistance to the Lord's authority could effectively undermine the quality of a life surrendered to the Lord. So, he urged Christians to trust God's direction in their lives and live as His children without complaint or argument. They should understand and trust the Lord Who saves them. He will also bring them safely through the experiences He ordains to that moment when they see Him face-to-face.

Paul's commendation of the Philippians' obedience was not empty praise. Rather, the Philippians expressed their obedience in lives that were fully surrendered to God. So he invited them to rejoice with him in his suffering because it served the advancement of the Gospel. He encouraged them to experience life as the expression of God's work in their changed life. He encouraged them to live in the fear of God, recognizing that the Holy Spirit alone was the Helper and Teacher Who constrained their conduct, decisions, and actions in everything they did. The Spirit empowers and encourages the redeemed to express their salvation through changed lives that manifest God's redemption through a life of obedience. The same applies to everyone who has been redeemed through Christ by God's saving grace.

Philippians 2:19–24

2:19–20 ***[19]I hope that the Lord Jesus will allow me to send Timothy to you soon so that I can receive some encouraging news about you. [20]I don't have anyone else like Timothy. He takes a genuine interest in your welfare.***

Even though his suffering was hard and seemed to be undeserved, Paul accepted his circumstances as his God-appointed life of service. His suffering for the ministry was an integral part of his appointment to ministry *(Acts 9:16)*. Instead of becoming bitter toward God, he rejoiced in his suffering for Christ. He was happy that God used his suffering to enrich the life of his children in the Gospel.

More surprising is Paul's attitude in all this. Instead of abandoning all hope of getting out of prison, Paul was actually making plans to visit the Philippians. He personally wanted to witness the continuing growth in their commitment to the Gospel. He was so anxious to hear from them that he promised to send Timothy because he could not wait for his freedom from Roman bonds. His spirit would be lifted up in spite of his circumstances. Paul was not naïve about the future. He told the Philippians that he hoped to send Timothy to them if the Lord Jesus Christ would allow him to do so.

Paul chose Timothy to be his emissary to the Philippians. Paul loved Timothy and considered him to be his spiritual son in the Lord *(1 Corinthians 4:17; 1 Timothy 1:2)*. Paul met Timothy in Lystra during his first missionary journey a.d. 49–50 *(Acts 16:2)*. Timothy was the son of a Jewish mother and a Greek father. His mother Eunice and grandmother Lois taught Timothy the Scriptures, even though he was raised in a Greek household *(2 Timothy 1:5)*. Timothy and his mother were both Christians when Paul met them *(Acts 16:1)*.

Paul considered Timothy the most suitable emissary to go to the Philippians. His life exhibited exactly what Paul taught. Timothy shared Paul's love and concern for the saints in Philippi. He was also deeply committed to the Gospel. Timothy was genuinely interested in their welfare and unmatched in his trustworthiness.

2:21–22 [21]*Everyone else looks after his own interests, not after those of Jesus Christ.* [22]*But you know what kind of person Timothy proved to be. Like a father and son we worked hard together to spread the Good News.*

Paul compared Timothy to others who were self-serving in their ministries. Some were unwilling to be completely committed to the proclamation of the Gospel. These people were more interested in their own welfare instead of working selflessly for the benefit of others. In Paul's view, many of his fellow servants were more interested in avoiding persecution even at the risk of compromising the Name of Jesus Christ.

On the other hand, Timothy was completely dependable because he was not self-absorbed. Like Paul, his spiritual father, Timothy understood that God had absolute claim on his life. Because Timothy was completely dedicated to the Gospel, it was an easy decision for Paul to appoint him as his messenger to Philippi.

The Christians in Philippi knew Timothy as well as they knew Paul. Timothy accompanied Paul when he first crossed the Aegean Sea from Asia Minor to Europe. He worked side by side with Paul as they taught both Jews and Gentiles about salvation through Jesus Christ. Timothy's character and commitment were evident by the way he served God alongside Paul, his spiritual father. His life and service to the Lord was an open book.

Timothy faithfully served God with Paul, undeterred by their drastically changing circumstances. He experienced the hostilities from both the world and the Judaizers. Timothy was a tried and true soldier of the Gospel, tested by the circumstances which befell the servants of Jesus Christ. Both Paul and Timothy were united in a common goal. As spiritual father and son, they lived to proclaim the Gospel and nurture those whom the Lord saved. Paul was confident that Timothy would faithfully serve the Lord as his emissary to the Philippian church.

2:23–24 ***23I hope to send him as soon as I see how things are going to turn out for me. 24But the Lord gives me confidence that I will come [to visit you] soon.***

Paul promised to send Timothy to the Philippians regardless of his future circumstances. As soon as God's will about Paul's future was revealed, whether he was acquitted or sentenced, he had already decided to send Timothy to them. Nevertheless, Paul was reasonably sure that the Lord would give him the opportunity of visiting with his spiritual children.

Notes/Applications

A quick reading of Paul's thoughts in the preceding passage might lead the reader to think that Paul contradicted himself. But a thorough study under the guidance of the Holy Spirit reveals a profound revelation of God's truth. In this chapter, Paul urges the Philippians to be like Christ in person and character. Then, he introduces them to the humble and obedient Lamb of God and the glorious Lord and King. This is not a contradiction, but the clear expression of the work of Jesus Christ Who is both the Lamb of God and the glorious King. When He came to earth His sole purpose was to die as the sacrifice for sin. When he finished His task on earth, He returned to heaven where He is seated at the right hand of the Almighty Lord God.

After telling them about the transforming power of the Spirit's sanctifying work, Paul invites the Philippians to join him in rejoicing over his suffering for the sake of Jesus Christ and His message of salvation. At one point, Paul seems to have given up any hope of getting out of prison *(17–18)*. He was prepared to die and be with his Lord. He seems eager to do this.

Later, Paul expresses his confidence that the Lord was going to release him from prison so he could visit the Philippian Christians.

He longed to see them. Was Paul confused as he expressed his acceptance of God's will no matter if he lived or died? Most certainly not. Paul was actually expressing the depth of his faith, confidence, and enduring hope in God's will in both life and death. Paul simply placed his total confidence in God's will and surrendered his personal hopes to his Lord and Savior. In one sweeping conviction of faith and hope Paul taught the saints of God to deny themselves and live for Christ. Depend on Christ, Who holds the future.

Absolutely surrendered yet confident in faith and hope, Paul lived a life of obedience and courage with an attitude of peaceful acceptance of God's will and bold anticipation of the future. James the apostle, a fellow pillar of faith, said: "Instead, you ought to say, 'If it is the Lord's will, we will live and do this or that'" *(James 4:15)*. Like James, Paul effectively said: "If the Lord wills, I am prepared to die and still expect to visit my children in the Lord. Or, if the Lord wills, I am anxious to go to Philippi, but I am still prepared to be killed for the Gospel."

Such a life of surrender and confidence is given to all who confess Jesus Christ as Lord and Savior. Such a life of faith, confidence, and enduring hope is bestowed upon those who look to God for strength and perseverance. With absolute assurance, God's people can say with Paul: For me to live is Christ, and to die is gain *(1:21)*.

Philippians 2:25–30

2:25 *I feel that I must send Epaphroditus—my brother, coworker, and fellow soldier—back to you. You sent him as your personal representative to help me in my need.*

Paul planned to send Timothy to Philippi and hoped to be set free so he could visit his children in the Lord. Paul now told them that he also planned to send Epaphroditus back to his home in Philippi. Epaphroditus came to Paul as the personal representative of the Philippian church to assist Paul while he was still imprisoned by the Roman authorities. Paul fondly referred to Epaphroditus as a brother in the Lord, a co-worker in the advancement of the Gospel, and a fellow soldier in Christ. Paul received Epaphroditus gladly, happy for his help and encouragement. He was grateful for the financial support of the Philippian church. Now Paul was going to send him back to Philippi even though he personally wanted to keep him around for the foreseeable future.

2:26 *He has been longing to see all of you and is troubled because you heard that he was sick.*

Paul also understood that Epaphroditus was concerned for his fellow compatriots in Philippi. He longed to return home and see his brothers and sisters in Christ. He knew that they were troubled by the news of his sickness. He was so eager to return home in good health and assure them about his own welfare.

Both the Philippians and Epaphroditus cared deeply about each other instead of being concerned about their own conditions. Epaphroditus was upset over the concern expressed by the Philippians. The Philippians wondered if they would ever see their brother again. Paul recognized the selfless love between Epaphroditus and the Philippians and decided to nurture their relationship further by sending Epaphroditus home at the earliest convenient time.

2:27 ***Indeed, he was so sick that he almost died. But God had mercy not only on him but also on me and kept me from having one sorrow on top of another.***

Paul was forthcoming as he candidly told the Philippians about Epaphroditus' health. He informed them that Epaphroditus had almost died. Paul honestly expressed his emotional distress because of the perilous condition, which befell Epaphroditus. Perhaps, Paul may have felt guilty because Epaphroditus may have endangered his health as he sacrificially took care of Paul.

Nevertheless, Paul was comforted by the mercies of God Who restored Epaphroditus' health. From Paul's point of view, Epaphroditus' healing was nothing less than a miracle, a gift of divine mercy for undeserving mortals. Paul considered Epaphroditus' healing as God's providence that kept him from unspeakable sorrow.

2:28 ***So I'm especially eager to send him to you. In this way you will have the joy of seeing him again and I will feel relieved.***

Even though Paul was fond of Epaphroditus and would have preferred to keep him, he was eager to share his joy with the saints in Philippi. He was anxious to send Epaphroditus back home so they could see him and rejoice in his good health. In his God-instilled selfless love, Paul was more than happy to give up Epaphroditus' help and companionship so that they could rejoice in their reunion.

2:29–30 ***[29]Give him a joyful Christian welcome. Make sure you honor people like Epaphroditus highly. [30]He risked his life and almost died for the work of Christ in order to make up for the help you couldn't give me.***

Paul instructed the Philippians to receive Epaphroditus with a warm welcome. Paul did not want the Philippians to misunderstand God's blessing. He urged them to look beyond the obvious and discern the mighty revelation of God's power through Epaphroditus' experience.

Paul explained how Epaphroditus endangered his health for the sake of the Gospel. He was very helpful to Paul even at the expense of his own health in ways that the Philippians could not understand. Epaphroditus was helping him personally while the Philippian saints were too far away to offer anything more than their prayers. Paul urged the Philippians to hold Epaphroditus and others like him in high esteem because Epaphroditus represented the Philippians well both in his ministry and companionship to Paul. Paul reminded the Philippians that it was important to recognize Epaphroditus' selfless service both in representing them and in serving Jesus Christ on their behalf.

Notes/Applications

This passage holds a unique, personal lesson to all the saints of Christ. Paul praised Epaphroditus and urged the Philippians to hold him in high esteem because of his selfless service and for the manner in which he represented them in Paul's ministry. Paul reminded the Philippians to be consciously aware that Epaphroditus was not only their messenger, but also selfless in his representation of the Philippians who sent him to minister to Paul on their behalf. He represented them so well that his service to Paul's personal needs made it seem that his friends were with him in the Roman prison.

Epaphroditus effectively exhibited a wonderful attitude of obedience and selflessness. Paul commended such spiritual excellence and celebrated it as the fruit of God's salvation at work in the changed life of this selfless servant of the Lord. He wanted the Philippians to pay tribute to Epaphroditus for his selfless and diligent service. Paul wanted the saints to see Jesus Christ's humbleness and obedience at work in the life and service of their messenger and brother in Christ. In truth, they should hold the image and glory of Christ living in him in high esteem.

There is an important lesson for believers in this passage. More often than not, any hint of excellence in the life and service of God's children is ridiculed as arrogance or conceit, which must be resisted at all cost. Rather, believers should discern the truth instead of smothering the witness of Jesus Christ and the power of the Gospel with jealous criticism. The saints of God instructed to acknowledge the presence of God in the life and service of those who serve God as obedient bondservants of the Gospel.

While God's people cannot and should not deny the reality about the sinful ego, they should understand that the life of the redeemed is a work in progress and the outworking of Christ's person and character. Along with His grace, mercy, and power, God has given His children the capacity to discern the truth, all the more making Paul's instruction a very significant admonition to observe. Ultimately, believers are encouraged to worship God by expressing their gratitude for the selfless dedication observed in the lives of the servants of the Gospel.

PHILIPPIANS 3

Philippians 3:1–11

3:1 ***Now then, brothers and sisters, be joyful in the Lord. It's no trouble for me to write the same things to you, and it's for your safety.***

Paul's instruction to the Philippians featured two basic aspects. He used both encouragement and warning as he continued to strengthen the faith of the saints. He commended them for their faithfulness while warning them about the enemies of the Gospel around them. Using both commendation and warning, he encouraged them to be joyful in the Lord Jesus Christ in spite of the hostilities they continued to face. He urged them to have confidence in Jesus Christ and, therefore, to persevere no matter what the circumstances.

Paul was probably referring to the more general warning he gave earlier. He encouraged them to stand firmly against the adversaries of the Gospel. He also strongly urged them to recognize these hostilities as the natural result of an unregenerate heart. He encouraged them to rejoice in the Lord while being aware of the animosity directed toward them by the enemies of the Gospel. They should be joyful, not because of the hostilities they are facing but in spite of it, recognizing that Jesus Christ had overcome these evil forces and the enemies of the Gospel *(John 16:33)*.

3:2 *Beware of dogs! Beware of those who do evil things. Beware of those who insist on circumcision.*

Paul had already issued warnings to the Philippians about the hostilities waged against them by the enemies of the Gospel. Now, however, his warnings were deliberate and unambiguous. He specifically called their attention to those who insist on circumcision as a necessary component to ensure salvation. He referred to such rabble-rousers as "dogs" and "those who do evil things." The term *dogs* is the same derogatory designation with which the Jews labeled the Gentiles. This derogatory connotation was voiced often by the Jews of the first century. Paul warned the Philippians to beware of those who refused to accept the Good News of God's redemption through Jesus Christ.

Paul turned the tables on these people and identified the Judaizers as the ones who were truly evil. In truth, they were the "dogs and evildoers." These "dogs and evildoers" relentlessly tried to mislead the redeemed and draw them back into bondage by insisting that circumcision was necessary to complete their salvation *(Acts 15:1)*. Here the issue was not so much that the Judaizers required circumcision for salvation, but that they viewed earthly rituals of sinful men as something necessary to validate God's grace in Jesus Christ. Such false teachers were indeed evil, unclean, and unrighteous. They spent all their waking energy to relegate God's sovereign work of divine grace to the province of human rituals and man's validating consent. The Philippian believers needed to discern the true identity of the Judaizers and be aware of their false message and godless endeavors.

3:3 ***We are the [true] circumcised people [of God] because we serve God's Spirit and take pride in Christ Jesus. We don't place any confidence in physical things,***

As a matter of principle, Paul did not summarily dismiss the concept of circumcision. The believers needed to understand the truth about circumcision. He explained clearly that true circumcision is spiritual in nature and takes effect only in the heart of a regenerated spirit.

True circumcision happens in the heart of God's children as the Holy Spirit cuts away the old sin nature through regeneration. This is not a physical act, but a spiritual action performed by Christ Himself *(Colossians 2:11)*. Christ completely cuts away the sin nature, disconnecting those He saves from their old nature and replacing it with a new nature *(2 Corinthians 5:17)*. As God's redeemed children, believers should recognize the spiritual circumcision of God's redeeming work in their own hearts. As the children of the Lord's circumcision of God's redemption, they know the truth and remain unimpressed by the demanding rigors of compliance to physical rituals. They recognize the fruitlessness of outward appearances and useless practices. They take confidence in Jesus Christ, refreshed by the cleansing work of the Holy Spirit, and reject the dead works of the flesh. By recognizing the true meaning of spiritual circumcision and understanding its far-reaching implications, the redeemed should understand the emptiness of outward rituals and courageously resist any demand for compliance to human religious practices by firmly standing on the truth.

It is abundantly clear that believers remain anchored only too closely to their sin nature. Why is the evidence of earthly passions still so prevalent in God's redeemed people? It should be understood that the Holy Spirit effectively applies the sacrifice of Christ's blood to the heart of those He saves. The act of spiritual circumcision by Jesus Christ removes the guilt of sin, the consequences of sin, and the penalty of sin from the heart. Thereafter, the believer lives in the constant tension between the old sin nature and his God-given redeemed nature. At the moment of death, the believer then becomes in fact what spiritual circumcision accomplished at the time of regeneration. *"And the Lord your God will circumcise your heart and the heart of your offspring, so that you will love the Lord your God with all your heart and with all your soul, that you may live" (Deuteronomy 30:6).*

3:4 *although I could have confidence in my physical qualifications. If anyone else thinks that he can trust in something physical, I can claim even more.*

Even though Paul possessed the physical qualifications that met the criteria the Judaizers demanded, he selflessly rejected the idea that these qualification had any effect on his salvation. He had been set free by the Christ's redemption. It was in this context that Paul appealed to his own background, which was the same as the Judaizers. He knew the entire structure of their religious traditions from his personal experience. Thus, he was well qualified to unmask the well-disguised denial of the true Gospel of Jesus Christ by these religious zealots.

Paul knew what he was talking about. He was a prominent Pharisee, the leading Judaizer, until he was rescued by God's irresistible grace. He was a zealous defender of the law and tradition until he was brought to his knees by the blinding light of Christ's overpowering glory. Fully aware of his lifelong experience and by the inspiration he received from God, Paul assured the Philippians that he was well qualified to expose the dead promises inherent in the physical observance of the law and to affirm the truth of salvation in Jesus Christ alone.

3:5 *I was circumcised on the eighth day. I'm a descendant of Israel. I'm from the tribe of Benjamin. I'm a pure-blooded Hebrew. When it comes to living up to standards, I was a Pharisee.*

The religious practice of the Judaizers was based on the observance of the Law. From a purely human point of view, Paul here shows how he uniquely meets all of their criteria. For the benefit of the Philippians and in a direct confrontation of the Judaizers, Paul told them about his heritage and religious zeal. He was born of Jewish parents whose lineage could be traced back directly to Benjamin, Jacob, Isaac, and even to Abraham, the patriarch himself. He was a "pure-blooded" Hebrew born to Hebrew parents. He was from the warrior stock of Benjamin, one of the two tribes which committed itself to defending and preserving the Jewish heritage. He kept the law from infancy. He was circumcised on the eighth day. He zealously observed the rabbinical law and jealously defended its precepts. He was a high-minded and self-righteous Pharisee who believed in persistently fulfilling the demands of the rabbinical law in order to earn his reward and qualify for a spot in heaven. He surpassed all of his compatriots in his compliance to the rabbinical law and in his knowledge of the Hebrew Scriptures and Jewish tradition.

3:6 *When it comes to being enthusiastic, I was a persecutor of the church. When it comes to winning God's approval by keeping Jewish laws, I was perfect.*

Paul carefully explained that he was consciously, willingly, and aggressively Jewish in everything he did. He zealously defended everything Jewish. He persecuted everyone who did not follow Jewish teachings. He also persecuted the disciples of Jesus Christ because they taught a Gospel that was different from Judaic traditions.

Paul honestly believed that he possessed God's truth and was, therefore, uncompromising in his zeal to defend Judaism. He was relentless in his self-discipline. He faithfully observed the tenets of Judaism that he taught and enforced. By his own admission, Paul was enthusiastically brutal against everyone who did not observe Judaic precepts. He subjected himself to the rigors of perfect compliance to the Law, convinced that he was earning God's approval. Paul was more than enthusiastic in his zeal as a leader of the Jews. The Judaizers could not claim any superiority over Paul's Judaic qualifications. He lived it and defended it zealously with a burning passion, which surpassed the fervor of his Jewish opponents.

3:7 *These things that I once considered valuable, I now consider worthless for Christ.*

Paul willingly discarded all his earthly qualifications that he formerly cherished. Before he was saved, he took great pride in his love of his Jewish traditions. His reason for rejecting these traditions did not come from a deterioration of his commitment to them. Instead, his conviction stemmed from the profound change that occurred in his life. In light of his relationship with Christ, his Savior, their value vanished. Everything he previously valued became worthless, because his new life in Christ did not depend on human accolades. What he thought to be a valued service to God became the glaring evidence of his sin and bondage. Now redeemed, everything that had been so important to him became trivial when compared to his new life in Jesus Christ. In comparison to what he had gained in Christ, everything he once treasured now seemed like garbage and rubbish. The King James Version uses the word "dung" (3:8). His perspective was completely transformed by his encounter with Jesus as he entered Damascus. Therefore, Paul completely rejected his glamorous past in favor of a more glorious gain assured by the work and authority of His Savior, Jesus Christ.

3:8–11 *[8]It's far more than that! I consider everything else worthless because I'm much better off knowing Christ Jesus my Lord. It's because of him that I think of everything as worthless. I threw it all away in order to gain Christ [9]and to have a relationship with him. This means that I didn't receive God's approval by obeying his laws. The opposite is true! I have God's approval through faith in Christ. This is the approval that comes from God and is based on faith [10]that knows Christ. Faith knows the power that his coming back to life gives and what it means to share his suffering. In this way I'm becoming*

like him in his death, [11]with the confidence that I'll come back to life from the dead.

For Paul, the change in his life was far more than his rejection of his Jewish tradition or the accolades of his colleagues. Knowing Christ was infinitely more valuable than anything this world had to offer him. Here Paul takes great care in providing the details about the profound change on his preference for his relationship to Jesus Christ to his past life as a righteous Jew. Paul did not reject his past simply because some new religion appeared on the horizon. He did not discount the worth of his past qualifications because of any inherent defect in what he previously valued.

Paul recognized the incomparable difference between the new life he received in Jesus Christ and what he once treasured. He realized that his new life in Jesus Christ was far more valuable than what his Jewish heritage promised to offer him. His earthly prestige offered only personal satisfaction that did not last. Knowing Jesus Christ provided boundless joy in this life and greater joy in the courts of heaven for all eternity.

Recognizing the difference, Paul fixed his focus on the eternal promises of Jesus Christ, forgetting what he left behind. Jesus Christ Himself was the reason for rejecting his past and embracing life eternal secured and given by the Lord Himself. In the past, everything he had or enjoyed required his personal effort. The life he received in Jesus Christ was secured and given to Him by God with no contribution from Paul himself. Paul thoroughly understood that the new life given to the redeemed by Jesus Christ was more than a gift. It was a profound transformation resulting in an irreversible and enduring change from death to life and from darkness to light *(John 5:24)*. It was the death of the old nature and the birth of the new man in Jesus Christ. It was a transformation initiated and sustained by the same authority that raised Jesus Christ from death. It was implemented in the heart of the redeemed by the regenerating action of the Holy Spirit. Paul explained the truth about God's transforming power by underscoring the difference between Saul of Tarsus, the zealous persecutor, and Paul the apostle, the servant of the Gospel.

Paul recognized that his salvation in Jesus Christ resulted in a life of service. His redeemed life included hardships and suffering at the hands of the enemies of the Gospel. That suffering only confirmed God's actions in his life. Paul gladly shared in Christ's suffering, realizing that this blessing further assured him that he would come back to life as his Savior had. Paul no longer served his own interests, but he served the Savior Who had bought him. He had been joined to Christ—His life, suffering, death, and resurrection. Nothing could be compared to knowing and serving the incomparable Christ.

Notes/Applications

Paul's instruction to the redeemed across the ages is characterized by encouragement and practical admonition. Paul encourages believers to be joyful and confident in Jesus Christ while warning them at the same time to be aware of the hostile world in which they are commissioned to live and serve God. Those who are ransomed by the blood of the Lamb of God are secure in Christ. Nevertheless, the hostilities of the world are just as real and persistent. Paul's instruction confronts a complacent Christianity that submerges real trials and persecution in a feel-good denial. Jesus Christ also told His disciples about the persecution they would certainly suffer at the hands of His enemies *(John 15:14–21)*. Paul only restated the truth disclosed by Jesus Christ and affirmed by the Holy Spirit. Paul's message encourages God's redeemed people to rejoice in their salvation and be well grounded in faith, discerning the hostilities surrounding them.

By recalling the details of his own heritage and religious background, Paul effectively exposed the patronizing attitude of the Judaizers who always felt religiously superior to everyone else. More importantly, Paul showed how such a condescending attitude not only feeds the ego, but also fuels the flames of false doctrine. His personal background and experience were far superior to theirs. He had better qualifications than the Judaizers. But he considered all of these assets to be worthless in light of his relationship to Jesus Christ.

Believers today will probably never encounter Judaizers. However, any doctrine not supported by scriptural affirmation will inevitably undermine genuine faith in Jesus Christ. The hostilities of the unregenerate world harbor a burning hatred for the truth.

Nevertheless, believers should know truth from error in order to guard against any false teaching that attempts to undermine the message of the Gospel. Paul's inspired words encourage all believers to be firmly established in God's redemption, living a godly life cultivated by the joy of God's salvation, knowing truth from error, and resting in a deeply-rooted faith in the finished work of Jesus Christ. Knowing Jesus is worth more than anything this world can offer. Living in Him and for Him, believers experience confidence and joy, sharing His sufferings and living in the power of His resurrection.

Philippians 3:12–16

3:12 *It's not that I've already reached the goal or have already completed the course. But I run to win that which Jesus Christ has already won for me.*

Paul knew that the practical application of embracing the redeemed life given by Jesus Christ and rejecting the natural tendencies of the unsaved life required wisdom and strength beyond man's inherent resources. Nevertheless, the rejection of the past and the unreserved acceptance of the new was the very essence of the life of God's redeemed children while they lived and served the Lord here on earth.

Paul honestly admitted his mortal shortcomings, which prevented him from fully attaining the goal of his transformation. Even though Jesus Christ had already completed his salvation and won the race of this life for Paul, he acknowledged that he had not yet crossed the finish line. Everything necessary for redemption and transformation into a fully redeemed life had been fully accomplished by Jesus Christ; but, practically speaking, it is progressively revealed in the process of daily life. Paul had not yet attained the ultimate goal of his new life in Christ. Rather, his daily encounter with his Lord was the means by which he personally experienced the victory that Jesus Christ had already accomplished on his behalf. Living in this hostile world as the servant of God meant running the race, which Jesus Christ has already won. Believers live out their redemption in the framework of the victory Christ has already secured on their behalf.

3:13–14 *[13]Brothers and sisters, I can't consider myself a winner yet. This is what I do: I don't look back, I lengthen my stride, and [14]I run straight toward the goal to win the prize that God's heavenly call offers in Christ Jesus.*

Paul was careful, deliberate, and patient as he unwrapped the paradox of living in an accomplished victory that must be conquered still. He confessed that he did not consider himself a winner yet, even though he boldly asserted that he lived in the victory already secured by Jesus Christ. His life as the servant of the Gospel consisted of a daily journey engaging him in a lifelong race that he is called and empowered to finish as a winner.

Instead of looking back at his own weakness, Paul looked forward to his Lord Who had won the race on his behalf and was waiting for him at the finish line. Instead of thinking about his dark past, Paul continued onward, focusing on his victorious future in Jesus Christ. Paul told the Philippians that the race of a Christian's life will end in the victory already secured by Christ. The final outcome is affirmed by the call and the provision of God's redemption. The redemption of those the Lord chooses to save is absolute and executed with His sovereign authority. God's call is irresistible and the outcome is unchangeable. He explained that his life as God's redeemed child was, therefore, comprised of a lifelong race. Every step of the journey, Paul leaned on every stride that Jesus Christ Himself had already taken on behalf of the redeemed.

3:15 *Whoever has a mature faith should think this way. And if you think differently, God will show you how to think.*

Paul felt that the truth he just explained should not come as a surprise to the saints. Anyone with a mature faith will agree with this conclusion. Paul understood that such a divine mystery was not easily discernible by human effort. However, redeemed and indwelt by the Holy Spirit, and united in mind and spirit, those who continue to mature in faith should gradually come to the realization of the victory secured by Jesus Christ and recognize their own journey toward the finish line. If any believer fails to understand this due to spiritual immaturity, then God Himself will eventually correct the error of their underdeveloped faith.

3:16 *However, we should be guided by what we have learned so far.*

The only way to guard against spiritual immaturity and stagnation is to apply what has already been learned. Paul instructed the Philippians to hold fast to the truth they had already been taught. No matter where believers are in their journey of faith, they should always cling to what the Spirit has taught them and continue to build on that growing knowledge. God's Word is life-giving and guards the growing Christian against the evil intentions of this hostile world. God's Word protects the saints from the relentless onslaught of the sin nature within them. Therefore, by being guided with the truth that has been learned, God's redeemed children are strengthened and encouraged to make steady progress forward in their journey toward the finish line where Christ waits to greet them.

Notes/Applications

Using his own personal testimony to illustrate Christ's Gospel, Paul carefully led the Philippians away from the Judaizers' claim of perfection by the Law, and introduced them to true perfection in Jesus Christ. Here, Paul instructed the Philippians to set a goal, which was absolutely attainable. Paul told the Philippians that he was running a race, which he was sure to win. He forgot everything he left behind and focused on what was ahead. Paul's focus was set on reaching the finish line as a winner.

Paul's goal setting is completely different from what is commonly taught and practiced in the world today. Most known motivational teachings discuss goal setting as an attainable, measureable, and sustainable objective. Goals that are well-defined by these criteria cultivate expectation and elicit commitment from the goal setter. The goal setter depends on his personal effort supported by his inherent resources to reach his objectives successfully. Such goal-setting theories anticipate success or failure on the basis of the goal setter's level of commitment and quality of performance.

In sharp contrast, Paul confessed that he was not perfect and could not reach his goals by his own efforts. However, his passion was to pursue Jesus Christ and share with his Lord in His victory and in His suffering. Paul planned and expected to succeed in his goal setting by depending on the One Who attained the objectives of his redemption on his behalf. Paul's goals were not objectives, which he could earn through his successful obedience to the Law. Rather, his commitment and goal setting reflect his attitude of obedience and surrender to his victorious Lord and Savior. Only in Christ could he gain an indisputable assurance of reaching the finish line with victory.

In this way, Paul assures all believers that because of Christ and by His assurance, we can confidently believe God's promise of winning the race. We can forget our past and run forward to the finish line in spite of our imperfections and inabilities. Because of Jesus Christ Who called us to follow Him through life's victory lane, we refuse to dwell in the past and, instead, step up to face today's situations and the challenges of the future. We know that the One Who called us is also faithful and will keep us until we meet Him face-to-face *(John 10:27–29)*. We can set our goals to pursue the victory of our Lord because it has been already secured for us. Our human outlook has been freed from our faulty perspectives by the godly perspectives instilled in us as we lean on the truth declared by the Word of God and on its author our Lord Jesus Christ.

Yes, we are all winners because we have been made winners by the One Who won the race. So let us run the race by following Jesus Christ Who leads us straight to the finish line.

Philippians 3:17–21

3:17 *Brothers and sisters, imitate me, and pay attention to those who live by the example we have given you.*

It may sound puzzling that Paul advised the Philippians to "imitate" him after admitting that he was imperfect and had not yet arrived at the finish line. What was in Paul's mind when he set himself up as an example to be followed? What did he mean?

The Gospel of Jesus Christ is life giving. It is knowledge and wisdom but also life. Paul knew that what was taught must be reflected in real life. So, he offered his own life as an example to be followed. Indeed, Paul wanted the Philippians to see how the life-changing power of the Gospel worked through his imperfections. He wanted them to observe the fragments of Christ-likeness that the Holy Spirit was steadily building in him. Since the Philippians did not yet have the full text of God's written Word, the teachings of the apostles and the exemplary life of God's saints were the main sources through which God's revealed truth was declared. Regardless of individual circumstances and struggles, Paul counseled the Philippians to emulate the exemplary lives of God's saints who lived and served the same true Gospel revealed by the Holy Spirit and declared by God's chosen servants.

3:18 *I have often told you, and now tell you with tears in my eyes, that many live as the enemies of the cross of Christ.*

Paul was well aware of the human tendency to follow individuals who appeared to possess an impressive air about them. His warnings implied that everyone was not as good as they appeared. Such people were not honest and failed to live up to their own standards. Paul told the Philippians to be aware of those people who appeared harmless but were actually enemies of the cross of Christ.

Paul was intensely passionate about his warning regarding teachers who showed no integrity or commitment to what they preached. He alerted the Philippians to be aware of the deceitful practices of such people. Paul had been warning the Philippians about the enemies of the Gospel for some time. But now we hear him pleading with them in tears to watch out for those who disguised their deceptions with a well-crafted presentation of illusive teachings. Paul was especially concerned about those false teachers who cleverly disguised their poisonous doctrine by expressing their message in words that sound like the true Gospel. These people are wolves in sheep's clothing who are really the enemies of the true Gospel of liberty in the Lord and the supreme message of confidence in the finished work of Jesus Christ.

3:19 ***In the end they will be destroyed. Their own emotions are their god, and they take pride in the shameful things they do. Their minds are set on worldly things.***

Paul identified the teachers and preachers that the Philippians should recognize as enemies of the Gospel. The conduct of these individuals exposes the true nature of their character. The enemies of the Gospel are committed primarily to their own self-interests. Everything they do is motivated by an inherent desire to satisfy their emotions, feed their appetite, or appease their intense drive for self-fulfillment. They pride themselves in disgraceful practices and disreputable events. They have no shame in distorting the truth and presenting it as the "gospel." In the end, God will destroy these people by His righteous judgment.

3:20 ***We, however, are citizens of heaven. We look forward to the Lord Jesus Christ coming from heaven as our Savior.***

Paul helped the Philippians recognize the difference between themselves as God's redeemed people and the enemies of the Gospel. While the enemies of the Gospel live in committed hostility to the Good News of God's redemption, those who are transformed by God's saving grace embrace their new life in Jesus Christ. Unlike the enemies of the Gospel, the redeemed no longer live in darkness and death. They have been brought from darkness to light and from death to life. They have been made citizens of heaven. Their future is certain. They look forward to that time when Jesus Christ returns from heaven and their salvation is complete. Unlike the enemies of the Gospel whose hope is fixed upon their own selfish pursuits in this present world, those who belong to Jesus Christ live and serve their Lord focused on the sure hope of eternal life with their Savior.

3:21 *Through his power to bring everything under his authority, he will change our humble bodies and make them like his glorified body.*

When Christ comes to earth again, He will bring everything under His authority. That authority and power will physically transform the bodies of the saints even as they have been spiritually transformed by the effective work of the Holy Spirit. Jesus will make their bodies like His body was following His resurrection.

The redeemed of God will no longer be the same. Their mortality will be replaced by immortality. Corruption will be displaced by incorruption *(1 Corinthians 15:51–54)*. God Himself, as the Creator and the Redeemer, will make His children fit for eternal life in heaven. Their humble bodies will be transformed into a glorious body fit for those who are exalted to be joint heirs with their Savior the Lord Jesus Christ. Paul encouraged them to live by the power and grace of their Savior as citizens of heaven, confident in their hope in Jesus Christ and fully aware of His power to complete their salvation in this way.

In his letter to the Corinthians, Paul gave this description of the transformation of the saints when Christ comes again:

> [51]*Behold, I tell you a mystery: We shall not all sleep, but we shall all be changed–* [52]*in a moment, in the twinkling of an eye, at the last trumpet. For the trumpet will sound, and the dead will be raised incorruptible, and we shall be changed.* [53]*For this corruptible must put on incorruption, and this mortal must put on immortality.* [54]*So when this corruptible has put on incorruption, and this mortal has put on immortality,*

then shall be brought to pass the saying that is written: "Death is swallowed up in victory." [55]*"O Death, where is your sting? O Hades, where is your victory?"* [56]*The sting of death is sin, and the strength of sin is the law.* [57]*But thanks be to God, who gives us the victory through our Lord Jesus Christ. (1 Corinthians 15:51–57,* NKJV*)*

Notes/Applications

Paul made a very strong case for the need to know and understand the implications and benefits of knowing Jesus Christ. Paul made a passionate plea with the Philippians to mature in their knowledge of their salvation in the Lord, and to be wise in identifying the enemies of the Gospel. Even though Paul admitted that he had not yet arrived at the finish line, he pointed to his own life as an example to be followed. This might appear strange in light of Paul's self-assessment. However, since Paul's point of reference had always been Jesus Christ and His finished work, his bold statements always struck a godly balance between arrogance and false modesty. Following Paul's example, the Philippians should imitate him and avoid the enemies of the Gospel of Jesus Christ.

Burdened by the weight of pastoral concern, Paul advises believers to be deliberate in their faithfulness to the Gospel. Paul's insistence on knowledge, wisdom, and understanding comes from his realization that the essential meaning of the power of the Gospel can be fully observed only through the lives and conduct of the redeemed. Therefore, Paul insists that the redeemed must always follow saintly examples modeled by saints who are fully committed to the Gospel and faithfully persevere in every aspect of their daily lives. The truth preached and modeled by such saints is consistent, predictable, and attainable regardless of the human condition.

We must exercise caution lest we erroneously conclude that sinless perfection is attainable by human effort. This is not the thrust of Paul's instruction. What Paul teaches is that salvation is the transformation of a lost life to a redeemed life only through the righteous and perfect work of Jesus Christ on Calvary. The salvation of the redeemed is complete and flawlessly perfect despite the imperfection, which remains in the earthly lives of God's saints. Nevertheless, the Holy Spirit continues to nurture the redeemed sinner with the person and character of Jesus Christ, progressively cultivating aspects of Christ-likeness in the moment-by-moment experiences of the believer as building blocks of the redeemed life.

The benefits of such divine work in the life of the redeemed cannot be fully enjoyed unless the believer actively participates in the process by growing in knowledge and maturing in experience. Therefore, Paul admonishes all believers to know the truth of God's redeeming grace in their lives and to guard against the enemies of the Gospel who seek to lead the sheep away from the fold.

Despite our imperfections, we who are among the redeemed are urged to reflect the image of Jesus Christ and display the depths of God's infinite grace. Such confidence can only take place when we are firmly rooted in the truth of God's salvation and guided by the precepts of God's Holy Word in all matters of life and action. We do so, not in our own strength, but with the support of the One Who has saved us and will one day come again to complete our salvation. At that moment, the struggles of our lives in Christ will grow dim for we shall be made like Him and share in the power of His resurrection for all eternity.

PHILIPPIANS 4

Philippians 4:1–9

4:1 ***So, brothers and sisters, I love you and miss you. You are my joy and my crown. Therefore, dear friends, keep your relationship with the Lord firm!***

After thoroughly schooling the Philippians on the importance of understanding their salvation and fulfilled hope in Jesus Christ, Paul affectionately encouraged them to stand firm in their relationship with their Savior. They were to continue building on the foundation of the faith that had already been given to them. Scriptural knowledge and understanding are essential to a maturing faith, because the strength to resist the relentless onslaught of the enemies of the Gospel is cultivated and implemented in the believer's heart under the guidance of the Holy Spirit.

The Philippians held a special place in Paul's heart. He addressed them with warm expressions of love and fondness. He told them how much he loved them and missed them. Paul's heart overflowed with joy as he thought of them and remembered his labor for Christ among them. The Philippians were his crown. They were the fruit of his labor, reflecting the work of God's redeeming power working through the ministry that God had given him. To Paul, the changed lives of the Philippians portrayed everything that serving Christ truly meant. His only prayer was for them to guard their relationship with Christ and to remain deeply rooted in His love.

4:2–3 ***[2]I encourage both Euodia and Syntyche to have the attitude the Lord wants them to have. [3]Yes, I also ask you, Syzugus, my true partner, to help these women. They fought beside me to spread the Good News along with Clement and the rest of my coworkers, whose names are in the Book of Life.***

Paul singled out two women by name and pleaded with them to resolve their differences. Paul was anxious to deal with anything that had the potential to undermine the unity of the church at Philippi. So he urged Euodia and Syntyche to make peace with each other and come to a mutual agreement. They should be able to do this since they were both disciples of Christ, governed by the same Holy Spirit. Paul did not want their disagreement to undermine their walk with Christ and their service to Him. More importantly, he did not want their disagreement to affect the testimony of the church.

Paul solicited Syzugus, one of his partners in ministry, to help resolve the conflict between the two women. These women had labored side by side with Paul in the Gospel. Their disagreement broke his heart. These had served the ministry of the Gospel with Clement and others whose names are written in the Book of Life. Paul sought to impress his ministry partners at Philippi with the importance of reconciliation between Euodia and Syntyche because both of them had been deeply involved in the work of the Gospel. Even though the conflict was between two individuals, Paul realized that their reconciliation would benefit the entire congregation. So he charged the leadership of the church and other influential members to be peacemakers within the congregation. In doing so, Paul underscored the principle that any difficulty within an assembly of believers was the problem of the whole congregation. He alerted the Philippians that they could not ignore any conflict among their members as it would negatively impact the entire assembly.

4:4 *Always be joyful in the Lord! I'll say it again: Be joyful!*

In contrast to the conflict between Euodia and Syntyche, Paul encouraged the Philippians to cultivate a much more positive attitude among the saints of the Philippian church. He exhorted them to rejoice always and to be filled with the joy of the Lord. This admonition was so important he had to say it twice. So, he charged his co-laborers in Philippi to facilitate peace between its two members so that the joy of the Lord would be a church wide reality collectively felt and experienced by the whole membership as well as by individual members.

4:5 *Let everyone know how considerate you are. The Lord is near.*

Paul urged the Philippians to exhibit a positive witness for the Gospel by doing everything in the strength of the Lord Jesus Christ. He wanted them to relate to one another with heartfelt consideration. He did not want their testimony for Christ to be marred by petty conflict. The child of God should always be aware of the unchanging reality that the Lord is near—that He is coming soon. Certainly, the Lord is present in each one's heart in the person of the Holy Spirit. Therefore, the church should be known for their gentle consideration of each other so that the joy and peace of the Lord would rule in each and every heart.

4:6 *Never worry about anything. But in every situation let God know what you need in prayers and requests while giving thanks.*

Even though the full consummation of God's redemption occurs after death, the blessings of God's salvation are available to the redeemed while they are still living on this earth. So Paul encouraged the Philippians to live a life of faith and trust in God, knowing that nothing can separate them from His love or deprive them of His joy and blessings.

For this reason, the life of God's people should be marked by quiet confidence, not deeply concerned about immediate circumstances. Even though some situations may be stressful on the human level, believers have full access to the throne of grace, drawing on the vast resources of God's abundant goodness. Surely God knows the situations of His children, but Paul wants them to express their needs to the Lord, not in the context of worry, but in the joy of thanksgiving. Therefore, freed from anxiety and worry by the Lord's grace, believers have the opportunity to submit their petitions and praises to God. Since He has ordained everything that happens to the children of God for their benefit, believers may rest confidently in the arms of the Lord Who cares for them—for their salvation, their growth in faith, and even the daily situations they encounter.

4:7 *Then God's peace, which goes beyond anything we can imagine, will guard your thoughts and emotions through Christ Jesus.*

When God's people approach the throne of grace in the spirit of thanksgiving, they are assured of His answer. Paul wants all believers to know that the expression of their concerns in the context of thankfulness will always be answered by the filling of God's peace. When believers reflect on their circumstances with a deep and abiding awareness of God's care for them, the stress and anxiety of the immediate moment vanishes, replaced with an outpouring of praise for God's goodness. The peace that God bestows on those He loves far outweighs earthly concerns. His peace makes such an impact on their outlook that the world can never understand how they face life's problems with such calm assurance. In fact, even believers are amazed at the peace that courses through their beings as God surrounds them in His peace. They experience deeply the benediction that Jesus expressed to His apostles on the night before He died: "Peace I leave with you; my peace I give you. I do not give to you as the world gives. Do not let your hearts be troubled and do not be afraid" *(John 14:27,* NIV*)*. The people of this world who do not belong to the redeemed family of God in Jesus Christ can never know this peace.

4:8 *Finally, brothers and sisters, keep your thoughts on whatever is right or deserves praise: things that are true, honorable, fair, pure, acceptable, or commendable.*

A life freed from worry and anxiety by God's surpassing peace will eventually reach a level of mature faith. Believers will come to the point where they desire the godly virtues Paul has enumerated here. So Paul encouraged the Philippians to fill their hearts and minds with the commitment to be godly in their conscience and emotions. He exhorted them to think on things that are right, praise-worthy, true, honorable, pure, fair, acceptable, or commendable. Instead of being driven by chronic worry and acute anxiety resulting in prayerful complaints to God, the redeemed are encouraged to overcome their natural tendencies by God's peace so that they pursue a life in which these virtues are displayed.

4:9 *Practice what you've learned and received from me, what you heard and saw me do. Then the God who gives this peace will be with you.*

Paul encouraged the Philippians to practice what they learned from him. He wanted them to imitate his way of life and his service to the Lord. Paul was confident that the work of God's peace in him was so obvious that any one who observed his demeanor—the way he faced life's challenges, the way he responded to the enemies of the Gospel, the way he loved the brothers and sisters who shared their faith in Jesus Christ—could certainly know the same peace that was given to the redeemed by God. From the time of his conversion, Paul was filled by God's peace and was no longer distracted by the worries and anxieties of this world. So he encouraged the Philippians to listen to what they heard him say and do what they saw him do. Then they, too, would experience the peace that the Lord gives to His people.

Notes/Applications

With deeply felt affection, Paul made an urgent appeal to Christians to live within the framework of their faith in God and their hope in Jesus Christ. He urged them to look at the world and their circumstances through the eyes of their redeemed lives. Their personal conduct and their relationship with each other should reflect the living Christ within them. They should live peaceably with each other and rest in the peace that the Lord gives to them. The redeemed children of God should live within the framework of quiet prayer without worry or anxiety.

The essence of Paul's admonition to believers should not be taken as some unattainable goal. Often, such advice as "do not worry" or "do not be anxious" challenges us because our emotions are beyond our control. We are overwhelmed by them. But Paul did not instruct us to manage our emotions. Instead, he teaches us to submit every situation which causes us to worry to our Lord through prayers of faith, thanksgiving, and confidence. When our hearts are open toward God through prayer, God graciously pours out His peace to calm our lives battered by worry and anxiety. Paul is really telling us to practice what we are taught. Trust God! Believe what He says! Take Him at His Word! As we exercise our faith in our Lord and submit ourselves to Him, His peace will begin to nurture confidence in our hearts, cultivating His peace in every aspect of our lives.

Philippians 4:10–14

4:10 *The Lord has filled me with joy because you again showed interest in me. You were interested but did not have an opportunity to show it.*

After having identified the points of struggle within the Philippian congregation, Paul turned his attention to acknowledging God's goodness manifested in the actions of his spiritual children at Philippi. Paul was filled with joy because of the kindness the Philippians exhibited toward him. His joy was great because God's goodness was reflected in what he received from the Philippians. Some time had lapsed before the Philippians could do anything for Paul. However, that was not a concern for Paul. He acknowledged that the occasion for good deeds did not present itself for some time. But when the time came the Philippians were ready to glorify God with unreserved obedience by sharing God's blessings with Paul. In doing so, the Philippians were ready to share God's goodness at the opportune time.

4:11 *I'm not saying this because I'm in any need. I've learned to be content in whatever situation I'm in.*

Paul carefully expressed his praise of his friends in Philippi. He wanted to make sure that his joy was not mistaken for self-serving gratitude shown for what he had gained from their kindness toward him. In his statement, he carefully separated himself and his interest from the manifestation of God's mighty work in the hearts of the Philippians.

Paul assured the Philippians that his affirmation of their kindness was not motivated by selfish ends. As far as Paul was concerned, he had come to a point in his life where he was content with whatever conditions defined the circumstances of his life. He did not need any form of human intervention unless it was ordered and directed by God and, therefore, his needs did not generate his testimony of God's goodness in them. As their teacher and exhorter, Paul saw God's good work in them and rejoiced in the transformation that God's goodness brought into their lives.

4:12 *I know how to live in poverty or prosperity. No matter what the situation, I've learned the secret of how to live when I'm full or when I'm hungry, when I have too much or when I have too little.*

God had brought Paul to a remarkable level of trust and maturity in his faith. He had learned to accept every situation in which he found himself. He was satisfied with His Lord. It did not matter if he had a lot or very little. It did not matter whether he had a lot of money or no money at all. It did not matter whether he was hungry or starving. He was content! Paul's contentment was not influenced by the conditions which dictated the circumstances surrounding his daily life. He was strengthened by God's immutable strength working in his weakness, which was brought on by the severity of life's conditions.

4:13 *I can do everything through Christ who strengthens me.*

Paul knew that his assertion about his contentment was not compatible with normal human thinking. So, he confessed that his strength came from Jesus Christ, his Lord and Savior. He said that he could do everything in Jesus Christ Who strengthened him. Despite everything he experienced as a result of his faithfulness to the ministry to which God called him, Paul found that his Lord provided both strength to survive and contentment to accept His will for his life. Jesus Christ's strength constantly worked in every aspect of his life. He could live above the influences of life's circumstances, which normally cause human beings to become frustrated, rebellious, and angry. Paul was content in all life's situations because he was supported by Christ's strength.

4:14 *Nevertheless, it was kind of you to share my troubles.*

Nevertheless, Paul appreciated what his friends in Philippi had done for him. Even though Paul had expressed his total dependence on

Christ's strength, he was very careful to thank them for the charity they showed to him. Paul did not measure the value of their kindness by the nature of his contentment in the circumstances of his life. So, he expressed his gratitude for sharing his troubles and providing the gift Epaphroditus brought to him on their behalf.

Notes/Applications

As God's appointed emissary of the Gospel, Paul was always careful to delineate the truth so that the essence of his teaching would not get confused with inaccuracies or false ideas. As the founder of the Philippian congregation, he took great care in helping the Philippians understand the significance of their conduct as Christians in light of their relationship with God. In the opening verses of this chapter, Paul instructed the Philippians to deal with the conflict within the church. They should be thankful, faithful, and virtuous believers as they make their petitions and praises known to God through prayer.

After commending them for their generosity, Paul embarked on a parenthetical remark separating himself both from the cause and the object of their godly behavior. Paul did not show ingratitude nor did he deny the significance of their gift to him. However, he emphatically underscored both the generosity of the Philippians and his own self-sufficiency. Both are a response to teaching of the Holy Spirit in their lives. He wanted the Philippians to understand that their generosity must be viewed primarily as obedience to God. By the same token, his own self-sufficiency was also God's unfailing providence. The generosity of the Philippians was a way of life cultivated in them by the Holy Spirit. The same behavior was also used to provide for Paul, God's servant. Obedience to the Lord should not be confused with human goodwill. Neither should self-sufficiency be mistaken for one's resilience or prudence. Jesus Christ is all in all!

Philippians 4:15–23

4:15–16 [15]*You Philippians also know that in the early days, when I left the province of Macedonia to spread the Good News, you were the only church to share your money with me. You gave me what I needed, and you received what I gave you.* [16]*Even while I was in Thessalonica, you provided for my needs twice.*

Paul continued to thank the Philippians for their kindness to him. The Philippians were the only ones who stood with him in supplying everything he needed during his ministry in Macedonia. They wholeheartedly received the Good News Paul preached to them, and in grateful partnership, continued to support him with money and supplies.

Paul saw a man in a vision who asked him to come to Macedonia and preach the Gospel (*Acts 16:9–12*). During his stay in Macedonia, Paul was persecuted primarily by the Jewish communities that stirred up the people against the Gospel (*Acts 16:20–24; 17:5–7, 13*). Paul was beaten and imprisoned in the various towns of the Macedonian region where he preached the Gospel. But every time he was in trouble, his fellow-believers smuggled him out of the troubled area into a safer town where he continued to preach. Eventually, he arrived at Athens where he continued to proclaim the Gospel while waiting for his ministry companions to arrive from Macedonia. Through it all, the Christians in Philippi remained true and faithful ministry companions. Paul also implied that the Philippians continued to support his ministry even after he left Macedonia.

4:17 *It's not that I'm looking for a gift. The opposite is true. I'm looking for your resources to increase.*

Paul took time to clarify his intentions for expressing such glowing praise. His commendation was not given lightly or frivolously. He was not trying to flatter them in order to secure more gifts. As he stated earlier, Paul was content with whatever circumstances he was in at any given moment.

Certainly, the Philippians understood that their gifts continued to provide the resources needed by Paul to spread the Gospel. Their gifts would bring an abundant harvest of souls into the Kingdom of God. In this way, their own riches as children and servants of God would increase.

The idea that Paul expected the resources of the saints to be increased can be misunderstood. It is clear that Paul was not speaking of increasing their financial resources. Rather, the Lord would bless them for their part in the work of the ministry to which Paul had been appointed.

4:18 *You have paid me in full, and I have more than enough. Now that Epaphroditus has brought me your gifts, you have filled my needs. Your gifts are a soothing aroma, a sacrifice that God accepts and with which he is pleased.*

Epaphroditus had brought their gifts to him. Paul explained the two essential ways in which their gifts were of great value. First, their gifts were of great significance and value to Paul personally. He felt that he had been fully paid. He was blessed. All of his needs were met. Paul was grateful and deeply appreciative of what the Philippians had done for him and for his ministry.

Second, Paul showed how their gift to him was also a pleasing sacrifice to God. Their gift was an offering of soothing aroma to God, which reflected their obedience. Their gift blessed Paul with the abundance of God's provision and pleased God as a selfless action of obedience.

4:19 *My God will richly fill your every need in a glorious way through Christ Jesus.*

The Philippians' obedience to God would not remain unrecognized. Paul was confident that God would bless them by supplying their needs through Jesus Christ. The obedience of the Philippians did not obligate God to respond to them. They did not earn what they received from God. God was simply pleased with their obedience. The work of the Spirit in their lives had moved the Philippians to be such selfless givers. Just as Paul was content in wealth or in poverty, so the saints should also be content. Their giving should never be motivated by their financial resources but by the richness of the Lord's provision. It is the heart, which responds to God's mercy, grace, and salvation. God is glorified when those who have little give generously to the work of the Gospel. The Lord is exalted as He makes consistent givers from saints who are poor.

4:20 *Glory belongs to our God and Father forever! Amen.*

Paul redirected the focus of his letter back to God following his commendation. There was danger if his remarks were misunderstood as reasons for pride. So it was important to praise the Lord for everything that transpired in the relationship between Paul and the saints in Philippi. Christ's strength provided Paul's contentment in every situation. The Spirit's direction made poor saints generous, supporting Paul's ministry among the Gentiles. Christ's measureless resources would provide for the needs of these friends. God alone had done everything in their redeemed lives, and He alone would continue to guide, support, and strengthen His saints in the days to come. So Paul gave glory to God and sealed it with a hearty amen.

4:21–23 *21Greet everyone who believes in Christ Jesus. The brothers and sisters who are with me send greetings to you. 22All God's people here, especially those in the emperor's palace, greet you. 23May the good will of our Lord Jesus Christ be with you.*

Paul closed his letter with his heartfelt salutation. He sent his personal greetings directly to the believers in Philippi. They, in turn, were to greet everyone who believed in Jesus Christ on his behalf. He also sent greetings from everyone who was with him, including those believers who were in Caesar's household. He prayed for the grace of the Lord Jesus Christ to be present with them and in them. It is Christ's grace that sustains the saints in every experience that the Lord brings into their lives, giving them contentment in the supremacy of their Lord Who makes all earthly circumstances an opportunity to glorify God in heaven. Believers should, therefore, be encouraged by the grace of God and rejoice in the truth that the power of the Gospel continued to accomplish God's purposes in Rome, in Philippi, and to the ends of the earth.

Notes/Applications

Paul dedicated the closing verses of his letter to the expression of his gratitude for the lengthy friendship of the Christians in Philippi. His closing thoughts basically reflected three specifically related elements. First, he acknowledged their support for him and his work that came at a crucial time when he was struggling with his imprisonment. Second, their perspective on what they had done for him should be understood in the correct spiritual framework. Third, their faithfulness to the ministry of the Gospel would continue to facilitate their obedience to the Lord.

The charitable gift the Philippians sent to Paul accomplished God's purpose. It met his needs and enabled him to continue spreading the Gospel in spite of the difficulties he faced. However, it is absolutely necessary that believers understand that any godly thing they do is an act of obedience to God. It is one of the ways in which God brings to fruition the outcome that pleases Him. God's purpose can never be thwarted. He is able to make consistent givers out of poor believers. For that, we have His unfailing grace and rich providence. Therefore, it is important to remember that obedience to God destroys the stronghold of excuses, clearing the way to draw nearer to our Father in heaven. God receives His children's obedience as a sweet smelling aroma that pleases Him.

In this way, God's children bring glory to Jesus Christ, Who left heaven's throne to bring salvation to the lost race of humankind. For this reason, at the Name of Jesus everyone will bow and confess that Jesus Christ is Lord to the glory of God the Father.

COLOSSIANS

INTRODUCTION

Colossae was an ancient city in Asia Minor, located in the southwestern part of present-day Turkey, and remembered primarily for the apostle Paul's letter to the church there *(Colossians 1:2)*. Colossae was located 100 miles (160 km) east of Ephesus in the Lycus River valley. The city flourished during the sixth century B.C. An ancient Greek historian, Xenophon, related that Cyrus the Great, founder of the Persian Empire, had passed Colossae with his army on his way to battle in Greece. According to Herodotus, another ancient Greek historian, when the Persian king Xerxes came to Colossae in the fifth century b.c., it was already a city of great size.[1]

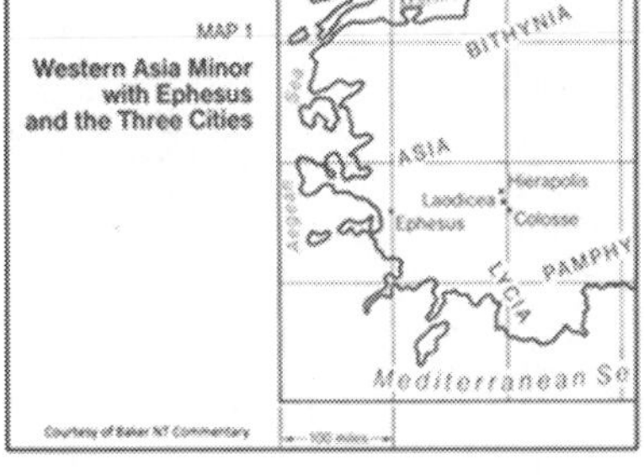

Colossae was situated in the region known as Phrygia and was a trading center at a crossroads on the main highway from Ephesus to the east. In Roman times relocation of the road leading north to Pergamum brought about both the growth of Laodicea, a city 10 miles (16 km) away, and Colossae's gradual decline. Nevertheless, Colossae was a significant commercial center through the third and fourth centuries as part of a prosperous triangle with two other cities of the Lycus Valley, Hierapolis and Laodicea, both of which are mentioned in the New Testament.[2] Colossae and Laodicea shared in the wool trade. The name Colossae was derived from a Latin name *collossinus*, meaning "purple wool."[3]

Epaphras was Paul's coworker in Ephesus and a native of Colossae. He was responsible for the city's evangelization, as well as that of Laodicea and Hierapolis. Through him Paul learned of the progress of the Colossian church and thus wrote his letter to the Colossians. Paul's high regard for Epaphras was expressed when he spoke of him as "beloved fellow servant," "faithful minister of Christ" *(Colossians 1:7)*, and "servant of Christ" *(4:12)*, a title of esteem Paul bestowed only on one other person—Timothy *(Philippians 1:1)*.

Following his third missionary journey, Paul was confined to a long period of imprisonment, first in Jerusalem and eventually in Rome, A.D. 59–62. During that time, Paul wrote several letters to churches that had been established during his missionary journeys—Colossians, Ephesians, Philippians, and Philemon. Most Bible scholars have come to the conclusion that these letters were written while Paul was in Rome about A.D. 61–62.

Philemon, Colossians, and Ephesians belong together. Paul wrote them at the same time from his prison. Tychicus delivered all three letters under Paul's direction. Philemon lived in Colossae and was the leader of the Colossian church. Paul wrote to plead with Philemon to accept his runaway slave, Onesimus, as a newly redeemed brother in Christ. Paul dispatched Tychicus to accompany Onesimus on his return journey. Tychicus also carried letters to the Ephesians and the Colossians. Philippians was probably written later and Epaphroditus, a representative of the Philippian church, carried Paul's letter to this small Christian community.[4]

Epaphras was in prison with Paul at the time the letter to Philemon was written *(Philemon 1:23)*.[5] During their imprisonment, Epaphras told Paul about his work in the Colossian church. Even though Paul never visited Colossae, he felt the familiar tug of Christian kinship and penned this letter as though they were his own children in the faith.

Colossians and Ephesians share a similar message with slightly different emphases. The outlines are parallel, first explaining the theological foundations of the Christian faith and then making practical application of the theological underpinnings. In Ephesians, Christ is exalted as the head of the Church, His Body. In Colossians, Christ is the transcendent sustainer of His creation. The language of Colossians, like Ephesians, is generally an expression of worship in the opening the sections. As readers follow Paul's thinking through these letters, spirits are lifted and hearts sing with praise. Then, walking with the exalted Christ, readers are urged to let the expression of praise be seen in their daily activities.

In the confused and shifting sands of the theologies of today's church, Paul's letter to the church at Colossae sounds a clarion call to make Jesus Christ the center of Christian worship. This short letter is a challenge to today's believers to again lift up Christ, exalt His Name, and live with thanksgiving as an expression of their worship.

COLOSSIANS 1

Colossians 1:1–8

1:1–2 ***[1]From Paul, an apostle of Christ Jesus by God's will, and from our brother Timothy. [2]To God's holy and faithful people, our brothers and sisters who are united with Christ in the city of Colossae. Good will and peace from God our Father are yours!***

Paul opens his letter to the Colossian church in the same way that other writers of his time did. He provides the sender's name, the recipient's name, and a greeting. However, his greeting is distinctly Christian in character.

Paul identified himself in his usual manner as an apostle of Jesus Christ, God's appointed messenger. When Paul says that this happened as a result of God's will, it is clear that Paul did not seek this appointment. However, Christ intervened in his life and gave him a specific task to complete. Paul also identified Timothy, not necessarily as coauthor of this letter, but as a partner in ministry (*1 Corinthians 1:1; Philippians 1:1*). He had accompanied Paul during much of his time in Ephesus and was with Paul now as he wrote this letter.

Paul wrote to the faithful people in Colossae, those people who belonged to the community of the Christian faith. They were holy and faithful because they were united to Christ, both individually and corporately. As each one was saved by the work of the Holy Spirit, they joined others who had likewise been redeemed.

In his greeting, Paul expressed his confidence in God the Father Who had already saved them. As a part of that salvation, God had established a relationship with His holy and faithful people, giving them His grace and peace.

1:3 *We always thank God, the Father of our Lord Jesus Christ, in our prayers for you.*

When Paul wrote about the prayers offered on behalf of the church in Colossae, he emphasized the thankfulness that permeated those prayers. The testimony of this church gave Paul every reason to be thankful. The thanksgiving was directed toward God, the Father of our Lord Jesus Christ. It is important to understand that the reason for the faithfulness of God's people was that God through the Holy Spirit had brought them to this stage of maturity in the faith. They did not do this because of their personal efforts, but because God had orchestrated this transformation in their lives.

Paul used the plural pronoun *we*, showing that he was not alone in his prison, but that others shared his prayers for this church. During this first imprisonment in Rome, Paul was under house arrest, guarded by a Roman soldier. Nevertheless, he was able to speak freely, entertain guests, and share time with other believers. We know from his salutation that Timothy was with him.

1:4 *We thank God because we have heard about your faith in Christ Jesus and your love for all of God's people.*

When Paul wrote his letter to the church in Galatia, he immediately scolded them for their failure to keep Christ at the center of their faith. The church in Colossae was dramatically different. Their faith remained focused on Jesus Christ, what He had done for them at the Cross and what He was doing in them. For Paul, Christ Himself was the very essence of the gospel message. Without Christ there was no salvation; there was no transformation; there was no eternal life. Without Christ, religion was useless *(1 Corinthians 15:14)*. Paul was grateful that the Christians in Colossae remained faithful to their calling in Jesus Christ, and kept Him the centerpiece of their faith.

When believers experience the forgiveness of their sin and restoration to fellowship with their Creator and Redeemer, they join with others whom Christ has redeemed. This was the experience of the Colossian church. They rejoiced in their salvation and shared that spirit of thanksgiving with others who had been saved. God's people in Colossae lived together in the bond of Christ's love and forgiveness.

1:5 ***You have these because of the hope which is kept safe for you in heaven. Some time ago you heard about this hope in the Good News which is the message of truth.***

This hope is fully secure, not because Christians hold on to it with all their strength, but because Christ Himself keeps it for them "in heaven" where no power, human or otherwise, can touch it. Both *faith* and *love* are based on *hope (Romans 5:1–5; 1 Corinthians 13:13; Galatians 5:5–6; 1 Thessalonians 1:3; 5:8)* which here means "the content of hope," "the thing one hopes for."[1] Though hidden from their view, this *hope* is centered in Christ *(1:27)* and will be revealed when He returns *(3:4)*. That is why Christians are to direct their minds toward heaven and to let their thoughts about Christ rule their lives *(3:1–4)*. Paul was telling the Colossians nothing new. It was the Gospel that had been already delivered to them when he was in Ephesus. They had already heard about this hope in the Gospel when they were converted. As the Word of Truth, the Gospel is completely reliable. It is God's Word and reflects His character.

1:6 ***This Good News is present with you now. It is producing results and spreading all over the world as it did among you***

from the first day you heard it. At that time you came to know what God's kindness truly means.

It seems that Paul describes the *Good News* as a power separate from the One Who is the Good News. It is not the written Word of God. It is not simply a message. Rather, it is the living, moving power of God making its way into the lives of the believers in Colossae and then throughout the world. In this case *"all over the world"* does not mean to each and every individual in the world, but in all those population centers throughout the Roman Empire in which the Gospel was preached. The evidence of the power of the Gospel has been displayed in the lives of countless people whose hearts have been changed. The Colossian Christians were only one example of what God was doing throughout the world.

That grace continued in their hearts at that very moment. It continued to grow in their hearts and minds from the time they were first converted. The reality of God's presence in their lives could not be disputed. It could be seen in the way that they grew in faith, and in the love with which they treated each other.

1:7–8 ***7You learned about this Good News from Epaphras, our dear fellow servant. He is taking your place here as a trustworthy deacon for Christ 8and has told us about the love that the Spirit has given you.***

Epaphras was the evangelist who took the Good News to Colossae, his native city. He also evangelized the cities of Laodicea and Hierapolis. Paul's high regard for Epaphras was evidenced by his use of such terms as "beloved fellow servant," "faithful minister of Christ" *(Colossians 1:7)*, and "servant of Christ" *(Colossians 4:12)*, a title of esteem Paul bestowed only on one other person, Timothy *(Philippians 1:1)*.[2]

Epaphras was imprisoned with Paul when he wrote the letter to Philemon, asking him to receive his slave, Onesimus, as a brother in Christ *(Philemon 23)*. It appears Epaphras was still in Rome, although it is not clear if he was still in prison. In Paul's prison, Epaphras told

Paul everything that the Lord had done in Colossae, emphasizing the love that was evident in the lives of the Christians. The Holy Spirit instilled this love in the believers. It was not like the normal regard that people have for one another as friends. It was a love that flowed from hearts filled with the love of Christ that had redeemed these people.

Notes/Applications

No church is perfect! As Paul continues his letter to the Christians in Colossae, this will become evident. But how many churches would love to hear the words that began Paul's letter, identifying them as God's holy and faithful people, united in Christ. These words would lift the spirits of Christians in many churches throughout the land. If Paul wrote to your church, would he say these same things?

The characteristics of a strong, believing fellowship are hallmarks of what it means to be Christ's disciple as individuals and partners in fellowship with other believers.

- Faith in Christ Jesus
- Love for all the saints
- Trust in the hope secured for the saints by Jesus Christ
- Living in the Word of Truth, the Gospel
- Bearing fruit in an unbelieving world
- Understanding the grace of God in truth
- Love in the Spirit
- Shepherded by a faithful minister of Christ

Everyone knows that no church is perfect. But that is really a misdirected observation. The criteria by which we evaluate the effectiveness of our churches are found in these characteristics Paul has spoken of in this introduction. These should be the thrust, the theme, and the centerpiece of every body of believers that calls itself "Christian." Any deviation from these Spirit-filled distinctives fails to fulfill God's purpose for His Church, which He has identified as His Body.

The practical trilogy of faith, hope, and love is common in Paul's letters. They are the distinctive characteristics by which God's people are identified, showing to everyone that they do not behave like the rest of people in the world. By this conduct, they show that they have been redeemed, that they belong to God, that they have experienced the forgiveness of their sin by Christ's sacrifice.

Perhaps the best-known expression of this kind of conduct is found in Paul's letter to the Corinthians. *"So now faith, hope, and love abide, these three; but the greatest of these is love"* (1 Corinthians 13:13, ESV). While these distinctives are not perfectly applied within any believing community, they are perfectly reflected in Jesus Christ, Who is the Head of His Church. He is the One Who has saved, is saving, and will save His redeemed people. He is the only truly reliable hope on Whom the faith of the saints securely rests. Then, the Holy Spirit instills these characteristics in the lives of God's redeemed people, setting them apart from the world and, at the same time, showing the world what it means to be a part of God's family.

Surely no church is perfect. Nevertheless, Christ's Church exhibits the transformation that takes place when God saves people from the tyranny of their sin. Then, like the Colossians, we are happy to hear Paul's words spoken to our churches, commending us for our faith in Jesus Christ, our love for all the saints, and our hope in the inheritance that is secured for us in heaven.

Colossians 1:9–14

1:9 ***For this reason we have not stopped praying for you since the day we heard about you. We ask [God] to fill you with the knowledge of his will through every kind of spiritual wisdom and insight.***

Paul informed the Colossians of the content of his intercessory prayer. Even though he had already commended them for their faith and their love for all the saints, Paul continued to pray for continued growth in their faith, particularly in their knowledge of God's will in their lives. This knowledge was not some humanly determined wisdom, but wisdom that came from the Holy Spirit. That kind of wisdom, God-given wisdom, would give them spiritual insight, the ability to discern what God wanted them to do.

1:10 ***We ask this so that you will live the kind of lives that prove you belong to the Lord. Then you will want to please him in every way as you grow in producing every kind of good work by this knowledge about God.***

Paul did not want God's people to have some rationally developed theology about God. Rather, the *spiritual wisdom and insight* that he asked the Lord to give them was to result in lives that proved they belonged to God. That kind of wisdom not only engaged the mental capacity of believers, but engaged the heart as well. Surely Paul wanted them to understand that God had given them their vibrant faith. But the deeply abiding presence of the Spirit should also produce lives that exhibit that presence to those around them.

In this way, the believing community in Colossae had one overriding objective—to please the Lord in everything they did. Every aspect of their daily lives was to be impacted by their knowledge of the Lord. As that knowledge grew in both mind and heart, their relationship with the Lord Jesus would grow and deepen. Although they already demonstrated their relationship to Christ by the love with which they treated each other, Paul's prayer exhibited a deep pastoral concern that this love would continue to blossom throughout the Colossian church, impacting their individual and corporate lives and providing a consistent witness to their surrounding community.

1:11 *We ask him to strengthen you by his glorious might with all the power you need to patiently endure everything with joy.*

Paul asked the Lord to strengthen their faith, not by their human effort, but by the Lord's *glorious might*. Only the Lord's strength could help them endure the rigors of their daily lives. The thrust of Paul's prayer did not ask the Lord for great, impressive miracles that could provide the impetus for their spiritual growth. Rather, Paul asked the Lord to give them the strength needed to provide what the believers required to patiently endure everything with joy. As the believers in Colossae faced opposition to their faith, they needed the Lord's strength, wisdom, and insight to help them understand who they were in Christ and the nature of the opposition. Nevertheless, they were to serve the Lord daily with the joy that He imparted to them.

1:12 *You will also thank the Father, who has made you able to share the light, which is what God's people inherit.*

Not only were the believers to serve the Lord with joy as they endured opposition to their faith, they were to do so in the spirit of thanksgiving. This was Paul's prayer for the Colossian Christians. He wanted them to live the way the Lord wanted them to, not begrudgingly, but with the joy and thanksgiving that flooded their lives ever since they were converted.

The phrase "*able to share the light*" has the idea that God's people should share the light of their salvation with others. While this is a well-established biblical principle, the meaning of the Greek phrase really emphasizes that the Father is the One Who has qualified the saints to share in the inheritance that God has prepared for them. It is impossible for people to be "*able to share the light*," as if they could do this by their own design and effort. Rather it is a gift that God gives to those He saves.

1:13 *God has rescued us from the power of darkness and has brought us into the kingdom of his Son, whom he loves.*

This is Paul's affirmation of the faith that had transformed the lives of the believers. It is God's action that had saved them. He is the One Who rescues people from the tyranny of the darkness that permeates the lives of the unsaved. He is the One Who has brought people into the Kingdom of His Son, the Son that He loves. God declared His love for His Son, Jesus, at His baptism *(Matthew 3:17)*, and when He met with Moses and Elijah *(Matthew 17:5)*. Paul made very sure that the Colossians understood that they had nothing to do with their salvation. He had emphatically made this same statement in his letter to the Roman Christians. "[10] *...as Scripture says, 'Not one person has God's approval.* [11]*No one has understanding. No one searches for God.* [12]*Everyone has turned away. Together they have become rotten to the core. No one does anything good, not even one person'*" *(Romans 3:10–12)*. This idea was also the theme of the Psalmist: "[2]The Lord looks down from heaven on the children of man, to see if there are any who understand, who seek after God. [3]They have all turned aside; together they have become corrupt; there is none who does good, not even one" *(Psalm 14:2–3)*. Joy and thanksgiving are the natural outpouring of a thankful heart when believers realize the desperate condition from which God has rescued them.

1:14 *His Son paid the price to free us, which means that our sins are forgiven.*

This is the core of Paul's letter to the Colossian Christians. Jesus Christ stands alone at the center of everything Paul wants them to know. Jesus paid the price that sets them free from the tyranny of the power of darkness, from their sin. Jesus' sacrifice sets people free from that unshakeable burden. Through Jesus Christ, the sins of believers are forgiven. Because of Jesus Christ, those that He has saved can stand before the throne of God without fear of condemnation. Because of Jesus Christ, the redeemed of the Lord enter His presence with thanksgiving and praise. The struggles of this life pale in comparison to the joy that awaits those whose sins are forgiven through the blood of the Lamb.

Notes/Applications

If Paul's opening remarks have given rise to any sense of accomplishment by the Colossian Christians, the remarks that follow provide a strong incentive to reflect carefully on the status of their faith. While Paul's commendation at the outset is encouraging, it does not mean that these believers had any reason to boast. Every word of praise is fundamentally grounded in Jesus Christ—what He did for them on the cross and the way He was sustaining the hope of their inheritance in the heavens. So there is room for continued improvement. Paul's prayer is an intercession for continued growth in their faith, hope, and love.

Paul praised the saints for their understanding of *the grace of God in truth*. What does he ask God to do? The first thing he asks for is that they *may be filled with the knowledge of his will in all spiritual wisdom and understanding*. He commended the Colossian Christians for their *faith in Christ Jesus* and *their love for all the saints*. These disciples were obviously walking with the Lord on a daily basis. But what does Paul pray for? He asks God to help them *walk worthy of the Lord, fully pleasing Him*. He thanks God that the Gospel is bearing fruit in Colossae as well as throughout the whole empire. They, too, are faithful fruitbearers. But Paul goes on to pray that they continue *bearing fruit in every good work and increase in the knowledge of God*.

Paul's analysis of their status in the faith was praiseworthy, but such praise was not an invitation to sit down and take their status for granted. There was room for improvement. Paul's prayer built on the foundation of the faith that already existed in their church, asking God to continue working in their hearts and minds in such a way that their faith would grow even more.

How could they do this? Again, not by their church programs. Not by their clearly defined plans. Not by their sincere devotion. Only by understanding what God had done for them through Jesus Christ, His Son. It is God Who has saved them. It is God Who has qualified them to *share in the inheritance of the saints in light*. It is God Who has delivered them from the domain of darkness and transferred them to the kingdom of His beloved Son, through Whom they have received their redemption and the forgiveness of their sins.

Because of God's undeserved gift of mercy and forgiveness, Paul asked God to give them a spirit of thankfulness and joy as they lived in the light of His redemption. How could they do otherwise? If they understood the grace of God in truth, then their hearts would naturally overflow with thanksgiving and joy.

It is good to hear words of praise for our faith in the Lord. It is good to receive recognition for the way that we treat each other in the love that shows how much God has loved us. But let us bow our heads with Paul and ask for God's continuing work in our hearts, for our growth in faith and love, and for the joy of His salvation.

Colossians 1:15–20

1:15 *He is the image of the invisible God, the firstborn of all creation.*

Building on the work of Jesus Christ, in whom the saints have received redemption and the forgiveness of their sins, Paul continued to describe the Savior, not in terms of what He has done, but in terms of Who He is.

Jesus is the very manifestation of the eternal God. The very nature of the Lord of heaven and earth is perfectly revealed in Jesus Christ. The Greek word for *image* is a term of *revelation*, showing that Jesus is not some vague copy, but the very *revelation* of God.[3] This is the how the disciple, John, described Jesus. "[14]*The Word became human and lived among us. We saw his glory. It was the glory that the Father shares with his only Son, a glory full of kindness and truth. . . .* [18]*No one has ever seen God. God's only Son, the one who is closest to the Father's heart, has made him known" (John 1:14, 18).* Indeed, Jesus raised this question among His disciples on the eve of His crucifixion:

> [7]*"If you have known me, you will also know my Father. From now on you know him [through me] and have seen him [in me]."* [8]*Philip said to Jesus, "Lord, show us the Father, and that will satisfy us."* [9]*Jesus replied, "I have been with all of you for a long time. Don't you know me yet, Philip? The person who has seen me has seen the Father. So how can you say, 'Show us the Father'?* [10]*Don't you believe that I am in the Father and the Father is in me? What I'm telling you doesn't come from me. The Father, who lives in me, does what he wants." (John 14:7–10)*

The phrase "*the firstborn of all creation*" is easily misunderstood. While the English translation can carry the idea of the *first in a series*, this cannot be true of Jesus, since He is the One Who created everything *(Colossians 1:16)*. The phrase is better understood as *unique* or *supremacy*. Jesus is "*the image of the invisible God,*" and as such, He is also the Lord over all creation, the One Who supremely brought the world into being. He existed prior to that creation, and He is the supreme sovereign over all aspects of its existence, since He created the world *(John 1:1–3)*.

1:16 *He created all things in heaven and on earth, visible and invisible. Whether they are kings or lords, rulers or powers—everything has been created through him and for him.*

Jesus is the One Who created all things—in every location, both material and spiritual, seen and unseen. In perfect agreement, the writer of Hebrews says: "Faith convinces us that God created the world through his word. This means what can be seen was made by something that could not be seen" *(Hebrews 11:3)*.

Jesus created kings, lords, rulers, and powers, whether here on earth or in heaven. Many people are greatly impressed by the idea of angels, powerful beings that they believe intervene miraculously in their lives. Who are they? They are simply creatures created through the power and authority of Jesus Christ. The cherubim and seraphim, angelic beings who bow before the throne of God in perpetual worship, are only creatures brought into existence at the pleasure of Jesus Christ. These creatures, amazing as they are, serve the purposes of God the Father through the agency of His Son, Jesus. They have no power except that which has been given to them by Christ, the Creator.

On earth, there are kings, presidents, dictators, legislatures, and parliaments. These, too, exist in their designated positions under the sovereign will of Jesus Christ. Some of these earthly authorities are thought to be good and others evil. It makes no difference to believers. Christians know that earthly rulers, like the heavenly authorities, serve the purposes for which Christ created them.

Likewise, human beings are simply creatures created by the word of God. Nevertheless, they are special creatures, for God has created them in the image of the Triune God *(Genesis 1:27)*. Humans, like the rest of the created universe, were created by Jesus Christ and for

Jesus Christ. Like all other creatures in heaven and earth, they have no power except that which has been given to them by their Creator.

All of creation—all creatures in heaven and earth, great or small—contribute nothing to their existence. "They can only *render service* and this always in subjection to Christ and through *his* power."[4]

1:17 *He existed before everything and holds everything together.*

If Jesus created everything that exists, the entire universe both visible and invisible, then it is perfectly logical to conclude that He existed before the manifestation of His creation. Christ has always been, even before He made time and creation. "There never was a time when He was not; there never will come a time when He shall cease to be."[5]

The truth of the Scriptures affirms this reality. In one of His numerous debates with the scribes, Jesus stated: "I can guarantee this truth: before Abraham was ever born, I am" *(John 8:58)*. He told His disciples that He came from His Father and was about to return to His Father *(John 13:3; 20:17)*. As Jesus prayed in the Garden of Gethsemane, He asked His Father: "Now, Father, give me glory in your presence with the glory I had with you before the world existed" *(John 17:5)*. In the Book of Revelation, Jesus again made it clear that He was not subject to creation and time: "I am the A and the Z, the first and the last, the beginning and the end" *(Revelation 22:13)*.

The eternal essence of Jesus is consistently affirmed throughout the New Testament narrative *(John 1:1; 2 Corinthians 8:9; Philippians 2:6)*. The writer of Hebrews says: "[1]In the past God spoke to our ancestors at many different times and in many different ways through the prophets. [2]In these last days he has spoken to us through his Son. God made his Son responsible for everything. His Son is the one through whom God made the universe" *(Hebrews 1:1–2)*.

Jesus not only created everything that exists, but He also continues to sustain it, holding everything together. If He did not do this, the whole world would fall apart. There is a logical system by which the universe continues, not in chaos but in an orderly fashion. The human race has made gigantic strides in science and technology and, in their foolishness, believe that they know how everything works. But the magnificence of Christ's creation and the way that it functions will never be fully knowable by mere humans. The reason for this is simple. In the final analysis, in all things physical and spiritual, Christ is the One Who sustains and orders His creation. He sustains it by the weather systems that surround the planet, by the natural flow of the seasons, which provide times of planting and harvest. This, too, is the testimony of the Scriptural narrative. "*He makes his sun rise on people whether they are good or evil. He lets rain fall on them whether they are just or unjust*" (*Matthew 5:45*). Bible scholars identify this providential care as God's *common grace*.

1:18 *He is also the head of the church, which is his body. He is the beginning, the first to come back to life so that he would have first place in everything.*

Not only does the eternal Christ hold first place in the worlds that He has created, but He also holds first place in the Church that He has redeemed. Paul clearly described the preeminence of Christ as the transcendent Author of creation. Now he tells the saints in Colossae that He is preeminent as the Author of salvation. Christ entered His own creation, became a flesh and blood man, died on the cross as the only acceptable sacrifice for man's rebellion against the Creator, and came back to life by His own power. By these actions, He provided the inescapable evidence that He had power over sin, death, and hell. Only the One Who created everything that exists could do something like that. Paul shows how Christ now holds the first place in resurrection, guaranteeing that those who belong to Him can be confident of their resurrection as well.

1:19 *God was pleased to have all of himself live in Christ.*

In verse fifteen, Paul made it clear that Jesus is "*the image of the invisible God.*" Paul wanted to make sure that the Colossians understood what this meant. Jesus was not someone Who represented what God was like. He was not simply a vague copy of the eternal Lord God. Rather, Jesus is the very essence of the invisible God. He is the very same substance as the Father clothed in human flesh. Jesus Himself is the residence of God's glory, power, wisdom, Word, and Spirit. Because this is true, Jesus could tell His disciples: "The person who has seen me has seen the Father" *(John 14:9)*.

1:20 *God was also pleased to bring everything on earth and in heaven back to himself through Christ. He did this by making peace through Christ's blood sacrificed on the cross.*

As the supreme Lord over creation and the supreme Lord over man's redemption and resurrection, Jesus was the One, the only One, through Whom God and His creation could be reconciled. Through Christ, the Lord provided the pathway that brought His lost creation back to Himself. The world, fallen and corrupted by Adam's fall, has been separated from its Creator. Humanly speaking, there is no way to cross the chasm that separates a sinful, broken humanity from its righteous Creator. But God could bridge that chasm. Not only could He do that, but through the blood sacrifice of Jesus Christ, He did exactly that. Rather than a world ravaged by sin and rebellion, God made peace with mankind by providing His Son, Jesus, as the sacrifice to pay the price required to bring the world back into harmony with the One Who had created it in the first place.

Notes/Applications

Paul has described Jesus Christ in terms of His transcendent power by which the worlds were created. He has told believers that Jesus Christ holds first place in their redemption and their resurrection. Jesus Christ is, therefore, the living center of everything that exists, material and spiritual, in heaven and on earth, visible and invisible. He holds the keys to time and eternity. He locks and unlocks the gates of heaven, granting and forbidding entrance into His Kingdom. "[17]*I am the first and the last, [18]the living one. I was dead, but now I am alive forever. I have the keys of death and hell"* (Revelation 1:17–18).

This passage in Colossians is described by some as the most beautiful portrayal of Jesus Christ in all of Scripture. Some think that it was a recital of an early Christian hymn.[6] Regardless of these different ideas, the passage establishes the centrality and supremacy of Jesus Christ both in creation and redemption. Is it so difficult to understand why believers through 2,000 years have praised the Name of Jesus Christ?

In practical terms, what does this mean for believers? It means that they can have full confidence in Jesus Christ—in what He has done for them and in the very essence of Who He is. Since Jesus is the image and substance of the eternal God Who created all things for His pleasure by His sole determination, then He is *their* Creator. Since Jesus is the One Who makes peace between sin-ravaged humanity and the holy, righteous Lord, then He is *their* Redeemer. Since Jesus is the first to come back to life, then He is their *resurrection* as well. Since Jesus is the One Who is God clothed in human flesh and the perfect sacrifice for sin, how can believers be afraid of life or death? How can they be unsure of their salvation? How can they question the possibility of their resurrection?

Paul puts all of these questions to rest. For those whom God has saved through His Son, life and death are only an amazing journey that unfolds before them. It is a journey that brings the lost back to their Creator, making the journey a blessed communion. The redeemed sinners, now members of the Church, Christ's Body, take every step of that journey hand in hand with the One Who has created them and saved them. Together, the Church on earth, one with the Church in heaven, marches ever onward in song with hearts overflowing with thanksgiving and praise:

> Lift high the cross
> The love of Christ proclaim,
> Till all the world
> Adore His sacred name.[7]

Colossians 1:21–29

1:21 *Once you were separated from God. The evil things you did showed your hostile attitude.*

After writing about the supremacy of Jesus Christ, both in creation and redemption, Paul went on to tell Christians about the truth of their own situation before they were saved. Like the rest of humanity, they were separated from God. They were fully engaged in the warfare that had troubled the world nearly from the dawn of creation. They were hostile toward God. They wanted nothing to do with Him. In fact, they hated Him and made every effort to act like He did not exist or, at the very least, that He did not matter. Everything they did proved that they rebelled against the One Who had made them.

1:22 *But now Christ has brought you back to God by dying in his physical body. He did this so that you could come into God's presence without sin, fault, or blame.*

How did this hopeless situation get resolved? Christ intervened in the history of the human race—a people who were hopelessly resolved to die in their sin rather than appeal to the mercy of their Creator. Jesus died on the Cross. This was not some religious persuasion! This was a historically verifiable event. A human being, Jesus of Nazareth, the very image of the invisible God, died to satisfy the righteousness of God, the Father, paying the penalty for human rebellion. It was at the Cross that God consummated the legal transaction that saved those whom the Lord redeemed. When that transaction was completed, when God's righteousness was satisfied, then those who were saved could enter the presence of the eternal God "*without sin, fault, or blame.*"

Is Paul saying that the Colossian Christians were pure and holy, that they could enter God's presence because of their inherent goodness? Certainly not! He was telling these believers that they could enter God's presence because of what Christ had done on their behalf, not because they had achieved some level of behavior that satisfied a righteous, holy God. The people described in verse twenty-one, once alienated from their Creator, were the same people described in this verse. However, there was one clear distinction in Paul's description. These people had been saved by the work of Jesus Christ. Their physical description never changed at all, but their hearts had been wiped clean by the sacrifice of Christ and they were no longer the same. They were now clothed with the righteousness of Christ Himself.

1:23 ***This is on the condition that you continue in faith without being moved from the solid foundation of the hope that the Good News contains. You've heard this Good News of which I, Paul, became a servant. It has been spread throughout all creation under heaven.***

Paul seems to make an argument that supports the idea that one's salvation is contingent upon human effort, but that argument can only be supported if we forget other passages that assure believers of Christ's faithfulness in their salvation and sanctification. Paul himself assures the saints of their security, not in their human effort, but in Christ's continuing work in their lives *(Romans 8:28–39; Ephesians 2:8–10; 2 Timothy 1:12)*. Jesus Himself promises that those whom the Father has given to Him will never be lost *(John 10:28–29)*. Jude's short letter contains one of the most beautifully worded assurances of Christ's faithfulness:

> *24To him who is able to keep you from falling and to present you before his glorious presence without fault and with great joy—25to the only God our Savior be glory, majesty, power and authority, through Jesus Christ our Lord, before all ages, now and forevermore! Amen. (Jude 24–25, ESV)*

So what does Paul mean when he says, "This is on the condition that you continue in faith…?" The force of the Greek text is not so much conditional as it is the presentation of a logical relationship, which might better be translated, "Assuming you continue in faith…!" "The theological matter concerns the doctrine of the perseverance of the saints. Paul taught that those who know the truth will continue in the truth."[8] From the human perspective, no one really knows if another person is truly saved. One can only make an educated guess as believers relate to each other and observe the actions, which either tend to prove or disprove the condition of a person's faith. On this basis, Paul made a very strong appeal for the Colossians to energetically pursue the faith that had already been instilled in them by the Holy Spirit.

There is another consideration that flows from the context of this passage. Paul has presented the supremacy of Jesus Christ in creation and redemption. He then describes the condition of Christians *before* they are saved. Then he shows them how Christ's work on their behalf has brought them into the very presence of God—"*without sin, fault, or blame.*" This is what Christ has already done for them and this is their present position before God, which will be consummated when Christ comes again. Now Paul is showing the believers their present circumstances while still on this earth. Christ *has* saved them; He *will* save them; and, right now, He *is* saving them. The believers in Colossae were living in the divine tension that permeates every believer's life between that moment when they are saved and that future time when they will see their Savior face-to-face. They are struggling to work out their salvation "*with fear and trembling*" *(Philippians 2:12).*

Paul then tells them that he is a servant to this message—Who Jesus is; what Jesus has done; what Jesus will do; what Jesus is doing. It is Paul's way of providing an example of the scope of Christ's work in a person's life—past, present, and future. Paul, as a part of God's plan, had done his God-given best to proclaim this Gospel to the people in Asia Minor. But Paul looked beyond his personal passion for the message of Christ's salvation and saw that the Gospel was proclaimed to people everywhere. Paul could not mean everyone had literally heard the Gospel. If that were true, then there was no need for his missionary zeal. Rather, it is the message of salvation in Jesus Christ that was preached from city to city, reaching even to the people of Colossae, not directly through Paul, but through Epaphras. There is only one

Gospel that faithfully proclaims salvation in Jesus Christ alone. It did not matter who the messenger was. The message itself was a matter of utmost importance. This was universally true throughout all creation. Wherever people heard this message, God would redeem a people for Himself.

There is a logical progression that Paul follows in his presentation to the Colossian Christians. He has explained the cosmic nature of Christ's work to the specific work of Christ in the lives of the Colossian believers–progressing from Christ to Paul to Epaphras to the Colossians. It then moves from the Colossian saints back to the same message heard by all creation.

1:24 *I am happy to suffer for you now. In my body I am completing whatever remains of Christ's sufferings. I am doing this on behalf of his body, the church.*

Paul had just told the Colossians that he was the servant of the Gospel. Since most of the readers of this letter did not know Paul personally, he continued to explain his position in the work of Christ's Kingdom. His life as a servant of Jesus Christ had not been easy, but Jesus had told him at the very beginning that this was the way it would be. Those who opposed the Gospel would constantly threaten his life, resulting in a great deal of personal suffering. *"I'll show him how much he has to suffer for the sake of my name"* (*Acts 9:16*). At the time that Paul wrote this letter he was imprisoned in Rome. He was suffering, not so much from his confinement as from his restriction from telling people about Jesus. Thus, he shares the sufferings of Christ as all believers do until that time when Christ comes again. Indeed, it is through suffering–the suffering of Christ–that the saints enter the Kingdom of Heaven (*1 Thessalonians 3:3*). In that sense, Paul was suffering on behalf of Christ's Body, the Church, in which the Colossians had their part.

1:25 *I became a servant of the church when God gave me the work of telling you his entire message.*

This was not a task that Paul asked for. Rather, it was a task given to him by God. Before Jesus changed the path of his life on the road to Damascus, Paul, then known as Saul (his Hebrew name), thought that he was doing what God wanted him to do when he pursued and persecuted Christians. He did not believe in Jesus. He believed that Jesus and His followers were a threat to the "purity" of the Jewish religious structure. But Jesus stopped him and changed his thinking. When he met Jesus, Paul knew that he had been wrong. Jesus was not a threat to Judaism. Rather, He was the source of life, light, and forgiveness for both Jews and Gentiles *(Acts 9:1–20)*. In a moment, Paul discovered the Truth—God's Truth! Jesus was the only way to be reconciled to God, to enter the courts of heaven without sin, fault, or blame.

1:26 *In the past God hid this mystery, but now he has revealed it to his people.*

Once the message of God's salvation was a mystery. Shrouded in the prophecies and imagery of the Old Testament sacrificial system and its history, God slowly unveiled His character and His plan of salvation to His chosen people. When Jesus was born in the Judean village of Bethlehem, the ancient mystery was revealed when the angels sang, "Glory to God in the highest heaven, and on earth peace to those who have his good will!" *(Luke 2:14)*.

When Jesus' parents brought Him to the temple to be circumcised, a man named Simeon took the infant Jesus into his arms. Looking at the face of this infant, Simeon witnessed the revelation of God's mystery, not only to him personally, but to the whole world.

> 29"*Now, Lord, you are allowing your servant to leave in peace as you promised.* 30*My eyes have seen your salvation,* 31*which you have prepared for all people to see.* 32*He is a light that will reveal [salvation] to the nations and bring glory to your people Israel."(Luke 2:29–32)*

As Jesus walked among the people of Judea and Galilee, He gathered disciples and named some of them His apostles. These twelve men had a difficult time comprehending Who Jesus was even though He calmed the seas during a powerful storm, fed more than 5,000 people at one time from a few loaves of bread and some fish, and raised Lazarus from the grave. Jesus knew this and told these few men that they would understand everything He had told them when the Holy Spirit opened their eyes *(John 14:26)*. When that happened, the disciples understood the mystery of the Christ that had walked among them.

Jesus' execution on a Roman cross devastated those who followed the Man from Nazareth. After His resurrection, Jesus gently scolded two of those disciples on the road to Emmaus, telling them that the mystery of the ages had been fulfilled in Him.

> *25 Then Jesus said to them, "How foolish you are! You're so slow to believe everything the prophets said! 26 Didn't the Messiah have to suffer these things and enter into his glory?" 27 Then he began with Moses' Teachings and the Prophets to explain to them what was said about him throughout the Scriptures. (Luke 24:25–27)*

A few years later, Paul, once the scourge of the Christian community, met Jesus on the road to Damascus and his life was changed forever. The mystery of God's salvation was now clear to him. Jesus Christ was his Creator and his Redeemer. That which was hidden in the past was now clearly understood in the life, death, and resurrection of Jesus Christ.

1:27 *God wanted his people throughout the world to know the glorious riches of this mystery—which is Christ living in you, giving you the hope of glory.*

God's message of redemption through His Son, Jesus Christ, is no longer a mystery to those who have been redeemed. They see Jesus as their Creator and Redeemer as surely as Paul did nearly two thousand years ago. They see and comprehend how the death of Jesus and His victory over death assured their salvation, presenting them before the throne of God without sin, fault, or blame. They worship Him as the transcendent, all-powerful Lord of the universe. But the greatest revelation of this mystery is the way that this creating, saving, dying, rising Lord makes Himself known to those He saves. He lives within them! *(Galatians 2:20)*. He is greater than their sin, closer than the dearest friend, and nearer than their breathing. For believers, this revelation brings them to their knees. This revelation not only gives them the hope of glory. Jesus *is* the hope of glory! This revelation is based on the work of the transcendent God of the universe, the death and resurrection of the Savior, Jesus Christ, and the truth taught by the indwelling Holy Spirit *(John 14:17, 20, 23)*.

1:28 *We spread the message about Christ as we instruct and teach everyone with all the wisdom there is. We want to present everyone as mature Christian people.*

This revealed mystery, the message of Christ living in His people, the Gospel that saves people from their sin—this was the thrust of Paul's energetic proclamation of this great Good News. It is clear that Paul did not consider his God-given task to be limited to telling people about Jesus. After a person's salvation, he set about the task of instructing and teaching believers what the transformation of their lives required. For this reason, he taught in Corinth for eighteen months and in Ephesus for three years. The Colossian church was an outgrowth of his work in Ephesus. He wanted the saints to understand that following Jesus was not a religious pursuit. It was not a set of religious regulations. Rather, it was the worship and service of a Christ-centered life. The message was and continues to be the person and work of Jesus Christ—before a person's salvation at the cross, during the believer's life in sanctification, and consummating in His Second Coming. The saints are forever secure in Jesus Christ. For Paul, the purpose of this laborious task was to bring all the saints to a place of Christian maturity and endurance.

1:29 *I work hard and struggle to do this while his mighty power works in me.*

This message was the passion of Paul's redeemed life. He spent every ounce of his physical energy on the task assigned to him by Jesus Christ. He taught, argued, debated, scolded, and encouraged Christians, relentlessly and compassionately urging them forward into a deeper understanding and appreciation for what Christ had done for them as well as who they were in Christ. Nevertheless, he realized that his physical stamina was dependent on the power of the Lord Whom he served. Christ in him made it possible for Paul to suffer beatings, stoning, and multiple imprisonments. Despite his physical conditions, Paul could say that he was content no matter the physical circumstances, because Christ was worth more than all the hardship and suffering he experienced *(Philippians 4:11; Romans 8:18)*. In his letter to the Philippian church, Paul made this unambiguous statement: "It's far more than that! I consider everything else worthless because I'm much better off knowing Christ Jesus my Lord. It's because of him that I think of everything as worthless. I threw it all away in order to gain Christ" *(Philippians 3:8)*.

Notes/Applications

As the first chapter of Paul's letter to the Christians in Colossae closes, we take a step back and wonder what we have just experienced. Paul has opened the courts of heaven and given Christ's Church a glimpse of the unparalleled majesty of Jesus Christ. He is the One Who stretched forth His right hand and called the universe into existence. With the Psalmist, the redeemed sing: "The heavens declare the glory of God, and the sky above proclaims his handiwork" *(Psalm 19:1)*.

Why would this Creator leave His throne in the heavens and become an infant in a manger? Why would the all-powerful Lord of heaven and earth die on a Roman cross? When He looks at the race of mankind—stiff-necked, arrogant, and rebellious—He must surely see the hopelessness of their condition. They are a worthless bunch! What makes their condition so tragic is that they do not realize it. In their blind, misguided pride they believe they are really the masters of their lives. They do not know that they are doomed! Yet, Jesus came to this earth and dwelt among the darkness of man's sin and rebellion, showing them the way to return to the One Who had made them. What did people do? They killed Him! They executed Him like a common criminal! They did not realize that in that heinous act they accomplished the will of the eternal Lord. They executed an innocent Man, but God sacrificed His only Son to pay the penalty for their sin and reconciled all things to Himself, "*making peace by the blood of His cross.*"

But what is the most amazing thing this creating, saving Lord does? He lives within those He has saved. He does not just live among them. He does not simply walk with them throughout their life's journey. He lives *within* them! Once He saves them, He enters their lives and continues to work His will in and through His people.

Because He does this, the saints praise Jesus as the Alpha and the Omega, the beginning and the ending of their faith. They embrace the proclamation of the writer of Hebrews: "Let us fix our eyes on Jesus, the Author and Perfecter of our faith, who for the joy set before him endured the cross, scorning its shame, and sat down at the right hand of the throne of God" *(Hebrews 12:2,* NIV*)*. The saints praise Jesus for what He has done for them, and with eyes opened by the Holy Spirit, they see Him in all His transcendent glory and majesty. With the Psalmist, they shout the praise of Him Who remains faithful to His redeemed people.

> 1 *Hallelujah!*
> *Praise the Lord, my soul!*
> 2 *I want to praise the Lord throughout my life.*
> *I want to make music to praise my God as long as I live.*

3 Do not trust influential people,
mortals who cannot help you.

4 When they breathe their last breath, they return to the ground.
On that day their plans come to an end.
5 Blessed are those who receive help from the God of Jacob.
Their hope rests on the Lord their God,
6 who made heaven, earth,
the sea, and everything in them.
The Lord remains faithful forever.

–Psalm 146:1–6

COLOSSIANS 2

Colossians 2:1–7

2:1 ***I want you to know how hard I work for you, for the people of Laodicea, and for people I have never met.***

Paul continued to tell the saints in Colossae the intensity of the struggle that occupied his mind and heart on behalf of their faith *(1:29)*. This struggle is not external, that is, between Paul and others opposed to the Gospel of Jesus Christ. Rather, this is an ongoing internal anxiety for their continued growth in their knowledge of Christ, expressed in his prayers to the Lord. Paul then included the saints in Laodicea, a city just eleven miles west of Colossae.[1] Paul had taught the Gospel in the school of Tyrannus in Ephesus, but he had never visited Colossae, Laodicea, and Hierapolis *(4:13)*. The evangelization of these cities became the task for Epaphras *(1:7; 4:12)*, who was imprisoned with Paul at the time this letter was written. There were many Christians throughout Asia Minor who had been saved through the ministry of others who had been influenced by Paul. Even though Paul had never met these Christians personally, he wanted them to know of his pastoral concern for their spiritual welfare.

2:2–3 ***[2]Because they are united in love, I work so that they may be encouraged by all the riches that come from a complete understanding of Christ. He is the mystery of God. [3]God has hidden all the treasures of wisdom and knowledge in Christ.***

Most translations interpret the beginning phrase as the purpose for Paul's struggle concerning these Christians. Kenneth Wuest translates the phrase: "in order that their hearts may be encouraged, having been knit together in the sphere of love."[2] Paul works hard on their behalf so that they *will be* united in the love that Christ has poured out on them. Following his explanation of Christ's supremacy in all things, His majesty and power in creation and redemption, Paul wants these believers to bask in the riches that are a part of their inheritance in Jesus Christ. Paul encourages the readers to look to Christ as the only person in Whom these "*treasures of wisdom*" are available. *Mystery* does not mean "concealed" but "deposited" or "stored up" *(1:26)*. Jesus Christ is the only resource where godly wisdom and knowledge are *stored up*. Other sources of knowledge apart from Christ are useless.[3] Christ alone is the storehouse of the wealth that He bestows on those He has saved.

2:4 ***I say this so that no one will mislead you with arguments that merely sound good.***

Paul struggled for these Christians, not only for their encouragement in the faith and their unity in love, but also for their protection from people who did not faithfully uphold the message of the Gospel. Such people could make arguments that sounded good, maybe even persuasive. But this kind of thinking could mislead them into a false hope, a hope that was not centered on the person and work of Jesus Christ.

2:5 ***Although I'm absent from you physically, I'm with you in spirit. I'm happy to see how orderly you are and how firm your faith in Christ is.***

Paul was imprisoned nearly 1,500 miles (2,415 km) from Colossae. That was a considerable distance, but that did not stop Paul from thinking about and praying for them. The Lord's strength, encouragement, and compassion are not confined to time and space. Thus, Paul could be close to them in spirit as though he were with them. That closeness and Epaphras' reports gave him great happiness. He knew the saints in Colossae, Laodicea, and Hierapolis lived in a way that demonstrated they were under the control of the Holy Spirit. Their faith in Christ was firm, deeply rooted, and secure, helping them to live in a way that showed they belonged to God through Jesus Christ.

2:6 *You received Christ Jesus the Lord, so continue to live as Christ's people.*

Christ had entered their lives, just as He had entered Paul's life, stripping away their sinful perspectives and filling them with His Holy Spirit. Because of this dramatic transformation in their lives, Paul asked them to live within the framework of their salvation. They were people who now belonged to Jesus Christ. Their changed lives should reflect the work that Christ had done in them.

2:7 *Sink your roots in him and build on him. Be strengthened by the faith that you were taught, and overflow with thanksgiving.*

The tenses of the Greek language are important here. They show how Christ's work has been both completed and continues to work in the routines of their daily lives. The opening phrase expresses something that has already happened in the past—the moment when they received Christ—and then the progressing, continuing development of their redeemed lives in and through Jesus Christ. The phrase literally states: "having been rooted and being built up in Him."[4] Notice also that the phrase is passive. This action comes from Christ by the work of the Holy Spirit. He is the One Who has rooted the believers in their faith and He is the One Who continues to build on that foundation, Jesus Christ Himself.

This was nothing less than the Gospel, Who is Christ, the mystery of God, hidden from the world but revealed to His saints. They had received Christ by His work in their lives. They have received Christ by the ministry of Paul, who had been assigned this task by Jesus. Thus, they not only received the gift of faith, but they also received Paul's authoritative instruction in that faith. They could trust the hard work, the struggle, the intercession of the man through whom God had revealed His Gospel.

Since the Lord had saved them and continued to work in and through them, they had every reason to be overflowing with thankfulness. It is in the framework of thanksgiving and praise that the saints show the world that they belong to God.

Notes/Applications

The mystery of God is not some well-hidden secret available only to a few intelligent people. It is not some well-developed philosophy that appears to be intellectually coherent. The mystery of God is not some religious expression of God's love for mankind. The mystery of God is not even the message of salvation expressed by Paul and other biblical authors. The mystery of God is a Person—Jesus Christ *(v. 2)*.

Jesus Christ is at the core of our understanding about God, salvation, judgment, mercy, forgiveness, and reconciliation. Without Jesus Christ there is no creation *(1:16)*. Without Him, His creation would fall apart *(1:17)*. Without Him, there is no reconciliation (1:20). Without His cross, there is no peace with God *(1:20)*.

Jesus Christ is salvation. He is mercy. He is the Author and Finisher of our Faith *(Hebrews 12:1–2)*. He is our Mediator with the holy, righteous God *(1 Timothy 2:15)*. He Himself is peace *(1:20)*. He is the image of the invisible God *(1:16)*. He is the repository of all wisdom and knowledge *(2:5)*. He is the Head of His Body, the Church *(1:18)*.

The mystery of Christ is the thrust of Paul's message to all Christians. This is the message for which he labored without thought to his own health and safety. This was the substance of his prayers. He was deeply concerned for the welfare of Christ's Church—those whom he knew and those whom he had never met.

For this reason, Paul could say to the Corinthians: "For I resolved to know nothing while I was with you except Jesus Christ and him crucified" *(1 Corinthians 2:2,* NIV*).* For this reason, Paul could say to the Galatians: "But even if we or an angel from heaven should preach a gospel other than the one we preached to you, let him be eternally condemned!" *(Galatians 1:8).* For this reason, Paul could say to the Colossians: "[6]You received Christ Jesus the Lord, so continue to live as Christ's people. [7]Sink your roots in him and build on him. Be strengthened by the faith that you were taught, and overflow with thanksgiving" *(Colossians 2:6–7).*

Any other doctrine, any other philosophy, any other religious scheme is futile and meaningless. Jesus is everything to those who have been redeemed. There is nothing else that captures the heart and mind of a redeemed sinner as the supreme glory of the One Who died on Calvary's cross. With Paul, let all the saints throughout the ages exclaim: "Indeed, I count everything as loss because of the surpassing worth of knowing Christ Jesus my Lord. For his sake I have suffered the loss of all things and count them as rubbish, in order that I may gain Christ" *(Philippians 3:8,* ESV*).*

Colossians 2:8–15

2:8 *Be careful not to let anyone rob you [of this faith] through a shallow and misleading philosophy. Such a person follows human traditions and the world's way of doing things rather than following Christ.*

Paul described the faith of the Colossian Christians as firmly established *(2:5)*. Nevertheless, there are always challenges that face even the most mature Christians. Despite the depth of faith, God's people always need to guard what they have been given with clarity of thought based on the pure doctrine of God's Word. Sometimes a mature faith can be easily misled, because that maturity can become a matter of spiritual pride. Then, in pursuit of "greater wisdom," such people begin to look to other sources for what they believe will make them appear more spiritual.

Paul now began to warn believers of the danger that surrounds "*shallow and misleading philosophy.*" Listening to the opinions of people about their religious convictions can be an exercise in foolishness. Paul has made it clear that Jesus Christ is supreme in all matters of faith, but human traditions and worldly thinking oppose Christ's position in creation and redemption. Instead, they elevate man and support the vanity and foolishness of his self-indulgent idolatry. Tradition may appear to have the weight of history, adding dignity, authority, and revelation to a particular philosophy, but such traditions can actually create barriers to faith that centers on Jesus Christ and His work.

2:9–10 [9]*All of God lives in Christ's body,* [10]*and God has made you complete in Christ. Christ is in charge of every ruler and authority.*

Earlier Paul had told believers that Jesus was the image of the invisible God, the firstborn over all creation *(1:15)*. Now he told them that the fullness of God lives in Jesus Christ. In other words, Jesus, as Creator and Redeemer, was completely the eternal Lord. There was no part of

Him that was not God. He was the very substance and essence of God in bodily form *(John 1:14–18)*. Any other philosophy or human tradition that failed to build on this eternal truth opposed the Christ of the Gospel. No human can add to or take away from Jesus Christ.

Because Christ is the fullness of God, it is only logical that believers also have received the fullness of their salvation in and through Him. They do not need anything else to complete what has already been completed in Christ. They do not need to follow human traditions or philosophies in order to receive their salvation. Such a philosophy would make Jesus less than God, inadequate to save people from their sins. Anyone who made such ridiculous claims angered Paul, causing him to say: "If anyone preaches any other Gospel than what we preached to you, let him be accursed" *(Galatians 1:8–9, paraphrased)*.

2:11 *In him you were also circumcised. It was not a circumcision performed by human hands. But it was a removal of the corrupt nature in the circumcision performed by Christ.*

The Law of Moses, given by God, required the circumcision of male infants eight days after birth. This circumcision marked them as children of God's covenant with Abraham, making his heirs God's chosen people and setting them apart from the rest of humanity.

In a metaphoric comparison, Paul told believers that they were also circumcised in Christ, Who is God in the flesh. Spiritually speaking, Christ circumcised those that He saved, removing their corrupt nature. In this way, Christ marked them as His children, not in the flesh, but in spirit. He set them apart from the rest of the human community, reconciling them to Himself by the shedding of His blood on the Cross *(1:20–21)*. When Jesus died, God completed the transaction necessary to make peace with His rebellious creation. When the Holy Spirit applies this transaction to a person's life, that person also dies to the world's way of thinking, knowing the unsurpassed fullness of his salvation in Jesus Christ.

2:12 ***This happened when you were placed in the tomb with Christ through baptism. In baptism you were also brought back to life with Christ through faith in the power of God, who brought him back to life.***

The Jews had developed intricate rituals of ceremonial cleansing. This was a source of bitter controversy between the Jews and Jesus *(Mark 7:3–9)*. Jesus took issue with people who performed external rituals, but failed to understand that God was more interested in a person's heart. Like Jesus, Paul is not speaking here about the external ritual of baptism. The rite of baptism never saved anybody. Here Paul is talking about what baptism symbolizes. When the Holy Spirit saves a sinner, that person is baptized spiritually. That person is buried with Christ in the tomb. He dies to the things of this world, even as Jesus died physically. Then he rises with Christ to a new life, a resurrection of the human spirit, transformed from within. A redeemed person literally is made spiritually alive, resurrected from slavery to sin to new life in Christ *(Ephesians 2:5–6)*.

2:13 ***You were once dead because of your failures and your uncircumcised corrupt nature. But God made you alive with Christ when he forgave all our failures.***

Sin keeps people separated from God. Outside of the saving mercy of the Lord, people are dead. They have no idea what real life, abundant life in Christ, is all about. They know only the pursuit of their own selfish goals and ambitions. They do not know what it means to breathe the clean air of forgiveness. Rotten to the core, people go through life as though they are the ones who make the choices that bring them success or failure. But this vanity does not consume the lives of those who have been redeemed. Believers are no longer captive to their sin nature with all its folly and foolishness. Why? Certainly not because they are able to see their sin, foolishness, and rebellion, but because Christ has forgiven them. Christ has opened believers' blind eyes, forgiven their sin, and set them free from the shackles of sin and the stench of death.

2:14 ***He did this by erasing the charges that were brought against us by the written laws God had established. He took the charges away by nailing them to the cross.***

How did Christ bring believers to life? Certainly not by His teaching, although His words stir the human heart. Certainly not by His miracles, although those miracles stagger the human mind. Words and miracles, as persuasive as they are, do not save the sinner from the wrath of a righteous, holy God. No! A sacrifice must appease God's anger, replacing God's judgment with His salvation. Jesus was that sacrifice! He bore the sins of many when He died on a Roman cross. This was the testimony of Peter, the leader of Christ's apostles: "He himself bore our sins in his body on the tree, that we might die to sin and live to righteousness. By his wounds you have been healed" *(1 Peter 2:24, ESV)*. When Jesus died in full agreement with the sovereign will of His Father, the sins of God's people were erased, wiped away, eradicated. People saw Roman soldiers drive the nails through Jesus' hands and feet. God saw His Son accept the sins of the human race and nailed them to that cross. The debt was paid. The sentence was lifted. The sins of God's people were forgiven.

2:15 ***He stripped the rulers and authorities [of their power] and made a public spectacle of them as he celebrated his victory in Christ.***

When the Sanhedrin, the high court of the Jews, sentenced Jesus to death and received Pilate's reluctant permission to execute that sentence, they thought they were getting rid of a powerful religious enemy. Jesus upset their traditions and infuriated their religious sensibilities. As Jesus was dying on the Cross, they made Him a spectacle of their ridicule and scorn.

> [29]*Those who passed by insulted him. They shook their heads and said, "What a joke! You were going to tear down God's temple and build it again in three days.* [30]*Come down from the cross, and save yourself!"* [31]*The chief priests and the scribes*

> *made fun of him among themselves in the same way. They said, "He saved others, but he can't save himself. [32]Let the Messiah, the king of Israel, come down from the cross now so that we may see and believe." Even those who were crucified with him were insulting him. (Mark 15:29–32)*

What these powerful rulers and authorities did not realize was the way the sovereign God was using them to accomplish His purpose in these events. They saw only the physical aspect of Jesus' execution. They saw His agony; they saw Him thirsty; they heard Him cry out to His Father, "My God, My God! Why have you forsaken me?" *(Matthew 27:46)*. But they never saw that God was offering His Son as the perfect sacrifice for the sins of those who executed Him as well as the sins of all mankind. While they ridiculed the Man on the Cross, the Father was celebrating His victory of over sin and death.

Notes/Applications

Things are not always what they appear to be.

When the leaders of the Jews arrested Jesus in the Garden of Gethsemane, they thought they finally got the upper hand on this self-appointed rabbi from Galilee. When the Sanhedrin found Jesus guilty of blasphemy, they thought that their law gave them the right to put Him to death. When they went to Pilate, they incited the crowd to demand Jesus' crucifixion, and eventually Pilate conceded to their wishes. When Jesus was hanging on the Cross, struggling for every breath, they laughed at His predicament–a prophet from Galilee Who could not save Himself.

These proud, vain religious leaders had no idea what was really happening. They did not realize that their hatred and scorn for Jesus was used by the eternal God to provide the only perfect sacrifice for the sins of the world. While the leaders of the Jewish people congratulated each other on the success of their mission to destroy Jesus, the Father in heaven was celebrating His victory over sin and death by the sacrifice of His Son, Jesus Christ *(2:15)*. While the disciples cowered in fear in the upper room, distraught over this turn of events, the Creator was rejoicing over the reconciliation that His Son provided for His wayward creation.

People have their religions, but religion is only an external, man-made system that is designed to make man feel good about himself. The Jews had developed an intricate web of religious tradition over the centuries. Yet, when their Messiah entered their history, they never understood what was going on. They executed Him in order to preserve the sanctity of their religious traditions. No one knew these traditions better than Paul, educated as a Pharisee and mentored by the great Jewish theologian, Gamaliel.

When Paul met Jesus Christ, he discovered that these religious traditions were meaningless. Following these traditions passionately saved no one. Only Jesus saved people from their sins. When he talked about baptism, he showed the Colossian Christians how the external rite was only an expression of what the Spirit had done to the heart. When redeemed, the sinner dies to the things of the world and rises to new life in Jesus Christ. It was the same as circumcision. Although the Jews held to this tradition passionately, and some believed that Gentiles needed to be circumcised in order to fully receive their salvation, Paul knew that the circumcision of the Spirit cut the sinner loose from his sin nature.

Things are not always what they appear to be. This is true for the events that led to the sacrifice of Jesus Christ for the sins of the world. It is equally true for the work of the Holy Spirit, applying the satisfaction of that sacrifice to those whom He saves. Religion comes from the misguided ambitions of mankind. Salvation and transformation comes through Jesus Christ.

Colossians 2:16–23

2:16 *Therefore, let no one judge you because of what you eat or drink or about the observance of annual holy days, New Moon Festivals, or weekly worship days.*

Paul continues to show Christians the hopelessness of man-made religions. Living in a religious society devoted to numerous gods, the Colossian Christians were raised in the observance of many traditions that had no significance for those who were the Lord's redeemed. Before they were saved, these people were thoroughly engaged in the worship of these false gods. When they became Christians, they were baptized into Jesus Christ and separated from their corrupt nature by the circumcision not made with hands.

Now the Colossian believers no longer engaged in the practices of their former religious worship. However, the pressure to continue in their old ways did not go away. Family and friends wanted them to join in their festivities. Paul reminded Christians that they were no longer subject to the opinions of those who were outside the household of faith. Now that they were in Christ, the saints should remember what Christ had done for them. This was the priority of their redeemed lives. Their allegiance to their Lord superseded their obligations to family and friends, to the old ways of living, and to the false religion out of which they had been saved.

Many of the converts were residents of the Jewish community in Colossae. The traditions of the Jewish society also imposed rules and regulations on their people. It was the Jewish people who were Paul's most adamant opponents to his message of salvation in Jesus Christ. Some became Christians and still observed the rules of their Jewish faith. In their opinion, a Gentile who became a believer should also submit to circumcision and adopt the Jewish regulations to fully receive their salvation. Although educated as a Pharisee, Paul knew better than anyone that these regulations had no impact at all on salvation.

2:17 *These are a shadow of the things to come, but the body [that casts the shadow] belongs to Christ.*

Christ Himself is the only reality to which the saints should cling. The history of the Jewish people was simply a shadow that forecast God's Messiah. They exhibited a dim representation of everything that the Messiah would accomplish by the sovereign will of the Lord God. Jesus Christ was the sum and substance of shadows that predicted His life and work of salvation among the nations. Jesus is the full revelation of God's salvation that was hidden in these shadows until He came to earth and saved His people by His sacrifice on the Cross.

Greek and Roman culture was profoundly religious. The most magnificent buildings of those days were the temples erected to the worship of numerous gods and goddesses. This culture also imposed its ideas and rules on the people. Like the traditions of the Jews, these pagan practices should no longer impact those who had been redeemed. In their religious devotion, special days had been set aside to focus their devotion. But Christ is sovereign over this pagan culture just as He was over the Jewish religious traditions.

All of Jewish history culminated in the Cross of Jesus Christ. All of human history is the story of the God's redemption. Jesus is the central figure of that history. Since that Cross, every person stands or falls on what they think of Jesus Christ. Since that Cross, every person is either saved or condemned by what happened on that Cross.

2:18 *Let no one who delights in [false] humility and the worship of angels tell you that you don't deserve a prize. Such a person, whose sinful mind fills him with arrogance, gives endless details of the visions he has seen.*

In every age within the context of differing religious structures, there have been those who achieve what they believe to be spiritual superiority by their pursuit of dreams and visions. *Humility* here means "self-denial" and describes fasting and other bodily disciplines, which were self-denying practices in some Jewish circles where mystical piety was supposed to open the way for receiving visions of heavenly mysteries.[5] In that mystical environment, adherents of mystical piety addressed their worship to angels, those beings that occupied the spirit world. Because of their "religious experiences," they thought they were better informed, more blessed, and spiritually superior. They thought that Christians were not worthy to receive God's blessings.

Angel worship was a predominant aspect of religious worship in Asia Minor. The region of the three cities, Colossae, Laodicea, and Hierapolis, was the center of this worship. It continued for several centuries. The Synod of *Laodicea*—one of the three cities of the Lycus Valley, in the year A.D. 363 declared, "It is not right for Christians to abandon the church of God and go away to invoke angels" (Canon XXV).[6]

Paul does not say that their "religious experiences" were not genuine. He did say that they bragged about their experiences in great detail. But these experiences were the outcome, not of a mind and heart under the care and guidance of the Holy Spirit, but the mind and heart of an arrogant person consumed by his corrupt nature. Those who had been redeemed should never be impacted by these false religious practices. They have Christ, and He reigns supreme over all of these man-made religious traditions.

2:19 *He doesn't hold on to [Christ,] the head. Christ makes the whole body grow as God wants it to, through support and unity given by the joints and ligaments.*

Why is it so wrong to seek a deeper religious experience? Because, Paul says, that it does not honor Jesus Christ, Who is the Head of His Church. So many crave a "religious experience," and fail to understand that believers need a closer relationship with Jesus. Humanly derived "religious experiences" spring up from the human heart's desire to be someone special, to be given special knowledge that the average person cannot know. Christ is not the center of such devotion. Self is the center of this devotion. Paul tells Christians that they can grow in faith as God directs only in Christ, only within the Church, which is the

Body of Christ where He rules as its supreme Head. Personal spiritual growth that is nurtured within the community of God's saints is reliable and faithful to the desires of the Lord, because it receives the support, unity, and guidance of the whole of Christ's Body.

2:20 *If you have died with Christ to the world's way of doing things, why do you let others tell you how to live? It's as though you were still under the world's influence.*

Paul then poses a question, which brings everything that he has been saying into sharp focus. Why do Christians continue to act as though they are influenced more by the world than they are by the Lord Who saved them? God has made peace with them through the blood of Christ's Cross *(1:20)*. He has circumcised their hearts, cutting away their corrupt nature *(v. 11)*. He has brought them through the baptism of their faith, where they die to their old nature and are raised to new life in Jesus Christ *(v. 12)*. He has given them life eternal by forgiving their sins and paying the debt imposed by God's Law *(v. 14)*. When Christ has done all these things for the benefit of those He has saved, why do Christians still listen to and seek guidance from those who are not redeemed? It seems as though the pull of the world's influence is stronger than the experience of their salvation.

2:21 *People will tell you, "Don't handle this! Don't taste or touch that!"*

Everywhere Christians go, people tell them what to do. They exert their worldly influence on God's people so that they fade into society, rather than stand out as those who belong to God through Jesus Christ. According to the world's philosophy, Christians should just be another member of society, quietly going about their daily routine without upsetting others with the distinctive calling of the gospel message.

2:22 *All of these things deal with objects that are only used up anyway.*

The Gospel sets people free from the rules and conventions of human traditions. The context seems to point back to food that the Jews were allowed to eat, and refrain from eating those foods that were forbidden (*v. 16*). Paul showed the saints in Colossae how foolish such regulations were. Once consumed, they pass away. Such taboos frustrated the liberating message of the Gospel, imposing obligations based on human traditions.

2:23 *These things look like wisdom with their self-imposed worship, [false] humility, and harsh treatment of the body. But they have no value for holding back the constant desires of your corrupt nature.*

While such rules and regulations may appear to have value by restraining a degree of human indulgence, they really have no impact on controlling man's sinful nature. It may give some reason to be proud that these "religious" people follow the rules faithfully, but it does nothing to change their true nature. Looking simply on the outside, such people may appear to be wise and pious. This is confirmed by their faithfulness to this self-imposed worship, their humility, and their self-discipline. However, their hearts are not changed and they are still slaves to their human appetites. It is a counterfeit religion that cannot save people from their sins. Only Jesus Christ can do that!

Notes/Applications

Paul's theme can be summarized with one short phrase: "Only Christ!" The Church of Jesus Christ should rise up and shout this message from shore to shore: "ONLY CHRIST!"

Paul has gone through a list of rituals, regulations, and religious instructions that were common in his day. After each one, he has made it clear that none of this works. People have contrived their own religions, which leaves them in despair. They have bet their lives on counterfeit religions. In the end, they will learn that their religious devotion was worthless, and they will die in their sin, lost and condemned to eternal damnation.

Circumcision is worthless, unless it the circumcision of the heart made by Christ Himself. Baptism cannot save a person, unless it is that baptism by the Holy Spirit, which transforms the heart and mind. Heavenly visions may stimulate devotion, but only the worship of Jesus Christ exalts the One Who has created and redeemed. Rules and regulations do not control sensuous desires, unless the Holy Spirit imposes those principles. Religious traditions making rules on things like food and drink save no one. Ultimately, religion itself is worthless. Religion saves no one!

"ONLY CHRIST!" He is the focus of worship for all the Lord's redeemed people. He circumcises their hearts. He baptizes them in the truth of His Word. He transforms the hearts and minds of sinners. He guards and protects the hearts of those He has saved.

The Christian faith centers on a person's relationship to Jesus Christ, a relationship that is bestowed on those He saves. Jesus sets the sinner free from human traditions. Jesus breaks the bonds of slavery to religious worship of anything or anyone other than Jesus Christ. Jesus tears down the strongholds of religious tyranny. Jesus raises His people to an abundant life where they breathe the fresh air of sins forgiven and rest in the peace of Christ that no one can humanly comprehend.

Let Christ's Church remain faithful to the One Who has brought it from death to life. Let His Body always follow the lead of its faithful Head. Let every knee bow and every tongue confess that Jesus is Lord to the glory of God the Father.

COLOSSIANS 3

Colossians 3:1–8

3:1–2 ***[1]Since you were brought back to life with Christ, focus on the things that are above—where Christ holds the highest position. [2]Keep your mind on things above, not on worldly things.***

The antidote to all counterfeit religious pursuits is to focus on the things that are above, the place where Jesus sits at the right hand of the Father. If believers continue to be influenced by the things of the material world, which will pass away, then they have lost their focus. They have turned their eyes away from Jesus, Who is the image of the invisible God, their Creator and Redeemer. Looking to anything other than Jesus is a formula for disaster in the Christian's life. To counteract this very human tendency, Paul urges believers to keep their mind focused on Jesus. Like the Colossian believers, all those who have been saved are already raised with Christ. They no longer belong to the world. They are no longer subject to the world's way of doing things.

The Greek tense of the verb has the idea of continuing to focus on things above. This does not come automatically, even to God's redeemed people. It is a lifelong commitment to remember Jesus, Who He is and what He has done. When looking to heaven, the saints see Jesus exalted on His throne, where He reigns as their King. The stunning glory of the angels pales in comparison to the majesty of Jesus Christ. When God's people see the Lord and bow their knee to His rule in their lives, they are driven to assess their ambitions, their goals, and their very thinking. Every thought, every decision, every action should be perceived through the lens of their redemption, and Jesus Christ is their redemption, the Author and Finisher of their faith.

3:3 *You have died, and your life is hidden with Christ in God.*

Obviously, Paul was not speaking of their physical demise. Rather, he is reminding them that, when they were saved, they had died to the world's influence with all of its regulations, visionary experiences, and self-exalting worship *(2:20)*. They have been pulled away from the counterfeit religious structures derived from man's self-centered ambitions. Their former lives have passed away, and they now belong to Christ.

More than dying to their old nature, Christ has hidden their life in God. Believers are joined to Christ in His death and resurrection *(2:12)*. Paul was reminding them of what he had said earlier: "[9]All of God lives in Christ's body, [10]and God has made you complete in Christ. Christ is in charge of every ruler and authority" *(Colossians 2:9–10)*. Jesus and His Father are one *(John 10:30; 17:11)*. Since believers are joined with Christ, they are also joined with God. Since Christ has redeemed them, He has brought them to the very throne of the Father where their salvation will be kept securely until that day when Jesus comes again. All believers are secure in Christ not only in this life, but for all eternity. Nothing on this earth can touch the redeemed. They are safe and secure from all the dangers, which surround them every moment of every day throughout their earthly lives.

3:4 *Christ is your life. When he appears, then you, too, will appear with him in glory.*

Believers should focus on things above where Christ reigns over all His creation. They should never forget what Jesus has done for them. But Paul wants believers to realize something even more important. While Jesus is the focus of worship, He is also life itself *(John 14:6)*. He is the very essence of their redeemed lives. He is the very air they breathe. Not in some future eternity, but here and now! The abundant life Jesus promised is given to everyone who receives the gift of salvation *(John 10:10)*.

Christ is the very life of His redeemed people, giving them an immeasurable joy throughout their earthly days. Saints would never trade their life in Christ for anything this world can offer them. But the joys of this life are only a foretaste of what happens when believers meet Jesus face-to-face. At the time when Jesus comes again for His Bride—His Church—all believers will be transformed, not only in heart and mind, but in body as well *(1 Corinthians 15:50–57)*. In John's letter to Christians of the first century, he said: "Dear friends, now we are God's children. What we will be isn't completely clear yet. We do know that when Christ appears we will be like him because we will see him as he is" *(1 John 3:2)*.

3:5 *Therefore, put to death whatever is worldly in you: your sexual sin, perversion, passion, lust, and greed (which is the same thing as worshiping wealth).*

When Jesus prayed to His Father, interceding for those who would come to faith, He said: "I'm not asking you to take them out of the world but to protect them from the evil one" *(John 17:15)*. When Paul asked believers to focus on Jesus Christ, he was not asking them to live with their head in the clouds. Like Jesus, he was asking them to remain in the world to complete the tasks assigned to them, but with their minds and hearts focused on things above. Such a focus would keep them from the clutches of the evil one. This focus would result in their obedience to the practical instructions that Paul now gives to them.

Since Christ has saved them, believers are already dead to their sin nature. The corrupt nature has been cut away by the circumcision made by Christ. But, practically speaking, this is more easily said than done. It is an ongoing struggle to keep one's focus on Jesus Christ. A person does not readily fall into step with the direction of the Spirit, and dreamy reflections cannot achieve what Paul is saying here. Nevertheless, believers are not left to struggle in self-defeating isolation. Rather, the Holy Spirit continues to work in the lives of those that belong to God. With the Spirit's direction, discipline, and encouragement, the execution of those sinful desires that stand in the way of living the abundant life have already been given to those He saves. Every human being is beset by these evils, which are only the exhibition of the depravity of the sinful heart. Nevertheless, that is no excuse! With the Spirit's help, God's people are to cut out deliberately those relationships, circumstances, and temptations that lead them back into their old ways of thinking and behaving. These are idolatrous behaviors that exalt human ambitions above the salvation that has been given to them in Jesus Christ.

3:6 *It is because of these sins that God's anger comes on those who refuse to obey him.*

God meets sin with His anger. God's anger is simply the outflow of His righteousness. People who offend the Lord may always expect His anger. Since all people sin, all people may expect His judgment. Nevertheless, God's judgment is always seen in the context of His salvation. The opposite is also true! His salvation is always understood in the context of His judgment. It is the outworking of God's holiness against all unrighteousness.[1] William Hendriksen states: "By means of what is sometimes called 'a prophetic present tense' (cf. John 4:21; 14:3) Paul stresses the fact that the coming of the wrath of God, to be visited upon those who live in such sins, is so certain that it is as if that wrath had already arrived."[2] The Lord is always the same, yesterday, today, and forever. His anger always comes on those who do those things that offend the nature of His righteousness. Even those who are redeemed, who live under the protection of Christ's blood, can be assured of the Spirit's discipline when they fall into sins which grieve the Holy Spirit.

3:7 *You used to live that kind of sinful life.*

Such behavior consumes the life of the unredeemed. It is the natural expression of the sin nature. Everyone lives this way until that moment when the Spirit breathes new life into the dead soul destined for hell and applies the work of Christ's cross to his life. Self-consumed, people spend every waking moment trying to satisfy the desires of their heart in sexual immorality, perversion, lust, and greed.

3:8 *Also get rid of your anger, hot tempers, hatred, cursing, obscene language, and all similar sins.*

The sins outlined in 3:5 could be seen as sins that characterize the relationships involving all people—saved and unsaved alike. The sins described here are simply the expression of an individual whose whole personality is steeped in a seething rebellion against the Lord. Such a rebellion is nothing more or less than a deep-seated self-love. Such a person is angry at everything and erupts in fits of uncontrolled temper that are verbally expressed by cursing and obscene language. Such a person is completely consumed by an uncontrolled evil that exhibits a profound dissatisfaction with life and hatred toward the Lord. But believers, who were once likewise consumed by their passions, are to get rid of these expressions of their former lives.

Notes/Applications

Paul could not have drawn a sharper contrast between the lifestyle of the unbeliever and that of a person who has been saved. The contrast is so razor sharp it seems too hard to really understand. As an unbeliever are we really that bad? As a believer, are we able to achieve the standards that Paul sets before us? Everything in our being tells us that we are not really that bad. At the same time, without any difficulty, we know that we cannot comply with the behavioral patterns that Paul requires of believers. We do not see any contradiction in this. We simply do not think of ourselves as terrible people, but we know we are not really good either.

In the trenches of our daily routines, we see too much of the old nature and very little of the redeemed life that has been given to us. We get angry at the smallest things. We say things a believer should never say. As someone has said, "If we were put on trial because of our Christian faith, is there enough evidence to convict us?" Sadly, for many of us, we would be released for lack of evidence. We fully agree with James: "Praise and curses come from the same mouth. My brothers and sisters, this should not happen!" *(James 3:10).*

We are so desperately tied to our earthly existence that it is virtually impossible to fix our minds on things above. We talk about the disciples who, though they walked physically with Jesus, just never quite seem to see what is happening around them. Now, two thousand years later, long after that remarkable Pentecost, we look back, read the gospels, and wonder why they did not understand. Since Pentecost, the Holy Spirit infused those disciples with a heaven-sent understanding of those three years with Jesus. We live in a post-Pentecost age, when believers are given this gift at the beginning of their salvation.

But, honestly, are we so different? With thousands of books published every year, we still stand cemented firmly to this world, clinging with all our strength to our egos, our possessions, and religions. The result is a weak, anemic church, divided into thousands of little pieces, scattered across the landscape, fighting each other for theological superiority. All this while the world dies at the hands of our neglect of the Gospel.

With James, we exclaim, "This should not happen!" With Paul we cry out, "Who shall save me from this body of death?" *(Romans 7:24).* With Paul we also exclaim, "Thanks be to God through Jesus Christ our Lord!" Let us fix our minds on things above, on Jesus Christ, the hope of our salvation, rising with the Spirit's help above a life of continual struggle.

Colossians 3:9–17

3:9–10 *[9]Don't lie to each other. You've gotten rid of the person you used to be and the life you used to live, [10]and you've become a new person. This new person is continually renewed in knowledge to be like its Creator.*

Paul continued to make a list of the things that believers should avoid. He had challenged them to put to death idolatry and other earthly passions *(v. 5)*. He had urged them to clean up the way they talked—to avoid anger, slander, and filthy language *(v. 8)*. Now he tells Christians to stop lying to each other. Such behavior is part of the old nature and should not characterize someone who has been redeemed by Jesus Christ.

Paul then provides two reasons why believers should get rid of these traits that had defined their character before they were saved. Before they became followers of Jesus, they were ruled by their old nature, their sinful humanity in Adam. But that nature has been removed by the circumcision not made with hands. The Holy Spirit has applied the work of Christ's sacrifice to their lives. But the Lord not only excised their old nature, but gave them a new nature—the nature of their redemption in Jesus Christ. This took place when they were joined to Christ in baptism—dying to their old nature and rising with Christ in His resurrection *(2 Corinthians 5:17; Galatians 6:15)*. Not only was this new nature given to believers at the moment of their redemption, but the Holy Spirit continues to work in their lives, clarifying and sharpening the knowledge of their Creator and Redeemer.

3:11 *Where this happens, there is no Greek or Jew, circumcised or uncircumcised, barbarian, uncivilized person, slave, or free person. Instead, Christ is everything and in everything.*

Economic, cultural, and social distinctions are wiped out within the community of God's saved people. Many Jewish believers thought that the Gentiles had to adopt Jewish religious practices to fully implement their salvation and receive God's blessing. But Paul wipes out that distinction. Paul had made it clear that religious practices, Jewish or non-Jewish, have no impact on a person's salvation. The distinction between those who are thought to be sophisticated members of society could worship the Lord next to those who are generally considered uncivilized. The slave could sing hymns of praise next to the master who owned him. Just as Christ was Lord over all creation *(1:15–16)*, so He is Lord over His Body, the Church *(1:18)*. The same Lord saves each one without any preference of one over the other. All of His saved people stand equally before the throne of God, because of Jesus Christ Who lives in them.

3:12 *As holy people whom God has chosen and loved, be sympathetic, kind, humble, gentle, and patient.*

Since the whole Church stands without preference before her Lord, it is only reasonable for God's people to treat each other in the same way as the Lord treats them. The fact that Jesus saves people without partiality to their ethnic, cultural, social, or economic status should be reflected in the way people treat each other in the community of the redeemed. It may not be that way in the world, but in Christ's Church no one has an excuse to behave badly toward others simply because they come from a different background. Those who have money should not feel superior to those who do not. Those who do not have money should not feel jealous of those who do.

But Paul did not list just the negatives. He also provided positive guidelines for the way Christians should treat each other. All of God's people have been chosen by God Himself to share their faith in Christ in a spirit of unity and peace. The Lord's love has been showered upon them. Because they are chosen and loved by God as seen in Jesus Christ, believers should discover the joy of treating others with a large measure of gracious love. The Greek text has the idea of getting dressed with these characteristics, which are really a reflection of the nature of Christ, Who has redeemed them. Just as God's saints should put off their old nature, they should put on Christ's nature, treating each other with sympathy, kindness, humility, gentleness, and patience. After all, isn't this the way that Christ has treated them?

3:13 *Put up with each other, and forgive each other if anyone has a complaint. Forgive as the Lord forgave you.*

Paul was not ignorant of the difficulties that arise between people, even people who have been saved. So Paul advises Christians to forgive those things that may offend. Living successfully within the Body of Christ requires a determined effort to absorb the pain of the offense rather than remaining bitter about some passing remark. Even as Christ's forgiveness overlooks the sins that offend His righteousness, so should believers live together in a spirit of forgiveness toward each other.

3:14 *Above all, be loving. This ties everything together perfectly.*

All of the characteristics that Paul has outlined in the previous verses may be summarized by the overriding (or underlying) characteristic of love. This love is not the normal love of one family member for another. Sometimes that can turn very bitter. But the love of Christ was showered upon His people before they ever asked for it *(1 John 4:19)*. That kind of love is patient and kind; it is not jealous; it does not brag; it is not arrogant *(1 Corinthians 13:4)*. This kind of love overcomes a host of minor annoyances as well as major offenses. Paul told the Christians in Corinth of the supreme importance of love in the Christian community: "So these three things remain: faith, hope, and love. But the best one of these is love" *(1 Corinthians 13:13)*. Paul told the Roman Christians: "Love does no wrong to a neighbor; therefore love is the fulfilling of the law" *(Romans 13:10)*.

3:15 *Also, let Christ's peace control you. God has called you into this peace by bringing you into one body. Be thankful.*

People worry about everything in their lives. They wonder what their future holds. They wonder if someone loves them. There is no peace! There is no rest! But that should not be true for God's people. Paul told the Colossian saints that God had made peace with them through the blood of Christ's cross *(1:20)*. There is no reason to be anxious about things that are beyond human control. Believers should rest in the peace that has been given to them. They should walk confidently every day, knowing that the great Lord and Creator of the universe has also saved them and walks with them every step of their earthly journey as their sustainer.

However, it is important to recognize that the peace of Christ that controls the individual Christian is expressed within the Christian community. Everything the believer does is best expressed within a community where love covers everything. There is no lying. Everyone tries to support and encourage those around them. Knowing that every member of the redeemed community fully understands their former nature as well as the new nature given to them in Jesus Christ, believers can relax and experience God's peace. It is only in this environment that people can experience the love and support that helps them grow in grace. It is only as members of Christ's Body that everyone diligently pursues those virtues that Paul has enumerated—compassion, kindness, humility, gentleness, and patience all wrapped up with love and forgiveness, controlled by Christ's peace.

3:16 *Let Christ's word with all its wisdom and richness live in you. Use psalms, hymns, and spiritual songs to teach and instruct yourselves about [God's] kindness. Sing to God in your hearts.*

Paul's theme in this letter centers on the work and person of Jesus Christ. The resource that provides the full revelation of Jesus Christ is not found in human interpretations or philosophies about God, but in the Word of Truth, the Gospel *(1:5)*. When believers search this resource, they find a rich storehouse of wisdom that overflows into an abundant life. Joy and thanksgiving bubble to the surface and believers sing to God in their hearts, humbled and, at the same time, lifted up in the expression of praise and adoration to the Lord, Who has poured out His goodness, mercy, and salvation on sinners.

Paul often instructs, defends, and encourages people with a logical progression that leads to the Cross. He urges people to be transformed by the renewal of their minds, proving and testing the will of God and the good works that they do *(Romans 12:2)*. But people are deeply emotional in much of their daily routines, making decisions that are not necessarily the result of clear, godly thinking. Knowing this, Paul here encourages believers to express that emotion in songs and hymns of thanksgiving. However, there is a clear purpose for the musical expression of faith. This music is designed to teach and admonish the Church, Christ's Body, building and deepening the relationship with her Lord and with each other.

3:17 *Everything you say or do should be done in the name of the Lord Jesus, giving thanks to God the Father through him.*

Still focused on Jesus Christ, believers should determine to do everything, both individually and corporately, in the Name of the Lord Jesus. It is through Jesus Christ—the reconciliation of His Cross *(1:20)*—that the saints approach the Father in the spirit of thanksgiving. Such actions are comprehensive, affecting every aspect of believers' lives—in the home, in the workplace, in the church, in the community.

The home and the workplace are often areas of conflict because many of the people surrounding believers are not among God's saints. For this reason, the church is the place where Paul's instruction can best be implemented. Everyone in the church should be among the redeemed, acknowledging their sin and their salvation through the work of Jesus Christ. Perhaps this is the reason that Paul has placed so much emphasis on the Body of Christ and the Church throughout this letter. Within the community of the redeemed, the Word of Truth is explained, its authority exalted, and its praises expressed in song—all centered on the work and person of Jesus Christ, hearts overflowing with thanksgiving, doing everything—no matter how big or small, individually or corporately—as though they were done for the Lord Himself.

Notes/Applications

The word picture that Paul paints shows the Church of Jesus Christ in awe-inspiring beauty. Christ is at the head, sitting at the right hand of the Father in heaven. There, the Prince of Peace intercedes for His redeemed Bride, having bought her by His blood. On earth, the bliss of heaven is bestowed upon God's people as they go about their daily lives in a world wracked by sin, corruption, and spiritual slavery. Those who belong to the community of faith have been set free from the tyranny of a world that is ruled by greed, domination, and anarchy.

Instead, Christ's Church is bound together in the same love they have experienced when they have been brought into Christ's Kingdom. Living in the environment of the peace that transcends human understanding, the saints support, strengthen, and encourage each other with compassionate hearts, kindness, humility, and patience. They do not strike out at one another. The stronger do not humiliate the weak. Rather, the weaker saints are instructed, encouraged, and guided by the stronger saints.

When they gather together, the peace of Christ rules the day, and individual hearts are quieted from the chaos of the outside world. Christ is lifted up! The cross of Christ, the blood of Christ, the sacrifice of Christ is brought to center stage and the redeemed bow down while tears of thanksgiving line their faces. Voices are raised and the sound of psalms, hymns, and spiritual songs grace the ear with praise. The thanksgiving and joy of the redeemed flows among the saints as they worship the One Who has redeemed them.

O Lord Jesus Christ, let it be so!

Colossians 3:18–25

3:18 *Wives, place yourselves under your husbands' authority. This is appropriate behavior for the Lord's people.*

Paul had just enumerated the activities that believers should abandon and those virtues that should characterize their daily lives. Believers should bathe in these virtues, both individually and corporately—compassion, kindness, humility, gentleness, and patience all wrapped up with love and forgiveness, controlled by Christ's peace under the direction of the Holy Spirit.

But how are these virtues expressed in the routine of daily living? Paul goes on to give practical instruction on the relationships that most deeply affect the lives of all people. He follows a pattern much as he did in his letter to the Ephesian Christians *(Ephesians 5)*.

The most intimate relationship among humans exists between husband and wife. The home is the most important place where peace should hold sway over everything that is said and done. Paul instructs wives to place themselves under their husband's authority. He provides no reasons why this is the appropriate behavior among Christian women. He simply makes the statement, expecting his apostolic authority to be followed. His letter to the Ephesians provides greater detail about his reasons for this instruction *(Ephesians 5:22–24)*. All Christians are to be submissive to each other, selflessly surrendering their egos for the sake of peace in the Body of Christ. Wives are to be examples to the world around them of this kind of submission, honoring their husbands and respecting his authority in the home.

3:19 *Husbands, love your wives, and don't be harsh with them.*

Paul described how the virtues outlined were to be clothed in love—the kind of love that Christ showers upon those He has saved *(14)*. In his Ephesian letter, Paul instructed the men to love their wives as Christ loved the Church and gave Himself for her *(Ephesians 5:25)*. Here Paul simply instructs men to love their wives. From the context it is easy to see that Paul wants men to relate to their wives in the environment of Christ's love. Loving their wives in this way, Christian men would never treat their wives harshly, just as Christ has not treated His people with harshness.

3:20 *Children, always obey your parents. This is pleasing to the Lord.*

The relationship between husband and wife is the most important in the Christian home. The parents set the tone in their relationship to each other and to their children. In the intimacy of family life, Paul instructs children to obey their parents always. This general principle has been in effect since the Lord God of Israel gave the commandments to the generations He brought out of captivity in Egypt. *"Honor your father and your mother, so that you may live for a long time in the land the Lord your God is giving you" (Exodus 20:12).* Since the Lord gave this to His people so many centuries ago, it is obvious that the behavior of children in the home is important to Him. When children behave this way, the Lord is pleased. The environment of the home is bathed in Christ's peace, providing a haven of rest and quiet from the noise and chaos of the world.

3:21 *Fathers, don't make your children resentful, or they will become discouraged.*

The Lord expects children to obey their parents, but it is important that fathers realize their responsibility in the relationship. Paul has asked husbands to treat their wives in the love of Jesus Christ. It is equally important that fathers treat their children in the same loving environment. Certainly, children should never be permitted the freedom to do whatever they want. They need to be schooled in the Scriptures and in those behaviors that please the Lord. Fathers need to exercise consistent, supportive discipline, but never to the point that the child becomes discouraged. If children feel that they can never make the father happy with them, they will give up trying. The father, therefore, must maintain discipline within the framework of love, concern, and compassion.

3:22 ***Slaves, always obey your earthly masters. Don't obey them only while you're being watched, as if you merely wanted to please people. Be sincere in your motives out of respect for your real master.***

Paul then addresses relationships outside the boundaries of the immediate family. In his day, citizens of modest means had slaves to support their lifestyle. "Slaves performed domestic tasks in many households as well as working in agriculture, the civil service, industry and mining, where slave gangs were often leased. The institution was part of the social fabric in Palestine as well as elsewhere in the Roman Empire."[3] This was a huge social institution in the first century. Paul does not comment on the institution, supporting it or criticizing it.

However, Paul sees a definite contribution that slaves can make to the witness of Christ's Church. Like children obey their parents, slaves are always to obey their masters. Submission to authority, right or wrong, demonstrates the way believers submit to the authority of their Lord. For Paul, faithful obedience is not required because of social position or from a sense of duty. Rather they are to obey their earthly masters out of respect for their real Master. They should apply the principle that Paul laid as the foundation of this section of the letter. *"Everything you say or do should be done in the name of the Lord Jesus, giving thanks to God the Father through him" (3:17).* As in everything that the saints do, they should always do everything in submission to their heavenly Lord—in the Name of the Lord Jesus.

3:23–25 ***[23]Whatever you do, do it wholeheartedly as though you were working for your real master and not merely for humans. [24]You know that your real master will give you an inheritance as your reward. It is Christ, your real master, whom you are serving. [25]The person who does wrong will be***

paid back for the wrong he has done. God does not play favorites.

Whatever the slave does, he is to do it with an eye toward his inheritance in heaven. His salvation, his real citizenship is in the Kingdom of God, administered by the Head of the Church, Jesus Christ. Therefore, it is reasonable for Paul to remind slaves who have been redeemed to submit to Jesus and perform their tasks to the best of their human ability, pleasing their Lord and, hopefully, their earthly master as well.

Earthly masters may be cruel and arbitrary in the administration of their slaves. They may punish harshly for minor offenses, but that is not true of the Lord's judgments. The Lord will punish disobedience as surely as He rewards faithful labor. Disobedience brings damage on the Name of Christ, whereas faithful labor exalts the Name of Christ.

Notes/Applications

Paul's picture of the Church, ruled by the peace of Christ, has practical application. It is not only in corporate worship that believers are instructed in the ways of the redeemed. It is also in the rigors of daily living that God's saints are to express their faith in the Lord.

Believers do not live in isolation, but in the community of the redeemed as well as in the world from which they have been rescued. Paul urges believers to express that faith in all the relationships, which intersect their lives. It is in these relationships that the Gospel can best be expressed to those who have not yet been saved. In the home and the workplace, the same distinctive behavior should characterize the behavior of God's saints just as it does within the community of faith.

Husbands and wives should live together in quiet, peaceful harmony, the wife submitting to her husband and the husband loving the wife. Children of Christian parents should be obedient to their parents' instruction, rules, and discipline, showing that they have already submitted to the rule of Christ in their lives. Fathers should rule their homes with patient compassion, remembering their younger days and Christ's compassion for them.

Slaves (employees) should do their work diligently, carefully, and as effectively as possible, not just when the boss is watching them, but when he is not. The testimony of their faith in Christ is expressed in the quality of their work, not in some falsely exhibited busyness. After all, they do not simply work for the boss, but they are in the service of the King Who owns them, having purchased them with His blood. They should always do their best for Him, knowing that He rewards those who are faithful and punishes those who fail to do their work to the best of their ability. Likewise, masters (bosses) must realize that they are also under the authority of their Master in heaven.

There is a sense in which Paul is telling Christians that their labor is qualified, not by their earthly associations, but by their Lord. His standards are more exacting than any earthly criteria. When speaking to His disciples, Jesus warned them that the tasks He assigns should be expected. His people should then perform those assigned tasks to the best of their human ability without thought for payment, recognition, or rewards. When all is finished, Christ's servants should be happy to say, "We are unworthy servants; we have only done what is our duty" *(Luke 17:10)*.

Certainly the Christian will experience conflict, jealousy, and hostility in the home and the workplace where others have not yet been redeemed. There will always be strife, but Paul's hope and prayer is that the example of the believer will impact the life of the unbeliever and the Holy Spirit will work redemption in his life as well. Life in the world clashes with life in Christ. The Christian should not be surprised when confrontations arise that threaten earthly security. Nevertheless, the saints should always remain faithful to their Master in heaven no matter the place where they are called to serve.

COLOSSIANS 4

Colossians 4:1–6

4:1 *Masters, be just and fair to your slaves because you know that you also have a master in heaven.*

Paul has provided practical advice to families and then to slaves. This advice is designed to express godly virtues among the saints, showing the world a way of living that is drastically different from the normal routines of daily life. If the world could see people living in submissive, supportive relationships, then they, too, may be attracted to the message of the Gospel.

When Paul wrote this letter in the first century, earthly masters exercised absolute authority over their slaves. One word from them and a slave could lose his life. But Christian masters were never to treat their slave in that way. Whether their slaves were members of the Body of Christ or not, they were to treat them fairly, not with anger and vindictiveness. To insure that Christian masters understood that they, too, had boundaries on their earthly authority, he reminded them that Jesus was their master, just as He was the master of those slaves who had been saved. Their heavenly Master would punish the masters for disobedience as well as reward them for a testimony that honored their Lord. Jesus has no regard for social status. Both masters and slaves are subject to His correction, discipline, and reward.

4:2 *Keep praying. Pay attention when you offer prayers of thanksgiving.*

As Paul opened this letter to the church in Colossae, he informed them of his prayers on their behalf. He thanked God for their faithful testimony of their salvation in Jesus Christ. He interceded for them, asking the Lord to fill them with the knowledge of the Lord's will through the wisdom and understanding that only comes from the Holy Spirit. He urges believers to keep on praying in everything they do. But their prayers are not to be mindless repetitions of well-worn phrases. Rather, their prayers are to be thoughtfully expressed in the framework of thanksgiving *(Ephesians 5:20)*. He wants believers to know what they are saying. He wants them to think about all the benefits that Christ's salvation has showered on them and, reflecting on these benefits, to thank the Lord specifically for what He has done for them, what He is doing in them, and for what He will do when they see Him face-to-face.

4:3 *At the same time also pray for us. Pray that God will give us an opportunity to speak the word so that we may tell the mystery about Christ. It is because of this mystery that I am a prisoner.*

Just as Paul prayed so earnestly for the Colossian saints, he now asks them to pray for him. He was in prison. Humanly speaking, his future looked grim. Nevertheless, he took every opportunity to explain the mystery of Christ to those who had not yet been saved. Even though he was imprisoned in Rome because of his faithful presentation of the Gospel, he used that time to speak to those around him about the salvation that Christ offered them.

4:4 *Pray that I may make this mystery as clear as possible. This is what I have to do.*

Paul did not simply ask for general prayer on his behalf. He asked specifically for their prayer to open the doors to the Gospel, even though the door to his personal freedom was securely closed. More than that, he asked the Colossian Christians to pray for clarity of thought as he explained the mystery of the Gospel to those for whom the message may sound strange. Clarity and simplicity—the faithful explanation of the Cross of Christ—was essential so that others could be brought into the Kingdom of God by the work of the Holy Spirit.

Paul often spoke about the mystery of Gospel in this letter. He has forcefully reminded them that Christ's salvation is no longer a mystery to His saints *(1:26)*. Through his appointed apostleship, Paul has also presented the mystery of the Gospel to the Gentiles, resulting in the salvation of many Gentiles who now know the riches of this mystery—Christ in them, the hope of glory *(1:27)*. It is in the framework of this glorious mystery that the saints are joined together in the bonds of love with full assurance of understanding and knowledge of this mystery, which is Christ Himself *(2:2–3)*. Now, imprisoned against his will, Paul still pushes forward, asking that the mystery be revealed to others as it has been revealed to them.

4:5 *Be wise in the way you act toward those who are outside [the Christian faith]. Make the most of your opportunities.*

Within the Christian community, the Body of Christ, Paul urged believers to put on godly virtues surrounded by love in the spirit of patient endurance and forgiveness, living in peace and tranquility that is provided by the Spirit of God. Does that mean that the saints can revert to the ways of the world when dealing with those who are not saved? That is unreasonable! Irrational! Foolish!

Earlier Paul asked the Colossian Christians to pray for him, asking the Lord to help him present the mystery of Christ with simplicity and clarity. Would Paul ask for anything different for those who have, like him, received forgiveness through the Cross of Christ and reconciliation with the Creator? Of course not! Those same virtues expressed within the Christian community should likewise be expressed to those outside the Church. Paul instructs believers to walk wisely among the unbelievers of the world, that is according to God's will with spiritual understanding and wisdom *(1:10)*. Paul wants believers to walk in a manner worthy of their calling in Jesus Christ, bearing fruit in every good work *(1:11)*. When unbelievers see the way believers represent those characteristics Paul has outlined, opportunities will arise, and God's people should be prepared to present the mystery of Christ in all its fullness. Those who have been redeemed may be the only witness others will see.

4:6 *Everything you say should be kind and well thought out so that you know how to answer everyone.*

In their endeavor to walk wisely in a lost world, Paul instructs God's people to consider every situation carefully. What a believer may say in one situation may not be helpful in another circumstance. Instead, believers should choose their words carefully so that they can say the right thing at the right time to the right person. Obviously, believers must be well schooled in the Scriptures to insure that everything they say will be faithful to the message of the Gospel. While engaged in the environment of the world, believers must be prepared to season their conversation with salt, expressing the grace by which they have been redeemed. What Paul says here is much the same as the instruction in Peter's letter: "But dedicate your lives to Christ as Lord. Always be ready to defend your confidence [in God] when anyone asks you to explain it. However, make your defense with gentleness and respect" *(1 Peter 3:15)*.

Notes/Applications

As Paul draws his instructions to a close, he outlines some very clear actions that every Christian should follow. If they listen carefully to these instructions, they will discover the distinctive virtues by which Christians should relate to their Lord, to each other, and to the world.

First, Paul instructs believers to pray—continuously and earnestly. Every aspect of the Christian's life should be part of a never-ending conversation with the Lord. Every thought, every motive, every gesture, every action should reflect an inner prayer life that results in a clear impression that the person belongs to Jesus Christ. If the behavior of a person is an expression of their thought, then the Christian's behavior should express their relationship to their Creator and Redeemer.

Paul also wants believers to converse with their Lord in the spirit of thanksgiving. Jesus has reconciled them to their Creator by His sacrifice on the Cross. He has given them the Holy Spirit to instruct them in the ways of truth. They have been made one with the eternal Father by the blood of His Cross. Why should they not be happy—overflowing with thanksgiving? Looking to Jesus takes the focus of their lives from their own shortcomings and turns their attention to everything the Lord has done.

The substance of that prayer should center on open doors for the Gospel. When those doors open, the saints should be equipped by the Scriptures and the indwelling Holy Spirit to express that Gospel with clarity and conviction. This is what Paul wanted the Colossian saints to ask the Lord on his behalf. But this prayer should be on the heart of every believer.

With that prayer flowing out of a heart that is continuously engaged in a meaningful conversation with the Lord, believers will be able to walk in wisdom among those in the Church and those outside. The words they speak will be carefully expressed to each person they meet. In this way, the Gospel will go forth in the light and power of the Holy Spirit, convicting the world of sin, and righteousness, and judgment.

This is Paul's prayer for God's redeemed people. Sadly, the reality of our daily lives clashes harshly with the picture that Paul has portrayed in these words. Many people claim to be Christians, yet live so closely tied to the world's way of doing things that it is hard to reconcile their words with their actions. For this reason, many people outside the church do not want to be associated with these people who say one thing with their mouths and another with their actions. When the unsaved see this, they come to the conclusion that Christians are the hypocrites, the phonies. They are not to be believed! They are not to be taken seriously! May God forgive us!

It is a good idea to read this short letter from Paul to the Colossian saints often. It will remind believers of the majesty, power, and glory of the One Who came to save us. It will remind us of the depth of our sin and the wonder of His grace. And perhaps, by the instruction of the Holy Spirit our actions will reflect our words, and our words and actions will exalt the Name of Jesus Christ.

Colossians 4:7–18

4:7–8 [7]*I'm sending Tychicus to you. He is our dear brother, trustworthy deacon, and partner in the Lord's work. He will tell you everything that is happening to me.* [8]*I'm sending him to you so that you may know how we are doing and so that he may encourage you.*

Tychicus was a native of Asia Minor, probably from the city of Ephesus. Tychicus was a close companion to Paul and a brother in the faith. He accompanied Paul on his return to Jerusalem at the close of his third missionary journey *(Act 20:4)*. Tychicus was the courier of Paul's letter to these Colossian Christians, to Philemon who was a native of Colossae, and the letter to the saints in Ephesus *(Ephesians 6:21–22)*. At the end of his ministry, Paul dispatched Tychicus to Ephesus as his emissary *(2 Timothy 4:12)*.

Paul told the Colossian Christians that he was going to send Tychicus to them so that they could be fully informed about Paul's personal condition and the Lord's work. This information would help them know Paul's specific needs and intercede with the Lord on his behalf. Paul introduced Tychicus as a dear brother, a trusted leader (a deacon), and his partner in the Lord's work. Tychicus would share the testimony of God's power in the ministry of the Gospel and encourage them with the truth that Paul had just expressed in this letter. Paul was anxious to educate the Colossian saints in their knowledge of the abundance of a life lived in and for the Gospel.

4:9 *I'm sending Onesimus with him. Onesimus is from your city and is our faithful and dear brother. They will tell you about everything that's happening here.*

None of Paul's letters say that Tychicus carried the letter from Paul to Philemon. However, it generally assumed that this is what happened. Onesimus had been Philemon's slave. He had stolen some money or valuables from his master and run away to Rome. He found Paul there, and through Paul's ministry became a disciple of Jesus Christ. After serving Paul while he was in prison, Paul encouraged him to return to his master, Philemon, and put the conflict behind them. Onesimus returned to Philemon, not only as his slave but also as his brother in Christ. Since Philemon lived in Colossae, it is likely that Tychicus accompanied Onesimus to Philemon's home, delivered the letter, and conveyed Paul's greetings and request verbally, substantiating Paul's written request. For the third time in as many verses, Paul told the church at Colossae that Tychicus would provide details about Paul's imprisonment and the progress of the Gospel in the capital city of the empire.

4:10–11 ***[10]Aristarchus, who is a prisoner like me, sends greetings. So does Mark, the cousin of Barnabas. You have received instructions about Mark. If he comes to you, welcome him. [11]Jesus, called Justus, also greets you. They are the only converts from the Jewish religion who are working with me for God's kingdom. They have provided me with comfort.***

Like Tychicus, Aristarchus was one of Paul's traveling companions. Paul taught in Ephesus for three years. At the end of that ministry, the silversmiths created a riot in an effort to stop Paul from preaching about Jesus. This hurt their business, since their main source of income came from the sale of silver medallions and icons honoring the goddess Artemis. Aristarchus is first mentioned when he was dragged into the theater because he was Paul's traveling companion *(Acts 19:29)*. He also accompanied Paul and Tychicus on Paul's return from his third missionary journey *(Acts 20:4)*. Aristarchus also traveled to Rome with Paul when he presented his case to the emperor *(Acts 27:2)*. Early Christian tradition claims that Aristarchus died as a martyr for his allegiance to Jesus Christ under Nero's persecution.

Mark is the younger man who traveled with Paul during his first missionary journey, and, for some unknown reason, left Paul in Perga and returned home to Jerusalem. This caused deep controversy between Barnabas and Paul, resulting in their separation before his second journey. However, there was reconciliation, because Paul later speaks of Mark with fondness. In his final letter, Paul says that Mark was very useful to him in his ministry *(2 Timothy 4:11)*. Mark is the writer of the gospel that bears his name. It is said that he accompanied Peter to Rome and that he received the details of his gospel from this great leader of the apostles. Tradition says that Mark died in Alexandria, dragged to death through the streets by a team of horses.

This is the only place in the New Testament where Jesus Justus appears. Nothing else is known of him. Along with Aristarchus and Mark, Jesus Justus sends his greetings to the saints in Colossae. These three men were Jews like Paul who had been brought into the family of God. Jews who believed that he had abandoned the traditions of their rabbis had pursued Paul throughout his ministry. In these three brothers who shared his Jewish background, Paul found great companionship and comfort.

4:12–13 ***[12]Epaphras, a servant of Christ Jesus from your city, greets you. He always prays intensely for you. He prays that you will continue to be mature and completely convinced of everything that God wants. [13]I assure you that he works hard for you and the people in Laodicea and Hierapolis.***

These verses affirm Epaphras as the evangelist from Colossae who took the Good News to his native city and to the neighboring cities of Laodicea and Hierapolis. Earlier, Paul informed the church at Colossae that Epaphras was also a prisoner with Paul in Rome. Since he cannot be with them personally, Epaphras sent his greetings to the church that was established by the Holy Spirit under his ministry. Paul now told them that this servant of Christ Jesus prayed for their continuing growth in the faith, *"convinced of everything that God wants."* Even though a considerable distance separated them, Epaphras knew that the Lord was present with them and his prayers on their behalf were heard.

4:14 *My dear friend Luke, the physician, and Demas greet you.*

Paul then extends greetings from Luke, who was a physician, and Demas, whose name appears here and in Paul's letter to Philemon.

Luke, a Greek, accompanied Paul on much of his travels, recording the events that took place. He was also the historian of the early church, the author of the gospel that bears his name as well as the Book of Acts. The Church is indebted to Luke's writings, which provide a wealth of information about the events that shaped the beginnings of Christ's Church, following Paul's journeys throughout the Roman Empire as he set forth the Good News of salvation in Jesus Christ. Little is known of his background, but one prologue to Luke's gospel states:

> *Luke was an Antiochian of Syria, a physician by profession. He was a disciple of the apostles and later accompanied Paul until his martyrdom. He served the Lord without distraction, having neither wife nor children, and at the age of eighty-four he fell asleep in Boeotia, full of the Holy Spirit.*[1]

Demas also sent his greetings to the saints in Colossae through Paul's letter. Paul provided no further information about this man. Paul does not say that Luke and Demas were prisoners. He does not say if they were among those who visited him. However, Paul's second letter to Timothy tells how Demas deserted Paul in Rome and went to Thessalonica because he was "in love with this present world" *(2 Timothy 4:10).*

4:15 *Greet our brothers and sisters in Laodicea, especially Nympha and the church that meets in her house.*

As far as can be determined, Paul never visited Colossae or Laodicea. Nevertheless, Epaphras' account of the churches in the three cities of the Lycus Valley aroused Paul's apostolic compassion, caring for them as he cared for the churches that grew under his personal ministry. Epaphras had told Paul about Nympha and the church that met in her house. So the prisoners, Paul and Epaphras, send their warm greetings to the saints in Laodicea.

4:16 *After you have read this letter, read it in the church at Laodicea. Make sure that you also read the letter from Laodicea.*

Even though Paul wrote letters to individual churches, they were often passed around to other churches in nearby regions. We know from these verses that Paul also wrote a letter to the church in Laodicea. He asked these two churches to exchange letters with the hope that Paul's instructions to both churches would help them in their faith. Paul's letter to Laodicea has been lost, although it was probably written at the same time as the Colossian letter and delivered by the same courier, Tychicus.

4:17 *Tell Archippus to complete all the work that he started as the Lord's servant.*

Archippus was a Christian who lived in Colossae. Some Bible scholars believe that he may have been a member of Philemon's household, perhaps Philemon's son.[2] Archippus must have impressed Paul because he calls the young man "a fellow soldier" *(Philemon 2).*

It seems that Paul addressed Archippus rather sharply. One wonders if Paul was scolding him or encouraging him. There is no clear explanation of the ministry that Archippus had begun. It is possible that he had been given a leadership position in the Colossian church, since Epaphras was in prison with Paul. In Paul's final letter written to Timothy, he tells his son in the Lord: "As for you, always be sober-minded, endure suffering, do the work of an evangelist, fulfill your ministry" *(2 Timothy 4:5, ESV).* In this instruction, it is clear that Timothy was to do the work of an evangelist. But the language to Archippus is short, clear and direct. Perhaps Paul simply wanted Archippus to remember the serious nature of his ministry and remain focused on a message that reflected the supremacy of Jesus Christ in all matters relating to the faith.

4:18 *I, Paul, am writing this greeting with my own hand. Remember that I'm a prisoner. God's good will be with you.*

Paul often dictated his letters and then signed them with his own signature *(Romans 15:22; 1 Corinthians 16:21; Galatians 6:11; Philemon 19)*. He did this for two reasons: (1) he wanted his readers to know that the letter was authentic *(2 Thessalonians 3:17)*; and (2) he wanted to discourage the spread of counterfeit letters *(2 Thessalonians 2:1–2)*.

Paul then asked the saints to remember that he was a prisoner. Paul was under arrest, not because of some criminal deed, but because he proclaimed the Gospel to the Gentiles. Angry Jews stirred up enough commotion to force the Roman government to arrest Paul, first for his protection, and second, to keep the peace *(Acts 21)*. Earlier, Paul appealed for their intercessory prayer *(4:2–4)*.

Paul closes his letter with this brief benediction. Although short, it conveys the richness of the faith that had been given to these believers in Colossae. Grace (God's good will) is the greatest blessing that he can express to them, summing up this letter in the context of God's goodness in Jesus Christ, given to undeserving sinners and transforming their lives. Paul opened this letter with God's grace *(1:2)* and with grace he closes the letter. It could be said that grace makes up the bookends of this letter just as grace is the opening and closing of the Christian's life. Everything is grace from beginning to ending.

Notes/Applications

Many times these passages at the end of Paul's letters go unnoticed. There is no deep theology here. There is no instruction in righteousness. There is no rebuke or correction. There is only the passing of greetings from one saint to another. Many of them have names that we cannot even pronounce. So little is known about them that we have difficulty getting excited about Christians who lived so long ago.

Yet, there is a poignant message here. It is the day-to-day expression of Paul's compassion for those who labor with him in proclaiming the Gospel of Jesus Christ. No one argues that Paul was a great thinker who was gifted by the Holy Spirit to express the meaning of Christ's sacrifice to Jew and Gentile alike. He certainly could be very stern if he sees that believers are not living up to their calling in Christ Jesus. But these expressions of instruction and correction are not seen here.

Here we see the love, compassion, and prayerful hope of a man who has given his entire life to the declaration of the Gospel in a pagan world. We see that expression from others who share Paul's passion for the Gospel. Although these men are often perceived as fearless warriors, in this passage we see men who feel vulnerable to the opposition they face. They ask for prayer—to be strong, to be faithful. And then they exchange their greetings and prayers for each other across the miles that separate them. All covered in the grace of the Lord Jesus Christ!

As today's saints, may the Lord give us the strength, courage, and confidence to be faithful to the message that has been written in His Word and then in our hearts. May the Lord also give us tender hearts that express that faith to each other in words of encouragement. May we be honest with each other, expressing our need for prayer that lifts us up to the task that the Lord has given us. May we, like Paul, do all these things in the framework of the grace that we have been given from the bounty of our salvation in Jesus Christ. In that way, may saints and sinners see Jesus Christ in all we say and do.

1st THESSALONIANS

INTRODUCTION

Thessalonica was the largest city in Macedonia and was the capital of one of the four Roman districts of Macedonia. It was located on the Thermaic Bay, making it a primary city of the Mediterranean trade routes. It was named in 315 B.C. by Cassander for his wife, the half-sister of Alexander the Great.[1] The population of the city may have been as much as 200,000 in Paul's day and boasted a large Jewish population.[2] The city retained its importance and continues to this day as Saloniki, the most important town in eastern Greece.[3]

Paul planted the church in Thessalonica about A.D. 51 on his second missionary journey. Paul did not stay in Thessalonica long enough to instruct the believers fully because the Jews who opposed the Gospel drove him out. He escaped to Berea about fifty miles (80 km) to the west. However, the Thessalonian Jews had followed him to continue their protest against his message, ultimately driving him out of the city. Paul again escaped but left Silas and Timothy there to

continue the ministry. Paul went further south to Athens, a journey of nearly two hundred miles (322 km).

When they reached Athens, Paul was so concerned about the young church in Thessalonica that he sent Timothy to help them. By the time Timothy returned from his trip to Thessalonica, Paul had traveled to Corinth. There Timothy told Paul that the believers in Thessalonica were enduring persecutions very well and that some had died for their faith. This prompted Paul to write this Thessalonian letter about A.D. 52, encouraging these believers to endure the persecution of those who did not believe. Even if they died for Christ's sake, they were at no disadvantage since they would ultimately be victorious when the Lord returned again.

The name *Thessalonica* means "victory over the tossing of law: victory over falsity."[4] Even though this Macedonian city was named for Cassander's wife, there is a sense in which the name of the city describes the Christians who lived there. Despite the persecution they faced on a daily basis, the truth of Christ's Gospel and the reality of the salvation bestowed upon them gave them confidence in Christ, their Savior, and victory over those who lived in the falseness of unbelief. Throughout the letter, Paul continued to emphasize the victorious truth found only in Jesus Christ, the true Messiah. He was also very encouraged by the faith these believers in Thessalonica demonstrated.

This first letter to the believers at Thessalonica was Paul's earliest letter written from Corinth. Even though Silas and Timothy told Paul about the loyalty of the Thessalonian Christians to Jesus Christ, they also reported some errors in the interpretation of Paul's teaching. As Paul encouraged them to continue faithfully in the face of persecution, he also corrected these misunderstandings. Both his encouragement and his corrections were couched in the context of the believers' enduring hope in the resurrection of the dead and Christ's Second Coming.

1 THESSALONIANS 1

1 Thessalonians 1:1–4

1:1 ***From Paul, Silas, and Timothy. To the church at Thessalonica united with God the Father and the Lord Jesus Christ. Good will and peace are yours!***

Paul wrote this letter with Silas and Timothy, his coworkers, to the young church in Thessalonica. These three men had founded the church in Thessalonica, became friends to many, and took a vested interest in the members' spiritual well-being.

Earlier, Paul had barely escaped the clutches of Jewish opponents to the Gospel in Thessalonica *(Acts 17:10)*. Some time later, Timothy had been dispatched to see how they were doing and to report his findings to Paul. Timothy returned to Paul in Corinth and reported all of the news about the believers in this thriving Roman city. Paul responded with this letter of encouragement and instruction.

As Paul began his letter, he greeted them in the unity they possessed because of their Christian faith. God's grace and peace are the inherited promise God gives to all believers when they are saved. Therefore, Paul encouraged the Thessalonians with these words, reminding them that they already possessed these blessings. Good will, kindness, and grace are given to human beings by God not because humanity deserves them but because God chooses to do so based solely on the work of His Son completed on Calvary's Cross. The work of redemption satisfies Almighty God's justice, removing the penalty of man's rebellion and showering believers with His grace, mercy, kindness, and good will *(John 1:17)*.

1:2 ***We always thank God for all of you as we remember you in our prayers.***

As Paul went about his daily tasks, he often thought about their Christian brothers and sisters in Thessalonica. Paul's concern for their spiritual well-being was not some momentary thought but an ongoing moment-by-moment prayer on their behalf. They rejoiced as they remembered their times together. The Good News received through Timothy's visit reported a blessed answer to their prayers. To see the fruit of their labor give birth to such genuine growth in the faith of these dear friends gave cause for rejoicing. Although the Holy Spirit was the One Who actually brought them to Christ and engendered their growth in the faith, Paul was happy to see how God had used them in the process.

1:3 ***In the presence of our God and Father, we never forget that your faith is active, your love is working hard, and your confidence in our Lord Jesus Christ is enduring.***

Paul asserted that he and his coworkers lived, worked, and prayed in the presence of God, the Father. How is this possible? Many assume that they enter God's holy presence when they die and enter the heavenly gates. However, that would leave believers in a woeful condition of despair. This is not what Jesus promised. One of Jesus' most powerful assertions was His promise that He gives His children an abundant life that overflows with His vitality and joy *(John 4:12–14)*. When individuals are born again, they are brought by the Holy Spirit into the presence of God, reconciled by the blood of His Son, Jesus. During moments of quiet prayer, believers can acknowledge their position in Christ and bow before the throne of the One Who created them, redeemed them, and provided the pathway for their reconciliation. While it is true that all people exist within the presence of the omniscient, all-powerful God, those who have been redeemed live within the scope of His love and forgiveness.

As Paul remembered the Thessalonian believers in his prayers, he acknowledged three aspects of their Christian experience. First, their faith was active. They did not rely on purely theological debate, but their faith resulted in acts of kindness to others (*John 6:27*). Second, their love was hard-working. Their love for the Lord motivated them to do those things that supported the faithful, helped the weak, and restored the lost. They selflessly served the needs and concerns of others (*1 Corinthians 13:4–7*). Third, they had an enduring confidence in the Lord Jesus Christ. Even though these believers were often challenged by opponents of the faith, their confidence in the Lord who had saved them was unshakeable. Because they had been redeemed by the only eternal, living God through the sacrifice of Jesus Christ, they knew that their lives were secure. This was true no matter what happened in this life because they were inextricably connected to the One Who had given them eternal life.

1:4 *Brothers and sisters, we never forget this because we know that God loves you and has chosen you.*

Paul addressed the Thessalonian believers as his brothers and sisters. Location made no difference to Paul—Athens or two hundred miles away. They were still children of the Lord Who had expressed His love for them by choosing them to be His own. As children of the saving Lord, all believers in Christ Jesus are brothers and sisters regardless of culture, nationality, or heritage. No matter where believers are around the world, they are related to each other because of their common faith in the finished work of Jesus Christ completed by His death on a Roman cross.

Notes/Applications

Paul, Silas and Timothy serve as wonderful Christian examples. They recognized that all believers live within the scope of God's redeeming presence. This became particularly evident as they prayed for each other. When they prayed, they recognized the wonderful way in which the Lord had blessed their lives. They already possessed the grace and mercy of their redemption, and this realization gave them God's peace regardless of their circumstances.

In submission to the will of God in Christ Jesus, believers who follow these examples of the faith will experience a similar Spirit-inspired vitality. Life in Jesus Christ results in lives lived to the fullest. Genuine believers do not become satisfied with a simple sermon on Sunday mornings. The true experience of Christ's love compels them to move into the world, bringing the Good News to the lost and instruction to those who share their faith in Christ.

1 Thessalonians 1:5–10

1:5 ***We know this because the Good News we brought came to you not only with words but also with power, with the Holy Spirit, and with complete certainty. In the same way you know what kind of people we were while we were with you and the good things we did for you.***

Paul was absolutely convinced of the position of the Thessalonian believers in Jesus Christ. They possessed the grace, mercy, and peace of God through Jesus Christ. This was evident by the way they served and supported each other in the faith regardless of the difficulty of the circumstances they faced.

These spiritual traits resulted from their inheritance in the faith and the changing of their lives through the power of the Holy Spirit that brought them into the presence of the living God. The "Good News" is the history of the birth, life, death, resurrection, ascension, and return of the Lord Jesus Christ (*Luke 2:10–11*; *Romans 1:16*; *John 10:14–15*; *John 2:19–21*; *Acts 1:9–11*). This brings the message and opportunity for reconciliation between the hopeless condition of the human race and the Lord God who created humanity in His image.

The consuming testimony of the Holy Spirit and the example that Paul, Silas, and Timothy lived while they were with the Thessalonians provided ample evidence of the Spirit's life-changing work among them. What was true for Paul, Silas, and Timothy was also true for these believers: their actions affirmed their life-changing experiences in the Holy Spirit and their eternal unity in Christ with absolute certainty.

1:6 ***You imitated us and the Lord. In spite of a lot of suffering, you welcomed God's word with the kind of joy that the Holy Spirit gives.***

These believers in Thessalonica imitated Paul, Silas, and Timothy, and that was good training because these men followed Christ.

Paul, Silas and Timothy proclaimed the Word of God to these people who suffered a great deal of opposition and tribulation because of their faith in Christ, yet the Thessalonians still embraced the truth when they heard the Good News. Their testimony to Christ's salvation cost them dearly, but the joy imparted by the Holy Spirit was far greater than their suffering. This perseverance came from God, and it enabled them to walk faithfully with the Lord despite their physical circumstances (*Romans 5:13*).

1:7 *This way, you became a model for all the believers in the province of Macedonia and Greece.*

These believers received God's Word with joy in spite of the difficulties they experienced when they became believers. When they received the forgiveness for their sins, their joy could not be contained. It was contagious. This joy provided a powerful testimony of Christ's redeeming action in their lives, making them models for all believers throughout Macedonia and Greece. Their reputation spread throughout the region and influenced many people near and far.

1:8 *From you the Lord's word has spread out not only through the province of Macedonia and Greece but also to people everywhere who have heard about your faith in God. We don't need to say a thing about it.*

The witness of these Christians' lives had spread all over Macedonia and Greece because their faith was evident despite their difficult circumstances. What is more, they lived with the joy of their salvation shining on their faces. Their faith shone in the actions that the Spirit produced. When a need arose, they arrived to help; they shared their possessions and comforted each other with words from the Lord. These believers lived in such a way that the truth of Isaiah 52:7 was plainly visible: "How beautiful on the mountains are the feet of the messenger who announces the good news, 'All is well.' He brings the good news, announces salvation, and tells Zion that its God rules as king." But their reputation spread even further. As travelers came from different countries, they would hear of their witness. Believers infused with the joy of the Lord's salvation and living in obedience to God's principles greatly impacted all who came into contact with them. The testimony of the believers in Thessalonica spread so widely that their faith in Christ was self-evident.

1:9–10 ***[9]They talk about how you welcomed us when we arrived. They even report how you turned away from false gods to serve the real, living God [10]and to wait for his Son to come from heaven. His Son is Jesus, whom he brought back to life. Jesus is the one who rescues us from God's coming anger.***

The hospitality shown to Paul, Silas, and Timothy exemplified Christ's love. Their relationship with other believers became so visible to everyone that many saw how Christ's salvation had affected their lives. Another example manifested itself in the dramatic change in the object of their worship. They had been worshipers of false gods. When the Good News was told to them, they immediately shunned their idols and served the real, living God.

Generally speaking, the Jews were not idol worshipers, which leads us to believe that most of these believers would have been Gentiles *(Acts 17:4)*. Notwithstanding, they turned from their dead idols to the living God. Their false gods were dead stone, wood, or precious metals. In contrast, the Lord alone is the living Almighty God. He is eternal, without beginning or end. They were no longer worshiping the false idols of man's imagination but, rather, the Creator who made all things. They now became the living members of the Body of the Lord Jesus Christ.

A very important part of the Good News was the promise of Jesus' return. Even though Paul complimented the Thessalonians' acceptance of the entire Gospel of Jesus Christ, here he emphasized Christ's return. As these believers turned from their false gods to serve the living God, they embraced this promise. Paul then clarified that the identity of God's Son Who would return was this same Jesus Who had been brought back to life by the power of God. This same Jesus rescued believers from God's coming anger.

Just before He ascended into heaven, Jesus promised that He would return *(Acts 1:11)*. However, His future return served a vastly different purpose than His first entry onto the world's scene. When that time comes, Jesus will return not as the suffering sacrifice for the sins of the world but as the righteous judge who will execute His justice among all people. Those that belong to Him will be granted entrance, as a result of salvation, into eternity with God. Those who do not belong to Him will be eternally punished for their rebellion and rejection of the Son's sacrifice. Perhaps this explains why Paul emphasized the fact that Jesus had saved the Thessalonian believers from God's coming anger.

Believers will not experience God's anger. They will not experience the eternal consequences of their sins because they are redeemed. God has saved them from the penalty of their sin. This verse does not imply that believers will not experience opposition and persecution while on earth *(John 15:20)*. In fact, believers often suffer under such circumstances as a result of their faith. However, no believer will ever experience God's wrath while on earth or in eternity.

Notes/Applications

If genuine redemption has occurred in a person's life, it simply cannot be hidden. A Christian witness naturally follows redemption as the sure outcome of the Spirit's work in the life of the redeemed. Such is further reflected in the way that Christians relate to each other. Unity and joy ensues when believers greet each other. As they share their experiences in the context of Christ's redemption, their joy cannot be constrained. Even if others criticize their actions, slandering their thoughts and intentions, the joy of Christ in their hearts remains unshakeable and can never be suppressed.

If individuals have been genuinely changed by the power of the

Holy Spirit, their lives will reflect the salvation that has been granted to them. This is the full impact of God's Good News. Whoever believes in Jesus Christ is saved—both in this world and the next. Whoever does not believe is already condemned because such individuals have not accepted what Christ did on their behalf on the Cross of Calvary *(John 3:16–18)*.

Paul commended the Thessalonian believers for accepting the message in its entirety. They did not leave any part of it out. They embraced the salvation that the Holy Spirit planted in their hearts. They embraced the sacrifice of Jesus Christ, God's Son, on their behalf. They actively lived out their faith by actions that served others rather than self. They eagerly looked forward to that time when Jesus would come again, executing the wrath of His righteous judgment and, at the same time, bringing those who have been redeemed to the joyful culmination of their salvation.

Paul commended the Thessalonians for the model of their redeemed faith, the testimony of their love for each other, and concern for others, even those who did not believe. Our prayer is simple: *Lord, help us to be like them!*

1 THESSALONIANS 2

1 Thessalonians 2:1–7

2:1 *You know, brothers and sisters, that our time with you was not wasted.*

As Paul expounded on the Thessalonian believers' reputation in the opening lines of this letter, it becomes evident that Paul's time with them proved beneficial. The believers' reputation of hospitality among their brothers and sisters in Christ showed how their salvation had impacted their lives. Their joy in the face of opposition and persecution spoke volumes about their unshakeable reliance upon the Lord who had saved them. Therefore, Paul's visit was eminently fruitful.

2:2 *As you know, we suffered rough and insulting treatment in Philippi. But our God gave us the courage to tell you his Good News in spite of strong opposition.*

Paul and his companions were not on vacation. This missionary journey involved much hardship and abuse by those who opposed the good news of Christ's redemption.

God directed Paul's journeys as he proclaimed the Gospel. In a vision, a man asked Paul to come to Macedonia *(Acts 16:9)*. Paul immediately left the city of Troas and began his journey toward Macedonia. Along the way, he stopped in Philippi and spoke quietly to some women along the banks of the river. One of those women, Lydia, immediately believed and was baptized *(Acts 16:14–15)*. Later, Paul cast a demon out of a young girl who told fortunes. The men who made money from her evil divinations were infuriated, so they had Paul and Silas beaten and thrown into prison *(Acts 16:22–40)*.

When Paul and Silas were finally released from prison, they continued on their journey and stopped in Thessalonica. Even there, the Jews heatedly debated with Paul as he attempted to show them how Jesus was the Messiah they had been looking for *(Acts 17:5–7)*.

2:3 *When we encouraged you, we didn't use unethical schemes, corrupt practices, or deception.*

Paul always preached the Gospel in a straightforward manner. He never failed to be completely honest with his audience. He told them the truth about their sinful condition and God's remedy for humanity's sin in the atoning sacrifice of His Son. Paul did not use any deceitful schemes to accomplish his goals. He knew that any human scheme would always fail to reconcile a person to God. Paul's message was not only honest but an encouraging presentation of Christ's redemption.

2:4 *Rather, we are always spreading the Good News. God trusts us to do this because we passed his test. We don't try to please people but God, who tests our motives.*

Paul and his companions always proclaimed the Good News wherever they went because God's sacred calling was laid upon their lives. The Lord had entrusted them with His mission because Paul had passed every test that the Lord gave him. They did not flee persecution. They did not succumb to pressure. They did not alter their message to fit someone else's philosophy. They remained steadfast and focused. In every effort, Paul attempted to please the Lord who had called him rather than the men who either praised him or cursed him *(Galatians 1:10)*.

2:5 *As you know, we never used flattery or schemes to make money. God is our witness!*

Many early traveling philosophers earned their living by lofty oratory. They often resorted to flattery in order to increase their income. Audiences in the ancient world readily recognized and despised such oratory devices.[1] In sharp contrast to this practice, Paul passionately stated that he refused to resort to this Greek practice.

Flattery was one way of extorting money from the audience, but Paul also pointed out that he did not use any other schemes to increase his income at the expense of an appreciative audience. In his letter to the Corinthians, Paul made a passionate defense of his practice of working to support himself rather than depending on others for his support *(1 Corinthians 9)*. In fact, Paul would rather die than have anyone think that he had resorted to common flattery, thus demeaning the glorious Good News of God's redemption through Jesus Christ *(1 Corinthians 9:15)*.

2:6–7 *[6]We didn't seek praise from people, from you or from anyone else, [7]although as apostles of Christ we had the right to do this. Instead, we were gentle when we were with you, like a mother taking care of her children.*

There are those who seek the praise of others by overwhelming the audience with big words and persuasive oratory. They often brag about their education and the great volumes of knowledge they have acquired in the process. People seek to receive the highest level of acclamation from others in order to give themselves some measure of self-worth.

Paul never attempted to do this. Although he was probably one of the most educated men of his time, he never relied upon his education to feel good about himself. He had been educated in the university in Tarsus. As a Pharisee, he was further educated at the school of Gamaliel, one of the most renowned rabbinical teachers of his time.

However, in his redeemed nature all of that meant nothing. Certainly the Lord had called him to the task of preaching the Good News to the Gentiles. He had the right to exercise his apostolic authority over the churches that sprang up as a result of the message that Paul brought to them, but Paul never sought to enhance his position among his brethren. Rather, he sought to please his Lord by carefully nurturing new believers much as a mother takes care of her newborn infant. The Gospel of Christ and the welfare of those who were brought into the Kingdom by the work of the Holy Spirit were much more important to Paul than the useless praise of any human being.

Notes/Applications

Paul was appointed by God to be the apostle to the Gentiles. He did not seek this assignment, but God tore Paul out of his pharisaical heritage and culture and set him apart for this task. It was not going to be easy, for Paul would face a lot of opposition. There were going to be times of beatings and torture, but he could not turn his back upon the task that God had laid on his shoulders. As God's appointed apostle, Paul had every right to expect the support of those who came to Christ as the outcome of his ministry.

As Paul entered the arena of human rebellion, he became obsessed with the faithful performance of his ministry. He grew so concerned about the integrity of God's work in his life that he literally refused to accept payment from anyone *(1 Corinthians 9:18)*. On the human level, he refused to employ the schemes that others used to influence their listeners. He refused to use flattery or flowery language *(1 Corinthians 2:4–5)*. Instead, he simply presented the gospel message in the power of the Holy Spirit, straightforward and unencumbered by foolish theological arguments.

Paul performed his task without regard for his physical safety or for the adulation of his audience. He served only the God Who had redeemed him and called him to this position. That was Paul's single-minded focus—to please God.

Believers today can learn from Paul. No, we cannot all be Paul because God has not appointed us to the same task, but we could learn to serve God with hearts that are devoted to Him. Our whole lives—body, heart, mind, and soul—should be unreservedly committed to His service with hearts filled with joy and worship.

Whatever the task God has placed on our shoulders should be performed with a transparent honesty that, so far as humanly possible, presents the Gospel in the power of the same Holy Spirit that guided Paul's ministry. Denying self, we should always act in such a way that seeks the well-being of those who have entered the Kingdom. While God's glory has existed from all eternity, in some small way our lives should provide further testimony to the glory of the Son of God.

1 Thessalonians 2:8–12

2:8 *We felt so strongly about you that we were determined to share with you not only the Good News of God but also our lives. That's how dear you were to us!*

Certainly no other passage in all of the Pauline letters employs such deeply felt language in describing Paul's relationship with his converts.[2] Paul often expressed his joy, love, and concern for converts in other cities, but this expression of affection is absolutely unique. In fact, it is rare to find it in any other early Greek writings.[3]

While Paul's special affection for these believers is evident, it is difficult to determine the reasons for such a special place in Paul's heart. It might be that the warm response of the Thessalonian believers in spite of the abuse and opposition that they faced overwhelmed him. This community of believers who simply rejoiced in what God had given them and expressed that joy by warmly greeting and supporting each other throughout the difficult experiences of their new life in Christ reflected their salvation in genuine and practical ways.

2:9 *You remember, brothers and sisters, our work and what we did to earn a living. We worked night and day so that we could bring you the Good News of God without being a burden to any of you.*

Paul's occupation was tent making *(Acts 18:1–3)*. He apparently decided at the beginning of his ministry that he would not solicit support from those who came to Christ through his ministry. There is a sense in which Paul felt that he would be like too many other itinerant philosophers, and his motives could be misconstrued. Using this method, he also would not be a burden to those who might be too poor to support him *(Acts 20:34–35)*. Whenever they were not telling others about Jesus, Paul and his co-ministers busied themselves making tents, selling their wares, and collecting sufficient funds to support the entire team that traveled with Paul.

2:10 ***You and God are witnesses of how pure, honest, and blameless we were in our dealings with you believers.***

Paul was not asking the Thessalonian believers to make some determination of his inner purity, honesty, or moral standing before God, for only God could determine this. However, he petitioned them to look at his actions which could be plainly seen. He did not ask the church to affirm things they could not know (matters of inner purity) but things they saw daily for weeks or even months.[4] What they saw would help them conclude that Paul was not bragging, but telling the truth. He never misrepresented the Gospel or the value of the physical labor that he performed to raise money for their expenses. Paul always conducted himself in this way wherever he proclaimed God's salvation: "With this belief I always do my best to have a clear conscience in the sight of God and people" *(Acts 24:16).*

2:11–12 ***11You know very well that we treated each of you the way a father treats his children. We comforted you and encouraged you. Yet, we insisted that 12you should live in a way that proves you belong to the God who calls you into his kingdom and glory.***

Earlier, Paul stated that he and his companions treated new believers like a nurturing mother *(2:7).* Now he stated that they treated the Thessalonian believers like a father. The Greco-Roman society adhered to the father's authority in the family. The father was responsible for the training of his children. He provided for their education and discipline. However, when unbelievers became believers, they were brought into a new family that required the education and discipline needed that reflected their new way of life.[5]

In the adventure of their new lives, Paul and his companions in ministry provided training and discipline in the context of comfort and encouragement. The rigors of the Christian life can be overwhelming to a new believer, especially when opposition and criticism from family and friends are their immediate reactions. From those who are closest, a person expects encouragement and support. When that was not the response, Paul and his colleagues provided the encouragement and comfort needed to overcome the obstacles that Satan threw in the pathway.

What instruction did Paul give to new believers? He urged them to remember what God had done for them and, remembering that life-changing moment, to submit to the new directions in which the Lord was leading them. As the believers matured under the guidance of the Holy Spirit, they proved that they now belonged to the Lord who had called them out of the darkness into the brightness of His kingdom and glory. What God had called them into could never be compared to the self-serving, sin-filled lives they had left behind.

Notes/Applications

The Thessalonian Christians were excellent examples of people who had truly been redeemed. Their lives provided visible expressions of the Spirit's work in their hearts. Once saved, they eagerly absorbed Paul's further instruction whereby he taught them that they should live in a way that clearly demonstrated they belonged to God.

God saves no one for the purpose of leading a meaningless life. Instead, His purpose is to bring glory to His Name. Every person who is born again by the power of the Holy Spirit is set apart by God to fulfill an appointed task for the welfare of His Kingdom. As believers are instructed in the Word of God, as they begin to understand their position in Jesus Christ, as the Spirit continues to open their hearts to receive His instruction, they cannot fail to show the fruit of the Spirit in their actions. How then is it possible for redeemed people to accept the instruction of the Word and then sit still and do nothing about that which the Spirit has taught them?

1 Thessalonians 2:13–20

2:13 ***Here is another reason why we never stop thanking God: When you received God's word from us, you realized it wasn't the word of humans. Instead, you accepted it for what it really is—the word of God. This word is at work in you believers.***

Obviously Paul spoke in the same way as every other human speaks. However, something happened in the Thessalonian believers' hearts when they heard what Paul said. Even though the words came from the mouth of a man, they seemed to possess a persuasive quality to them. However, that persuasiveness did not come from the words that Paul spoke but from the power of the Holy Spirit that gave wings to those words. The light of the Gospel dawned in their hearts, their sins were forgiven, and they were set free to live in the liberty of Christ's redemption.

Only under the authority of God's Word can human beings speak the words that convey the truth of the Gospel in the power of the Holy Spirit. Jesus made it very clear: "The Spirit gives life; the flesh counts for nothing. The words I have spoken to you are spirit and they are life" *(John 6:63, NIV).*

When the Thessalonian people heard Paul speak, the Holy Spirit convinced them that his words came from God's very mouth. The Spirit enabled them to look beyond the speaker and see the work of God. With that understanding, they accepted what Paul said as the Word of God. That Word of God transformed their lives and then expressed itself in the actions of those who were saved. When that transformation was observed, when the words were expressed in the actions of warm hospitality and mutual support, other people witnessed the work of God among the Thessalonian believers.

2:14–16 ***[14]You, brothers and sisters, were like the churches of God in Judea that are united with Christ Jesus. You suffered the same persecutions from the people of your own country as those churches did from the Jews [15]who killed the Lord Jesus***

and the prophets and who have persecuted us severely. They are displeasing to God. They are enemies of the whole human race [16]because they try to keep us from telling people who are not Jewish how they can be saved. The result is that those Jews always commit as many sins as possible. So at last they are receiving God's anger.

As a part of the redeemed family, the Thessalonian believers often suffered at the hands of those who hated the gospel message. They experienced the same thing that other believers had suffered. Many believers in Judea also suffered severe persecution at the hands of Jews who opposed the Gospel. Several years earlier, James, one of the Twelve and the brother of John, was executed for faithfully holding forth the Word of God *(Acts 12:1–2).*

Just a few months earlier when Paul and Silas were still in Thessalonica, a young believer, Jason, had been beaten severely by the Jews because he had welcomed them into his house *(Acts 17:5–9).* However, Paul pointed an accusing finger at the persecutors, identifying them specifically—these Jews refused to accept Jesus as their Messiah.

They were continuing their campaign against the Christians after Jesus had returned to His Father in heaven. Paul himself had persecuted the Christians with all the righteous zeal of his background as a Pharisee. When Paul was intercepted by Jesus on the road to Damascus, his life was immediately turned around, and from that moment on, he served the Lord with his whole heart. However, the Jews then relentlessly persecuted him, causing his arrest and torture on several occasions. They simply could not accept Paul's ministry to the Gentiles. They did not believe that their God would ever speak to people who were not the sons of Abraham.

However, even though Paul suffered the arrows of their hatred, he also understood that this battle was not against flesh and blood. Those that persecute believers and attempt to stop the progression of

Christ's kingdom by impeding the message of those who faithfully proclaim His Word of reconciliation and hope will self-destruct.

Just as Paul could not stop doing what the Lord appointed him to do, those who hate Christ will never stop opposing those who accept Christ as their Savior. Their continuing rebellion against the Word of the Lord ignites the wrath of God that will eventually consume them.

2:17 *Brothers and sisters, we have been separated from you for a little while. Although we may not be able to see you, you're always in our thoughts. We have made every possible effort to fulfill our desire to see you.*

Even though Paul and Silas had fled the persecution in Thessalonica and escaped with the help of some friends *(Acts 17:10)*, they really missed being with their Thessalonian friends. They wished with all their hearts to visit them again and share the joy belonging to them through Jesus Christ. Nevertheless, Paul assured them that even though they were unable to see them, they were always on their minds. Certainly, Paul and Silas prayed for them as he expressed later in this letter: "We pray very hard night and day that we may see you again so that we can supply whatever you still need for your faith" *(1 Thessalonians 3:10)*. They made plans to return to Thessalonica and thus fulfill their hearts' desire, joining with them in the fellowship of Christ's love.

2:18 *We wanted to visit you. I, Paul, wanted to visit you twice already, but Satan made that impossible.*

Paul personally expressed his intense desire to return to Thessalonica. Satan delayed his return, though not because of any unwillingness on Paul's part. These believers held a special place in Paul's heart. He treasured their fellowship. He wanted to encourage them and lift them up in the joy of the Lord.

We do not know specifically how Satan thwarted Paul's plans. It may have been some illness (his thorn in the flesh) or it may have been the continued opposition of the Jewish community in Thessalonica. We have too little information to be certain. Whether or not Paul ever got his wish, God's sovereign determination will always override Satan's intentions.

2:19–20 *[19]Who is our hope, joy, or prize that we can brag about in the presence of our Lord Jesus when he comes? Isn't it you? [20]You are our glory and joy!*

Paul asked a rhetorical question that expressed his special attachment to these believers. The answer was as simple as it was remarkably powerful in its praise for God's work in their lives. Paul never bragged about his personal importance in the scheme of God's plan. However, he certainly didn't hesitate to brag about the Thessalonian believers—their understanding that his message was the Word of God, that the Holy Spirit had removed the darkness of sin from their lives, and that their actions plainly showed that they were changed people. They had turned away from idols and turned immediately to worship the living God. They had done this even though they immediately encountered fierce opposition.

Paul's experience in Thessalonica affirmed his calling as God's apostle to the Gentiles. He rejoiced that their lives confirmed God's blessing on his ministry. It gave him the reason to be grateful for the results of the Spirit's regenerating power to change the lives of people who were once trapped in the darkness of their sin. In this way, the Thessalonian believers were Paul's pride and joy, the visible confirmation of God's call on his life.

Notes/Applications

Paul spent the first two chapters of this letter praising the congregation in Thessalonica. It seems that he could not stop outlining all the evidence that pointed to the extraordinary work of the Spirit among that persecuted congregation. His praise culminated in the greatest accolade that any believer can give to another—that their mutual experience abounds with the verification of God's salvation, grace, and goodness.

When we, as believers, see this in each others' lives, there is only one thing that anyone can say—God's Name be praised that we see the wonderful way that God has brought us together in the joy of His salvation to the honor and glory of His Name.

It is rare for believers to speak this way to each other. Maybe we should stop, take careful inventory of all that we have seen, and instead of seeing the numerous faults of our fellow believers, rejoice when we see God's loving, redeeming hand changing their lives. Maybe then we could join hands and hearts in the work of Christ's kingdom rather than criticizing each others' shortcomings. Maybe then we could join Paul and point to those dear friends who have shared our faith journey, bragging how they were our pride and joy.

1 THESSALONIANS 3

1 Thessalonians 3:1–6

3:1–3 ***[1]We thought it best to remain in Athens by ourselves. But, because we couldn't wait any longer for news about you, [2]we sent our brother Timothy to you. He serves God by spreading the Good News about Christ. His mission was to strengthen and encourage you in your faith [3]so that these troubles don't disturb any of you. You know that we're destined to suffer persecution.***

Because of difficult circumstances, Paul was unable to leave Athens and visit the believers in Thessalonica who were being persecuted. Paul grew concerned about the development of circumstances in Thessalonica. Even though Paul enjoyed his association with Silas and Timothy *(Acts 17:15–16)*, he decided to send Timothy to this thriving city to ascertain what was going on. What was the status of the church? To what degree did persecution affect the faith of the believers? Were the Jews still so hostile? Were people's lives threatened by their hostility? There were a whole host of questions that Paul wanted answered so that he could find some peace that would calm his concerns.

Paul sent Timothy to Thessalonica to encourage and strengthen the persecuted believers. He provided his strong commendation of Timothy's qualifications. Within the framework of that life-changing message, Timothy was eminently qualified to provide encouragement and support to the believers' growing faith.

Paul wanted the Thessalonians to understand their situation in the face of persecution. He did not want them to weaken as the opposition hurled threats at them. Paul knew what it was like to encounter people who hated the good news of Christ's salvation. He escaped the persecution of the Jews in Thessalonica when some of the believers helped him escape to Berea *(Acts 17:10)*.

Believers should not allow the opposition to disturb them. Insults and persecution were an integral part of the believer's experience. Jesus taught this *(John 15:18–21)*. Not only was this to be the expected response of unbelievers, but Jesus asserted that this kind of opposition would be a source of God's blessing. "[11]*Blessed are you when people insult you, persecute you, lie, and say all kinds of evil things about you because of me.* [12]*Rejoice and be glad because you have a great reward in heaven! The prophets who lived before you were persecuted in these ways*" *(Matthew 5:11–12)*. When Paul wrote his letter to the Romans, he echoed Jesus' words when he stated that "nothing can separate us from the love of God in Jesus Christ…death or life" *(Romans 8:35–39)*.

3:4 *In fact, when we were with you, we told you ahead of time that we were going to suffer persecution. And as you know, that's what happened.*

When Paul, Silas, and Timothy entered the city of Thessalonica, they immediately proclaimed the good news about Jesus. Many of the people, particularly Greeks converted to Judaism *(Acts 17:4)*, accepted Paul's message, and the Holy Spirit brought them into the family of God's redeemed people. As he continued to instruct them in their new lives, he told them that they were going to suffer persecution.

Paul knew the consequences of faithfully proclaiming the Gospel of Christ. Christ's message was not easy for the Jews to accept since it confronted their traditions and challenged their understanding of who the Messiah was. Paul understood that he and his companions would suffer further persecution. When the Jews in Thessalonica reacted in the same way, he was not surprised. The Thessalonian believers also should not have been surprised when Paul's prophecy came true.

3:5 *But when I couldn't wait any longer, I sent Timothy to find out about your faith. I wanted to see whether the tempter had in some way tempted you, making our work meaningless.*

Again, Paul exposed the intensity of his concern for the newborn believers in Thessalonica. Another reason for sending Timothy to them was to determine if Satan had somehow weakened their steadfastness in the faith and thus threatened the work that he had invested in them. Paul did not want his labor to be in vain, not for selfish reasons but because he truly loved these believing friends. They had a very special place in his heart and his spirit ached when he thought about what might be happening. He wanted some reassurance that the Thessalonian believers remained steadfast despite the opposition that confronted them.

The temptation to return to the safety of the old ways grows strong when a new believer suffers ridicule because of his faith. Satan plays on this weakness and attempts to redirect the believers' thoughts, foolishly hoping that they will return to the region of darkness and sin. Even though Satan has his schemes, Paul wanted the believers to know that God's power and protection far exceeded Satan's deceits *(1 John 4:4)*.

3:6 *But Timothy has just now come back to us from you and has told us the good news about your faith and love. He also told us that you always have fond memories of us and want to see us, as we want to see you.*

As it turned out, Paul's concerns were unwarranted. Timothy brought back amazingly good news *(Proverbs 25:25)*. The faith and love that

God had implanted in the Thessalonians' hearts empowered them to overcome those circumstances that would normally defeat the unsaved person. Instead of succumbing to Satan's deceits, they were growing and maturing in their Christian walk.

The kind of love that the Thessalonians demonstrated was the same kind of love that God had shown to mankind when He sent His Son to be the sacrifice necessary to satisfy His righteousness and release people from the penalty of sin.

Not only did that faith and love sustain the Thessalonians in their trials, but these believers expressed that same kind of love as they remembered Paul and Silas. Paul was relieved that the believers reciprocated his fondness for them. They loved him and wanted to see him as much as he wanted to see them.

Notes/Applications

The Scriptures contain numerous examples where believers suffered simply because they were God's people. It is as much a part of the believer's life as breathing is to the human body. This must be recognized and accepted by every believer. It is not something to be avoided. It is not something to be sought. It is not something to complain about. It is not something to rejoice in. It is simply a fact of the redeemed life:

> *16The Spirit himself testifies with our spirit that we are God's children. 17If we are his children, we are also God's heirs. If we share in Christ's suffering in order to share his glory, we are heirs together with him. 18I consider our present sufferings insignificant compared to the glory that will soon be revealed to us. (Romans 8:16–18)*

As we live in a hostile world and bear witness to the salvation of our Lord by our redeemed lives, we can be sure that people will challenge the validity of our salvation experience. Certainly, we will experience the normal adversities that every human being faces. There will be the simple pressure of surviving day to day. There will be disease. There will be the death of those we love, but Paul was not speaking of this kind of adversity. He spoke of the suffering believers face because they simply testify to the change that God has fashioned in individual lives. The darkness of this world cannot understand or accept the light of Jesus Christ. Believers find themselves deeply engaged in a spiritual battle that they cannot win without the support, instruction, and protection of God's indwelling Spirit.

The Thessalonian believers provide an excellent example of believers who faced this kind of persecution. Like them, we, too, can be happy that we belong to Christ. We can rejoice that we share in Christ's sufferings. We can accept whatever the world throws at us because we know with absolute certainty that nothing can separate us from the love of God in Christ Jesus *(Romans 8:38–39)*.

1 Thessalonians 3:7–13

3:7 *So brothers and sisters, your faith has encouraged us in all our distress and trouble.*

When believers live in the light of God's saving grace, they exhibit God's love and joy in their lives. It is impossible to suppress this kind of spiritual exuberance. Others who witness the Spirit's joy in the believers' lives are drawn to the witness of the Gospel. Other believers are greatly encouraged. As individual believers share their lives in the Body of Christ, they find numerous opportunities to share their faith, witnessing to the way God works in them, providing mutual support and comfort to the Body of Christ:

> [3]*Praise the God and Father of our Lord Jesus Christ! He is the Father who is compassionate and the God who gives comfort.* [4]*He comforts us whenever we suffer. That is why whenever other people suffer, we are able to comfort them by using the same comfort we have received from God.* (2 Corinthians 1:3–4)

In Paul's own experience of distress and trouble imposed upon him by his enemies, he rejoiced in the faith of the Thessalonian believers. Paul was encouraged by Timothy's report and the good news he brought lifted his spirits and engendered a spirit of thanksgiving in his troubled heart.

3:8 *Now we can go on living as long as you keep your relationship with the Lord firm.*

Thankful for Timothy's report, Paul put his concerns for their welfare behind him. He primarily wanted to know that the Thessalonian believers were growing in their relationship with the Lord. Now he prepared to go on with the tasks God had assigned to him, living to the fullest in the joy of God's providence for these dear friends.

3:9 *We can never thank God enough for all the joy you give us as we rejoice in God's presence.*

The evidence of God's work in the lives of believers brings overflowing joy to those who have proclaimed the good news of God's salvation to them. Paul found it difficult to find the words that could adequately express his joy about the way these believers abided firmly in their relationship with the Lord. The trials and persecutions they endured revealed the salvation that God had wrought in them. It was wonderful to hear how God's Word was so deeply rooted in these people's lives.

Paul's expression of thanksgiving exemplified selfless rejoicing in the spiritual welfare of other believers. The steadfastness of God's people as they faced the insults of unbelievers was cause for great joy.

Paul could not take credit for the results. It was the manifestation of God's miraculous power. Nevertheless, he knew that he was the instrument that God used, and to be used by God in the salvation of others gave the reason for his joy.

3:10–11 *[10]We pray very hard night and day that we may see you again so that we can supply whatever you still need for your faith. [11]We pray that God our Father and the Lord Jesus will guide us to you.*

Despite Timothy's good report, Paul, Silas, and Timothy prayed continuously, asking God to open the pathway for them to visit Thessalonica again. They knew that God had to provide the guidance that would enable them to share personally with these believers. The wonderful news about their faithfulness in the midst of suffering did not dampen their desire. Even though the believers demonstrated an outstanding degree of maturity in their relationship to the Lord, he wanted to come and share whatever they needed to continue building their faith.

Orthodox Christian theology has always held that the Father and the Son are one Person. Jesus and His Father are one, eternal, inseparable essence. Jesus often spoke of this divine oneness. *"The Father and I are one" (John 10:30)*. Paul did not submit his petitions to two different persons, but to the one, holy, immutable, and inseparable Being—Jesus being the visible manifestation of the invisible Creator.

3:12 *We also pray that the Lord will greatly increase your love for each other and for everyone else, just as we love you.*

As Paul and His companions continued to pray, asking the Lord to grant them a safe return to Thessalonica, they also raised another petition on behalf of these beloved believers. Even though he had continually praised the Thessalonian believers for the amazing expression of God's love by their actions toward others, he asked the Lord to continue to increase their love.

Again, Paul used the Greek word *agape*, the kind of love God has shown toward the lost despite their rebellion and rejection of His love. No matter how successfully believers express God's love for others, there is ample evidence that they often fail to be consistent in this regard. Therefore, Paul was not being critical of the believers. He simply wanted God to continue the work He had already begun.

3:13 *Then he will strengthen you to be holy. Then you will be blameless in the presence of our God and Father when our Lord Jesus comes with all God's holy people.*

Paul continued to pray and ask God to strengthen these believers, encouraging them to be holy. He affirmed that they would be able to stand in God's presence when Jesus comes again without fear of His righteous judgment. They would, in fact, be blameless in the presence of the holy God who had created and redeemed them.

Paul repeatedly praised the testimony of the Thessalonian believers. However, he also prayed for them to continue to grow in God's love to the point that they would be holy and blameless when Jesus comes again. So what was Paul saying? He spoke of the testimony of Christ's redemption that becomes evident in the life of believers as they mature under the instruction of the Word by the Holy Spirit who leads them into the truth of God's Word *(John 16:13)*.

The Thessalonian believers had already matured to the point that their witness to Christ in their lives was well-known to everyone who heard about them. Notwithstanding, Paul justifiably prayed for their love to continue to grow so that their salvation would be even more evident than it already was.

Many times believers encounter circumstances with other believers in which *agape* love is desperately needed. It is obligatory for the believer to deal in all confrontations with God's *agape* love *(1 Corinthians 13:1–8, 13)*. That means that we should often overlook offenses and leave the circumstances up to God's resolution. If there is to be a verbal exchange, then we must again express ourselves without any expectation for a satisfactory resolution. God treats us this way, and we should follow His commands and treat each other in the same way. Thus, we obey our Lord's command: "Love each other as I have loved you. This is what I'm commanding you to do" *(John 15:12)*.

Notes/Applications

How could Paul ask the Thessalonian believers to be holy when in fact he had already praised them for their very visible witness to everyone around them? How could they be praised in one breath and then encouraged to continue to grow even more so that they could be blameless at some future time? Is the Christian life nothing more than a struggle to do whatever God commands so that a person can merit God's salvation?

It is obvious that Paul was speaking of something else in these verses. We know that Christ's righteousness is imputed to the believer at the moment of his regeneration by the Spirit of God. We know that our sins were placed upon the Son of God's shoulders *(2 Corinthians 5:21)*. So from the moment of new birth, believers are set apart and made blameless by being clothed in the righteousness of Christ by the work of the Holy Spirit *(Jude 24–25)*.

So what was Paul saying? He spoke of the testimony of Christ's redemption that becomes evident in the life of believers as they mature under the instruction of the Word by the Holy Spirit who leads them into the truth of God's Word *(John 16:13).*

The Thessalonian believers had already matured to the point that their witness to Christ in their lives was well-known to everyone who heard about them. Notwithstanding, Paul justifiably prayed for their love to continue to grow so that their salvation would be even more evident than it already was.

Many times believers encounter circumstances with other believers in which *agape* love is desperately needed. It is obligatory for the believer to deal in all confrontations with God's *agape* love *(1 Corinthians 13:1–8, 13).* That means that we should often overlook offenses and leave the circumstances up to God's resolution. If there is to be a verbal exchange, then we must again express ourselves without any expectation for a satisfactory resolution. God treats us this way, and we should follow His commands and treat each other in the same way. Thus, we obey our Lord's command: "Love each other as I have loved you. This is what I'm commanding you to do" *(John 15:12).*

1 THESSALONIANS 4

1 Thessalonians 4:1–8

4:1 ***Now then, brothers and sisters, because of the Lord Jesus we ask and encourage you to excel in living a God-pleasing life even more than you already do. Do this the way we taught you.***

Paul addressed these dear friends in Thessalonica by calling them "*brothers and sisters.*" He urged them to continue growing in their faith. Although Paul had just spent the first three chapters of this letter praising their amazing exhibition of Christian behavior, Paul now let them know that they had not yet arrived. No matter what degree of Christian maturity had been achieved, it was vitally important that the Thessalonian believers understood that there was always room for growth in the vast, measureless grace of the Lord Jesus Christ. This had been a significant part of Paul's verbal instruction when he was with them. He had taught them how to live in the light of their new Christian lives.

4:2 *You know what orders we gave you through the Lord Jesus.*

While we do not know for certain what Paul had taught the new believers when he first brought them the Good News, the Thessalonian believers knew. Paul did not change his instructions. He simply restated his instructions, reminding them how they were to live as the redeemed in Christ. Both while he was personally with them and now in this letter, Paul gave them the instructions he had received through the Lord Jesus.

4:3 *It is God's will that you keep away from sexual sin as a mark of your devotion to him.*

One aspect of Paul's instructions on living the Christian life centered on one of the most powerful aspects of human existence. Outside of the drive for food, the sexual urge given by God for the procreation of the species is one of the powerful influences on human behavior. It is the most beautiful expression of love between a man and his wife. In contrast to God's design and under the burden of the sin nature, the human race has virtually demolished God's design for this covenantal relationship between man and woman.

In contrast to normal human behavior, believers have been restored to a positive, supportive relationship with their Creator. Under the sanctifying influence of the Holy Spirit, believers are to keep away from sexual sins that often mar the human experience, defile the body that is the temple of the Holy Spirit, and rebel against the design and purpose of the Creator. If believers follow the Word of God and submit to the Holy Spirit's teaching, they behave as their Creator intended—living as man and woman united in a life-long, loving relationship that honors God, both as the Creator and as their Redeemer. This was also emphasized by Paul in his letter to the Romans:

> *11So consider yourselves dead to sin's power but living for God in the power Christ Jesus gives you. 12Therefore, never let sin rule your physical body so that you obey its desires. 13Never*

> *offer any part of your body to sin's power. No part of your body should ever be used to do any ungodly thing. Instead, offer yourselves to God as people who have come back from death and are now alive. Offer all the parts of your body to God. Use them to do everything that God approves of.* [14]*Certainly, sin shouldn't have power over you because you're not controlled by laws, but by God's favor.* (Romans 6:11–14)

4:4–5 [4]*Each of you should know that finding a husband or wife for yourself is to be done in a holy and honorable way,* [5]*not in the passionate, lustful way of people who don't know God.*

Once redeemed, the believer's life—both body and spirit—belong to the Lord. This action, initiated and sustained by the Holy Spirit, restrains the behavior that normally controls the unsaved person. Under the authority of God's Word and in obedience to its instruction, the believer is constrained to control sexual urges. It must be clearly understood that the Holy Spirit does not remove the common sexual urges. He does not remove the deeper need for an intimate, satisfying, lasting relationship with a life-long mate.

However, God gives the divine framework of marriage in order to express His purpose for this gift. Therefore, believers are admonished to exercise God-given constraint while searching for a mate. Believers should behave properly toward prospective spouses, carefully learning to know them within the borders of God-given friendship.

Such considerations do not typically characterize unbelievers' relationships. In fact, the biblical framework for both dating and marriage is counter-cultural and not the manner in which so many people live their lives. However, God's design provides spiritual, emotional, and physical safety and support for individuals to enrich their lives through His design for sexual intimacy.

4:6 ***No one should take advantage of or exploit other believers that way. The Lord is the one who punishes people for all these things. We've already told you and warned you about this.***

Believers should not behave as unbelievers when searching for a spouse. Rather than following the sexual urges of the unsaved person, the believer should follow the counsel of the Lord, carefully evaluating the characteristics of the proposed spouse. When believers behave in the same way as unbelievers, all of the consequences visited upon unsaved people are likewise visited upon believers.

The most heinous consequence of this behavior becomes the image presented to the world. Such practices do not demonstrate that believers belong to Christ, but that they are subject to the same temptations and often succumb to those temptations. Unbelievers see no reason why the good news of Christ's salvation should even apply to them. This behavior among believers tarnishes Christ's image, and He holds them accountable for such offenses. Therefore, Paul warned believers everywhere about the dangers of sexual sin:

> [15]*Don't you realize that your bodies are parts of Christ's body? Should I take the parts of Christ's body and make them parts of a prostitute's body? That's unthinkable!* [16]*Don't you realize that the person who unites himself with a prostitute becomes one body with her? God says, "The two will be one."* [17]*However, the person who unites himself with the Lord becomes one spirit with him.* [18]*Stay away from sexual sins. Other sins that people commit don't affect their bodies the same way sexual sins do. People who sin sexually sin against their own bodies.* [19]*Don't you know that your body is a temple that belongs to the Holy Spirit? The Holy Spirit, whom you received from God, lives in you. You don't belong to yourselves.* [20]*You were bought for a price. So bring glory to God in the way you use your body. (1 Corinthians 6:15–20)*

4:7 *God didn't call us to be sexually immoral but to be holy.*

The opposite of living in a sexually immoral way is to live in the light of God's salvation. In this way, believers fulfill the sacred calling on their lives, living as individuals redeemed by the Lord, holy in His sight. Believers who commit sexual sin not only sin against their own bodies, but they also sin against God.

4:8 *Therefore, whoever rejects this order is not rejecting human authority but God, who gives you His Holy Spirit.*

Man did not establish the principle of remaining sexually pure. God established these precepts from the very beginning of creation. Any degradation of God's holy design for His creation directly offends and defies God's will. Paul appealed to the witness of the Holy Spirit in the believer's life as undeniable confirmation of the eternal truth he was teaching them. In summary, the Scriptures affirm the testimony of the triune God—Father, Son, and Holy Spirit—as the source of this principle.

When sinners are born again, they are restored to fellowship with the eternal God who has created them. Once redeemed, it should be clearly understood that the Holy Spirit has taken up the task of giving believers the mind of Christ. The redeemed mind finally understands with absolute clarity God's will that was established from the dawn of creation.

Furthermore, God wants His children to live in the harmony of marriage between a man and a woman throughout the course of this life. This is God's will as well as His blessing on those that belong to Him. Believers, therefore, possess not man's wisdom but the God-bestowed wisdom, knowledge, and understanding as well as the ability to think upon these matters with the mind of Christ. They have the capacity to develop in holiness and purity by the ongoing work of the Holy Spirit. Therefore, the redeemed child of God has no excuse for surrendering to those urges that consume the passions of the unredeemed person.

Notes/Applications

Even though the Thessalonian believers were exceptional in the way that they exemplified Christ, there was still room to grow. Paul, therefore, embarked on further instructions concerning how they should live in a way that displayed Christ's distinctive ownership of their lives—the forgiveness of sin, past, present, and future, as well as the future, never-ending work of the Holy Spirit that continued to bring them into the full knowledge of the mind of Christ.

One of the most important ways showing the distinctiveness of the Christian's life as opposed to the life of the unsaved person is the way that we approach the subject of sexual purity and responsibility. "*It is God's will that you keep away from sexual sin as a mark of your devotion to him*" *(4:3)*. Christian behavior in this matter is one of the clearest marks testifying to the unsaved world that we belong to Christ. However, in today's culture, it is the one area that shows the world that we are not so different at all.

We know that the Scriptures teach us how God created man in His image, how He designed the relationship between man and woman, and that He asks His people to live in full accordance with His eternal will. We know that He pronounced His blessing on marriage. We know that God meant marriage to last throughout this lifetime *(Hebrews 13:4)*.

Yet, we behave as though God has never spoken on this subject. We go on our way, behaving just like the world behaves. The percentage of marriages that break up in divorce among professing Christians is the same as the percentage among those who do not profess belief in Christ. The percentage of unwed mothers and fathers and couples living together prior to being married parallels those who do not claim to be Christians.

If we really believe what God's Word tells us, we would never behave this way. We have said that believers possess not man's wisdom but God-bestowed wisdom, knowledge, and understanding as well as the ability to think with the mind of Christ. We have the capacity to develop in holiness and purity by the ongoing work of the Holy Spirit.

Therefore, as redeemed children of God, we have no excuse for surrendering to those urges that consume the passions of the unredeemed person.

Like King David, we need to acknowledge our sin, confessing it to the Lord, and prayerfully ask: "Have pity on us, O God, according to Your mercy!" *(Psalm 51:1, paraphrased).* We need to bask in the light of His instruction. If believers submit to the direction of the Holy Spirit, remaining true and obedient to God's instructions, we will enjoy the blessings of pleasing Him, showing both individually and corporately that we belong to God and to each other *(1 Thessalonians 2:6; Romans 12:1–5).*

1 Thessalonians 4:9–12

4:9 *You don't need anyone to write to you about the way Christians should love each other. God has taught you to love each other.*

Throughout this letter, Paul expressed his thanks to Almighty God for the way that the Thessalonian believers showed that they belonged to God. Nevertheless, he also encouraged them to excel in their God-pleasing behavior *(4:1)*.

The Greek text uses two different words for *love* in this context. Paul was saying that the Thessalonian believers already demonstrated that they belonged to God in the way that they related to each other with brotherly affection (*philadelphias*). Paul then stated that God had also shown them how to love (*agapao*) each other even as Jesus commanded them to do *(John 13:34–35)*.

It is one thing for people to relate to each other in the natural order of human relationships. However, it is impossible for any human being to love another in the same sense that Jesus has loved them. Only the redeemed sinner who has experienced the unconditional love of God by the regeneration of the Holy Spirit can begin to express love among the believers without conditions or human expectations. Only after this life-changing experience can believers understand that they love their brothers and sisters because of the *agapao* love flowing through them as the Spirit continues His sanctifying work in their hearts.

4:10 *In fact, you are showing love to all the Christians throughout the province of Macedonia. We encourage you as believers to excel in love even more.*

These Thessalonian believers provided an outstanding testimony of the change that God had produced in their lives by the way that they loved each other. Nevertheless, there are no limits to God's love for those that belong to Him. Therefore, Paul encouraged them to live in the process of ongoing growth, never failing to express God-given love (*agapao*) to everyone they met.

4:11 *Also, make it your goal to live quietly, do your work, and earn your own living, as we ordered you.*

Living in a growing relationship with the Lord and expressing that relationship in a clear demonstration of love for others, Paul provided additional advice that was designed to shape their redeemed lives, further enhancing their testimony to all observers.

Paul advised believers to live "*quietly*." This word carries the connotation of undisturbed rest. Believers who live within the framework of God's love are to live their lives in quiet acceptance not only of God's salvation given to them but also the circumstances surrounding them. Believers who live within the dynamic, motivating teaching of the Holy Spirit do not need to be upset about anything that might affect their lives because they possess the stabilizing assurance the Holy Spirit provides.

Believers are also to live productive lives, earning an honest wage for the provision of their families. They are to do this also in the quiet comfort of the Spirit's care and guidance, not with a rebellious or ungrateful attitude. Believers who respect their employers, even if these overseers are not believers, should perform their assigned tasks faithfully to the best of their human abilities, providing a living testimony of their contentment within the context of their life in Christ.

4:12 *Then your way of life will win respect from those outside the church, and you won't have to depend on anyone else for what you need.*

The Christian way of living provides a testimony to everyone that believers are dramatically different from the unbelieving world. The way they love each other, their mutual support for each other, the quiet demeanor regardless of circumstances, and their diligent application to their occupation demonstrate the changes that God has made in their lives. Paul stated that the application of these principles would win the respect of the unbelieving world.

Notes/Applications

Paul encouraged the Thessalonian believers to continue growing in the love that Christ had shown to them, even though they already excelled in the testimony of their Christian lives, providing a powerful witness to God's life-changing work in their lives.

Paul then proceeded to advise them how to live in the common areas of their lives within the framework of God's uncommon love. It is virtually impossible to live under the teaching of God's Holy Spirit without having that special relationship affect all areas of the believer's life. Everyone agrees that the Spirit brings His counsel into the life of the believer as well as the life of the Church, Christ's Body. Paul, however, showed how the Spirit's influence in the believer's life affects the public arena of employment and the very private arena of the home. Once a sinner is redeemed, the Holy Spirit directs the learning, behavior, and ongoing growth of his relationship with the Lord in every area of the believer's life. Nothing is outside the Spirit's influence, authority, and direction. Thus, believers should show the world that they have been redeemed by living in quiet contentment; resting in the Lord; working diligently; rejoicing in their liberty in Christ; thanking the Lord for their redemption; and living in Christ's abundance, fueled by God's uncommon love.

1 Thessalonians 4:13–18

4:13 ***Brothers and sisters, we don't want you to be ignorant about those who have died. We don't want you to grieve like other people who have no hope.***

Paul had just demonstrated how the lives of the Thessalonian believers reflected a living witness to God's redemption in their lives. He showed them how their redemption should be exhibited in their homes and in their work.

Now, Paul led them into an understanding that the uncommon love God had shown to them, although experienced in this life with faulty human perceptions, also had a future aspect in which their salvation would be completed. Such confidence in Christ's promise should have provided additional motivation to live their lives in consummate surrender to the ongoing work of the Holy Spirit, showing to everyone that they belong to Christ.

No doubt many believers had died. Paul recognized that, from the human perspective, the death of someone could cause excessive grief. The vision of the lifeless body of some beloved person convinces many people that they are witnessing the end of that person's life. Paul now set out to alleviate those misunderstandings and to bring hope to those who grieve.

4:14 ***We believe that Jesus died and came back to life. We also believe that, through Jesus, God will bring back those who have died. They will come back with Jesus.***

It must be clearly understood that Paul was speaking to believers versus making some universal statement, claiming that everyone will come back to everlasting life. Believers come back to everlasting life because Jesus was first brought back to life by the authority of His heavenly Father. Jesus, therefore, brings those who belong to Him into His eternal Kingdom *(1 Corinthians 15:20)*. On the other hand, those who do not believe will rise to their everlasting destruction.

This is the firm assertion of the biblical record, both Old and New Testament. The prophecy of Daniel states: "Many sleeping in the ground will wake up. Some will wake up to live forever, but others will wake up to be ashamed and disgraced forever" *(Daniel 12:2)*. Jesus also affirmed this immutable fact: "Those who have done good will come back to life and live. But those who have done evil will come back to life and will be judged" *(John 5:29)*.

The resurrection of Jesus the Christ assures the resurrection of every believer. *"Does the Spirit of the one who brought Jesus back to life live in you? Then the one who brought Christ back to life will also make your mortal bodies alive by his Spirit who lives in you" (Romans 8:11)*. The Old Testament saint, Job, made this astounding statement of confident belief in the resurrection of the body: "[25]I know that my Redeemer lives, and that in the end he will stand upon the earth. [26]And after my skin has been destroyed, yet in my flesh I will see God; [27]I myself will see him with my own eyes—I, and not another. How my heart yearns within me!" *(Job 19:25–27, NIV)*.

4:15 *We are telling you what the Lord taught. We who are still alive when the Lord comes will not go into his kingdom ahead of those who have already died.*

Paul reminded the Thessalonians what the Lord had already taught during His earthly ministry. When this awesome day comes and the Lord Jesus Christ returns, believers still living on the earth will not meet the Lord before the saints who are already dead in Christ. Instead, those who are alive and those who are dead in Christ will meet the Lord at the same time. Those whose bodies are alive will have to be changed into eternal bodies. Those who are in the grave will have to be resurrected and changed into eternal bodies:

> [51]*I'm telling you a mystery. Not all of us will die, but we will all be changed.* [52]*It will happen in an instant, in a split second at the sound of the last trumpet. Indeed, that trumpet will sound, and then the dead will come back to life. They*

will be changed so that they can live forever. [53]*This body that decays must be changed into a body that cannot decay. This mortal body must be changed into a body that will live forever.* (1 Corinthians 15:51–53)

4:16–17 [16]***The Lord will come from heaven with a command, with the voice of the archangel, and with the trumpet call of God. First, the dead who believed in Christ will come back to life.*** [17]***Then, together with them, we who are still alive will be taken in the clouds to meet the Lord in the air. In this way we will always be with the Lord.***

The Lord Jesus Christ ascended to heaven when He left the earth forty days after His resurrection. Now, Paul further explained the events that will occur when He returns *(Acts 1:11)*. When He does, all creation will be subjected to the authority of His command. We do not know all the details—how the archangel will shout, who will blow the trumpet—but we do know that everything proceeds according to God's sovereign plan.

This will be a great day of victory for those who have been washed in the blood of the Lamb:

"[8]*He will swallow up death forever. The Almighty Lord will wipe away tears from every face, and he will remove the disgrace of his people from the whole earth. The Lord has spoken.* [9]*On that day his people will say, 'This is our God; we have waited for him, and now he will save us. This is the Lord; we have waited for him. Let us rejoice and be glad because he will save us'*" *(Isaiah 25:8–9)*.

The great driving force in a Christian's life comes not only in the salvation given through the sacrifice of the Lord Jesus Christ but also in the ultimate consummation of that salvation when the resurrected Christ returns and all mortality dissolves into the bliss of immortality. The human mind will never be able to grasp how this will occur.

How will the bodies that have been burned to ashes be resurrected? How will those who have been buried at sea and consumed by sea life be resurrected? What about those who have decayed into dust? Even their ashes no longer exist. Nevertheless, believers affirm that their Creator spoke all of creation into being out of nothing. Therefore, the God of all creation can easily reconstruct bodies, bringing them to life from the earth and the sea, resurrecting them to their immortality *(1 Corinthians 15:35–43).*

After the dead have received their heavenly bodies, the believers who are still alive on the earth will be caught up to meet Jesus in the air. This cannot occur unless their earthly bodies have been changed. Dead bodies are brought back to life in their eternal form and living bodies are changed into their eternal form and together they rise up to meet the Lord Jesus Christ in the air. This same theme was emphasized by Paul in his letter to the Corinthian church: "It will happen in an instant, in a split second at the sound of the last trumpet. Indeed, that trumpet will sound, and then the dead will come back to life. They will be changed so that they can live forever" *(1 Corinthians 15:52).*

When Jesus returns, He gathers all those who belong to Him so that they can be with Him forever. This event is the consummation of Jesus' prayer spoken the night before He was crucified: "Father, I want those you have given to me to be with me, to be where I am. I want them to see my glory, which you gave me because you loved me before the world was made" *(John 17:24).* Once believers are gathered to the Lord in heaven, they will see their Savior face-to-face and worship Him forever in the glory of His eternal presence.

4:18 *So then, comfort each other with these words!*

For Paul, the historical record of Jesus' life, death, and resurrection provided ample evidence that Jesus' testimony was absolutely reliable. When he explained the content of Jesus' teaching about His return, Paul was not basing his thesis on unfounded desire. He was absolutely confident that Jesus was fully capable of bringing to pass what He promised. Thus, his discussion of Jesus' return provided absolutely reliable reasons to rejoice in the life that the Thessalonian believers received by the regenerating work of the Holy Spirit.

The promise of Christ's return and the consummation of the believer's salvation in the sudden transformation of mortality into immortality should be a source of great comfort. Not only does this future event provide comfort, but it also gives tremendous confidence as believers move onward in this life under the direction of the Holy Spirit. When this life becomes difficult with all of its trials, tribulation, and suffering, believers can rely on their future with Jesus Christ. On the basis of this future event, believers can live without fear of any of their temporary circumstances, knowing that they will be with their Lord when these trials are over *(Romans 8:18)*.

Christians are to comfort each other with "these words," knowing that when a beloved person who believes in Christ dies, peace and comfort soothe the grief, knowing that immortality awaits. When our bodies become weak and begin to fail, that pain and suffering will pale in the light of Christ's promise. When life becomes exceptionally burdensome, rejoice in that day when we will be united with the Lord.

Paul did not want believers to be ignorant of what the future held for them. Christians, therefore, should remember Paul's reiteration of what Jesus taught, keeping an eternal perspective and remembering that this life is only preparatory for their eternal union with Jesus Christ, God's beloved Son and our beloved Savior *(1 John 3:1–3)*.

Notes/Applications

On the Resurrection Morning

On the resurrection morning,
soul and body meet again.
No more sorrow, no more weeping,
no more pain.

Here awhile they must be parted,
and the flesh its Sabbath keep,
Waiting in a holy stillness,
wrapped in sleep.

For a while the wearied body
lies with feet toward the morn;
Till the last and brightest Easter
day be born.

But the soul in contemplation,
utters earnest prayer and strong,
Bursting at the resurrection
into song.

Soul and body reunited
thenceforth nothing shall divide,
Waking up in Christ's own likeness
satisfied.

O the beauty, O the gladness
of that resurrection day,
Which shall not through endless ages
pass away!

On that happy Easter morning
all the graves their dead restore,
Father, mother, sister, brother,
meet once more.

To that brightest of all meetings
bring us, Jesus Christ, at last,
By thy Cross, through death and judgment,
holding fast.[1]

1 THESSALONIANS 5

1 Thessalonians 5:1–6

5:1 *Brothers and sisters, you don't need anyone to write to you about times and dates.*

As Paul wrote to the believers about the hope that was theirs in Jesus Christ and the wonderful anticipation of His Second Coming, he told them how their bodies would be changed from their mortal formulation to their immortal constitution. All believers, those who have died and those who are still alive, will join in one happy throng to meet the Lord in the air.

Again addressing the Thessalonians with the endearing terms of brothers and sisters, Paul now wanted them to know that even though Christ's coming was certain, there should be no presumption on the times and dates of that glorious event. The surety of that future event should be sufficient to provide comfort throughout their lives. The actual times and dates of this event were known only to the Father. Paul affirmed what Jesus had already told His disciples: "[6]So when the apostles came together, they asked him, 'Lord, is this the time when you're going to restore the kingdom to Israel?' [7]Jesus told them,

'You don't need to know about times or periods that the Father has determined by His own authority'" (*Acts 1:6–7*). Jesus explained some specific details about His return without outlining any specific times or dates (*Matthew 24*).

5:2 *You know very well that the day of the Lord will come like a thief in the night.*

"*The day of the Lord*" is a subject that ripples through much of Old Testament prophecy. The tone of those prophecies is frightening, telling of the wrath of the Lord that will be visited upon the arrogant and rebellious:

> *[9]The day of the Lord is going to come. It will be a cruel day with fury and fierce anger. He will make the earth desolate. He will destroy its sinners. [10]The stars in the sky and their constellations won't show their light anymore. The sun will be dark when it rises. The moon won't shine. [11]I will punish the world for its evil and the wicked for their wrongdoing. I will put an end to arrogant people and humble the pride of tyrants. (Isaiah 13:9–11)*

No one really knows when Jesus will return to execute His judgment on those who have rejected His salvation. Scripture affirms the reality of this day in Matthew 24:42–44; 1 Peter 3:10; and Revelation 16:15. The entire New Testament witness exposes the waywardness of the human race, going its own way without any consideration of Jesus Christ and, therefore, completely surprised when He descends from heaven in all of His glory.

5:3 *When people say, "Everything is safe and sound!" destruction will suddenly strike them. It will be as sudden as labor pains come to a pregnant woman. They won't be able to escape.*

Unbelieving people will go on their usual way, self-absorbed with the activities of their lives and convinced that the world was safe. Governments will live in the confidence of their treaties, believing that they have arrived at a time in history when there will be peace. This is Satan's deception. At that time, God's judgment will be visited upon the world, destroying every vestige of security and peace:

> [36]"*No one knows when that day or hour will come. Even the angels in heaven and the Son don't know. Only the Father knows.* [37]"*When the Son of Man comes again, it will be exactly like the days of Noah.* [38]*In the days before the flood, people were eating, drinking, and getting married until the day that Noah went into the ship.* [39]*They were not aware of what was happening until the flood came and swept all of them away. That is how it will be when the Son of Man comes again.* [40]"*At that time two men will be working in the field. One will be taken, and the other one will be left.* [41]*Two women will be working at a mill. One will be taken, and the other one will be left.* [42]"*Therefore, be alert, because you don't know on what day your Lord will return.* (Matthew 24:36–42)

Paul illustrated the timing of this coming event with the description of a pregnant woman about to give birth. No one knows exactly when the birth will occur because every birth progresses on a slightly different timetable. The doctor does not know. Even the pregnant woman does not know; but when the moment of birth arrives, no doubt remains about what is happening, and the birth proceeds with tremendous pain. Just as such a birth is inevitable, so is the time when Christ returns to earth. It will be so sudden, so frightening, so overwhelming that no one will be able to escape.

5:4 *But, brothers and sisters, you don't live in the dark. That day won't take you by surprise as a thief would.*

In stark contrast to the unbelieving world, those who have been saved no longer live in spiritual darkness. They have the instruction of the Scriptures. They have the guidance of the Holy Spirit that leads them into the truth of God's Word.

They, therefore, realize that Jesus is going to return to earth. For them, it is not a day of destruction in the wrath of God's judgment but the consummation of their salvation. Believers anticipate the time when Jesus will return to earth for they will see the face of the One Who died for them. Their faith will become sight, and their joy will know no bounds.

5:5 *You belong to the day and the light not to the night and the dark.*

When God's regenerating work intersects a sinner's life, that individual is reborn into the light of God's glory. "*You will open their eyes and turn them from darkness to light and from Satan's control to God's. Then they will receive forgiveness for their sins and a share among God's people who are made holy by believing in me*" *(Acts 26:18).* Believers no longer live in the terrible darkness and inescapable bondage of their sin. They now belong to Jesus Christ. They belong to the One Who is the Light of the world *(John 8:12).* For this reason, the day of the Lord for them is the day of the Lord's salvation when they will see Jesus in the brightness and majesty of His glory.

5:6 *Therefore, we must not fall asleep like other people, but we must stay awake and be sober.*

Because believers live in the light of Christ's glory, they should not fall asleep like other people. There may be some confusion about Paul's instruction in the previous chapter *(4:13).* Other translations use the word *sleep* in that verse as well. However, these are two different Greek words. The translation used in this commentary correctly translates this in the context of those who have died. In this verse, a different Greek word is used which indicates normal rest and sleep.

Paul was not saying that believers should never lie down and rest, but they certainly shouldn't be lazy, wasting the valuable time the Lord has assigned to their earthly lives *(Proverbs 19:15).* In other words, Paul urged them to be industrious, working diligently for Christ's Kingdom until this same Lord comes again.

The command to be sober is not a suggestion. Paul gave this command throughout his ministry *(Romans 13:11–14)*. He instructed Titus: "[11]God's saving kindness has appeared for the benefit of all people. [12]It trains us to avoid ungodly lives filled with worldly desires so that we can live self-controlled, moral, and godly lives in this present world. [13]At the same time we can expect what we hope for—the appearance of the glory of our great God and Savior, Jesus Christ" *(Titus 2:11–13)*.

Notes/Applications

Almighty God's eye constantly watches over all of His creation. He is sovereign over everything that happens. His children can rest under His watchful care. Nevertheless, these facts do not negate our responsibility to listen and obey His instructions.

The Scriptures advise us as believers to avoid a preoccupation with the events surrounding Christ's return to earth. Many of us, however, become so preoccupied with Christ's Second Coming that we lose all perspective on our current situations. Therefore, we eagerly look forward to the consummation of our salvation when Christ appears in His glory.

Nevertheless, the strong admonition of Jesus and other New Testament writers remains. We should occupy our lives with the work that the Holy Spirit has assigned to us. Look forward to that day, but live like Jesus may return at any moment. In that divine tension, we can find the deepest satisfaction and the greatest joy in serving Him until that time when we see Him face-to-face. There is joy in serving the Lord and comfort in knowing that one day our faith will be rewarded when we are personally ushered into His presence.

1 Thessalonians 5:7–13

5:7 *People who sleep, sleep at night; people who get drunk, get drunk at night.*

After the work of the day, people sleep. They also drink wine and sometimes enter slumber in a drunken stupor. Building on his instruction in verse six, Paul emphasized a daily routine that presents a metaphor that describes people who have not been redeemed. Paul was clearly drawing an analogy to the spiritual world.[1]

This world is under sin's curse, which is often described in Scripture as a condition of darkness. The world without Christ revolves in the sphere of night that cannot be removed or overcome. Unbelievers are "asleep" to spiritual realities. Unaware of the fact that Jesus is going to return to earth, they sleep in the ignorance of their spiritual blindness, not knowing that they live on the precipice of the Lord's wrath.

5:8 *Since we belong to the day, we must be sober. We must put on faith and love as a breastplate and the hope of salvation as a helmet.*

In contrast to the spiritual darkness that blinds those who do not believe, Christians have been redeemed and the light of their Lord and Savior lives in their hearts. This has been the consistent message of the prophets and the apostles: "So we regard the words of the prophets as confirmed beyond all doubt. You're doing well by paying attention to their words. Continue to pay attention as you would to a light that shines in a dark place as you wait for day to come and the morning star to rise in your hearts" *(2 Peter 1:19).*

From the moment of salvation, believers belong to God through Jesus Christ's sacrifice. The spiritual darkness that overshadowed every moment of their lives is dispelled and the dawn of the light of the Gospel begins to rise in their hearts. From that moment on, they live in the light of that redemption. It is therefore reasonable, even necessary, that the redeemed live in the light of their spiritual day.

In the context of that new day, Paul urged the believers to be sober. That does not mean that they had no joy in their salvation. It simply means that they are to be watchful and careful. They should no longer live as though they had not been saved from their former darkness. Walking in the light of Christ's salvation, believers should carefully exercise God-given discretion in every action of their lives.

Paul not only told them that they should live with sober discretion, but he also told them how they could accomplish this Spirit-induced objective. They must put on the breastplate of faith and love.

The breastplate is the piece of armor that protects the vital organs. When believers put on the breastplate of faith and love, they are nurtured by the ongoing work of the Spirit. The Spirit so captures the believer's heart that newly found faith and love mature until they faithfully reflect the life Christ lives within them.

Believers are also to put on the helmet of salvation, which is the crown that the Spirit gives to those who belong to Him. Under the light of salvation, believers' minds are renewed moment by moment, moving ever forward toward the mind of Christ. The greatest hope of salvation is that Christians will one day be completed in Christ. On that day Christians will live forever in His awesome presence *(1 John 3:1–3)*.

5:9 *It was not God's intention that we experience his anger but that we obtain salvation through our Lord Jesus Christ.*

God's judgment on unbelief is inescapable. The testimony of Scripture assures all people that they will feel the heat of His anger when He comes again. Only those who have been redeemed by the blood of the Lamb will escape His judgment, for God does not intend for those who belong to Him to experience His wrath. Surely, Christians will sometimes suffer the Lord's corrective chastisement, but they will never be subjected to Christ's judgment. "[6]*The Lord disciplines everyone he loves. He severely disciplines everyone he accepts as his child.*" [7]*Endure your discipline. God corrects you as a father corrects his children" (Hebrews 12:6–7).*

5:10 *He died for us so that, whether we are awake in this life or asleep in death, we will live together with him.*

Predicated on Jesus' sacrificial death when the sin of the world was placed upon Him by His loving Father, those who accept His sacrifice will live together with Him. Physical life and death make no difference to the Lord, whose power and authority overcomes the circumstances of this life as well as the threat of the grave. He will bring all those who belong to Him into His presence. "[8]*If we live, we honor the Lord, and if we die, we honor the Lord. So whether we live or die, we belong to the Lord. [9]For this reason Christ died and came back to life so that he would be the Lord of both the living and the dead" (Romans 14:8–9).*

Without the redeeming sacrifice of Jesus Christ, God's Son, and His resurrection from the dead, the whole world would be without hope. Nevertheless, the gospel message affirms over and over again that Christ died to reconcile the lost world to the Creator. "[20]*God was also pleased to bring everything on earth and in heaven back to himself through Christ. He did this by making peace through Christ's blood sacrificed on the Cross. [21]Once you were separated from God. The evil things you did showed your hostile attitude. [22]But now Christ has brought you back to God by dying in his physical body. He did this so that you could come into God's presence without sin, fault, or blame" (Colossians 1:20–22).*

5:11 *Therefore, encourage each other and strengthen one another as you are doing.*

Christians are to encourage, exhort, comfort, strengthen, and edify each other. All those who have been redeemed belong to Christ's Body. Nothing happens within this redeemed Body that does not affect the entire structure. Christ's Body is the dynamic, growing, helping evidence of Christ on earth. Always learning, always growing, always helping, always witnessing, the Body of Christ fulfills the task that the Spirit gives to its members.

Paul encouraged these believers in Thessalonica to continue doing what they had done in the past. Paul had commended them for the way that they supported and helped each other. When doing this, they showed that they belonged to Christ and exhibited numerous scriptural instructions. He wanted them to continue behaving in this manner and adopt these Christian virtues as their way of life.

They encouraged each other: "Encourage each other every day while you have the opportunity. If you do this, none of you will be deceived by sin and become stubborn" *(Hebrews 3:13).*

They supported and strengthened those who were sometimes troubled by sin's entrapment. "[1]*Brothers and sisters, if a person gets trapped by wrongdoing, those of you who are spiritual should help that person turn away from doing wrong. Do it in a gentle way. At the same time watch yourself so that you also are not tempted.* [2]*Help carry each other's burdens. In this way you will follow Christ's teachings*" (Galatians 6:1–2).

5:12–13 ***[12]Brothers and sisters, we ask you to show your appreciation for those leaders who work among you and instruct you. [13]We ask you to love them and think very highly of them because of the work they are doing. Live in peace with each other.***

Paul instructed these Christians to show their appreciation for their spiritual leaders. This was true in the sense of common courtesy, but also as a matter of godly obligation. These leaders were their appointed shepherds. They had been set apart for this task in very difficult circumstances. Charged with the responsibility of guiding, directing, and nourishing their flock in the instruction of God's Word, they bore a heavy burden. Coupled with this fundamental task, they were often attacked by those who opposed the Good News of Jesus Christ. *"Remember your leaders who have spoken God's word to you. Think about how their lives turned out, and imitate their faith" (Hebrews 13:7).*

Not only were the believers to show their appreciation, but they were to love their spiritual leaders. This may seem like a daunting task for the Church, but the word used for *love* is the same as the love that God has shown to this fallen world. Paul instructed the Thessalonians to love their spiritual leaders without any expectation of personal gain. These leaders worked under very difficult circumstances. More importantly, they labored under the authority of Christ Himself.

Under these circumstances, the Church of Christ in Thessalonica could fulfill Paul's injunction to "live in peace." Peace and tranquility among the brethren is one of the most powerful testimonies that any church can provide to an unbelieving world. This accomplishes the Lord's will: "Everyone will know that you are my disciples because of your love for each other" *(John 13:35)*.

Notes/Applications

The Lord "is the same, yesterday, today, and forever" *(Hebrews 13:8, NKJV)*. Those who have been saved by the sacrifice of God's Son, Jesus Christ, have the unique gift of the Holy Spirit living in them. Under the Lord's divine guidance, believers of all ages can experience the joy of living in a community of peace and love, showing God's transforming work in everything they do and everything that they are and in their relationships with one another.

1 Thessalonians 5:14–22

5:14 *We encourage you, brothers and sisters, to instruct those who are not living right, cheer up those who are discouraged, help the weak, and be patient with everyone.*

Paul had commended the Thessalonian church numerous times throughout this letter. Interspersed within these commendations was the encouragement to do even more—to grow in the love of Christ, to share the joy of Christ with each other, to look forward to that day when they will be united with Christ, and to show their appreciation for their spiritual leaders. While the church lived by these God-given precepts, it is obvious that there were some who still needed special support and consideration in their Christian lives. This could be accomplished as mature believers continually gave themselves to the service of the Lord.

Within this context, Paul encouraged the more mature believers to take up the task of ministering to others in their congregation who needed a helping hand through the rigors of Christian growth. Some did not live uprightly within acceptable standards of Christian behavior. These believers needed further instruction in God's Word so that they could align their thoughts and actions with those precepts that God had laid out for His people.

Some believers were discouraged by their circumstances. Whatever they were experiencing in their lives became a source of contention. Discouraged believers sometimes become angry with God and develop into rebellious believers. More mature believers could offer a valuable service by cheering them up and showing them how the Lord's promises were always reliable. They were God's children, brought into God's Kingdom through Jesus Christ. They had every reason to rejoice no matter what their circumstances were.

Some of the believers did not have a very strong faith. They may have been newborn babes in Christ that had not yet learned how wonderful their salvation really was. They needed loving, careful instruction in the basics of the Scriptures so that they could grasp the measureless grace that had been given to them when they first believed. They may have been believers who never really developed in their Christian walk and needed the admonition of a more mature believer to motivate them to study the Word and understand who they were in Jesus Christ.

In such circumstances with all of their Christian brothers and sisters, the more mature believers were to exercise their instruction, correction, and encouragement with carefully controlled patience. Only this God-given patience could provide all of these ministries without becoming frustrated by the slow progress of some of their fellow believers.

5:15 *Make sure that no one ever pays back one wrong with another wrong. Instead, always try to do what is good for each other and everyone else.*

If the Thessalonian believers followed Paul's earlier instructions, they would perform these ministries in the framework of Christ's redeeming love. They would express their love and support for each other without any thought for repayment of any kind.

Sometimes supporting and helping others in the Christian community can produce unexpected results. Instead of expressions of thanksgiving and appreciation, unruly, discouraged, or weak believers may react with violent rejection of any offers of help. Though the believer offering the assistance could respond with anger and ungodly remarks that could make the situation worse, Paul urged the stronger believer to remain quiet and never to respond in the same manner as addressed. No one should ever pay back one wrong with another.

In addition, Paul advised all believers to use every opportunity of doing whatever is possible for the good of every other believer in their congregation. Always, without any hesitation, and without any thought for personal welfare, believers are to be continually directed toward the welfare of others and the Church as a whole. They are to be Christ's witness to the unsaved world around them.

In the end, Paul even pushed the believers to go beyond the walls of their believing community and to treat everyone, even unsaved people, with Christ-like love and support. This is the hardest of all of Paul's instructions. If believers have difficulty getting along with each other because they allow their human nature to override the Spirit's direction, how much more difficult will it be to provide love and support to those who are enemies of Jesus Christ and His Church, yet Paul was only following the Lord's instructions: "Rather, love your enemies, help them, and lend to them without expecting to get anything back. Then you will have a great reward. You will be the children of the Most High God. After all, he is kind to unthankful and evil people" *(Luke 6:35).*

5:16 *Always be joyful.*

At first this may seem to be easy advice to follow, yet many believers complain loudly when things do not go their way. What about the physical attack of some dreaded disease? What happens when a good job is lost for no more reason that one company buys out another? What happens when a family member dies? Even believers wonder why God has dealt them this sudden reversal of health and fortune.

Nevertheless, Paul taught believers to be joyful in all circumstances. Fully immersed in the Word of God as instructed by the Holy Spirit, stronger believers are overwhelmed with the joy of salvation that floods their soul. They are certainly afflicted with the same circumstances as everyone else, but their spirits never seem to relinquish the joy that God has planted in their hearts.

This goes back to Paul's earlier encouragement to rejoice in the hope that the Spirit instills in believers' hearts when they look to the future return of their Redeemer and realize that all human experiences pale in comparison to the joy that belongs to them when they will meet their Savior and be with Him for all eternity *(1 Thessalonians 4:13–18).*

5:17 *Never stop praying.*

Many Christians live with only a minimal awareness of who they are in Jesus Christ. Then, when some crisis hits their lives, they quickly remember that they can turn to the Lord in prayer.

However, believers are to be praying all of the time. God means for His children to live in dynamic, intimate relationship with Him. Even as they communicate with the world around them, they are to be communicating with the Lord, acknowledging His presence and relying upon His guidance. This is the source of the believer's strength, joy, and direction for every moment of their lives.

5:18 *Whatever happens, give thanks, because it is God's will in Christ Jesus that you do this.*

Contrary to praying only in a time of crisis, Paul urged Christians to give thanks no matter what was happening. If the believer prays continually, the major aspect of that prayer should be the expression of gratefulness not only for everything that God has done through Jesus Christ but also for His providence in the smallest details of daily experience. There may be times when circumstances are so difficult that it may be difficult to be thankful. At those moments, it is wise to thank God anyway as a matter of obedience, believing in the hardest of times that God is working through the circumstances to accomplish His purposes *(Ephesians 5:20 and Colossians 4:2).*

5:19 *Don't put out the Spirit's fire.*

The Holy Spirit works in the heart of sinners, bringing individuals to repentance, and washing them in the water of the Word. "[25]*He [Jesus] gave up his life for her [the church]* [26]*to make her holy and clean, washed by the cleansing of God's word" (Ephesians 5:25–26,* NLT*).* The main purpose of the Spirit is to teach believers the truth about Jesus Christ, to convict unsaved persons of their sin, and to show them God's judgment *(John 16:8).* Believers should never behave in such a way that they hinder other believers from living in the context of that sacred relationship.

Very often, believers become stagnant in their relationship with Jesus Christ. The problem of stunted growth does not lie within the Spirit's responsibility. Instead, it falls squarely on the shoulders of the half-hearted believer. By avoiding fellowship with other mature Christians who love and cherish the Word of God revealed in them by the Holy Spirit, the spiritual growth of many believers is arrested at a rather infantile stage. That was the major problem at the Corinthian church. Because they were infantile in their understanding of the Word, they became subject to a host of conflicts and controversies that virtually tore the church apart. Paul's advice was clear: "Don't ever put out the Spirit's fire!"

5:20 *Don't despise what God has revealed.*

When speaking of the gifts of the Spirit, Paul emphasized the value of those who spoke what God revealed. Everything that God has revealed to the human race is found within the pages of His Holy Word. That does not mean that God has revealed everything that He knows. Many people have questions about all sorts of matters for which God never provided the answers. However, God has provided everything that mankind needs to know about its true identity, God's plan of redemption, and the pathway to reconciliation between the Creator and His creation. To despise this revelation of God's love and salvation is to despise its Author. The consequences for such disrespect are too horrible to imagine.

In his letter to his son in the faith, Timothy, Paul summarized the preeminent place of God's Holy Scriptures in the lives of those who belong to the Father through the sacrifice of His Son, Jesus: "[16]Every Scripture passage is inspired by God. All of them are useful for teaching, pointing out errors, correcting people, and training them for a life that has God's approval. [17]They equip God's servants so that they are completely prepared to do good things" *(2 Timothy 3:16–17).*

5:21 *Instead, test everything. Hold on to what is good.*

Rather than despising God's message, believers are to test every message put forth for their edification, no matter if the message is written or spoken. Believers should not sit passively under the teaching of some spiritual leader. Instead, they should actively listen to the message and constantly filter the message through their knowledge of the Word. That is very difficult to do if the believer has very little knowledge of the Word. Thus, it should be clearly understood that all believers must be fully engaged in the study of God's Word, pursuing the high mark of God's calling on their lives in Christ Jesus *(Philippians 3:14)*.

Late in the first century, the last living member of the Twelve, the apostle John, emphasized the same message when he felt the believers were threatened by teaching that did not fully agree with the message of Jesus and the later teaching of His apostles. *"Dear friends, don't believe all people who say that they have the Spirit. Instead, test them. See whether the spirit they have is from God, because there are many false prophets in the world" (1 John 4:1).*

When all is said and done, believers need to weed out that which contradicts the instruction of God's Word and hold to everything that affirms its authority. In this way, false teaching is eliminated, and God's instruction is faithfully communicated to the Body of Christ.

5:22 *Keep away from every kind of evil.*

In testing everything, holding on to the good is not simply making good choices in the daily activities that believers encounter. Testing must also include the complete rejection of every evil that can get in the way of the Christian's growth in the faith that the Spirit has given to them. The King James Version translates this verse to mean that believers are to avoid every *appearance* of evil. Very often, immature believers attempt to live in the unholy alliance of being with the Lord and still doing what they want to do. The result is disastrous. The testimony of that person's faith both within the community of believers and to the unsaved world brings shame on the Name of the One Who has redeemed them as well as to Christ's Body.

Paul's instruction is clear. Stay away from any kind of evil. Don't try to remain attached to the world when the Savior has torn the believer from the evils of the world and married the believer to Himself as His Bride.

Notes/Applications

In his letter to the Romans, Paul set forth the foundation by which believers live in a way that pleases the Lord. God's compassion provides the fountain from which springs all godly actions:

> [1]*Brothers and sisters, because of God's compassion toward us, I encourage you to offer your bodies as living sacrifices, dedicated to God and pleasing to him. This kind of worship is appropriate for you.* [2]*Don't become like the people of this world. Instead, change the way you think. Then you will always be able to determine what God really wants—what is good, pleasing, and perfect. (Romans 12:1–2)*

When a person is redeemed, the overwhelming emotions of relief and irrepressible joy often assault the person. Shortly thereafter, the day-to-day task of living in the context of this new life begins to moderate those emotions and the believer begins to ask, "Now what?" Genuine repentance and regeneration forces the believer to ask this question, but the answer is sometime elusive. How does the believer live in such a way that the Lord is pleased? How does the believer determine what the Lord wants? Paul answers that question simply: "Offer your bodies as living sacrifices!"

In this Thessalonian letter, we find that the believers had done just that. They were living in a way that pleased the Lord and showed the region around them that they belonged to Jesus Christ. Nevertheless, Paul urged them to continue growing in the faith that the Lord had given them. In the course of his letter, Paul summarized two major aspects that affect Christian lives: there is massive evil in the world and there is joyful thanksgiving for God's salvation in Jesus Christ. These two influences on the Christian's daily life are mutually exclusive. There is no logical or spiritual way for them to coexist in the life of someone who has been redeemed.

The redeemed, who once lived in the bondage of sin and now live in the light of the Lord's salvation, are profoundly aware of both influences. They feel these influences affecting every move, every decision they make. There is the pull of the old nature to return and do what they want. There is also the indwelling Holy Spirit, leading them into the truth of God's Word. The tug of war that ensues follows the believer the rest of his life *(Romans 7).*

However, Paul did not abandon the believer to the apparent hopelessness of this struggle. Instead, he provided them with some very practical advice to help them grow in their faith and, in that maturing confidence, please the Lord. Indeed, the struggle is not hopeless, but it is the testimony of God's ongoing work in the life of believers.

Christian people support and help one another. The overriding expression of their redeemed lives is the joy that pervades every moment, reminding them that they will one day be with the Lord. They forget the offenses that may come their way. They pray continually. They thank God for every evidence of His care that they see in their lives. They do not put a damper on the Spirit's work in other believers. They respect the authority of God's Word. They test everything they hear and read through the filter of God's Word. They avoid every kind of evil.

In summary, they love the things of the Lord. They love the instruction of His Word. They love what the Spirit is teaching them. On the other hand, they hate every kind of evil. They hate the denigration of God's Word. They hate opposition to Christ's message.

As believers, we should be profoundly aware of these two aspects of our earthly lives. Heeding Paul's advice, we must walk circumspectly in this hostile world until the Lord comes again and our salvation is consummated in Him.

1 Thessalonians 5:23–28

5:23 *May the God who gives peace make you holy in every way. May he keep your whole being—spirit, soul, and body—blameless when our Lord Jesus Christ comes.*

After everything that Paul said in this letter to the Thessalonians, after every commendation for the outstanding testimony of their lives, after all of the instructions that should help them understand the circumstances in which they live, and after encouraging them to look forward to the day when believers will be reunited with their Savior, Paul offered this glowing benediction.

In the end, Paul placed the Thessalonian church under the Lord's authority and blessing. Even though he had advised them on various activities they should do to ensure their continued spiritual growth, he concluded by acknowledging that the Lord was the One Who gave them His peace and Who made them holy. The Lord alone could keep them–spirit, soul, and body–blameless until Jesus Christ returns. In the end, it is the Lord Himself that perfected their faith, bringing them home to be with Him forever.

5:24 *The one who calls you is faithful, and he will do this.*

While all believers waver from time to time in their attempt to please the Lord, the Lord Jesus Christ never wavers. He is always faithful. He will finish the work that He has begun in them. That is their confidence. That is their joy, and that is their victory.

5:25 *Brothers and sisters, pray for us.*

As Paul rejoiced in the testimony of the Thessalonian church, even as he had committed them to God under the authority of his faithful Lord, he now asked them to pray for him. Just as they needed Paul's encouragement and support, so Paul also needed their encouragement and support through their prayers.

5:26 *Greet all the brothers and sisters with a holy kiss.*

In Paul's Middle Eastern culture, greeting each other with a kiss on the cheek was common. Regardless of the culture, Paul encouraged believers to greet each other in a way that was normal for them. The expression of high regard that believers hold for each other should be shown with physical gestures that inform others that they are loved, supported, and cared for.

5:27 *In the Lord's name, I order you to read this letter to all the brothers and sisters.*

Paul lived under the divine authority of God's ordination upon his life. He had been set apart for this task to bring the good news of salvation to the Gentiles. Powerfully and remarkably redeemed on the road to Damascus, Paul never again questioned the hand of God that was operating in his life. Thus, with the authority of the Lord's Name, Paul demanded that this letter be read to everyone. The contents were not the opinions and instructions of Paul but were the inspired exhortation of God's Spirit to the believers in Thessalonica.

5:28 *The good will of our Lord Jesus Christ be with you.*

With a closing benediction, Paul pronounced the benefits of the good will [grace] of the Lord Jesus Christ to accompany them throughout their lives. They had been born again under the auspices of God's matchless grace, and Paul submitted them to that same grace as they lived for Him day by day.

Notes/Applications

The words of the hymn, "Love Divine, All Loves, Excelling," summarizes not only Paul's benediction, but the thrust of his entire letter to these believers who excelled in their testimony for Christ yet who also submitted further to the continuing work of the Spirit as they looked forward to that day when they would join the Lord forever.

Love divine, all loves excelling,
Joy of heav'n to earth come down;
Fix in us Thy humble dwelling;
All thy faithful mercies crown.
Jesus, Thou art all compassion,
Pure, unbounded love Thou art;
Visit us with Thy salvation;
Enter ev'ry trembling heart.

Breathe, O breathe Thy loving Spirit,
Into ev'ry troubled breast!
Let us all in Thee inherit,
Let us find the promised rest;
Take away our bent to sinning;
Alpha and Omega be;
End of faith, as its beginning,
Set our hearts at liberty.

Come, Almighty to deliver,
Let us all Thy grace receive;
Suddenly return, and never,
Nevermore Thy temples leave.
Thee we would be always blessing,
Serve Thee as Thy host above,
Pray, and praise Thee without ceasing,
Glory in Thy perfect love.

Finish, then, Thy new creation;
Pure and spotless let us be;
Let us see Thy great salvation
Perfectly restored in Thee:
Changed from glory into glory,
Till in heav'n we take our place,
Till we cast our crowns before Thee,
Lost in wonder, love, and praise.[2]

2nd THESSALONIANS

INTRODUCTION

It is difficult to determine the date of Paul's second letter to the Thessalonians. As in the first letter, Timothy and Sylvanus were still with Paul. It is possible that Paul was still in Corinth since he stayed there for eighteen months. Sometime during that eighteen-month period Paul received an update on the condition of the church and felt compelled to write this second letter. The church was still persecuted by those who rejected the Gospel and needed Paul's encouragement to remain faithful to the One Who had called them from the darkness of their sin.

Paul's first letter to the church in Thessalonica was written shortly after he arrived in Corinth. Some Jews had pursued Paul from Philippi and caused a lot of trouble for him in Thessalonica about A.D. 51. The Christians helped him escape to Berea and then to Athens *(Acts 16–17)*. Paul left Silas and Timothy in the city to further encourage and instruct them in their Christian faith.

Paul moved on to Corinth *(Acts 18)*. A short time afterward Silas and Timothy arrived in Corinth and told Paul about the condition of the church. This report gave rise to the first letter Paul penned to this church that was suffering intense persecution. This first letter to the believers at Thessalonica was Paul's earliest letter written from

Corinth. Even though Silas and Timothy had reported the loyalty of the Thessalonian Christians to Jesus Christ, they also reported some errors in the interpretation of Paul's teaching. As Paul encouraged them to continue faithfully in the face of persecution, he also corrected these misunderstandings. Both his encouragement and his corrections were couched in the context of the believers' enduring hope in the resurrection of the dead and Christ's Second Coming.

However, it seems that some in the church interpreted Paul's letter to mean that Jesus was coming back in the near future and some held the opinion that Jesus had already returned *(2:2)*. In this second letter, Paul tried to correct this misconception telling them that Jesus had not yet come. Certain events had to take place before Jesus returned in glory. While Paul assured the faithful that Christ's Second Coming was certain, he emphasized the events that preceded that great day.

Paul closed his second letter with the same encouragement that he gave them in his first letter. Those who follow Christ should labor for Him even in the face of persecution looking forward to that day when the Lord will vanquish His enemies, punish those who have rejected Him, and save those who have endured. It was not a time for laziness, but for industrious enterprise in and for the Gospel of Jesus Christ.

2 THESSALONIANS 1

2 Thessalonians 1:1–5

1:1 ***From Paul, Silas, and Timothy. To the church at Thessalonica united with God our Father and the Lord Jesus Christ.***

As they did in the first letter, Paul, Silas, and Timothy also joined together to write this letter to the church at Thessalonica. Paul stated the facts of their position in Christ—they were united with God their Father and with the Lord Jesus Christ, their Savior. In his first letter, Paul encouraged the believers to look forward to that day when they would join the Lord forever *(1 Thessalonians 4:13–18)*. Even though this was still a future event, Paul recognized that all believers are immediately united by the work of the Holy Spirit with Christ at the moment of their salvation.

1:2 ***Good will and peace from God our Father and the Lord Jesus Christ are yours!***

The Father and the Son dispensed grace and peace to this congregation. An inextricable link exists between the believer's union with the

Lord and the receipt of God's providence and grace. God extended love and grace to members of the human race when He gave His Son to die as the atoning sacrifice for their offense against God. These people received that life-changing grace and continued to live under the auspices of that grace. John's gospel supports the affirmation that believers not only are redeemed by this grace but also live within the framework of that grace: "16For out of His fullness (abundance) we have all received [all had a share and we were all supplied with] one grace after another and spiritual blessing upon spiritual blessing and even favor upon favor and gift [heaped] upon gift. 17While the Law was given through Moses, grace (unearned, undeserved favor and spiritual blessing) and truth came through Jesus Christ" *(John 1:16–17, AMP).*

1:3 *We always have to thank God for you, brothers and sisters. It's right to do this because your faith is showing remarkable growth and your love for each other is increasing.*

Paul, Silas, and Timothy expressed their thanksgiving to God for these dear brothers and sisters. Just as they had in the first letter, Paul, Silas, and Timothy commended the believers for their faith, which showed remarkable spiritual growth that was visibly observable in their lives. The sense of the Greek reveals that this growth exceeded normal expectations. The love that they had for each other was tangible. No human reasoning could explain such an extraordinary display of mutual affection. The only possible explanation was the fact that they continued to grow so remarkably because of the Spirit's continuing work in their lives.

1:4 *That's why we brag in God's churches about your endurance and faith in all the persecutions and suffering you are experiencing.*

The Thessalonian believers' visible testimony was so extraordinary that Paul and his companions literally bragged about their conduct as they traveled to different churches. The Thessalonians endured persecution and suffering because of that powerful witness to God's life-changing work. Opposition to their testimony only resulted in more God-given grace and endurance, making their witness even more persuasive.

Any believer would be overjoyed to see God's hand working so mightily in the lives of other believers. The Thessalonians' faith, endurance, and testimony outgrew the hostile attacks of those who opposed Jesus Christ. Paul also expressed this same confidence in the witness of the Roman church: "[3]We also brag when we are suffering. We know that suffering creates endurance, [4]endurance creates character, and character creates confidence. [5]We're not ashamed to have this confidence, because God's love has been poured into our hearts by the Holy Spirit, who has been given to us" *(Romans 5:3–5).*

1:5 *Your suffering proves that God's judgment is right and that you are considered worthy of his kingdom.*

The persecution that the Thessalonian believers suffered was not just the opposition of a hostile crowd. It occurred as the result of God's sovereign determination. Because their suffering demonstrated persuasively God's working among them, God used their suffering to provide a powerful testimony of His saving, sustaining grace. Suffering at the hands of those who oppose the Gospel of Jesus Christ visibly showed God's plan for this growing, faithful body of believers. Therefore, Paul could safely tell them that God considered them worthy of His Kingdom.

Jesus had warned His disciples that they would suffer even as He was about to suffer. "[18]If the world hates you, realize that it hated me before it hated you. [19]If you had anything in common with the world, the world would love you as one of its own. But you don't have anything in common with the world. I chose you from the world, and that's why the world hates you" *(John 15:18–19).*

It is extremely difficult to endure insult and persecution. It raises all sorts of questions about the reasons for the suffering. Surely, Jesus warned His disciples that they *would* endure suffering. However, it is difficult to accept that God would use the suffering of His people to further His Kingdom-building plan. Nevertheless, this is exactly what Paul told the Thessalonians.

Notes/Applications

Christians cannot take credit for their salvation, the evidence of God's work in their lives, the direction of their lives, nor the eternal destiny of their lives *(Ephesians 2:8–10)*. All is accomplished at the direction of the eternal God.

Because of God's work, the Thessalonian believers were united in God the Father and in His Son, the Lord Jesus Christ. They were the recipients of God's grace and peace. They also experienced exceptional spiritual growth in their faith and in their love for each other. They suffered persecution at the hands of those who hated the gospel message.

We cannot imagine what these Thessalonian believers were going through. We might whimsically wish for the kind of faith and love they exhibited, but would we be willing to endure the suffering that came along with such growth in faith?

Too many believers find it difficult to join the assembly of believers if it is too cold outside or maybe too hot. Bible study might be held on some evening that is not convenient to our schedules. Our children may have a soccer game on Sunday morning, and we have so many other "commitments." If we are not willing to give up the slightest inconveniences to our daily routines in order to make a worthwhile spiritual investment, how do we think that we could become like these Thessalonian believers?

These believers invested in their redeemed lives. They joined to worship God. They invested their time and effort in the study of God's Word. They prayed continually, remembering all of the saints. They rejoiced in the Spirit's work that took place in their lives.

If we are to grow in the Lord, if we are to experience the Holy Spirit teaching and correcting us, if we are to grow in love for our brothers and sisters in the community of faith, then we must give up and give over. We must surrender our selfishness and self-centeredness and seek to serve God and others. We must willingly invest our time and efforts in those activities that nurture our faith and understanding of the Word.

Only when we continually seek the Lord with our whole heart can we expect to grow spiritually as these Thessalonian believers did. Only when we study God's Word with single-minded yearning to discover God's will can we expect to know what God wants us to do. Only when we suffer the slings and arrows of our enemies can we rejoice that we are found worthy to share in the sufferings of our Lord *(Acts 5:40–41)*.

2 Thessalonians 1:6–12

1:6 *Certainly, it is right for God to give suffering to those who cause you to suffer.*

As the Thessalonian believers suffered the anger of those who opposed Christ, it was natural for them to hope that the Lord would destroy their enemies. Even though Paul had shown them how the Lord had determined their persecution for the testimony of His Name, he recognized that human nature would begin to hate their persecutors. He acknowledged the genuineness of these feelings. It was right for God to punish those who caused their suffering.

David, King of Israel and writer of many of the Psalms, expressed this deeply felt hostility. "[1]*The Lord is a God who punishes. God, show your greatness and punish!...* [21]*They join forces against people who do right and sentence to death the innocent.* [22]*But the Lord is my defender; my God is the rock of my protection.* [23]*God will pay them back for their sins and will destroy them for their evil. The Lord our God will destroy them" (Psalm 94:1, 21–23,* NCV*).*

As Paul acknowledged the deeply felt desire for God's revenge and punishment upon their enemies, he also advised believers that God acts in His own time to fulfill His purposes. "*My friends, do not try to punish others when they wrong you, but wait for God to punish them with his anger. It is written: "I will punish those who do wrong; I will repay them," says the Lord" (Romans 12:19,* NCV*).*

1:7 *It is also right for God to give all of us relief from our suffering. He will do this when the Lord Jesus is revealed, coming from heaven with his mighty angels in a blazing fire.*

Not only was it right for the Thessalonian believers to feel animosity toward their persecutors, it was also right for God to relieve their suffering. However, very often believers attempt to rush God, demanding that He relieve their suffering immediately. Paul answered this impatient tendency by describing the time when the Lord will finally end the suffering of those that belong to Him. Christian suffering will be ended at a time when Jesus returns to earth again. At that time, Jesus will be accompanied by a host of angels with the blazing fire of His righteous judgment. Therefore, believers may expect to suffer throughout their earthly lives until Jesus comes again.

Peter, the leader of the Lord's disciples, described the same event in his letter. The fury of the Lord's judgment is a frightening thing to behold: "The day of the Lord will come like a thief. On that day heaven will pass away with a roaring sound. Everything that makes up the universe will burn and be destroyed. The earth and everything that people have done on it will be exposed" *(2 Peter 3:10).*

1:8 *He will take revenge on those who refuse to acknowledge God and on those who refuse to respond to the Good News about our Lord Jesus.*

When Jesus returns, He will end the suffering of those who are redeemed, whose robes are washed in the blood of the Lamb *(Revelation 7:14).* While the suffering of the saints ends, the suffering of those that opposed the Good News of Jesus Christ begins. In the blazing light of God's justice, the situations will be reversed. This is exactly what Jesus described in His conversation with Nicodemus, a ruler of the Jewish Sanhedrin: "Those who believe in him won't be condemned. But those who don't believe are already condemned because they don't believe in God's only Son" *(John 3:18).*

As Jesus continued to talk with Nicodemus, He clearly stated the reason why His judgment must be executed. The Creator had given life to His creation. He had made man in His own image. Yet man had turned away from Him and defied the One Who had made them. God then outlined His plan for redemption in His Word, showing how a Savior would enter the world and save people from their sins. That man was Jesus. Rejection of Jesus' work as the atoning sacrifice for sin constitutes an offense that the Father cannot and will not overlook *(John 3:19).*

1:9 *They will pay the penalty by being destroyed forever, by being separated from the Lord's presence and from his glorious power.*

Those who oppose God's message of salvation, those that reject the salvation He has provided, those who have persecuted His saints will one day pay the penalty for their offense against the Almighty. The Lord God has done everything necessary to satisfy His righteousness when He sacrificed His Son on Calvary's Cross. He will not do anything more. If these enemies of God reject Him throughout their earthly lives, He will likewise reject them for all eternity. They will never again have the opportunity to consider the tremendous cost God paid for salvation. They will never again have the opportunity to enter the Lord's presence and experience His glorious power. God's salvation will not always be available to those who have rebelled against Him. *"By God's word, the present heaven and earth are designated to be burned. They are being kept until the day ungodly people will be judged and destroyed" (2 Peter 3:7). "God's anger is revealed from heaven against every ungodly and immoral thing people do as they try to suppress the truth by their immoral living" (Romans 1:18).*

Many times people make some statement that Jesus shows the love of God for lost humanity. While this is absolutely true, it is only part of the picture that portrays Christ's nature. Jesus Himself told His disciples about a time when He would return to execute His justice on the earth. He carefully explained what His illustrations meant:

> 38*The field is the world, and the good seed stands for the sons of the kingdom. The weeds are the sons of the evil one,* 39*and the enemy who sows them is the devil. The harvest is the end of the age, and the harvesters are angels.* 40*"As the weeds are pulled up and burned in the fire, so it will be at the end of the age.* 41*The Son of Man will send out his angels, and they will weed out of his kingdom everything that causes sin and all who do evil.* 42*They will throw them into the fiery furnace, where there will be weeping and gnashing of teeth.* 43*Then the*

> *righteous will shine like the sun in the kingdom of their Father. He who has ears, let him hear. (Matthew 13:38–43,* NIV*)*

1:10 ***This will happen on that day when he comes to be honored among all his holy people and admired by all who have believed in him. This includes you because you believed the testimony we gave you.***

On the same day that the Lord executes His judgment upon those who reject His salvation, those who have been redeemed will see the One Whom they have trusted for their salvation. They will at last honor Him and stand in His presence, amazed by the glory of the One Whom they have worshiped by the faith the Spirit instilled in them *(Ephesians 1:6 and 12).* The Thessalonian believers will be among the great crowd of the redeemed on that day because they believed Paul's testimony of God's Good News.

Those who have been redeemed have no reason to fear the day when Jesus comes again. They will not stand in Almighty's presence in the shame of their sin but in the righteousness of His Son. Likewise, all who have accepted the sacrifice of Jesus Christ for their sin will stand with the Thessalonian believers in this crowd of amazed worshipers. Those who have never accepted this sacrifice will face Jesus as their judge, standing in abject fear before the One Whom they have rejected.

1:11 ***With this in mind, we always pray that our God will make you worthy of his call. We also pray that through his power he will help you accomplish every good desire and help you do everything your faith produces.***

Remembering both God's salvation and the execution of His judgment on the day when Jesus returns to earth, Paul told the Thessalonian believers that he prayed that God would make them worthy of His call.

Even though he praised the testimony of their Christian lives, Paul prayed in such a way that revealed his awareness that God Himself was the one working in and through these saints—perfecting their faith in the midst of persecution. As he wrote this letter, he also made the Thessalonian believers aware of God's action that enabled them to endure their suffering, and despite their physical circumstances, to demonstrate the power of God that had transformed their lives.

Realizing that God was the source of their extraordinary testimony, Paul further prayed that God would continue to accomplish everything that He desired by the application of His power in their redeemed lives. Only God could help them do everything that He wanted their faith to produce.

1:12 *That way the name of our Lord Jesus will be honored among you. Then, because of the good will of Jesus Christ, our God and Lord, you will be honored by him.*

Paul's prayer for the Thessalonian believers had already been answered because their lives already showed the world that they belonged to God. Nevertheless, he prayed for God's power to continue to work in their lives so that the testimony of the Lord Jesus would continue to be honored among them. There is no better prayer than this—that believers honor the Lord Jesus by the way that God works in them. There really is no other purpose for which believers should pray than that the Lord's Name would be respected in the body of believers. Those outside the fold may harass them; they may throw verbal insults at them; they may curse the Name of Christ. However, inside the community of faith, the Lord's Name should be lifted up with songs of praise for the gift of His salvation.

When God's people honor Jesus Christ and extol the message of His salvation, they simultaneously experience the blessing of God's grace in their hearts. The relationship between believers and their redeeming Lord is one of reciprocal respect. In the context of the preceding verses, God's work prepares His people to do His work, fulfilling His will. The expression of faith is the result of God's work, but the blessings that result from that work belong to God's people.

Notes/Applications

Humanly speaking, people react negatively to unwarranted attacks that threaten their security and well-being. No one likes to be insulted, ridiculed, or belittled. The natural reaction is to pay back with a stronger insult. The Thessalonian believers were being insulted and ridiculed because they belonged to Christ. Those that insulted them merely reacted to the message of Christ's salvation that offended their sensibilities. They, therefore, resorted to verbal and physical attacks, subjecting God's people to imprisonment and beatings.

In response to the hostilities the Thessalonian believers faced, Paul encouraged them by reminding them that God would eventually repay their persecutors with the fury of His anger. God's justice would be imposed upon those who rejected His Son on that day when Jesus returned to earth again:

> [11]*I saw heaven standing open. There was a white horse, and its rider is named Faithful and True. With integrity he judges and wages war.* [12]*His eyes are flames of fire. On his head are many crowns. He has a name written on him, but only he knows what it is.* [13]*He wears clothes dipped in blood, and his name is the Word of God.* [14]*The armies of heaven, wearing pure, white linen, follow him on white horses.* [15]*A sharp sword comes out of his mouth to defeat the nations. He will rule them with an iron scepter and tread the winepress of the fierce anger of God Almighty.* [16]*On his clothes and his thigh he has a name written: King of Kings and Lord of Lords. (Revelation 19:11–16)*

On that same day, God's people will see Jesus face-to-face and bow down in worship. In the light of his unveiled glory, the suffering of God's people will be ended forever.

Paul's letter offered little relief from their present situation. Waiting for some future event to correct the inequities of their persecution provided no consolation. The inescapable solution demonstrated that as long as there was breath, believers would suffer at the hands of those who do not belong to Christ. The only relief from such persecution arrives only at the point of death or at the time when Christ returns. Nevertheless, Paul's concluded the opposite. He stated that he prayed for God's power to be revealed in their lives even more so that Jesus would be honored.

Strangely, history shows that the Gospel of Jesus Christ flourishes in a time of persecution. Conversely, the Gospel becomes subverted in the minds and hearts of people who live in unchallenged prosperity. Somehow, believers who live in adversity, maybe even under the yoke of unwarranted persecution, discover strength and joy when they are forced by their circumstances to depend wholly on Almighty God and on each other—praying together and studying God's Word together. On the other hand, prosperity deceives some believers to rely upon their own resources rather upon the resources of their faith.

In the end, Paul wanted the believers in Thessalonica to continue to be dependent upon the work of the Lord that was so visibly evident in their lives. When these believers relied steadfastly upon God's power to sustain them, they showed how much they honored God no matter what their circumstances were.

That should be the prayer of every believer. It makes no difference whether believers live in a culture of relative wealth or relative poverty. It makes no difference if they live under the yoke of bondage or under the human guise of freedom. It makes no difference if they are persecuted or if their faith is praised. In everything that is done, believers should demonstrate that they belong to God through the sacrifice of His Son, revealing His power while looking to His return, which will end all suffering.

2 THESSALONIANS 2

2 Thessalonians 2:1–8

2:1 ***Brothers and sisters, we have this request to make of you about our Lord Jesus Christ's coming and our gathering to meet him.***

Continuing the theme from the previous chapter, Paul asked the Thessalonians for their attention as he made a special request. This request centered on Christ's return to earth when all believers will be gathered with Him *(1 Thessalonians 4:17)*. Earlier, Paul had described the way in which Jesus would return to punish evildoers and be united to those that belong to Him *(2 Thessalonians 1:6–10)*. He now returned to this theme to address some issues surrounding that future event.

2:2 ***Don't get upset right away or alarmed when someone claims that we said through some spirit, conversation, or letter that the day of the Lord has already come.***

We do not possess any information about a fictitious letter that was reportedly written by Paul in which he claimed that Jesus had already returned. Obviously, there must have been some rumor that was circulating among the churches. Paul did not want the Thessalonian believers to be upset when they heard reports of this letter. This may have been the reason for writing this second letter and maybe even the first letter to the Thessalonian church.

2:3 *Don't let anyone deceive you about this in any way. That day cannot come unless a revolt takes place first, and the man of sin, the man of destruction, is revealed.*

Paul did not want the Thessalonian believers to be deceived by this false rumor. Jesus had not yet returned, and Paul denied any association with such rumors. Paul then began to explain some of the events that had to occur before the Lord would return to earth to gather His people and judge those who had opposed Him.

First, a tremendous revolt had to take place. In the Greek text, there is the idea of a defection from the truth, a falling away from what God has said in His Word. This can occur in the church or throughout the world. An attitude of resistance toward God's moral law will wrench people even further from the precepts of the Word. The world attitude will be openly defiant and ungodly. In his letter to Timothy, Paul also described the evil environment pervading the entire world order:

> *¹You must understand this: In the last days there will be violent periods of time. ²People will be selfish and love money. They will brag, be arrogant, and use abusive language. They will curse their parents, show no gratitude, have no respect for what is holy, ³and lack normal affection for their families. They will refuse to make peace with anyone. They will be slanderous, lack self-control, be brutal, and have no love for what is good. ⁴They will be traitors. They will be reckless and conceited. They will love pleasure rather than God. ⁵They will appear to have a godly life, but they will not let its power change them. Stay away from such people. (2 Timothy 3:1–5)*

Another event will be the unveiling of "the man of sin, the man of destruction." Other translations use the phrase "man of lawlessness" or "the son of perdition." The "man of destruction" cannot be specifically identified. However, his personage is easily identifiable. He is someone who opposes Christ and so is called the antichrist. The prophet Daniel further describes this person: "He will speak against the Most High God, oppress the holy people of the Most High, and plan to change the appointed times and laws. The holy people will be handed over to him for a time, times, and half of a time" *(Daniel 7:25)*. He will be a deceptive and satanic opponent of the true Christ. Jesus Christ will ultimately destroy the pretender at the genuine return of Jesus.[1]

2:4 *He opposes every so-called god or anything that is worshiped and places himself above them, sitting in God's temple and claiming to be God.*

This evil man epitomizes a complete defection from the truth. Completely deluded by his megalomania, this religious imposter will set himself up above all other objects of worship—not only Jesus Christ but also all of the false entities that deceived men had set up as an outcome of their evil imaginations. This antichrist is well exposed in the prophecy of Daniel: "The king will do as he pleases. He will highly honor himself above every god. He will say amazing things against the God of Gods. He will succeed until God's anger is over, because what has been decided must be done" *(Daniel 11:36)*. Although he is ultimately doomed to destruction, his arrogance is so pervasive that he dares to set himself up in God's sanctuary and actually claims to be a god.

Nothing seems to stop this juggernaut. He destroys everything in his path and annihilates those people who belong to God:

> *5The beast was allowed to speak arrogant and insulting things. It was given authority to act for 42 months. 6It opened its mouth to insult God, to insult his name and his tent—those who are living in heaven. 7It was allowed to wage war against God's holy people and to conquer them. It was also*

given authority over every tribe, people, language, and nation. [8]Everyone living on earth will worship it, everyone whose name is not written in the Book of Life. That book belongs to the lamb who was slaughtered before the creation of the world. (Revelation 13:5–8)

2:5 *Don't you remember that I told you about these things when I was still with you?*

Paul expected the Thessalonian believers to remember what he had taught them. This was not new subject matter. Paul had discussed this subject when with the Thessalonians on a previous visit. Realizing Christ's return gave believers encouragement even though they faced persecution.

The Scriptures thoroughly and completely reveal the unique position that Jesus Christ holds in the redemption of believers and the condemnation of sinners. Jesus, the Son of God, is the Lord's Anointed, the Ruler of the universe, the righteous Judge, the King of kings and the Lord of lords. He alone fulfills the Law, satisfies the Father's righteousness, reconciles sinners to their Creator, and judges those that reject His salvation.

2:6 *You know what it is that now holds him back, so that he will be revealed when his time comes.*

Because Paul had discussed this subject with the Thessalonians when he was with them, they already knew what it was holding the "man of destruction" back. However, Paul's letter only described some unspecified restraint that was placed on this antichrist, keeping him from doing what he wanted to do—pronounce his claim to be god, replacing all other gods, both the true, living God and man's imagined deities. Paul had told these believers, but he does not specifically identify the force that restricts the actions of this lawless imposter. Since Paul was not specific, the reader can only agree that God Himself ultimately is the One Who restrains this godless beast of a man until that time when

God sets him free to accomplish his God-defying plans. Satan himself operates only within the parameters that God has defined.

2:7 *The mystery of this sin is already at work. But it cannot work effectively until the person now holding it back gets out of the way.*

The mystery of sin was already at work at the time that Paul wrote this letter. In truth, sin had always haunted man's existence from the time when Adam and Eve disobeyed God. Not only had the consequences of sin haunted man's existence, it was the very nature of man that corrupted the smallest details of thought and action. The mystery of sin continues to this day. However, sin has not yet reached its consummate act of rebellion against God. The "man of destruction" will be the person who ultimately will defy the Creator and establish himself as "god."

Paul then moved from the general to the specific. Although Paul did not identify who or what restricted the activities of the "man of destruction," he now stated that it was a person who was standing in the way of the ungodly imposter. Since Paul also did not specifically identify this person, many scholars have made numerous suggestions. However, all of those suggestions are purely conjecture since there is no biblical way to substantiate their claims. It should be sufficient to say that, whoever the person is, he operates under the sovereign authority of God, Who determines the times and the seasons according to His own private counsel.

2:8 *Then the man of sin will be revealed and the Lord Jesus will destroy him by what he says. When the Lord Jesus comes, his appearance will put an end to this man.*

The "man of sin" will deceive and confuse the world for a period of time allotted by Almighty God. This defined time period will begin when the person who restrains him is taken out of the way. Then the man of sin will rise to unprecedented heights of power, displaying his arrogance by claiming to be "god." That defined time period will end when Jesus comes again, ending the rule of this godless imposter and destroying him completely.

Jesus will destroy this person "by what he says." Paul was probably alluding to the Isaiah prophecy that described the way that the descendent of Jesse would judge the earth: "He will judge the poor justly. He will make fair decisions for the humble people on earth. He will strike the earth with a rod from his mouth. He will kill the wicked with the breath from his lips" *(Isaiah 11:4).*

This self-deluded demigod will establish himself and behave in a way that is the antithesis of the Lord's behavior. When the Lord, Who is the very essence of God's Truth, speaks, that Truth will utterly demolish the one who is the embodiment of untruth. This antichrist will never be able to stand in the blinding light of Jesus' unveiled glory—His truth, righteousness, and power. Untruth will be unmasked by God's truth. Dark unrighteousness will fade away when He Whose Name is righteous appears. Lawlessness will be replaced by God's justice. The fleeting power of this self-appointed ruler will crumble under the power of the almighty and eternal God. When Jesus speaks, His words forever expose the hideous realities of sin as He pronounces His unrelenting judgment on all who oppose Him. *"A sharp sword comes out of his mouth to defeat the nations. He will rule them with an iron scepter and tread the winepress of the fierce anger of God Almighty" (Revelation 19:15).*

Notes/Applications

Ever since Jesus ascended into heaven and returned to His Father, people have tried to determine when He will come again. Some have used Bible prophecies to interpret current events, believing that they can reliably predict the time when Jesus will return to earth. Some have been bold enough to stipulate a specific day. Not one of them has been correct.

The Church of Jesus Christ has had to defend itself from these unwarranted pursuits and face the ridicule of the unsaved world for the obvious blunders of a few misguided, though passionate, persons.

The Scriptures reliably tell believers that no one can make this prediction:

> [3]*As Jesus was sitting on the Mount of Olives, his disciples came to him privately and said, "Tell us, when will this happen? What will be the sign that you are coming again, and when will the world come to an end?"* [4]*Jesus answered them, "Be careful not to let anyone deceive you.* [5]*Many will come using my name. They will say, 'I am the Messiah,' and they will deceive many people. (Matthew 24:3–5)*

Jesus even more pointedly advised His disciples that these end times were none of their concern. In that same discourse, Jesus made it very clear: "No one knows when that day or hour will come. Even the angels in heaven and the Son don't know. Only the Father knows" *(Matthew 24:36)*. On the day that Jesus ascended into heaven, the disciples again pursued the subject: "[6]So when the apostles came together, they asked him, 'Lord, is this the time when you're going to restore the kingdom to Israel?' [7]Jesus told them, 'You don't need to know about times or periods that the Father has determined by his own authority'" *(Acts 1:6–7)*.

Why do people insist on predicting a time that Jesus has said is unpredictable? Why do multitudes of people follow the teaching of leaders who are inordinately preoccupied with the Lord's return to earth? The minute that any human being says that he or she knows something that Jesus Himself said that none of us would ever know is the same minute that Christians should understand that such a person is an imposter.

When we as believers encounter such charlatans, we should immediately recognize the heresy and withdraw from their false teaching. We can make these observations with absolute assurance because we pronounce the heresy with all the authority of God's Word from the mouth of Jesus Himself.

Believers should search the Word. Either Jesus is correct or the person making the prediction is correct. Either Jesus is God in the flesh, or the person who claims to know more than Jesus is making himself "god." Let the warning go forth to all God's people in all locations and in all times—search the Scriptures and do not be deceived by imposters who elevate themselves above the authority of that Word.

2 Thessalonians 2:9–12

2:9 *The man of sin will come with the power of Satan. He will use every kind of power, including miraculous and wonderful signs. But they will be lies.*

When this "man of sin" assumes the role of "god," he will be able to do so because he is Satan's human pawn. He will be the visible representative of the archenemy of God. Consumed by the power of Satan, he will perform wonderful miracles and signs. When Jesus described the religious leaders in Jerusalem, he also described Satan well: "You come from your father, the devil, and you desire to do what your father wants you to do. The devil was a murderer from the beginning. He has never been truthful. He doesn't know what the truth is. Whenever he tells a lie, he's doing what comes naturally to him. He's a liar and the father of lies" *(John 8:44).*

The man of sin will build his entire kingdom on a web of lies and deceit. It will be difficult to distinguish between the genuine and the fraudulent. He and his emissaries will deceive the world by miracles and lie so successfully that the world will swarm to their adoration and worship. *"False christs and false prophets will appear. They will work spectacular, miraculous signs and do wonderful things to deceive, if possible, even those whom God has chosen" (Matthew 24:24).*

2:10 *He will use everything that God disapproves of to deceive those who are dying, those who refused to love the truth that would save them.*

This person will be the exact opposite of Jesus Christ. He will be fully consumed with evil. He will therefore use every deceitful trick he can employ to deceive the world population. Through that deceit he will mislead people who are already dying, not physically but spiritually. Why are they dying? Not because of any dreaded physical disease but because they turned their backs on the Truth. Many philosophers and innumerable hosts of misled people spend tremendous amounts of energy searching for truth. However, the Greek manuscript uses the definite article. These people are deceived by their pursuit of truth and they will find their answer in the "man of sin." In that vain pursuit, they will never discover the one and only Truth of Jesus Christ that could save them.

2:11 *That's why God will send them a powerful delusion so that they will believe a lie.*

In the end, this powerful antichrist will function under the sovereignty of the all-powerful God. Through his deceit, God will actually send unbelievers a powerful delusion that they will believe. Unbelievers will believe what this person tells them and all things for which he stands. However, everything the man of sin represents will be a lie that will deceive unbelievers to the point that they will suffer the wrath of God's judgment. This is what God will do to those who follow the antichrist. Paul described the same situation in his letter to Timothy: "The Spirit says clearly that in later times some believers will desert the Christian faith. They will follow spirits that deceive, and they will believe the teachings of demons" *(1 Timothy 4:1).*

But why would God do something so heinous, so patently destructive to these people? Many people, even people who profess to follow Jesus Christ refuse to accept this portrayal of the loving God who sent His Son into the world to save sinners. However, if Christians accept God's Word about His salvation, it is mandatory that they also accept God's Word about His judgment.

The answer is as simple as it is frightening. The answer was already given in the previous verse. God sends this delusion to those people who have rejected the love of "the truth." God provided to everyone the pathway of reconciliation to the Creator. That pathway lies through the atoning, substitutionary sacrifice of Jesus Christ. Once that pathway is rejected, there is no more hope for salvation.

2:12 *Then everyone who did not believe the truth, but was delighted with what God disapproves of, will be condemned.*

For the unbeliever, God's condemnation is a sure thing *(Mark 16:16)*. Everyone who rejects God's plan of salvation given through Jesus Christ will suffer the consequences of his or her actions. Those who enjoy doing those things that demonstrate their defiance of God's precepts will be hopelessly cut off from any further opportunity for salvation. God will no longer wait. He will no longer exercise His patient observation of man's rebellion. His judgment must come to the fore because His righteousness cannot tolerate sin. Either people are clothed in the righteousness of Christ through the forgiveness of their sin and are therefore exonerated from the consequences of their sin or they stand before the righteous Judge with all of their sin exposed to His watchful eye and will suffer terribly because they rejected God's Son. "[7]*He will give everlasting life to those who search for glory, honor, and immortality by persisting in doing what is good. But he will bring* [8]*anger and fury on those who, in selfish pride, refuse to believe the truth and who follow what is wrong*" *(Romans 2:7–8)*.

Notes/Applications

A terrible fate awaits those who reject the sacrifice of God's Son. This is God's unvarnished truth. Christ's Cross is not only the symbol of salvation to those who are being saved; it is also the symbol of those who are being condemned for their unbelief. There is no secret here, no hidden agenda, no clandestine conspiracy against the human race. God has spoken plainly and clearly to people of all ages through His Son *(Hebrews 1:1–2)*.

Yet, people don't like what they read in the pages of God's Holy Word. They want to believe that there is some merit to their lives. They want to establish their value in the eyes of their transcendent Creator. They want to prove to Him that they are not really as bad as His holiness proves them to be. They may nod to accept Jesus, His wonderful life, the way that He dealt with people, even the standards that He espoused as the guideline for their daily lives. They may acknowledge the cute, little baby in the manger. They may recommend the flowing oratory of his Sermon on the Mount, but they do not accept Jesus as God—the One Who will come again and destroy unbelievers with a fury that confounds the human mind. God's salvation and His justice are two aspects of the same changeless Truth. A person cannot stand before the holy God clothed only in the rags of his or her sin and live. A person only dares to stand in the presence of the eternal God clothed in the righteousness of Jesus Christ that has been unconditionally and without merit given to the sinner only by virtue of God's measureless grace and mercy.

Those who follow Christ wish with all their hearts that everyone understood this teaching of God's Word. However, many will never understand the awful simplicity of God's Word that condemns those who refuse the gift of God's salvation. Instead, they will believe the deceiver's lie and, with him, go to hell.

2 Thessalonians 2:13–17

2:13 *We always have to thank God for you, brothers and sisters. You are loved by the Lord and we thank God that in the beginning he chose you to be saved through a life of spiritual devotion and faith in the truth.*

In dramatic contrast to the future outlined for unbelievers, the Thessalonian church was reason enough to thank God. They were not hated by the Lord; they were loved. They were not under the judgment of God; they lived in the light of His salvation.

Why are these people so loved by the Lord? Because God chose them from the beginning to be saved. Matthew's gospel records Jesus' summation of a parable that further describes this affirmation: "Then the king will say to those on his right, 'Come, my Father has blessed you! Inherit the kingdom prepared for you from the creation of the world'" *(Matthew 25:34)*. Just before He died, Jesus prayed to His Father: "Father, I want those you have given to me to be with me, to be where I am. I want them to see my glory, which you gave me because you loved me before the world was made" *(John 17:24)*. Paul also affirmed this in his letter to the Ephesians: "before the creation of the world, he chose us through Christ to be holy and perfect in his presence" *(Ephesians 1:4)*.

2:14 *With this in mind he called you by the Good News which we told you so that you would obtain the glory of our Lord Jesus Christ.*

Paul asked the Thessalonian believers to remember what God had done for them from the foundation of the world. They were set apart by God before the world began, and God called them by the Good News of His salvation through Jesus Christ. Because they were set apart and called by God, they would eventually possess the glory of Jesus Christ. They already possessed it, but only by faith. When Christ came again, their journey in Him would be fully consummated, and they would thereafter walk in His presence. When this occurs, Jesus' prayer as recorded in John 17:24 will be fully answered by the Father in heaven.

2:15 *Then, brothers and sisters, firmly hold on to the traditions we taught you either when we spoke to you or in our letter.*

In light of everything Paul wrote to the Thessalonian church—the unveiling of the "man of destruction," the unbelievers' impending judgment, the believers' salvation from the foundation of the world, Paul encouraged them to hold fast to everything he had taught them when he was personally teaching them or by the message contained in his letters. Paul told them to remain steadfast, regardless of the circumstances they were facing. Because they had been chosen by God, because they were saved by His grace through the sacrifice of His Son, because they would one day obtain the glory of the Lord Jesus Christ, there was no earthly reason to weaken as they fought the battle that confronted them in light of the heavenly glory that awaited them.

When Paul asked them to hold on to his traditions, he was not speaking of some religious practice by which people could be saved. He was speaking of the doctrine that he had carefully laid out for their growth in Christ.[2]

2:16–17 *16God our Father loved us and by his kindness gave us everlasting encouragement and good hope. Together with our Lord Jesus Christ, 17may he encourage and strengthen you to do and say everything that is good.*

The believers' salvation provided convincing proof that God the Father loved them. With unhesitating confidence, Paul pronounced this benedictory declaration on the Thessalonian believers. Since he had just acknowledged how they had been set apart unto God since the foundation of the world, Paul's benediction demonstrated that

God's love for them was sufficient, not only for this life, but for all eternity.

Again, the preeminence of Jesus Christ came to the forefront of Paul's remarks. Most other translations start with "May the Lord Jesus Christ Himself...," showing that Jesus Christ was the One Who gave believers His grace and His encouragement. On this reliable foundation, believers may always draw confidence, strength, and encouragement both for this life and for the life to come. Under this loving, supporting authority, believers fall into step with their eternal Creator, doing and saying those things that please Him.

Paul also expressed this confidence beautifully and powerfully in his letter to the Roman church:

> *2Through Christ we can approach God and stand in his favor. So we brag because of our confidence that we will receive glory from God. 3But that's not all. We also brag when we are suffering. We know that suffering creates endurance, 4endurance creates character, and character creates confidence. 5We're not ashamed to have this confidence, because God's love has been poured into our hearts by the Holy Spirit, who has been given to us. (Romans 5:2–5)*

Notes/Applications

Why does God choose anyone to be his child? No one knows the answer to that question. Even those who have been delivered and reborn by the blood of Jesus Christ as revealed by the Holy Spirit through His eternal, unchanging Word cannot fully answer that question. Nevertheless, believers experience overwhelming gratitude that God has saved them, giving them comfort, strength, and encouragement both now and for all eternity.

Somehow the Holy Spirit makes Paul's words come alive in the hearts of the redeemed. Believers understand that God has chosen us to be His representatives in a world that slowly decays. Somehow the Holy Spirit uses His people to show by the things they do and the words they speak that they belong to God. Somehow the Holy Spirit infuses His truth into hearts that continue in the process of His sanctifying work, declaring the glory of God through the lips of broken, but redeemed sinners.

Under the authority of this saving, sanctifying Spirit, we feel the power of Paul's words wash over us, bringing newness of life like a breath of fresh air. The benediction sweeps through our souls, and we raise our voices in one accord: "Praise God from Whom all blessings flow!"

2 THESSALONIANS 3

2 Thessalonians 3:1–5

3:1 ***Finally, brothers and sisters, pray that we spread the Lord's word rapidly and that it will be honored the way it was among you.***

As Paul brought this letter to a close, he asked the Thessalonian believers to pray for him and his entire missionary team. In light of the terrible consequences of unbelief, as well as the alternative found in the joy of God's salvation through Jesus Christ, Paul knew that time was precious. He felt the pressure to spread the gospel message quickly so that belief could spread throughout the world. He asked that the believers pray that the Lord's Word would be accepted, respected, and honored by those who heard and believed the Gospel in the same way that the Thessalonian believers had responded to the good news of Christ's redemption.

Paul recognized that he was simply the mouthpiece that God used in proclaiming the Gospel to the Gentiles. He also recognized that people accepted his message because of God's work in their hearts, not because of any persuasive speeches that he gave. "*Here is another reason why we never stop thanking God: When you received God's word from us, you realized it wasn't the word of humans. Instead, you accepted it for what it really is—the word of God. This word is at work in you believers" (1 Thessalonians 2:13).*

3:2 *Also pray that we may be rescued from worthless and evil people, since not everyone shares our faith.*

Paul did not live in a fantasy world. He knew that some would embrace the Gospel and others would reject it. He did not ask believers to live in denial of the realities of their hostile surroundings. Opposition to the Gospel was real. People hated the Lord, and they hated the Lord's people. The Thessalonian believers had experienced this rejection first hand. They endured insults, beatings, and torture at the hands of the Jews who constantly harassed Paul and those who came to faith in Christ when they heard the Good News. Therefore, Paul urged them to pray for God's intervention in their circumstances, asking the Lord to rescue them from "worthless and evil people."

When Paul and Barnabas proclaimed the Good News to the people of Antioch, some were pleased by what they heard while others were furious. This pattern of reaction to God's Word repeated itself in Thessalonica and followed Paul throughout his ministry:

> *45When the Jews saw the crowds, they became very jealous. They used insulting language to contradict whatever Paul said. 46Paul and Barnabas told them boldly, "We had to speak the word of God to you first. Since you reject the word and consider yourselves unworthy of everlasting life, we are now going to turn to people of other nations. 47The Lord gave us the following order: 'I have made you a light for the nations so that you would save people all over the world.'" 48The people who were not Jews were pleased with what they heard and praised the Lord's word. Everyone who had been prepared for everlasting life believed. 49The word of the Lord spread throughout the whole region. 50But Jews stirred up devout women of high*

> *social standing and the officials of the city. These people started to persecute Paul and Barnabas and threw them out of their territory.* (Acts 13:45–50)

3:3 *But the Lord is faithful and will strengthen you and protect you against the evil one.*

Even as Paul urged the Thessalonian believers to pray for God's protection from their adversaries, he knew that God was already working in the midst of their circumstances. He was already bringing glory to His Name by the way these believers showed that they belonged to God, both in the way that they loved and supported each other and in the way that they endured the persecution that assailed them. Paul's own experience exemplified the Lord's faithfulness. He knew that the Lord would be faithful to them as well, strengthening and protecting them against not only their persecutors but also the evil one. They were not alone in this battle. God was their partner as well as their captain in this conflict between the forces of Satan and the Lord. "*God faithfully keeps his promises. He called you to be partners with his Son Jesus Christ our Lord*" *(1 Corinthians 1:9)*. The Lord's protection was also experienced by King David: "[7]The Lord guards you from every evil. He guards your life" *(Psalm 121:7)*.

3:4 *The Lord gives us confidence that you are doing and will continue to do what we ordered you to do.*

Paul's confidence in the Lord's protection provided further assurance that the Thessalonian believers would continue walking in the path of God's redemption as they had from the first time they heard the Gospel. Paul prayed that they would continue to follow his instructions, knowing that his teachings were the Word of the Lord. He had provided the guidelines that would direct their journey in Christ for the rest of their lives. The Lord would not allow them to deviate from His pathway and would protect them every step of the way. Paul also expressed this confidence in his letter to the Philippian church: "I'm convinced that God, who began this good work in you, will carry it through to completion on the day of Christ Jesus" *(Philippians 1:6).*

3:5 *May the Lord direct your lives as you show God's love and Christ's endurance.*

Paul then added his own prayer to his request for their prayers. He asked the Lord to direct their lives. He had already spoken of the Lord's protection and his instructions that, when followed, could guide them to living faithfully in the redemption they had received from God through Jesus Christ. He had often praised them for the way that these believers showed God's love to everyone so that their reputation was well-known throughout Macedonia *(1 Thessalonians 1:7–8).* Nevertheless, their remarkable witness for Christ did not dissuade Paul from asking the Lord to continue His work in their hearts as they showed "God's love and Christ's endurance."

Notes/Applications

Prayer is not some mystical experience far removed from the realities of our daily lives. Rather, it is a profoundly intimate, personal conversation between the living, almighty God and His children. Prayer invokes God's blessing and protection on those who share in the journey of their redeemed lives. It is not constrained by time and space since it involves a deep communion with the One Who is timeless and infinite, standing not only above and beyond His creation, but through Jesus Christ entering this world and becoming intimately involved in the most personal details of each of our lives.

Paul requested prayer as he pursued the task that the Lord had given to him. Prayer is the vehicle that expresses the intimate relationship that exists between the Lord and His people. It was a privilege for the Thessalonian believers to ask their eternal, saving Lord to intervene in the circumstances of their daily lives, asking Him to rescue them from those that hated the Good News. It made no difference that Paul served in Athens and these believers were two hundred miles away in Thessalonica. God was not limited by that distance. Believers from all corners of the world are as close as a prayer uttered through the agency of God's Holy Spirit.

As the prayers of the saints rise into the presence of their holy God, the Spirit responds with assurance that God hears and is answering their prayers even before they are spoken. That Spirit-given assurance induces confidence in the hearts of God's people, affirming God's love and protection no matter what the earthly circumstances are. By the Spirit's work, believers can continue to show God's love, not only to their companions in faith but also to the world that rejects God's salvation. They are upheld and sustained in all their battles by Christ's enduring work until that day when their lives are ended at the call of Christ or when Christ comes again. At that moment, prayers end and living in the glorious light of the Savior begins, at home with Jesus in the majesty of His presence.

2 Thessalonians 3:6–15

3:6 *Brothers and sisters, in the name of our Lord Jesus Christ we order you not to associate with any believer who doesn't live a disciplined life and doesn't follow the tradition you received from us.*

Paul rejoiced with the Thessalonian church. There were many ways that they portrayed the love of Christ to friend and foe alike. He urged them to follow his instructions as they would follow the Word of the Lord. He had just prayed that the Lord would direct their lives as they continued to show God's love to those around them, yet Paul was not ignorant of the follies of human nature. He understood that some of the believers would fail to follow the Lord's direction in their lives.

Paul described these believers as undisciplined. They seemed to live under the bondage of their old nature rather than reflecting the fact that they had been saved. The undisciplined living resulted from the failure of some believers to follow the instructions that Paul taught in all of the churches he had established. When they failed to follow Paul's instruction, they failed to obey the Lord's commands. Such believers struggled with their own passions, refusing to submit to the Lord's instruction and correction. They failed not only themselves but the Lord who had redeemed them. Therefore, Paul cautioned the Thessalonians to be aware of the undisciplined believers among them and guard against being influenced by them.

3:7 *You know what you must do to imitate us. We lived a disciplined life among you.*

Paul then reminded the Thessalonians of the example he set by his own life. He spent some time with them as he proclaimed the good news of Christ's redemption. Throughout that part of his missionary journey, Paul lived a disciplined life that demonstrated that he belonged to God through Jesus Christ. He urged them to imitate his example, following the Lord's instructions in everything he did.

Paul's example and encouragement that believers follow his example were vitally important. Living a disciplined life accomplished two major advantages in believers' lives: it kept believers out of trouble, and it provided a positive testimony to believers and unbelievers alike. This was Paul's instruction to Titus: "[7]Always set an example by doing good things. When you teach, be an example of moral purity and dignity. [8]Speak an accurate message that cannot be condemned. Then those who oppose us will be ashamed because they cannot say anything bad about us" *(Titus 2:7–8)*.

3:8 *We didn't eat anyone's food without paying for it. Instead, we worked hard and struggled night and day in order not to be a burden to any of you.*

How did Paul provide an example to the Thessalonian believers? One pragmatic example was that he always paid his own way. He always paid for the food he ate. He paid for it from the wages he earned as he worked at his trade, making tents and selling them in the marketplace *(Acts 18:3)*. It was common for teachers of the day to receive remuneration from those they taught. This often resulted in charges that the teachers cared nothing for their disciples or their disciplines but did what they did solely for the adulation and material gain it brought them.[1]

Paul never wanted anyone to say that he had taken advantage of anyone. No one could ever say that Paul paid homage to anyone in his messages so that he could gain favor among the more wealthy inhabitants of the city. Paul's message was never tainted by human need. It was always purely proclaimed without ulterior motives.

3:9 *It's not as though we didn't have a right to receive support. Rather, we wanted to set an example for you to follow.*

Certainly Paul had the right to be supported as the other apostles were. Paul provided a lengthy discourse on this subject in his letter to the Corinthian church *(1 Corinthians 9:4–18)*. He appealed to Moses' Law to prove that ministers appointed by God had every right to be supported by those they taught. Paul stood out as an apostle who never exercised this privilege. He disciplined himself in this matter so that he could be an example to believers, showing them how they should work to provide for their daily needs. This was not to become a "law" for the believers in other cases where God's minister needed to be supported.[2] This was simply the way that he chose to live in the sight of those to whom he ministered.

3:10 *While we were with you, we gave you the order: "Whoever doesn't want to work shouldn't be allowed to eat."*

Paul's letter supplied written force to his verbal teaching. It came to the Thessalonians in the form of a direct order. In this letter, Paul repeated his order in writing, lending direct adjuration to all believers: work or starve. Laziness was not permitted among the Thessalonian church. That does not mean that believers could not or should not help those who were in desperate need of support. However, every able-bodied citizen of the believing community was ordered to provide for his own support. Paul was simply emphasizing God's command to Adam and Eve when He punished them for their disobedience. He told them: "By the sweat of your brow, you will produce food to eat until you return to the ground, because you were taken from it. You are dust, and you will return to dust" *(Genesis 3:19)*. Solomon's Proverbs state: "A lazy person craves food and there is none, but the appetite of hard-working people is satisfied" *(Proverbs 13:4)*.

3:11 *We hear that some of you are not living disciplined lives. You're not working, so you go around interfering in other people's lives.*

Paul clarified that if a person was not willing to work, he was not living a disciplined life. When a person has nothing better to do, gossip results. "At the same time, they [people with nothing better to do] learn to go around from house to house since they have nothing else to do. Not only this, but they also gossip and get involved in other people's business, saying things they shouldn't say" *(1 Timothy 5:13)*. The human mind must be occupied with some direction. If work is avoided, the mind begins to dwell on other people's business. Such people stick their nose into other people's affairs, interfering in the tranquility of their lives. An undisciplined believer only causes disruption, thus impeding others' efforts to be productive.

3:12 ***We order and encourage such people by the Lord Jesus Christ to pay attention to their own work so they can support themselves.***

Paul repeated what he had told the Thessalonians in his first letter: "Make it your goal to live quietly, do your work, and earn your own living, as we ordered you" *(1 Thessalonians 4:11)*. The opposite of living a disciplined life is living a wasted life of laziness. It is clear that Paul urged lazy believers to get to work and support themselves rather than meddling in other people's affairs. Once redeemed, all aspects of believers' lives become sacred. They no longer live for their own selfish pleasures but live to please the Lord. Even a person's occupation is brought into the arena of the sacred. No matter what a person's occupation when performed as a service in the joy of the Lord, it takes on the aspect of work performed, not for an earthly boss but for the Lord who has redeemed them. Man's time on earth is limited. It is best lived in the service of the Lord. *"Whatever presents itself for you to do, do it with all your might, because there is no work, planning, knowledge, or skill in the grave where you're going"* (Ecclesiastes 9:10).

3:13 ***Brothers and sisters, we can't allow ourselves to get tired of doing what is right.***

Again, Paul demonstrates his uncanny awareness of human nature. Even believers who want to continue growing in the faith that the Holy Spirit provides sometimes grow weary. There are times when physical weariness so overwhelms the staunchest believers that they really wish they could just let go for a minute and forget about the labor that God has called them to do. Often they resort to their old nature and selfishly desire to do what they want to, but Paul urged even these believers to remain steadfast.

The Old Testament Scriptures support Paul's instruction to believers. They are to remain steadily working at those sacred labors the Lord has called them to do. The prophet Isaiah, speaking the Word of the Lord, promised God's people that the Lord Himself will be their strength in times of weariness: "Yet, the strength of those who wait with hope in the Lord will be renewed. They will soar on wings like eagles. They will run and won't become weary. They will walk and won't grow tired" *(Isaiah 40:31)*. Believers are thereby assured that they do not struggle alone, but that the Lord Himself is their refreshment and renewal, providing not only physical strength but also the spiritual fortitude to endure the daily routines of life as well as the opposition of the God-haters until He calls them home.

3:14 *It may be that some people will not listen to what we say in this letter. Take note of them and don't associate with them so that they will feel ashamed.*

Paul was adamant about his instructions. If some people refused to listen and do what he told them to do, then these people were to be avoided. Paul had already declared previously that he only commanded what the Lord commanded him. Those who refused to obey would not be rebelling against mere mortals but would be rebelling against God Himself. Therefore, Paul taught that such persons ought to be severely chastised.[3]

The Jewish synagogue community and the Essene community adopted varying levels of discipline. These levels of discipline were brought into the church community.[4] The method of punishment that Paul outlined here was for the active members of the faith community to avoid those people who didn't follow his instruction. However, the purpose of the punishment was not to hurt them either physically or spiritually but to embarrass them. Hopefully that embarrassment would result in a change in their behavior that would again reflect their salvation in Jesus Christ.

3:15 *Yet, don't treat them like enemies, but instruct them like brothers and sisters.*

Even though it seems that Paul instructed believers to avoid those who did not follow his instructions and lead a disciplined life, he apparently did not mean that believers should have nothing to do with these disobedient believers. The purpose of avoiding them was to shame them into obedience. The stronger believers were to instruct these wayward Christians as though they w ere brothers and sisters. The tone of Paul's instruction was certainly corrective but performed within the framework of support and further instruction that was designed to get them back on track. Only in this way could they also reap the benefits of Paul's prayer that the Lord would direct their lives. Paul's instructions were to be faithfully followed. From the implication of Paul's letter we can see how the community of faith was to act as the instrument of the Lord, chastising and instructing believers who did not fall in line with the Christian standards of conduct.

Notes/Applications

God's grace imparted to the sinner at the time of regeneration saves the sinner from the penalty imposed by the righteous, holy God on those who do not believe. That grace demonstrates the full outpouring of God's mercy on those who at one time lived in rebellion against their Creator. However, God's goodness does not eradicate all vestiges of sin in believers' lives. Rather, believers are destined in the providence of the Lord's grace to live in the divine tension that exists between their old sin nature and their new redeemed nature. Humanly speaking, they are neither sinless nor sinner. Under the blood of Christ, they are clothed in His righteousness, and their sin is no longer a barrier between them and their Lord. "*You will again have compassion on us.*

You will overcome our wrongdoing. You will throw all our sins into the deep sea" (*Micah 7:19*).

Under the continuing work of the Holy Spirit, believers are to live under His directives, neither claiming sinless perfection in themselves nor falling back to the passions of their old nature using the excuse that "they have been saved." Instead, believers are to live disciplined lives that reflect that they have been redeemed. Even though saved, directed, and sustained by the Lord's limitless grace, Paul orders believers to follow the Lord's instructions, the precepts outlined in His Word. Believers need to encourage each other to live in the light of Christ's redemption, always showing in word and deed that they belong to Jesus Christ.

As believers, we will always be at odds with the unsaved world. The world will always hate us. Within the community of faith, we who are constantly seeking the Lord's direction and correction in our lives, growing in the faith that the Spirit has imparted to us, will also encounter disunity with those believers who take their salvation casually.

Paul's instruction seems severe, but it seems obvious that believers who associate with undisciplined believers will eventually become like their associates. It is far better to live under the Spirit's direction and correction.

2 Thessalonians 3:16–18

3:16 *May the Lord of peace give you his peace at all times and in every way. The Lord be with all of you.*

Paul concluded his letter with his benediction of peace. In the troubled world of the Thessalonian believers, peace was not readily available. There was strife between the believing community and those that rejected the good news of Christ's redemption. Tension within the believing community arose because some followed the Lord's instructions and others did not. As these believers struggled to maintain some degree of normalcy in these situations, more strife than peace ensued. Despite his rather harsh correction of those inside the church that failed to live disciplined lives, Paul loved this church. On the whole, he loved these people who so quickly embraced the Gospel and proved that the Lord had changed their hearts by the way that they loved and supported each other.

In the midst of all these troubles, Paul pronounced his benediction of peace by asking the Lord of peace to give them His peace. This is one of the strange paradoxes of the Christian life. In the middle of life's battles, believers possess God's peace given to them through the indwelling Spirit of God. Even as Jesus faced His Cross, He told His disciples about His kind of peace:

> [25]*"I have told you this while I'm still with you.* [26]*However, the helper, the Holy Spirit, whom the Father will send in my name, will teach you everything. He will remind you of everything that I have ever told you.* [27]*"I'm leaving you peace. I'm giving you my peace. I don't give you the kind of peace that the world gives. So don't be troubled or cowardly. (John 14:25–27)*

Firmly established in God's Word, taught and sustained by the Holy Spirit's presence, following the instruction of the Lord, these believers possessed Christ's peace despite their surroundings, their circumstances, and their adversities. This peace shined on their faces and showed in their lives by the way they loved and helped each other and did good things for their enemies. Living this way, they demonstrated that God was with them at all times in every way. Not only was the Lord with them, but His Holy Spirit lived in them.

3:17 *I, Paul, am writing this greeting with my own hand. In every letter that I send, this is proof that I wrote it.*

Earlier Paul had written about a letter that had been circulated in his name. This letter stated that the Lord had already returned to earth, but this letter was false. Paul never taught anything like this, and he certainly never put it in a letter to the Thessalonian church *(2 Thessalonians 2:2)*. To thwart any further misrepresentation, Paul wrote this greeting with his own hand to prove that he indeed wrote it. He wanted the Thessalonian believers to distinguish between that which was false and that which was true. He, therefore, asserted the genuineness and authority of this letter because it bore his own handwriting.

3:18 *The good will of our Lord Jesus Christ be with all of you.*

Paul's closing benediction petitions the good will of our Lord Jesus Christ to be with all the believers in Thessalonica. This phrase was not some vague petition that everything will go satisfactorily with them. Rather it was God's special favor bestowed on these believers even though they did not deserve it by any personal merit on their part. It was a gift of God conferred on those that belonged to Him. It cannot be found among the human race except in those incidences in which people have been wrenched from their sin by God's unmerited grace and set on the lifelong journey of faith and service by the Holy Spirit's sanctifying work.

Notes/Applications

Paul wrote this greeting with his own hand, showing clearly that this letter was not a forgery. As such, he wrote this letter under the authority of God Himself. Its instructions were not to be taken casually but with full recognition that they came from the mouth of God. With the authority of his apostleship, Paul pronounced his benediction on the Thessalonian believers. By his benediction, Paul put the believers squarely in the hollow of God's hand under the peace that the Prince of Peace provides.

This is where believers dwell. In the hollow of God's hand, they dwell within the shadow of the Almighty Who is their fortress throughout life's battles. In God's hand, they have peace that the world cannot give regardless of the circumstances they face, even if death is imminent. There with Him they find direction and purpose to their lives, throwing the cares of this world aside to serve the One Who died and rose again for their salvation.

What else does anyone need? If the Lord of all offers this to the people of the world, why aren't they all rushing to join His family? The multitudes believe the lie that the world is telling them, and they are rushing headlong toward their own destruction.

When we look around and observe this mad rush toward death that many people choose, we can only fall on our knees and thank the Lord that He has reached down and touched our hearts of stone, melting our rebellion by the warm fire of His love. Thus we embrace the One Who has saved us. We have received the Lord's undeserved grace, peace, and salvation. With unending praise on our lips, we praise the Name of Jesus both now and for all eternity.

TEXT NOTES

Galatians

Introduction

1. Walter A. Elwell and Barry J. Beitzel, *Baker Encyclopedia of the Bible* (Grand Rapids, MI: Baker Book House, 1988), 1236.
2. Ibid.
3. William Hendriksen, *New Testament Commentary: Exposition of Galatians* (Grand Rapids, MI: Baker Book House, 1968), 2–3.

Chapter Six

1. Timothy George, "Galatians," *The New American Commentary* (Nashville: Broadman & Holman Publishers, 2001), 420.
2. Kenneth S. Wuest, *The New Testament: An Expanded Translation* (Grand Rapids, MI: Eerdmans, 1997), Galatians 6:6–10.

Ephesians

Introduction

1. Stanley E. Porter and Craig A. Evans, *Dictionary of New Testament Background: A Compendium of Contemporary Biblical Scholarship* (Downers Grove, IL: InterVarsity Press, 2000), s. v. "Ephesus."
2. Allen C. Myers, *The Eerdmans Bible Dictionary* (Grand Rapids, Mich.: Eerdmans, 1987), 88.

Chapter Six

1. Spiros Zodhiates, *The Complete Word Study Dictionary: New Testament*, (Chattanooga, TN: AMG Publishers, 2000), 5043, s.v. "*téknon.*"
2. William Hendriksen, *New Testament Commentary: Exposition of Ephesians* (Grand Rapids, MI: Baker Book House, 1967), 276.
3. George Duffield, Jr., "Stand Up, Stand Up for Jesus," lyrics, 1858, (public domain).

Philippians

Introduction

1. William Hendriksen, *New Testament Commentary: Exposition of Philippians* (Grand Rapids, MI: Baker Book House, 1962), 6.
2. Ibid., 7.
3. Richard R. Melick, "Philippians, Colossians, Philemon," *The New American Commentary* (Nashville: Broadman & Holman Publishers, 2001), 40.
4. *The Valley of Vision* (Edinburgh, UK; The Banner of Truth Trust, 1975), 341.

Chapter One

1. *PCF Devotional Commentary Series, 1 & 2 Timothy, Titus, Philemon,* (Lake Mary, FL: Creation House, 2011), 126–127.

Colossians

Introduction

1. Elwell and Beitzel, *Baker Encyclopedia of the Bible*, 496.
2. Ronald F. Youngblood, F. F. Bruce, R. K. Harrison, and Thomas Nelson Publishers, *Nelson's New Illustrated Bible Dictionary* (Nashville: T. Nelson, 1995), s.v. "Colossae."
3. Walter A. Elwell and Philip Wesley Comfort, *Tyndale Bible Dictionary*, Tyndale Reference Library (Wheaton, IL: Tyndale House Publishers, 2001), 299.
4. Melick, "Philippians, Colossians, Philemon," *The New American Commentary*, 171.
5. Elwell and Comfort, *Tyndale Bible Dictionary*, 431–432.

Chapter One

1. D. A. Carson, *New Bible Commentary: 21st Century Edition*, 4th ed. (Downers Grove, IL: InterVarsity Press, 1994), Colossians 1:3–8.
2. Elwell and Beitzel, *Baker Encyclopedia of the Bible*, 703.
3. Carson, *New Bible Commentary: 21st Century Edition*, Colossians 1:15–17.
4. William Hendriksen, *New Testament Commentary: Exposition of Colossians and Philemon* (Grand Rapids, MI: Baker Book House, 1964), 73–74.
5. A. W. Pink, *The Attributes of God* (Pensacola, FL: Chapel Library, www.sgbchapel.com).
6. Hendriksen, *New Testament Commentary: Exposition of Colossians and Philemon*, 70.
7. Sydney H. Nicholson, "Crucifer," score, "Lift High the Cross," George W. Kitchin and Michael R. Newbolt, lyrics, 1916.
8. Melick, "Philippians, Colossians, Philemon," *The New American Commentary*, 234.

Chapter Two

1. Porter and Evans, *Dictionary of New Testament Background: A Compendium of Contemporary Biblical Scholarship*, s.v. "Colossae."
2. Wuest, *The New Testament: An Expanded Translation*, Colossians 2:1–3.
3. Carson, *New Bible Commentary: 21st Century Edition*, Colossians 1:24–2:5.
4. John Peter Lange, Philip Schaff, Karl Braune, and M. B. Riddle, *A Commentary on the Holy Scriptures: Colossians* (Bellingham, WA: Logos Research Systems, Inc., 2008), 43.
5. Carson, *New Bible Commentary: 21st Century Edition*, Colossians 2:16–23.
6. Hendriksen, *New Testament Commentary: Exposition of Colossians and Philemon*, 126.

Chapter Three

1. Carson, *New Bible Commentary: 21st Century Edition*, Colossians 3:5–11.
2. Hendriksen, New Testament Commentary: Exposition of Colossians and Philemon, 147.
3. Porter and Evans, *Dictionary of New Testament Background: A Compendium of Contemporary Biblical Scholarship*, s.v. "Colossae."

Chapter Four

1. F. F. Bruce, *The Spreading Flame* (London: Paternoster, 1958), 230.
2. Hendriksen, *New Testament Commentary: Exposition of Colossians and Philemon*, 197.

1 Thessalonians

Introduction

1. Robert B. Hughes, J. Carl Laney, and Robert B. Hughes, *Tyndale Concise Bible Commentary*, The Tyndale Reference Library (Wheaton, IL: Tyndale House Publishers, 2001), 615.
2. Hughes, Laney, and Hughes, *Tyndale Concise Bible Commentary*, 615.
3. M. G. Easton, *Easton's Bible Dictionary* (Oak Harbor, WA: Logos Research Systems, Inc., 1996, c1897), 664.
4. Stelman Smith and Judson Cornwall, *The Exhaustive Dictionary of Bible Names* (North Brunswick, NJ: Bridge-Logos, 1998), 237.

Chapter Two

1. Charles A. Wanamaker, *The Epistles to the Thessalonians: A Commentary on the Greek Text* (Grand Rapids, MI: W. B. Eerdmans, 1990), 97.
2. Ibid., 102.
3. Ibid.
4. Martin, "1, 2 Thessalonians," *The New American Commentary*, 82.
5. Ibid., 84.

Chapter Four

1. *The Valley of Vision* (Edinburgh, UK: The Banner of Truth Trust), 86.

Chapter Five

1. Martin, "1, 2 Thessalonians," *The New American Commentary*, 165.
2. "Love Divine, All Loves Excelling," words by Charles Wesley, 1747, (public domain).

2 Thessalonians

Chapter Two

1. Martin, "1, 2 Thessalonians," *The New American Commentary*, 235.
2. John Calvin, *Calvin's Commentaries: 2 Thessalonians* (Grand Rapids, MI; Wm. B. Eerdmans Publishing, 1973), 2 Thessalonians 2:15, 411-412.

Chapter Three

1. Martin, "1, 2 Thessalonians," *The New American Commentary*, 278.
2. Calvin, *Calvin's Commentaries: 2 Thessalonians*, 2 Thessalonians 3:9, 418.
3. Ibid., 2 Thessalonians 3:14, 421–422.
4. Craig S. Keener and InterVarsity Press, *The IVP Bible Background Commentary: New Testament* (Downers Grove, IL: InterVarsity Press, 1993), 2 Thessalonians 3:14.

Contact Information

Practical Christianity Foundation
2514 Aloha Place
Holiday, Florida 34691
www.practicalchristianityfoundation.com